Mark J. B...

29 September 1993

S0-ADK-531

HENRY MILLER

a life

By the same author

Enigma: The Life of Knut Hamsun

HENRY MILLER

—————*a life*—————

Robert Ferguson

W·W·Norton & Company
New York   London

Copyright © Robert Ferguson 1991
First American Edition, 1991

All rights reserved.

Printed in the United States of America.

Manufacturing by Arcata Graphics/Fairfield.

ISBN 0-393-02978-6

W.W. Norton & Company, Inc.
500 Fifth Avenue, New York, N.Y. 10110
W. W. Norton & Company, Ltd.
10 Coptic Street, London WC1A 1PU

1 2 3 4 5 6 7 8 9 0

Contents

List of Illustrations

Illustration Acknowledgements

The author and publishers would like to thank the following for their kind permission to reproduce illustrations: Special Collections Library of the University of California at Los Angeles (1); The Pach Brothers, New York (2); Misha Erwitt/Magnum Photos (3, 8, 9); Museum of the City of New York (11); Jose Alemany (12); Popperfoto (14); Robert Fink (16); The Hulton Picture Company (20, 21, 23); UPI/The Bettman Archive (29, 45); University of Virginia Library (24); Hans Reitzel (26); William Webb (27); Arthur Knight, Petaluma, California (31); Coll. F. J. Temple (36); The Scotsman Publications Ltd, Ireland (37); Emil White (40); Pictorial Press (41, 49); William Webb (43); Pompeo Posar/*Playboy* Magazine (46); Bradley Smith (47, 48).

Whilst every attempt has been made to trace sources, this has not been possible in some cases. The publishers would like to apologise in advance for any inconvenience caused.

Acknowledgements

My thanks to the following: Joan Adler; Donald Anderle; Tove Bakke; George Barker; Diane and Ray Barnes; Sybille Bedford; Antonio Bibalo; David Braasch; Hans Jørgen Brøndum; Erik Burns; Dolores Buttry; Ann Caiger; Patrick Cody; Richard Cohen; Bernard R. Crystal; Mary Anne DiNapoli; Elisabeth Dyssegaard; Gloria Ferris; Paul Ferris; Benjamin Franklin V.; Victoria Glendinning; Yannick Guillou; Tullah Hanley; Lilace Hatayama; Cathy Henderson; Sara S. Hodson; Georges Hoffman; Anneli Høsier; Sidney F. Huttner; Anne Hyde; Helen Iggulden; Buffie Johnson; Jonathan L. Kirsch; David V. Koch; Star Lawrence; Gerson Legman; Anthony Levintow; Angela Lucas; Ian S. MacNiven; Linda McCurdy; Barbara Sylvas Miller; Tony Miller; Valentine Miller; Herbert Mitgang; Jack Moore; Gerald Nason; Michael Neal; Amelia E. Needham (née Pasta); Joe Nuttgens; Sigfrid P. Perry; Rupert Pole; Bern Porter; David Pryce-Jones; Hans and Mette Reitzel; Havard Rëm; Sheila Ryan; Pamela Scheffel; Carl Scheiner; Rivers Scott; Gunther Stuhlmann; Frédéric-Jacques Temple; The Society of Authors; Ursula Veit; Alice Wexler; Elizabeth L. White; George Wickes; David Wigdor; Patricia C. Willis; Melanie Yolles; Murray Zuckerman.

Particular thanks to Celia Conason; Vincent Birge; Petter Naess; the late Alfred Perlès and his wife Ann Barrett; Twinka Thiebaud.

For their help and co-operation I would also like to thank the following libraries and institutions: the Beinecke Rare Book and Manuscript Library; Harvard University; Harry Ransom Humanities Research Center, University of Texas at Austin; Library of Congress, Manuscript Division; the New York Public Library, Henry W. and Albert A. Berg Collection; University of California, Los Angeles; Yale University Library; University of Oslo; University of Virginia, Clifton Waller Barrett Library; Southern Illinois University at Carbondale; The Huntington Library; San Marino, California; the George Orwell Archive, University College, London; Brooklyn Public Library; Rochester Public Library, NY.

Thanks are also due to the following for their permission to quote from published works: Carcanet Press and New Directions Publishing Corporation for *Letters to Emil* and *Ends of the World* by Cecily Mackworth; Capra Press for *Reflections* by Twinka Thiebaud, *Gliding Through the Everglades, The Word of Lawrence* and *Hamlet Letters* by Henry Miller; Bern Porter for *The Happy Rock*; the Estate of John Cowper Powys for *Autobiography* by John Cowper Powys; New Directions Publishing Corporation for *The Smile at the Foot of the Ladder* by Henry Miller; W. H. Allen and Harcourt Brace Jovanovich for *Henry and June* by Anais Nin and *A Literate Passion: From the letters of Anais Nin and Henry Miller, 1931–1953* by Anais Nin and Henry Miller; New Directions and Faber and Faber Ltd for *The Durrel-Miller Letters 1935–1953* ed. Ian S. MacNiven; Houghton Mifflin.

Company for *Greenwich Village* by Caroline Ware; New Directions Publishing Corporation for *The Books in My Life* by Henry Miller and *Stand Still Like the Hummingbird* by Henry Miller; Alberts-Sittard for *Henry Miller: Colossus of One* by Kenneth C. Dick; Curtis Brown Literary Agency and Grove Press Inc. for *Sexus, Plexus, Nexus* and *Tropic of Capricorn* by Henry Miller; Routledge for *A Dictionary of Slang and Unconventional English* by Eric Partridge.

Introduction

Few literary reputations can have fluctuated as dramatically as that of Henry Miller. For over thirty years he was a hero to liberal society for the way in which he had written about his sexual life in *Tropic of Cancer*, *Black Spring* and *Tropic of Capricorn*, autobiographical novels written in the 1930s in Paris which were banned in the United States and England until the series of court cases in the early 1960s that permitted their publication in both countries. After less than ten years of legitimacy and acclaim, however, his reputation as a prophet of sexual liberation suffered a sea-change.

A school of feminist literary criticism arose which analysed his work from an ideological point of view and declared him a misogynist. The appearance of AIDS in the 1980s and subsequent media campaigns designed to persuade the public of the mortal dangers of sexual promiscuity sent his reputation on another violent downward spiral, and the posthumous publication in 1983 of *Opus Pistorum*, a collection of hard-core pornographic stories for which Miller always strenuously denied responsibility, completed the process. It appeared, after all, that he had been all along a simple pornographer and confidence trickster who had hoodwinked an entire liberal establishment into taking him seriously as a sexual philosopher. Such developments saddened, but did not dishearten, Miller's most loyal readers, those who felt that this focussing on the purely sexual aspect of his writing obscured his much more important rôle as a religious seeker of unorthodox method, who had successfully carried out the journey proposed by William Blake along the road of excess to the palace of Wisdom.

Even beyond the fields of special interest of feminism and public health, the perception of Henry Miller, both as writer and as the guru figure he had become during his years as a literary outlaw, underwent changes. This was particularly true once the legal victories had eliminated the need to present a united front against a prevailing moral establishment. An aura of slightly puzzled suspicion grew up around his person which has never quite been dispelled. Perhaps this had something to do with hubris. There is, after all, something fitting about the black pessimism of Mark Twain's last years, or Jack Kerouac's descent from the youthful exuberance of *On the Road* into alcoholism and reactionary middle age. We sympathise with the lecherous John Berryman and the boastful Ernest Hemingway because we can forgive the unhappy dead much – especially if they died young, or killed themselves. Miller, on the other hand, by the time of his death in 1980, had been publicly and shamelessly proclaiming his happiness for over forty years. Well into his eighties he was still riding his bicycle, playing ping-pong and falling violently in love with a succession of attractive young women. He was spared the horrors of alcoholism, loneliness, serious illness or anything else which in old age might have been taken as a sign of God's displeasure, and he died in his sleep. The suspicion engendered by this consummate display of getting away with it, coupled with a persistent unease about his real achievement and status as a writer, has led to neglect on the part of the scholastic establishment. In proportion to the size of his reputation, therefore, the number of biographies of Miller has been small. There have been shorter studies by the Frenchman, Frederic-Jacques Temple, and the German, Walter Schmiele, but the only full-length biography in English so far has been Jay Martin's thorough, respectful but trusting *Always Merry and Bright*, published in 1979. In the year of Miller's centenary, further studies are promised from Mary Dearborn and Erica Jong.

2

A biography of Henry Miller presents a number of interesting practical difficulties. On the one hand, the later life, from Miller's departure from New York for Paris in 1930, offers an embarrassment of material in the form of letters, unpublished manuscripts and drafts for novels, as well as numerous reminiscences from personal acquaintances. It is unlikely that any author is better represented in the libraries of American universities than Henry Miller.

By contrast, available documentary material relating to the years between his birth in 1891 and 1930 is sparse, consisting of the several manuscripts of two unpublished novels written in the 1920s, a handful of letters to his friend Emil Schnellock dating from the same period, sundry notes and letters to other friends and a letter to his mother written when he was eight years old. There are many possible explanations for this – the recipients of his letters may not have kept them, and he admitted himself that he rarely kept letters which were sent to him during his early years. Nor was the first- and second-generation immigrant culture in which he grew up one which documented itself to any extent.

Furthermore, though Miller wrote extensively about all phases of his life, including his childhood, it was with an almost religious refusal to choose between things: everything that happened to him struck him as being of equal and monumental importance. Straight autobiography was not his literary aim, and details such as the year or date, or his age at the time of a given episode, had little relevance to the subjective self-portraiture that was his real concern. Thus his unpublished novels, published novels, draft novels, outlines for novels and notebooks, all of which are otherwise replete with biographical detail, are entirely lacking in such reference points.

This vagueness particularly affects his adolescence, the period from 1908 and 1917, during which he suffered an agonising adolescent crush on an unattainable girl, left school and started work, had an affair with an older woman, changed jobs and travelled across America, all in a shifting, timeless, impressionistic vacuum that leaves us guessing at the exact order in which events took place, their duration and their real importance for him. The occasional reference to some specific event in the outside world which caught his attention – the outbreak of the First World War, for example – can provide a useful reference point, although Miller was an unreliable witness who often became confused himself about the details of his life.

The vagueness of Miller's autobiographical reminiscing is accentuated by the tentative status that was accorded proper names in the circles in which he moved. The outstanding example is that of his second wife, June, who used five different surnames at various stages of her life. His friend Emil Cohen changed his name to Conason as part of a process of Americanization. June's friend Martha Andrews, apparently on an artistic whim, was generally known under a completely different name. Miller's first mistress also used a variety of surnames at various times. The situation is further enlivened by the way in which Miller rechristened most of his friends, wives and lovers in writing about them, often simply redistributing the names among them, changing them sometimes between different draft versions of the same episode when writing, with the result that Miller himself often referred to friends in letters by the fictional names he had given to them in his books, as though he had lost the ability to distinguish between the created character and the real-life person.

Researches among Birth, Marriage, Divorce and Death Records, School Records, Brooklyn Street Directories and Naturalization

Records have enabled this difficulty to be overcome to some extent, permitting the establishment of a reasonably certain independent chronology for these earliest years. I was also fortunate in having the assistance of Mrs Celia Conason, the widow of Emil Conason, one of Miller's closest friends from about 1920 onwards, who provided me with a valuable independent perspective on aspects of Miller's life during this period.

3

The investigation of a man who turned himself into a myth might seem to cry out for 'psychobiography'; yet there are good reasons for not placing too heavy a reliance on a rigidly methodological approach to Miller's life and personality. One is a seduction inherent in the method itself, the invitation to create from speculative analysis a potential being to which we then attribute a greater reality than the mere flesh-and-blood, 'real' one who actually walked the earth. Another is that the successful application of the method may become an end in itself. A horse may be boxed, but the difficulties are great, and success is often at the cost of the horseness of the horse. The most compelling reason for not relying too heavily on orthodox analysis, however, is that Miller himself was, from the early 1920s onwards, thoroughly familiar with all the basic ideas put forward by Freud on the rôle of hidden motivation in human behaviour. This familiarity, allied to the single-minded assault on personal fame that saw him addressing letters – not wholly ironically – to 'Posterity', long before he was a published writer, meant that he was capable of playing the fox with his analytic pursuers, anticipating with some ease the questions potential huntsmen on the trail of the 'real Henry Miller' would be asking, and providing them with the answers they would be expecting to find. A simple example of this might be the baffled and apparently naive way in which he returned throughout his life to the subject of his poor relationship with his mother. Obviously there was much truth in his description of this relationship; just as clearly Miller was offering a large and juicy psychological morsel in hopes of satisfying his pursuers. One has to guard against an offensive cynicism on this score; but the realization that it was more fun to be the fox than the hunter might provide another explanation for the remarkable amount of detailed documentary material that Miller began producing after 1930 and made so readily available to scholars and interested parties, either by donation to college libraries or by commercial publication, and the corresponding dearth of material from before this date.

The most famous defence of Miller's reputation was probably that offered by George Orwell in *Inside the Whale*. Written in 1939, this essay put forward the view that a piece of literary art cannot be at the same time both political and honest, and praised Miller for the way in which his rude independence of the union mentality of his fellow-writers in the 1930s enabled him to introduce a new and valuable type of honesty into literature. Some forty years later, in 1984, Salman Rushdie published a refutation of Orwell's views in an essay entitled *Outside The Whale*, in which he wrote that 'Miller's reputation has more or less completely evaporated, and he now looks to be very little more than the happy pornographer beneath whose scatological surface Orwell saw such improbable depths.' The observation reminds us of how difficult it is to re-enter the past fully enough to understand it on its own terms, and in so doing to avoid that attitude of 'generational chauvinism' in which the present looks to the future with a mixture of reverence and apology while spurning, in an arrogant and unforgiving way, both the past and the invariably naive and illiberal simpletons who inhabit it. Yet somewhere between the sinister bully portrayed by the feminists, the holy man revered by the disciples and the worthless fraud dismissed by the contemporary literary establishment, there lurks a unique, interesting and necessary literary figure, and it is this individual I have tried to portray.

cunt 1. (In back slang, *tenuc*, the *e* being intruded for euphony.) The female pudend. In one form or another, it dates from OE; it is unlikely to be related to L *cunnus*, but is certainly cognate with OE *cwithe*, 'the womb' (with a Gothic parallel); cf modern English *come*, ex OE *cweman*. The -nt, which is difficult to explain, was already present in OE *kunte*. The radical would seem to be **cu** (in OE *cwe*), which = quintessential physical femininity (cf sense 2) and partly explains why, in India, the cow is a sacred animal. Owing to its powerful sexuality, the term has, since C15, been avoided in written and in polite spoken English: though a language word, neither coll, dial, nor slang, its associations make it perhaps the most notable of all vulgarisms (technical sense, *bien entendu*), and since circa 1700 it has, except in the reprinting of old classics, been held to be obscene, ie a legal offence to print it in full; Rochester spelt it *en toutes lettres*, but Cotgrave, defining Fr *con*, went no further than 'A woman's, &c', and the dramatist Fletcher, who was no prude, went no further than 'They write *sunt* with a C, which is abominable', in *The Spanish Curate*. Had the late Sir James Murray included the word, and spelt it in full, in the great OED, the situation would be different; as it is, no dictionary before the Penguin English Dict (1965) had the courage to include it. (Yet the OED gave **PRICK**: why this further injustice to women?) 2. (cf Romany *mindj* or *minsh*, the pudend; a woman.) In C19-20 it also means woman as sex, intercourse with a woman, hence sexual intercourse. (It is somewhat less international than **FUCK**.) 3. Anybody one dislikes: late C19-20.

fuck 1. An act of sexual connection: from circa 1800. (Ex the v, for which see etymology, etc.) 2. A person (rarely of the male) viewed in terms of coition, as in 'She's a good *f*': C19-20. These two senses are excellent examples of vulgarisms, being actually SE. 3. The seminal fluid, esp if viewed as providing the requisite strength (*full of* fuck, potently amorous): low coll: C19-20.

fuck 1. vt and i. To have sexual connection (with): vi of either sex, vt only of the male: vulg, C16-20. Almost certainly cognate with the Latin v *pungere* and n *pugil*, both ex a radical meaning 'to strike'; semantically, therefore, **fuck** links with **PRICK**. 2. Transitive synonyms, many of them SE, occur in Shakespeare (9), Fletcher (7), Urquhart (4), etc, etc; intransitive in Urquhart (12), D'Urfey and Burns (6), Shakespeare (5), etc, etc. See esp B & P (the Introduction); Grose, P.; and Allen Walker Read, 'An Obscenity Symbol' (sec II) in *American Speech*, Dec 1934 – all at this term. 3. See **FUCK** OFF.

From *A Dictionary of Slang and Unconventional English* by Eric Partridge, London 1961.

HENRY MILLER
a life

CHAPTER ONE

1891–1909
Childhood and first love

1

Henry Miller was an unusual person. He began life as a human being, and after a series of surprising and sometimes hazardous adventures succeeded in his self-appointed task of turning himself into a rare hybrid of man and book. To enter the world he created in the commission of this task is a strange, disorienting experience, and one does so with the same pleasantly nervy sense of anticipation Alice must have felt as she stepped through into the looking-glass world. The first impression is of a hall of mirrors, all reflecting the same face. Closer examination reveals that each face is slightly different, for the purpose of the world is myth-making, and the raw-material of myth is an abundant supply of images. The skills necessary for the task were a talent for fabulating, lying, improvising, exaggerating, and for telling and evading harsh truths. He had them all. It is a hilarious, wise, foolish and occasionally cruel and misguided world, but never a sinister one. Every fact within it is at risk and liable to be altered at a moment's notice, whether it be the sex of the phrenologist who felt his head in Union Square in 1912, or the age at which he first read the *Tao Te Ching*. Even in what one might call the official environment of the journalistic interview and the letter, the process of autobiographical reinvention goes on, obeying always a gospel of subjectivity so strong that he frequently proclaims the lie to be truer than the truth – which it is, but only sometimes, and within the context of a general contract of agreement about what truth is which Miller neither signed nor even recognised the existence of. He believed with all his heart that he owned himself, and that owning himself gave him the right to invent himself too.

Under the circumstances it was a small matter for him to dispense with the background provided for him at birth and by a simple act of literary will 'disavow my supposed heritage, and trace it back to very early times. Thereby concluding, in my own mind, that I am a mixture of Mongol, Chinese, Tibetan, and Jewish bloods.' His improvements on reality never made it duller than it was, and the 'supposed

1

heritage' he so casually wished himself free of was considerably more prosaic than the one with which he replaced it.

All four of his grandparents were immigrants, among the 1.5 million Germans who journeyed to the United States between 1840 and 1860 in flight from famine, religious and political persecution, and the draft. His maternal grandfather, Valentin Nieting, took a roundabout route, leaving his home in Stessfeld Stessen at the age of sixteen and making his way first to London, where he apprenticed himself to a Savile Row tailor named Isaac Walker. After ten years in London his boss emigrated to New York, and Nieting accompanied him. In 1866 he married Emelie Insel, from Neaglerburg in Prussia, in a Lutheran church on East 6th Street, and in due course they had a family of six girls and one boy. Four of the girls survived. Henry's mother, Louise, was the second of them. When she was about thirteen years old, her mother was taken away and placed in an insane asylum, where she remained until her death in 1891. Another sister, Emelia, suffered the same fate later in life.

Henry's paternal grandfather, Heinrich Mueller, was from Minden in Hanover, where he had worked as a journeyman tailor. He settled in the Yorkville district of New York City and married an immigrant girl from Bavaria named Barbara Krapp. They lived in a house on 85th Street in Manhattan, where Miller's father Henry was born on October 23rd 1865, the only boy in a family of four children. All were baptized with the Americanized form of the family name, Miller.

In 1890, Henry Miller senior and Louise Nieting were married, and shortly after midday on December 26th 1891 at 450 East 85th Street in Manhattan, Louise gave birth to a son, Henry Valentine. Shortly afterwards the family moved across the river to a house at 662 Driggs Avenue in Williamsburg, where they lived for the next eight years.

2

'The development of my environment was practically nil', Miller once wrote to a scholar who had presumed to trace it. 'I did not belong to any environment.'[1] Perhaps they attached different meanings to the word, for Miller was the product of a very definite environment, the immigrant Brooklyn which he captured with such impressionistic brilliance in *The Rosy Crucifixion*, the three volumes of auto-biographical romance which he worked on intermittently throughout his writing life. An impressionistic picture was perhaps all one could ever hope to give of a place like Brooklyn, since it changed character almost from decade to decade during the years in which his family lived there. It was a place teeming with newly-uprooted people, all of them looking to reinvent themselves under a new nationality and a new name.

A process like this, taking place on such a massive scale, was bound to be associated with nostalgia. Even the name Brooklyn is a corruption of Breuckelen, the name the first homesick Dutch-Americans of 1645 gave their settlement in memory of their home in the Netherlands. The population cycle thenceforth was one of constant settlement and displacement. The Dutch displaced the Indians and were in their turn displaced by the Yankees. In the nineteenth century the Irish began to arrive in large numbers, to be joined from about the middle of the century onwards by Germans, Swedes and Norwegians. After 1890 settlers began arriving in great numbers from eastern, central and southern Europe, particularly southern Italy. In one generation the mass migration of Jews from Russia, Hungary, Poland and Romania brought to Brooklyn the single largest element in its population, and made it, almost overnight, the largest Jewish centre in the world.

The immigrant Germans, Irish, Dutch, Poles, Syrians, Italians, Scandinavians and Jews settled in enclaves which, like the Irish one near the Navy Yard and Red Hook and the German one at Dutchtown, were often poor and overcrowded ghettos. There were frequent clashes between the various ethnic groups, usually over jobs. The Irish, being native English speakers, had a head start over other groups in establishing themselves in the new country; but the Germans, bringing with them the tradition of the seminar for the training of college teachers, formed an educational elite among the immigrants and were soon challenging the Irish for the leading position behind the long-established Yankees and the Englishmen.

By 1890 Brooklyn was America's fourth largest city. With the annexation of Flatbush, Gravesend, North Utrecht and Flatlands in 1894 it grew larger still, but by 1898 its status as an independent city was gone as, in its turn, it was swept up into 'Greater New York'. The ghetto mentality remained, however, and in the 1890s there were people in the remoter German-speaking areas of Williamsburg, where Miller grew up, who had never seen the Brooklyn Bridge ten years after it had opened. Right on into the 1920s there were people living in Brooklyn who spoke nothing but German.

This was the environment in which Henry Miller grew up, and which left its mark on practically every page of writing he ever produced. It was a threateningly unstable world; but for a boy with a curious and receptive mind it was also a rich, exciting and even mysterious place in which to grow up.

Henry's father followed Valentin Nieting into Isaac Walker's tailoring firm and was able to provide comfortably for his family. Santa could usually be relied on to bring the boy everything he put on his Christmas list, although once he had to substitute a spotted rocking horse for the live pony the young Henry had asked for. This was Henry's favourite toy for a long while, and he gave it the crisp name Dexter. From an early age he was conscious of the fact that he came from a better home than many of his schoolmates at the kindergarten in Fillmore Place. One Christmas when the teacher handed out socks and mittens to the class he refused to accept his, piously explaining that the poor could make better use of them.

Louise Miller had certain social graces, such as playing the guitar and the zither, but in the main Henry's parents were not cultured people or great readers. Louise had been fond of Marie Corelli in her adolescence, and once confessed to Henry that she had read Edward Creasy's *Fifteen Decisive Battles Of The World* while sitting on the toilet. Henry senior was hardly less original in his choice of reading matter: apart from a book by his son much later in life, the only one he could recall reading was Ruskin's *The Stones of Venice*. Both of them had great respect for education and culture, however, and when Henry showed an early aptitude for reading they encouraged him, showering him with books at Christmas. His earliest favourites were the fairytales of Hans Christian Andersen and the Brothers Grimm. Pinnocchio was another early favourite, and he retained a sympathetic sense of identification with the wooden boy of this pathetic tale for much of his life. He read most of the classics of children's literature, like *Robinson Crusoe, Gulliver's Travels*, James Fenimore Cooper's books, *Huckleberry Finn* and *Tom Sawyer*, though he would not have been able to borrow the Twain books from the local Brooklyn Public Library as both were excluded from the Children's Room in the belief that they would corrupt childish minds. G. A. Henty, the English author of historical romances for boys, was another great favourite.

Henry soon developed the habit of reading aloud to his grandfather Nieting as he worked at his tailor's bench in the house on Driggs Avenue. Nieting would try to distract him by urging him to make something that he could show to his father when he came home from work. With uncanny foresight he warned Louise that she might one day regret indulging her son's love of reading so freely. Henry also experimented with reading aloud to his own playmates and made the interesting discovery that while this tended to put the boys to sleep, the girls seemed to enjoy it very much.

Most children grow up with the idea that there is something special and unique about them simply because they are who they are. Henry had a particularly strong sense of this: so strong, in fact, that it seems reasonable to speak of a sort of reverse paranoia in which he suspected others of plotting secretly among themselves to find ways of increasing his happiness. It is almost as though he had taken to heart the words of the 23rd Psalm ('The Lord is my shepherd, I shall not want') which he was set to memorize, and for which the Sunday School gave him a Bible with his name stamped in gold letters on the front cover.

Louise Miller doted on her son and made sure he was always the best turned-out little boy on the street. She was proud of his intelligence and his fair good looks, yet Henry never felt that she was part of the conspiracy to favour him. The basic trouble was that she was the disciplinarian in his life, and he was an unusually headstrong, wilful boy who did not like to be told what to do. It was a common enough situation, but later in life it got dreadfully out of hand. Henry's later depiction of her as a cold, joyless, undemonstrative woman who never hugged or kissed him may be accurate, or it may be a picture considerably darkened by the bad feeling that later arose between them.

Certainly Louise did not have much to be cheerful about. The insanity of her mother and the feeble-mindedness of her elder sister had made her the responsible female in her family while still in her early teens. She was just twenty years old when she married Henry's father, but if she thought marriage might be her means of escape then she was mistaken. Brooklyn had thirty-eight working breweries in 1890, and her husband came from a culture which regarded beer-drinking for breakfast – even beer-drinking on Sundays – as normal. He was a heavy drinker, and though he was also a good tailor he had little ambition or drive. The task of managing the family's affairs, of being the force for sobriety, disapproval, prohibition and caution, fell to Louise. It was she, and not his father, who was responsible for keeping Henry in on Saturday afternoons and making him scrub the woodwork, polish the silver and the glassware before allowing him out to join the other boys in 'Nigger Heaven' for the matinée at the Novelty Theatre down the road.

Her difficulties increased with the birth of a daughter, Lauretta Anna, on July 11th 1895, who turned out to be feeble-minded and ineducable. Lauretta rarely features in Miller's many accounts of his childhood. Here and there he mentions occasions when he had to fight other children who liked to taunt her by calling her 'crazy Lauretta'.

Usually when he brings up her name it is to recall with anger and disappointment the way his mother used to treat her:

I'll never forget my mother standing over Lauretta in the kitchen, trying to teach her the simplest things on a little blackboard. In one hand she held a piece of chalk, in the other a ruler.

'What's two and two?' she'd ask. And Lauretta, who knew what was coming, would begin to rattle off any answer she could think of. 'Three, no five, no three . . .' and the harder she'd try the crazier my mother would get. It always ended up with a beating, then mother would turn to me with this exasperated look on her face, and she'd throw her hands up in despair. 'What did I do to deserve this?' she'd ask me, as if I were God and had all the answers, *me*, a little boy![2]

Lauretta had a nervous tic which caused her limbs to move uncontrollably. When she talked she would talk incessantly and swiftly, jerking her head from side to side, without continuity or point, and only stopping when ordered to do so.[3] Then her chin would droop on her chest.

If the arrival of Lauretta increased Louise's burden, Henry too felt the pressure. He became in effect an only child in whom all his mother's hopes and expectations resided. A neighbour, Agnes Snyder, recalls that when she visited the Miller's home with her mother the talk between the two women was always of 'little Henry', and that Henry was the idol of the local mothers. Louise apparently came to feel that she had married beneath herself, and was anxious to promote in her small son the virtues of industry, thrift and respectability which she felt were much more clearly represented by her side of the family than by her husband's. The walls of the parlour at home were decorated with pictures of her relatives, but not of his. Many of these relatives still lived in Germany and had the Old World's contempt for the New, a contempt in which Louise appeared to collude. On the occasion of their visits, great formality would be observed, and German would be spoken out of deference to the visitors. Once at the meal table Henry's little German cousin rebuked him, in German, for slurping his soup.

His father's relatives, in particular his three sisters and their husbands who still lived over the river on 85th Street, were not welcome in the Driggs Avenue house as far as Louise was concerned. They were uneducated, uncouth, and even the women drank too much. Amelia Miller's American-born husband Dave could not even write his own name. (Amelia herself died young of cancer, the first of a startling number of people in Miller's life to die of the disease.)

Henry liked his father's side of the family better, and the couple of weeks he spent each summer with his cousin Henry Baumann on 85th

Street were always looked forward to with the keenest anticipation. Perhaps only because it was always summer there, life on the other side of the river always seemed better to him. It seemed a more relaxed, less *secretive* life than Brooklyn. In old age, he even recalled that the summers were hotter then than they are now.

On one of these stays with the Baumanns, at the age of about seven, he had his first love affair. A girl called Weesie, short for Louise, developed a crush on him, apparently because his habit of reading made him seem so unusual, and invited him to come and play with her in her bedroom one afternoon. The episode developed chastely enough and ended in a kiss, leaving Henry to make the vague assumption that he and Weesie would one day get married.

5

Language is the key to success in an immigrant *milieu* like Brooklyn. The man who gets on in life, who gets the good job and engineers the family's escape from the ghetto to the middle class is the man who masters the native tongue. Henry became aware of the power of language at a very early age. He observed the esteem in which his grandfather Nieting was held locally on account of the excellent English accent he had acquired during his ten years in London, and the respect enjoyed by another possessor of an English accent, Dr Roberts, the superintendent of the Presbyterian Sunday School which Henry attended. He could not help but be aware of the way his reading ability impressed the adults he met, nor fail to pick up the signals of approval from his mother in the presence of a man like Dr Roberts. Education and culture were Good Things, and language was the key to them both. These realizations were the earliest roots of Henry's later obsessive desire to become a master of language himself.

He was lucky in that he seems to have been one of those rare individuals who find the mere sounds of words intoxicating, and to have been equipped with an unusually synaesthetic form of imagination which made it natural for him to say of a certain kind of person, 'I *glistened* in their presence'. Recalling visits to the home of his Polish friend, Stanley Borowski, he wrote of his ecstasy on hearing Poles speak together, the way they 'hissed their long polychromatic words through tiny sensual mouths' to make 'an intoxicating sort of music, a steel-gibber which could also register anomalous sounds like sobs and falling jets of water'.

Henry also learnt that the power of language had its darker and forbidden sides. At the age of six he was dragged off to the local police

7

station by an older girl who had caught him using foul language in the street. Louise and Henry senior were a respected couple in the area and the station sergeant contented himself with giving the boy a solemn talking-to. In the light of later developments, this clearly made little impression on him.

The early years on Driggs Avenue remained in Henry's memory as a period of continuous happiness. Despite the fact that he went to a different Sunday School from the rest of his friends, the majority of whom were Catholics, despite the fancy clothes which he was made to wear, despite the fact that this eyesight was poor (for which he later blamed his mother for feeding him pastry so often) and that his sister was funny in the head, and not least despite his mother's habit of walking along holding him by the hand in front of his friends, he was always accepted as one of the gang. Charles Gross, a slightly older boy who lived nearby, recalled him as 'a clean, attractive- looking blond, friendly, alert and eager, after contact had been made, but more inclined to shyness than dominant leadership'.

His closest friend was Stanley Borowski. Stanley was embarrassed by his family, and although he spoke Polish at home he was ashamed to do so in front of his friends. If his aunt spoke Polish to him when a friend was there he would always reply in English. Henry was a dangerously observant boy and noticed things like this, things which make people feel uneasy or embarrassed. But Stanley grew up quicker than he did. It was Stanley who told him there was no such person as Santa Claus, and who first acquainted him with what seemed the unbelievable fiction that babies come from a woman's stomach.

Like most small boys Henry had his heroes among the older ones, and youths like Lester Reardon and Johnny Paul became the focus of a powerful hero-worship which did not fade with the passing of childhood. 'Johnny Paul opened my eyes,' he once wrote. 'Not Jesus, not Socrates, not the Buddha.' This hero-worship later developed into one of his most striking characteristics, a remarkable willingness to mythologize normal people and pick his saints and his devils, his great men, his sages and criminals from within his own circle of acquaintances.

For scary amusement there was a rich gallery of mad people and eccentrics roaming the streets of Williamsburg, characters with names like Apple Mary, the Yellow Kid, Crazy George, Clarence the Cop, Billy Wheeler the oyster-seller, Ed and John the black chimney sweeps, and the fish-sellers, going about their business with an army of cats following them every step of the way. Every evening at about six o'clock a boy known as Crazy Willie who lived down the road from Henry would climb out of his window and masturbate on the windowledge. On fine summer evenings the motorman would stop his trolley car as it went by to give the passengers a better view. It was a life with all the cheerful violence of a cartoon film. Boys brawl with each other, get involved in territorial gang fights, are chased down the street with razor blades by drunken uncles, whack each other over the head with Christmas trees, have rock fights and snowball fights. They fiddle with girls in sheds and cellars, or climb drainpipes to get a hard-on, and in the afternoons gather in fascination outside Dr McKinney's the animal doctor to watch the stallions being castrated, argue with each other about the purpose of the operation, fight, forget about it, and go off with their air rifles to shoot sparrows which they roast over open fires on empty lots. In *Tropic of Capricorn* Henry even described how he and his cousin Henry Baumann killed a boy in a rock fight, though he withdrew the claim in later life.

It was a tough world, ugly in many ways, but honest and open. The tensions between the adults of different nationalities and races were reflected among the children, and if one boy called another kike, wop or little shit then he would expect in the natural course of things to be called kraut, thick mick, dumb Swede, dago or whatever in return and would not make too much fuss about it. If somebody did want to make a fuss about it then there were always the gangs, institutions which were 'as simple as North and South' in which 'a kid has no choice. He's either for or against. He either does or he doesn't. *He's got to belong*, that's the imperative thing. Nor does he do the choosing. He has to choose the side he's born on, whether good or bad.'[4]

Every now and then even a system as accommodating as this would break down, as it did the day Claude de Lorraine came to live in Williamsburg. No one could work out how to offend him. Henry recalled that 'we all thought it was a strange name, very alien. It was a Latin name, and in our neighbourhood there was not one Latin person, unless it was an Italian, and an Italian was not a Latin but a wop, a dago, an ice-man, a barber.' Henry, taking after his mother, was actually very impressed by Claude de Lorraine, and recognized in this silvery-named boy 'the first cultured person I ever met'.

The most outstanding event in the outside world during these Driggs Avenue days was the Spanish-American conflict of 1898 over Cuba and the Philippines. This provided Henry with heroes from both sides in the form of Admiral Dewey, who destroyed an entire Spanish squadron in Manila Bay without losing any of his own men, and the Philippino revolutionary leader Emilio Aguinaldo. Until he took an oath of allegiance to the USA after his capture in 1901, Aguinaldo was Public Enemy Number One for decent Americans, and Henry's romantic enthusiasm for him must have been a pleasantly shocking piece of contrariness. He recalled the visits to the house of men in uniform who were courting his aunts, and how his mother would play the guitar for them while his Aunt Caroline sang. Mobs roamed the streets chanting 'Spain, Spain, you ought to be ashamed', and with the discernment of mobs everywhere broke the windows of shops owned by local Jews. Neighbourhood boys were called up, went off to fight, came back heroes. Certain aspects of heroism baffled Henry though. He relished the welcome given to Rob Ramsay on his return home, the wonderful Rob Ramsay who'd been at San Juan and fought with Teddy Roosevelt's volunteer force of Roughriders, but he was puzzled and troubled by the sight of Ramsay later in the day, leaning on the lamp-post outside his father's house and vomiting. An uneasy confusion arose in his mind between 'heroism and puke, disease and medals'.[5]

Driggs Avenue gave Henry a good education. It gave him a natural appreciation of the richness and bizarreness of life, and taught him that there is no such thing as normality, and no such thing as a normal person. The generally unselfconscious and unreflecting nature of his eight years there became more precious to him as the years went by, and it became ever more clear to him that there was no way back to that kind of simplicity.

6

In the early winter of 1900 the family moved to the Bushwick section of Brooklyn, just south of Ridgewood, another predominantly German area. It was Valentin Nieting who bought the house. The move came just two years after the incorporation of Brooklyn as a part of the City of New York, and like those nostalgic citizens of Brooklyn who referred to this event as 'the mistake', Miller regarded the move from Driggs Avenue as his personal experience of the Fall.

In the shorthand of his own mythology the new address at 1063 Decatur Street was always the 'Street of Early Sorrows'. The house, now replaced by a school, was a three-storey brick and clapboard building, part of a block of connecting houses identical save for the bay windows on alternate fronts. In front was a small patch of grass big enough to sit on and watch people go by, and there was a garden at the back in which grandfather Nieting planted an elm tree. These were good middle-class homes, not to be confused with the windowless railroads flats further down the road. As Charles Gross recalled it, Decatur Street was 'no *locale* for dead end kids'.

Nine or ten is a difficult age for a boy to move to a new

neighbourhood. He has to prove himself with a new gang. The first time Henry showed himself on the street a boy walked up to him and put a chip on his shoulder. The ritual demanded that he defy someone to knock if off and then fight with his challenger. Henry could fight, and could call upon a blind rage when necessary, but he did not enjoy it and on this occasion refused to participate. Somewhat taken aback, but impressed, the Bushwick boys let him into the gang on his own terms.

Henry had the luck to inherit his mother's musical ability and at the age of about ten began taking piano lessons in the new house from an elderly German with bad breath and palsy named Mr Walther. He was a good pupil, and soon discovered that being musical was another factor that helped him to establish himself in the new neighbourhood. He was also good at running and swimming and boxing, and at about the same time as he began piano lessons he learnt how to play ping-pong on the dining-room table at home.

Henry attended Public School number 85 at Covert Street and Evergreen Avenue, two blocks away from Decatur Street. (School Song: 'Dear Eighty-Five we'll ever strive to honour thy fair name. We shall by creed, by word and deed our loyalty acclaim.') In retrospect, the education he acquired there disappointed him. What he missed above all was a sense of connection, some suggestion that everything hung together. He missed this especially in Dr Payne's history classes, recalling his disappointment in a passage in *The Books In My Life*, the autobiographical account of his life as a reader which he wrote in 1950:

He never gave us his own précis of the causes of the various wars. We followed the books he handed out, and if we had any ideas of our own, we smothered them. It was more important to have the right date, the exact terms of the treaty under discussion, than to have a wide, general integrated picture of the whole subject.[6]

This sense of history as an unresolved chaos was something that bothered him throughout his adult life, and to some extent accounts for his later indiscriminate attraction to any synthetic worldview which he came across. In theory at least, his educational background was sound, and included classes in History, Mathematics, Literature, Botany, Physics, Chemistry, German, Art and even Latin. He had a retentive memory, and did well in class, but it seemed to him a pointless game. All he could remember of his Latin was of the whole class shouting on cue 'Hic, haec, hoc . . . huis, huis, huis . . . huic, huic, huic'. Though he was recalled by classmates as the best scholar in school, he was a mischief-maker. Once he was severely rebuked by a teacher for taking a ruler and sloshing it about in the waters of the school fish-tank, terrifying the fish, and he was even briefly suspended from the school in October 1902 for some misdemeanour.

One of the pleasures of his boyhood years at Driggs Avenue and Decatur Street was the trip out to see his friends Joey and Tony Imhof in Glendale, which he recalled as 'a tiny village, boarded on one side by a golf links and on the other by two Catholic cemeteries'. It is a curious experience to read his descriptions of days spent walking in the woods looking for birds' nests, visiting a goat in a field or tending to the chickens, ducks and pigeons that the boys raised, and to contrast them with the urban sprawl that has replaced the rural idyll. This kind of drastic reshaping of a familiar environment, taking place within a short span of time, goes some way towards explaining the consistency and intensity with which Miller began suffering from nostalgia while still quite a young man.

Much as he enjoyed the visits to Glendale, he was a city boy, with his roots in the cobblestones, and apart from a bull he saw mounting a cow in a field one day, he was never much interested in nature or animals. On one of his visits in March 1899, on a dull day, he grew bored, and made a start on his career as possibly the most prolific letter-writer of all time:

Dear Mamma and Pappa.

As it is a dreary, rainy day, so I have plenty of time to write. We went to bed last night at 9 o'clock, and we did not fall to sleep until half past ten. In the morning we got up at seven o'clock, and after breakfast we went to Minnie's school. After school I wrote this letter. Dear Mamma, Mrs Imhof would like to have you to do her a favour. If the weather is fine Wednesday, you should come for dinner without fail, if not then come on Thursday, Mrs Imhof would like to go to the city while you are here, so somebody is with Gertrude. Dear Mamma, you can tell Aunt Annie and Aunt Emily and Grandpapa I sent my love on a long string from Glendale to 662 Driggs Avenue, Brooklyn NY and a bushel of kisses. I will close my letter with best regards to all, with lots of love and kisses to you, papa, and my dear little sister Lauretta. Hoping you are all well and happy as I am.

> I remain your
> loving son,
> Henry.[7]

He saw his first naked woman at Glendale. Joey and Tony's big sister Minnie slept in the same room as the boys, beneath a crucifix, and while she pretended to be asleep Henry and Joey would lift up the covers and take a good look at her. Hanging above the bed in which the boys slept was a reproduction of Leonardo's *The Last Supper* which haunted his imagination and which, in a curious way, also mingled religion and sex. What puzzled him was the portrayal of the disciples in robes: why should men with beards be wearing dresses? Or if they were women in long dresses, why did they have beards?[8] He might have asked Tony and Joey's father, John Imhof, a watercolour painter who also made the stained-glass windows for the local churches, but he didn't like to disturb him. The reverence with which his father spoke of this man as an 'artist' communicated itself to Henry, and set him on the road to his unquestioning acceptance in later life of the status of the artist as the highest type of human being. On their way to bed at night the three boys had to pass through John Imhof's studio. Bent over his work by the light of a student lamp, he seemed hardly to be aware of their presence. Miller recalled that it gave him a 'holy feeling' to see Mr Imhof like that.

7

In 1905, the year that his grandfather Valentin Nieting died and the house passed into the possession of the Miller family, Henry left PS 85. He still felt that his roots were in Williamsburg and chose to continue his studies at the Eastern District High School on Wythe Avenue rather than locally.

But Williamsburg was not as he remembered it. Many of the two million emigrant Jews who arrived in New York between 1890 and 1914 had settled there, radically altering the nature of a community in which it had been possible, just a short time before, for a Jewish boy to know by sight every other Jewish boy in the area.[9] At his new school he found himself isolated, along with about a dozen other gentiles, in the midst of a completely Jewish population. There were several waves of antisemitism throughout the 1890s and although Miller recalled that 'there was no open conflict between the gentiles and the Jews', there was little racial mixing between the boys. The teachers at the school were not Jews, and Miller and the other gentile pupils were generally favoured with good marks.

Some of the boys Miller met here remained his friends for life. One was the cynical, intelligent William Dewar. Another was Emil Schnellock, a boy who surprised and impressed Henry because he would draw for the love of drawing, not just because it was a time for the Art lesson. But the most decisive experiences of his schooldays commenced in his third year when, at the age of sixteen, he became infatuated with a girl named Jessie Cora Seward, the 'Una Gifford' to

13

whom he would refer so frequently in his writings. Cora was thirteen years old and she lived with her mother and father and brother Edwin at 181 Devoe Street, just round the corner from the old house on Driggs Avenue. She was a pretty, Germanic-looking girl, with clean white teeth, golden hair and China-blue eyes.

Even for an adolescent passion, this was a strangely tormented affair. Cora was definitely interested in Henry and they could blush in each other's presence. He danced with her when the occasion arose, and met her at student parties, where there would be games of *Kiss the Pillow* and *Post Office*. But their mutual shyness prevented them ever advancing beyond the most innocent pleasures. When they danced Miller was so tense he would stumble over his own feet, painfully reinforcing his mother's view that he was a clumsy boy.

He impressed Cora and her friend Edith Mitchell when he sat down at the piano and played rags for them to sing along to, but somehow he could never capitalize on her admiration. Twice he took her to the theatre, and on one occasion presented her with a bunch of violets which got dropped in the dark and trodden on. The symbolic potential of this incident did not escape Henry, and on each of the many occasions in later life on which he wrote about it he made slight but significant alterations to the story. Sometimes he was the one who trod on the flowers, sometimes it was Cora. Certainly it must have been embarrassing and distressing when it actually happened.

Their intense and unresolved affair persisted for something like three years, and at the end of it all almost nothing had happened. Both families had telephones, but the two never rang each other. They exchanged occasional letters on their summer holidays, but they were newsy letters, not love letters. He wearied his friends with accounts of his torment, and finally even ritualized it with its own music (phonograph recordings of music by Cantor Sirota, Caruso and John McCormack) and its own ceremony (a long walk or a ride on the bike past Cora's house on Devoe Street after the evening meal each day).

This prolonged and passionate stasis had a decisive effect on Henry. He believed that the reason he had failed to win the girl was because all along he had been too timid, too sensitive, too afraid of rejection, pain, ridicule and loss of face. The humiliation of not having dared to act remained one of the outstanding memories of his adolescence. It intensified as the years passed, and the realization grew of how easy it would have been to act, how it would have required no more than one moment of courage to overcome himself. One long-term effect of this was to make him for much of his adult life an over-realist in matters of sex, a man determined never again to be frozen in a sexual fetter. A more immediate effect was the resolve to avoid the mistake of ever again putting a woman on a pedestal.

14

Cora's position on high, however, was established and unassailable. She became in time an ikon, part of the permanent display in his vast personal museum, perpetually reminding him of his innocence, his failure, his oversensitivity. In *First Love*, a brief memoir written in late middle-age, he recalled her:

In all the years which have since elapsed she remains the woman I loved and lost, the unattainable one. In her China-blue eyes, so cold and inviting, so round and mirror-like, I see myself forever and ever as the ridiculous man, the lonely soul, the wanderer, the restless frustrated artist, the man in love with love, always in search of the absolute, always seeking the unattainable. Behind the iron curtain her image remains fresh and vivid as of yore, and nothing, it seems, can tarnish it or cause it to fade away.[10]

It was a banal, adolescent affair; but one of Miller's curious strengths was his refusal to recognize the concept of the banal. He saw the myth-making potential in everything, and allowed the affair to take on fantastic proportions in his mind. He remained faithful to what Cora symbolized for him, and at the age of 85 was still expecting to die with her name on his lips. 'On the other hand,' he wrote, 'if she is still alive and I should chance to run into her one day, what a calamity!'[11] He certainly persuaded a whole world of her enduring importance in his life: in 1978 a statue of 'Cora Seward' by one Hiro Shirai was solemnly deposited in the Henry Miller archives at the University of California in Los Angeles.

8

Miller graduated second in his class at Eastern District High in 1909, by which time he had received a total of eight years schooling. His outstanding memory of these years was of the pleasure he took in reading *Ivanhoe* and Tennyson's *Idylls of the King*. Apart from this, he claimed to have experienced nothing but anguish, despair and confusion. His German teacher, however, was sufficiently impressed by his achievements to encourage him to apply for a scholarship to Cornell University. He failed to get this and was instead matriculated as an Arts II student in the spring of 1909 at the City College in New York, where he took Latin, German, Physics, Gym and Chemistry.[12]

Henry had never had any ambition. As a small boy, he once said that he wanted to be a river pilot, like a friend of his father's. To his surprise, his parents took the statement seriously and instead of just saying 'Yes Henry' they argued with him about it. On another occasion, at school, the teacher had gone round the class asking each pupil what he wanted to do when he left. The other boys surprised him by the seriousness and realism of their answers. When his own turn came he said the first thing that came into his head – that he wanted to be a travelling salesman. From the way his father had spoken about the drummers who came to buy and sell at his place of work, Henry had picked up an image of them as 'wealthy vagabonds'. Another idea was to be a clown. Basically he hoped he would never have to make a choice, and that he could carry on going to school for the rest of his life.

The attempt to enter further education may have been no more than an expression of this vague desire. On the other hand, it may have been the serious expression of high ambition, in which case his failure to win the scholarship to Cornell would have wounded his pride. This was, after all, the street know-all, the top of the class, in Agnes Snyder's words 'the most brilliant scholar old 85 ever had – the ideal of all the teachers and the principal'. The failure to make a brilliant transition to the larger and more competitive academic world outside Brooklyn perhaps shocked and disappointed not only himself, but his mother and father too.

He left City College after one semester, disillusioned after an encounter with Spenser's *Faerie Queene*, and feeling like an outsider among the College's many Jewish students. Perhaps in leaving he was also rejecting a system which had rejected him. Miller was a man desperately anxious to prove himself, and the failure to get the scholarship to Cornell may partly account for the ferocious and desperate nature of the ambition he later displayed.

There was in any case something deeper than ambition in him: a desire to invent his own life and not simply take the one that was being sold to him. His father had just started up in his own business in partnership with Isaac Walker's son in premises off 5th Avenue, but Miller resisted family pressure to join him in the garment trade. Instead he began work as a filing clerk at the Atlas Portland Cement Company at 30 Broad Street, for a wage of twenty-five dollars a month, fifty cents a day extra for overtime. It was dull work. Shortly after commencing there, however, he met a woman, and suddenly the dullness didn't seem to matter so much. He was about to take the great nosedive into the world of physical sex.

CHAPTER TWO

1909–1916
The widow and the tailor shop

1

Henry had already had his first experience of sex by the time he met Pauline Chouteau, and a wretched one it was too. With another youth he had gone looking for excitement in the area known as the German Village, behind the Metropolitan Opera House, where they had been solicited by two prostitutes. By the end of the evening he had lost not only his virginity but his wallet, and picked up a mild case of gonorrhoea. This may have alarmed him, but in those days a dose of clap was considered a badge of manhood, and he was able to boast of the experience to his male colleagues at the office. He even repeated the experiment the following summer at a French brothel near the Herald Square Theatre.

Pauline was not a professional, however, and his relationship with her was the first serious sexual relationship of his life. To supplement his wage at the Atlas Portland Cement Company he had been giving piano lessons in the evening for 30 cents an hour, and Pauline was a friend of the mother of one of his pupils, a woman named Louise Ashley. Pauline, a thirty-two year old divorcee, lived on Sumpter, the same street as Louise, and was often at the house when Henry gave his lesson. He got into the habit of walking her home afterwards to her flat. To begin with it was Louise who flirted with him, but he didn't welcome her advances because he was nervous of her lover, a tough black man named Edward Perry who ran a bicycle shop at 21 Sumpter and used to maintain Henry's bike. Henry's interest vanished completely after Pauline confided to him that Louise had syphilis.

Pauline was born in Phoebus, Virginia, in 1877. At the age of seventeen she gave birth to an illegitimate son, George, whom she took with her when she moved to New York. George adopted the name Wilson, after his father, and his mother also used the name occasionally. Later she had a liaison with an army bandsman named Chouteau, and after this broke up she continued to call herself Chouteau – pronouncing it 'Shooter' – though it seems even her lover's use of the name was informal: the Chouteau family is prominent in St Louis, Missouri, and its thorough genealogical records contain no reference either to her or her army bandsman. A suggested explanation is that it was at one time common practice among working-class people to assume names with an aristocratic ring to them.*

To Henry, Pauline seemed a beautiful woman, with a 'sad, wistful beauty, like a thing that had been used too roughly'[1] and large, sorrowful eyes which he called 'Armenian eyes'. She was a stylish dresser and Henry was proud to be seen in her company. They began going out together, to the cinema and the theatre, for walks in the Botanic Garden, then on day trips to Coney Island to hear the bandstand concerts in Luna Park. For a while their relationship was that of companions; the fifteen-year difference in age between them seemed to Henry to preclude sex, and in the event it was Pauline who seduced him. The experience gave him a shock and his first reaction was that there must be no repetition.[2] There were immediate repetitions, however, and before he quite knew what had happened they were a couple.

Henry was not a particularly handsome youth, but his face was sensual, with large lips and a strong, broad nose, and he had an attractive, rumbling voice. He was also friendly and cheerful, a sympathetic listener and, in virtue of his enthusiasm for cycling and sports, fit and strong. To the divorced and lonely Pauline he seemed to have a great deal to offer, and she gave herself freely to him. She had no other lovers, and he was in the first flush of youth. As he recalled later: 'We were both hungry for it. We fucked our heads off.'

Apart from themselves, no one was pleased at this turn of events. Louise Miller in particular was hostile to the relationship. She may not have liked it much when her son grew up and began showing an interest in other women, but Cora Seward had at least been young, and Germanic, and if Henry had ever managed to marry her, Louise would soon have got used to the idea. Pauline, however, with her grown-up son, and a best friend who lived with a black man, was a wholly unacceptable proposition.

The affair also opened up a gap between Henry and his friends. After leaving school, a dozen or so boys had banded together in a group which they called the Xerxes Society. This was really only a more formal continuation of an earlier gang known as the Deep Thinkers, in sly honour of the silent and rather stupid youth whom they had elected as their president. The Xerxes Society had its own badge and ritual handshake; but the name probably had more to do

*Her given name was probably Laura May. Miller specifies that at one time her address was 366 Decatur Street. A search of the 1915 Census for that address turns up Laura May, a white housewife aged 38, as head of a household consisting of herself and her son George V. Wilson, aged 21, a salesman.

with a pun on 'exercises' than the legendary King of Persia, for the whole enterprise was only marginally more serious than the Deep Thinkers. The boys organized dances, went cycling together, attended wrestling matches at Coney Island, as well as boxing matches, or 'theatrical entertainments' as they were then legally known. They also followed the other major sporting events of the day like the six-day bike races at Madison Square Gardens. Now and then Henry tried to introduce an intellectual side to their activities, such as debates on religious and social issues, but without much luck. For most of them, the main idea was just to meet girls. They were a fairly conservative bunch of boys, and they expressed open disapproval when Henry presently took up with someone who was so very much more than a girl. Though Henry remained close to a couple of them – William Dewar and George Wright – he was drifting away from his other boyhood friends, and the affair with Pauline gave him his first real taste of being an outsider.

Henry and Pauline did have some supporters as a couple. Henry greatly admired an athletic youth named Ray Wetzler who worked with him at the cement company, and invited him to one of the dances organized by the Xerxes Society. Pauline was with him that night, and he was flattered when Ray Wetzler congratulated him at work next day on his taste in women. Another admirer was a man named Lou Considine who lived downstairs from Pauline on Sumpter. Considine was a middle-aged man to whom she must have seemed young, and he always treated her with deference and courtesy. Henry had begun spending a lot of time at Pauline's flat, where he took over some of her caretaking duties like putting out the rubbish, raking the boiler and carrying out the ash cans in the morning, and he struck up a good relationship with Considine. They talked about books and writers, and played chess together. Considine fulfilled a role as intellectual mentor which Henry's own father was unable to play. 'My Guide', he called him once, 'my Comforter, my Bright Green Wind'.[3]

Pauline was an uneducated woman, a gentle and undemanding companion, and their domestic life on evenings together at Sumpter had a peace and an ease which Miller's problems with women later in life led him to recall with wistful fondness. However, for all their good times together, Henry never quite managed to shake off the deep mood of uncertainty in which he had entered the relationship. The violence of his sexual feelings was, to begin with, overwhelming, shaming and frightening. It is unlikely that he received any kind of sexual education from his drunken father and his cold mother, and he was an easy prey to contemporary theories about sexual emission being debilitating for young men. For a while he tried to shame himself into moderation by making a note in his diary each time he and Pauline made love, but it was always too often, and he soon abandoned the check in alarm and disgust.

Instead he practised a driven athleticism with which he hoped to counteract the ill-effects of his sex life. He rose early each morning and cycled the six miles from Prospect Park to Coney Island, and sometimes took a swim in the sea before riding home again. Regularly every evening he went through the routines devised by Eugene Sandow, the leading professional Hercules of the period, in his physical fitness course. Henry was an energetic youth, however, and it took a lot to tire him out.

Other aspects of the relationship disturbed him. He felt that in becoming the lover of a woman, particularly an older woman, he had automatically assumed a binding moral responsibility towards her. Yet as soon as the pleasures of sex became commonplace, he found himself tormented by the age difference between them. He would double their years and visualise himself in his mid thirties, with Pauline approaching fifty. All the small, close-up signs of age he saw in her reminded him constantly of the problem. Her hair had once been red. Now she used peroxide on it and the sight of the discoloured roots, and of the tiny wrinkles around her eyes, was depressing and shaming. An early association between death and sex arose in him, and in speaking of her to his friends he began referring to her as 'the widow'.

His job as a filing clerk was tedious, and Pauline's lack of intellectual curiosity began to bore him too. He always took something to read with him as he rode the elevated line from Brooklyn Bridge over to the financial district – Carlyle's *Heroes and Hero-Worship* maybe, or one of the little literary magazines like *The Dail, Simplicissimus* or *The Little Review* – but even at work there was no-one with whom to share his interests. He enjoyed the company of the other workers in the Broad Street office, but it was the same sort of horse-play he shared with the Xerxes boys.

What made everything worse was that his romantic longing for Cora Seward continued unabated, heightened even. She was a guest at his twenty-first birthday party at 622 Decatur Street on December 26th 1912, and as Louise Miller was in charge of the arrangements it is reasonable to suppose that Pauline was not. The guests drank punch, and Henry danced with Cora. His parents gave him a meerschaum pipe as a present which might have made him *look* old and mature but could not make him feel that way. Later he recalled his twenty-first year as one of the least enjoyable of his life.

His great problem was that he still had no idea what he wanted to do with his life. Idling on a bench in Union Square one day, his eye fell on an advertisement for the services of a phrenologist. He went along and paid a dollar to have the bumps on his head felt and be told that he had all the makings of an architect, or maybe a good corporation lawyer.[4] It wasn't really what he wanted to hear. He was looking around for ways to escape Pauline and thought of becoming a student again. He discussed the idea with his parents and they agreed to provide him with enough money to enrol at Cornell. He took the money but never went, hiding out at Pauline's house and frittering it away. When he finally plucked up the courage to go back home again, with the money all gone, his mother only said: 'I know all about it, Henry. We won't talk about it.' At last, in the spring of 1913, he stirred himself enough to make the break.

2

In his essays and autobiographical novels Miller often told the same story at least twice, though rarely in the same way. A feature of his literary reminiscing is the ease with which he switches between the parallel universes of his past to provide superficially quite different sets of motives to account for the same course of action. He can work hard to convince his readers that the reason he went to California in 1913 was to try to start a new life for himself and Pauline, away from everyone who knew them in New York, and that he intended to send for her to join him once he had found the right place; on another page and in another book he can turn around and tell the story from a completely different angle that makes it appear to have had little to do with Pauline at all. Though in the end the different reasons usually connect somewhere along the line, this approach to autobiography has a way of making his life seem like an ever-changing hypothesis, a draft for a novel which is under continual revision and which might possibly be available in a final version one day – if the author can finally make up his mind what happened and why – but it probably won't be.

Though his primary reason for leaving New York for California in the spring of 1913 must indeed have been to escape the relationship with Pauline, he entertained with great seriousness a whole set of other motives only very indirectly connected with his love-affair. These constitute the first real signs of the spiritual quest which was to preoccupy him for the remainder of his life, a driven but formless pursuit of religion revealing the many striking links between the turn of the century *zeitgeist* which shaped his search, and the eclectic 'New Age' phenomena of the late twentieth century.

His mentor in this field was a youth named Bob Challacombe, the half-brother of Henry's Xerxes companion, William Dewar. The two brothers had been separated shortly after Bob's birth, and he had been raised in California. They were different types, William a worldly youth, clever and cynical and good with girls, his brother more interested in the spiritual side of life. There was some uncertainty about who Bob's real father was, and he arrived in New York from California in 1912, and lived with Dewar and his family for a while to try to solve the riddle. Dewar had no time for his half-brother. He called him a 'real skin-flint' who 'talked on a superior plane', but Henry liked him at once. He found the quest for the 'real father' pleasingly exotic, and in his disappointment with his own father's averageness and unintellectuality probably identified with it. Soon he considered Bob 'a fellow that next to myself I like better than anyone in this wide world'.[5]

Henry's attendance at Sunday School as a small boy had been largely a social matter, something that gave him the chance to thud on a drum in the Boy's Brigade. Since his family was not religious, he grew up with no focus for his strong religious instincts. It made him an easy target for some of the many eccentric philosophical cults which flourished around the turn of the century. The Christian Scientists and the New Thoughters were among the most successful of these, both profiting from an atmosphere of hostility to Calvinism and Rationalism. Old Thought was pessimistic, dwelling on sin, pain and suffering and offering the darkly stoical view of life Henry associated with his mother. New Thought associated itself with the idea of light, assumed the goodness of the natural man, and insisted that human beings had the capacity to transcend their own limitations. There were numerous other movements besides these, including – especially after Freud's visit to the United States in 1909 – the first stirrings of interest in psychoanalysis, which later picked up many converts from among the New Thoughters; Elwood Worcester's Emanuel Movement had also attracted many adherents with its combination of scientific medical theory and religious ritual. One of the most popular of the cults was the Theosophical Society, founded in New York in 1875 by Madame Blavatsky and Colonel H.S. Olcott to promote Madame Blavatsky's detailed revelations of the septenary structure of the universe, and the presence in Tibet of a secret brotherhood of *Mahatmas* who concerned themselves with the spiritual development of individuals in search of personal experience of the divine.

Bob Challacombe had much to tell Henry about these movements. Back home in California he had been a member of the local branch of the Theosophical Society at Point Loma. Latterly, however, he had developed an enthusiasm for the teaching of a former Evangelist preacher named Benjamin Fay Mills, who had left the orthodox church in 1897 on account of his liberal views to found a new religious organization which he called the 'Los Angeles Fellowship'. Between 1903 and 1915, Mills travelled the United States delivering lectures on philosophy, psychology and sociology designed to promote the work of the Fellowship. When he arrived in New York in 1912, Challacombe took Henry along to hear him.

Henry was deeply impressed by Mills, but the full course of lectures was more than he could afford. Mills was moved by his enthusiasm, however, and agreed to let Henry attend the lectures free if he would pass the plate at the end of each session. Later Miller recognized that these lectures were 'probably very bad', but that what Mills had to offer was 'the only thing of its nature obtainable in my American environment'.[6] 'I clutched at him as a drowning man clutches at a straw,' he wrote. 'I needed the interior serenity and poise which he gave me to fight my sexual battle.' Henry felt that through Mills he 'recognized for the first time the *mystic* side of my nature'.[7]

Challacombe came along at just the right time for Henry. Under the influence of Stanley Borowski he had been going through a dispiriting phase of 'passionate atheism'. By kindling his instincts for mysticism, Challacombe was the first to show him that the way to escape the banality and many of the unpleasant responsibilities of everyday life was by dramatizing and elevating personal conflicts to a higher plane. Between them, Challacombe and Mills put the business with Pauline on an idealistic footing. 'Their reasons are in accord with my own,' Henry wrote later. 'They do not represent my motives as selfish, but as the highest good, and such-like. I require the right, the justificatory motive. And they supply it.'[8] A passage in Miller's autobiographical novel, *Tropic of Capricorn*, suggests that Henry and Bob Challacombe even planned and discussed Henry's trip west as a spiritual rite of passage. Miller recalls how, stranded and homesick in an Arizona desert town, he began to address his thoughts to Challacombe ('Roy Hamilton') back home in Brooklyn:

I feel so terribly deceived and I begin to weep. It is dark now and I stand at the end of a street, where the desert begins, and I weep like a fool. Which me is this weeping? Why it is the new little me which had begun to germinate back in Brooklyn and which is now in the midst of a vast desert and doomed to perish. *Now, Roy Hamilton, I need you!* I need you for one moment, just one little moment, while I am falling apart. I need you because I was not quite ready to do what I have done. And do I not remember your telling me that it was unnecessary to make the trip, but to do it if I must?[9]

23

Discussing the incident elsewhere, however, Miller played down the spiritual aspect and claimed that he had travelled west on the advice of an oculist who assured him that the outdoor life in a warm climate would relieve him of the need to wear glasses for the rest of his life; and to a French biographer he stressed the decisive rôle played in his decision by his encounter with Teddy Roosevelt's enormously popular book *The Strenuous Life* which promoted an ideal of rugged asceticism to young American males. Whatever the relative importance of these factors on his plans, the quest aspect of the trip loomed large in Henry's mind at the outset, and he chose the Los Angeles area as his destination because Fay Mills had a brother there whom he intended to visit. Somewhere along the line, however, this seems to have faded out, to be replaced by a concentration on a more Jack London-like approach, and soon after arriving in California he found himself working on a cattle ranch outside San Pedro. This proved to be the first of several such casual jobs.

Most of his time was spent on a lemon grove in Otay, near Chula Vista, where he was given the job of collecting the branches pruned from the lemon trees, loading them onto a sled pulled by a jackass, then burning them all in a big pile. One of his tasks was to curry-comb the asses in the morning. It was hardly more exciting than the office job at Atlas, and he disliked it intensely. His eyebrows were singed, his lips cracked, and his office-worker's hands were torn and cut by the branches.[10]

He might perhaps have been bullied by the other men, but his naivety and friendly openness saved him. Instead they made a pet of him, encouraging him to entertain them with tall stories about New York, the subways, skyscrapers, nightclubs and women. He was not his mother's Little Henry here, nor his Pauline's 'Harry', nor Sunny Jim, which his father called him in honour of the athletic boy who leapt the fence on the front of the Force Flakes cereal packets. After the fashion of work-gangs everywhere, he was known simply as 'Yorkie', from his place of origin. 'I was such a city boy,' he recalled, 'a sissy compared with all those other men. But you know they treated me very well. They could have been a mean bunch of guys but they took a liking to me.'[11]

He could never remember himself how long the stay lasted and once suggested six months, which may have been a generous estimate. He felt homesick, missed Pauline, and wrote long letters telling her he wished he was back in her arms. Soon he was looking round for a way to leave and return to Brooklyn without losing face among his workmates. The chance came in an unexpected way.

His stay on the West Coast coincided with the height of a violent debate in the area on the subject of freedom of speech. Nearby San Diego in particular had developed a tradition that allowed considerable freedom in public speaking, and socialists, anarchists and the militant trade-unionists of the IWW often held open-air meetings there. In a wave of fear inspired by the revolutionary oratory of some of these speakers, a backlash developed, and the local authorities passed resolutions which put severe limitations on freedom of speech. A series of deliberate breaches of the new ruling were arranged, and in the rioting that followed eighty-four radicals were thrown into jail. Vigilante mobs ruled the streets. It was against the background of this atmosphere that Henry and a friend from the citrus grove named Bill Parr travelled to San Diego one day with the intention of visiting a Mexican whorehouse. On the way they passed a poster advertising a lecture on European literature to be delivered in town by the anarchist Emma Goldman. Henry decided he would rather hear her speak than go to the whorehouse, and he and Bill Parr went their separate ways.[12]

The lecture had a salutary effect on him, and afterwards he went forward to greet Emma's consort, Ben Reitman, from whom he bought two books, Nietzsche's *Anti-Christ* and Max Stirner's *The Ego and His Own*. On account of the dangerous atmosphere in the area, Reitman cross-examined Henry carefully before letting him have the books, fearing that he might be an *agent provocateur*. Here was further proof for Henry of the explosive social power of the word, written or spoken. On his way back to camp he thought hard about his life, and suddenly it dawned on him that he was not a cowboy and a plain man at all, but a reader of books, a thinker, a discusser, a complex and pleasingly-corrupted big-city boy, and he made up his mind to go home at once. Shamelessly anxious for the good opinion of others – though it is hard to imagine that the labourers in the lemon grove cared one way or another why the branch-burner was leaving – he gave instructions in one of his letters to Pauline that she was to send him a telegram in his father's name saying that his mother was dying and he was to come home at once.

This was Henry's own account of how his West Coast adventure came to an end in 1913. He was so open about his fabulating that to mention it seems almost pedantic, but Emma Goldman did not lecture in San Diego that year. She and Ben Reitman were in town but there was a riot and she was prevented from speaking by vigilantes. Though she tried again in May the following year, it was not until 1915 that she was finally able to deliver her long-postponed lecture on Ibsen's *An Enemy of the People*. In a letter to a friend in April 1939 Miller referred to Stirner's book as 'the book that set me off years ago, when I was in California –the book I bought from Emma Goldman at a lecture in San Pedro or San Diego'. Certainly he had a strong streak of solipsism in him, but surely not so strong that he would have failed to notice a riot going on around him. Clearly, San Pedro was the venue. Maybe he got mixed up, or maybe he was lying. Lying came easily to him, as the telegram hoax shows. Hearing Emma Goldman lecture undoubtedly had a great effect on him, and his instincts as a myth-maker would be to make as much out of the occasion as possible. This whole California episode of his life is steeped in the kind of woozy imprecision in which he thrived as an autobiographer, and if he says it all began one day when he was on his way to a whorehouse with a cowboy named Bill Parr from Butte, Montana, then the best we can do is nod our heads and wait to hear the next instalment.

4

Pauline was pleased and perhaps not too surprised to see her Harry back again. She gave him a '*hot* welcome',[13] though he had to do his flies up quickly when her lodger, Tex the motorman, walked into the room unannounced. When the initial relief at being back on home ground was over, however, Henry had to face the fact that, after his failure to start an affair with Cora, his inability to end one with Pauline constituted a second decisive defeat in love, and the cause of his defeat was once again his own lack of decision and passivity. In a mood of perverse and preposterous irritation he thereupon 'surrendered to Pauline completely, convinced that it was hopeless to evade my destiny':[14]

Nothing matters now, nothing but to live out this relationship which appears a hopeless enigma. I become in the eyes of those about me a saint and a martyr. I became at once extraordinarily good and extraordinarily satanic. I feel justified in doing anything, be it evil or good . . . I turn my strength into spiritual conquests.[15]

This new kind of fetter in which he was held was his first experience of the combination of sex and guilt. Pauline had been a wonderful mistress to him, and through her he had been spared many of the farcical and unhappy mishaps that adolescent boys often have to endure before they are able to relax and enjoy their sex-lives. She was an open and natural woman, able to laugh and have fun without indulging in neurotic problems. But it was sex, not love; and company, not friendship. Worst of all, he felt sorry for her. Her son George had contracted tuberculosis, and as part of his saintliness Henry got himself into debt in order to help Pauline meet her medical expenses.

26

Desperately anxious to avoid hurting her, he harmed them both by staying with her out of pity, knowing all the while that by his own standards of intense romanticism he was betraying love.

By the time he returned from California, Cora Seward was married. He met her once in the street and she invited him in to look around her new home. The apartment turned out to be in a block just behind Pauline's – he could see Pauline's flat from her windows. As they came to the bedroom, Cora pointed to the big double bed and in foolish embarrassment said 'This is where we sleep'. 'With these words', he wrote, 'it was as if an iron curtain fell between us.'[16]

Miller comforted himself by looking from the window of Pauline's flat across to Cora's, soulful and remote, puzzling Pauline, who can have had no idea of the intensity of his feelings for Cora. She became pregnant with his child, and while they were still working on the difficult and dangerous business of finding a doctor willing to carry out an abortion, Henry took her to hear a concert at Luna Park. Quite by chance Cora was there too. The thought of what she might think if she saw Henry walking hand in hand with his pregnant 'older woman' humiliated him, and he tried, unsuccessfully and ungallantly, to smuggle Pauline away before Cora could catch sight of them. Cora was the dream, Pauline the reality, 'the other one', the succubus:

Meanwhile the other one is waiting. I can see her again as she sat on the low stoop waiting for me, her eyes large and dolorous, her face pale and trembling with eagerness. *Pity* I always thought it was that brought me back, but now as I walk towards her and see the look in her eyes I don't know any more what it is, only that we will go inside and lie together and she will get up half-weeping, half-laughing, and she will grow very silent and watch me, study me as I move about, and never ask what is torturing me, never, never, because that is the one thing she fears, the one thing she dreads to know. *I don't love you!* Can't she hear me screaming it? *I don't love you!* Over and over I yell it, with lips tight, with hatred in my heart, with despair, with hopeless rage. But the words never leave my lips. I look at her and I am tongue-tied. I can't do it... .[17]

Yet already Miller seems to have discovered the trick of detaching himself from his misery and deriving a masochistic enjoyment from his suffering, watching himself as he looked forlornly across the yards to Cora's windows, thinking of himself as romantic and soulful, like the hero of a tragic love-story. His campaign of 'spiritual conquests' had also provided him with a number of ways of cutting himself off from Pauline on their evenings together. He rented a cheap upright piano which he kept at her flat and practised on it for hours, hoping and dreaming that he might one day become good enough to be a concert

27

pianist. He buried himself in chess problems, and became ever more deeply involved with the world of books. 'What good is all that reading going to do you?' Pauline would ask, and he would shake his head and reply, 'I don't know. I just like to read.'

5

In his twenty-third year, Henry was coming under increasing pressure from his family to settle down and join his father's firm on a full-time basis. He still had not the slightest idea what he really wanted to do, but he was fairly certain he did not want to be a tailor. Finding himself forced to make a decision he acted impulsively and put his name down for a four-year course at Watson L. Savage's newly-opened School for Physical Education on Columbus Circle, with the aim of becoming a qualified gymnasium instructor. There was a logic in this, given his interest in sport and the regime of physical culture he had been following since his adolescence, but as events turned out he was no more fated to be a gym teacher than he was a cowboy. The factor which decided his future for him was the ever-declining relationship between his mother and father.

One of the reasons he spent so much time at Pauline's was that her company was in many ways the lesser of two evils. The atmosphere at home at Decatur Street was bad. His father was not thriving under the pressures of running his own business, and his social drinking with clients, potential clients and friends had got out of hand. He regularly came home drunk, and he and Louise indulged in frequent and degrading brawls in front of their children.[18] Sometimes Henry would have to separate them physically. One night his father came home drunk with a friend and insisted that his friend be allowed to stay overnight. Louise was furious, and Henry never forgot the sight of their visitor on his knees to her in the morning, begging her for a forgiveness she would not grant. On another occasion the couple began to row as they were doing the washing-up together. Suddenly his mother slapped his father hard across the face with her wet hand. Henry senior responded calmly, telling Louise that he would leave her if she ever did it again.

At night, as Henry lay in his hall bedroom, he would hear his mother threatening to kill her husband because of his drinking; and when Henry senior stayed out until the small hours Louise would wake her son and tell him to call the police to go out looking for him. Henry survived these dispiriting scenes, but at the time, and for some years afterwards, he suffered from a nervous disorder which constricted his

28

throat at meal times and caused him to feel that the was choking on his food. He did what he could to bring his parents together, and on their wedding anniversary each year treated them to a piano recital, playing popular favourites such as *The Orange Blossom Waltz*, *The Midnight Fire Alarm*, *The Burning of Rome*, *Poet and Peasant* and *The Chariot Race*. On their Silver Wedding Day he bought them a recording of John McCormack's *Mother Macree*; but such moments of shared enjoyment in the family were rare.

As he got older, Henry saw his father's drinking as the retreat of a warm-hearted, generous and easy-going soul from the nagging of a pushing and joyless wife. At the time, however, his sympathies were with Louise, and he seems to have shared the weary contempt in which she held his father. Once Henry senior caught his son reading Balzac's *The Wild Ass' Skin*, and misunderstanding the allusion to an 'ass' confiscated the book. Later in life Henry had a connoisseur's affectionate appreciation for such mistakes, and as his anti-intellectualism grew he might even have wished himself capable of them; but as a young man it made him wince. In certain moods of disgusted despair it seemed to him that the best for all concerned would be for his father to kill himself and leave his insurance money to Louise. Lauretta, who was mimetic in her feeble-mindedness, also sided with her mother.

Things might have been different had the business at 5 West 31st Street been a success, but despite occasional periods of relative prosperity, such as that in 1912 which had provided the money for Henry's abortive attempt to go to Cornell, the business struggled all the way. A number of times Louise had to dip into her own savings to help the firm out, and it was obvious that unless something was done both father and firm would soon go under.

Guilt had become, by default, the most powerful motive force in Henry's life. Louise knew this, and she knew that the accumulating failures of her son's adolescence gave her a powerful emotional lever to use on him. After the City College fiasco there was the Cornell fiasco, his subsequent poor work record, his absurd attempt to leave home, and above all his craven relationship with a divorced woman in her late thirties. On the unpromising grounds that in making love to Pauline he had assumed 'a tremendous moral obligation towards her' and was 'guilty of violation and must pay the penalty',[19] he had once told his mother he intended to marry her. At this Louise 'blazed forth with incredible violence, taking the carving knife and actually threatening to kill me', according to one of several descriptions of the incident he later recorded. Under the circumstances it was hard for Henry to resist when Louise began to exert real pressure on him to forget about becoming a gymnasium instructor and to begin full-time

29

work at the tailor-shop, addressing himself seriously to the task of fulfilling his destiny as his father's successor in the business. She framed her appeal with care, avoiding undue concentration on her own – and his father's – wishes in the matter, focussing instead on the intimate problem of his father's drunkenness: there were now periods when Henry senior was drunk for days on end, so drunk that he was not always able to find his way back to the office after lunch.

Put like that, it was Henry's clear duty to save his father from himself, and after just two months at the Savage School he abandoned the course and agreed to join the firm and become a tailor. His parents were delighted. Straightaway his father had the stationery printed: Henry Miller and Son, Tailors and Importers, Madison Square 1199, 5 West 31st Street. In the top right-hand corner was the legend 'Opposite Hotel Wolcott', whose bar was the cause of so much of the trouble.

6

The garment industry in New York had been through many changes since the emergence of high-class tailoring as a profession after the Civil War. The years immediately following the Civil War had seen the establishment of a number of small businesses in New York, most of them run by German immigrants, catering to a small but wealthy clientèle. By the 1880s and 1890s these businesses were just becoming established when Jewish refugees from Eastern Europe and Russia began arriving in New York in large numbers. Many of the new arrivals were people with the same traditions in clothes-making as the Germans, and the subsequent competition led to a restructuring of the industry. After the turn of the century a typical tailor's shop might consist of a group of five or six tailors working under the same roof in a loose alliance in which each preserved their individuality and kept their own list of customers while employing the same pool of journeyman tailors. This was the arrangement at Henry Miller senior's shop. He shared it with five other tailors – a Frenchman named Wemlinger, Rente, Metz and Erwin the Germans, and an American named Chase. The boss-tailor might have the status, but it was often the case that the journeyman tailors earned more money than their employers, and with the exception of Metz, the Millers' great rival, none of the bosses in the shop were affluent.

Henry was already familiar with many aspects of his new life. As a young child he used to spend hours watching his grandfather Nieting dreamily pressing the seams of suits and coats with a hot iron in the house on Driggs Avenue. Sometimes, for fun, he used to cut out paper patterns of suits which he would lay on his father's bed as a surprise for him when he came home from work. In the days before drinking took the upper hand, his father would set up a big cutting-board down in the coal cellar at home, and work on after dinner in the evening. When the family went on summer holidays together they travelled only as far as Rockaway Beach so that his father could continue to commute to work. Later, as a boy of twelve or fourteen, Henry junior would be sent out with packages of clothes to deliver on Saturdays.

His duties now – apart from expanding his knowledge of the world of alpaca sleeve linings, soft-rolled lapels, bastings, vicunas, flap pockets, silk waistcoats and braided cutaways – included familiarizing himself with the accounting, selling and social side of the business. One of his regular tasks was to try to claim on outstanding bills. Another, which he seems to have hit upon himself, was to drum up trade by going from door to door locally with a package of samples to display to prospective customers. He would try his luck at, among other places, the American Express, and the Woolworth Building on Broadway. Since an important part of his later career as a writer involved the difficult business of selling his personality, this was a useful first experience of persuading people to buy something they did not actually realize they wanted, as well as providing valuable insights into the special pleasures of being rebuffed and rejected. His line of approach was pleasingly naive: he would simply go up to prospective customers and ask if they were interested in clothes. An elderly gentleman surprised him one day by replying: 'Why yes, seeing as I'm obliged to wear them.'

As anticipated, much of his time was spent in the business of minding his father. Henry senior would generally stroll over the road to the bar of the Wolcott at about ten in the morning, easing along until it was time for lunch at about twelve. The meal itself might last until four or five in the afternoon,and then it was back to the shop in time to switch out the lights. If his father were too drunk, or had wandered too far from the Wolcott, Henry would have to go out to look for him. Often they lunched together. Henry senior wanted his son to grow up and take over the business, and he would invite Henry to join him and his cronies at the Wolcott so that he would get the hang of the social side of the life. Understandably, however, Miller was practically teetotal at the time, and though he enjoyed the food at the Wolcott he never drank anything but water with it.

What hurt him most was the humiliation his father suffered because of his drinking, and the way in which this humiliation reflected on him. It pained him to be at the shop with the cutter and the workers from

31

the busheling room at the back, where the suits were finished and pressed, when his father turned up at the end of another quiet day in his dirty straw hat, drunkenly informal, friendly, vacuous, wiping his moustache, 'nonchalant-like, reckless, devil may care, in his little boss-tailor way',[20] and to have to listen as he called up a few of his customers on the phone, speaking to them with the 'slightly defective lisp of the half-drunk man'.

One of their oldest and best customers was a lawyer named Corbett. Corbett knew that young Henry could not serve him properly, and he disliked Jews so intensely that he refused to be measured by Berg the cutter either. Instead he would humiliate Henry by obliging him to telephone the bar at the Wolcott with instructions for his father to return to the office immediately. On one occasion, after a French salesman in a bar called his father a drunken bum, Henry's self-control cracked.[21] He attacked the man and nearly throttled him before he was pulled away by others in the bar.

The humiliations he suffered on account of his father's drinking took root in Henry. It was a period of 'bitter estrangement' between father and son during which they 'communicated in monosyllables'. He felt that he had become a martyr for his mother's sake, having 'sacrificed my whole career to make her happy, to protect her from my father whose life is destroying her'.[22] Soon he developed ways of compensating for the disappointments and frustrations of his life. When he got sick of watching his father kowtow to rich customers, and of thinking of Pauline and how he could never escape her, he would relieve himself by writing long, 'sarcastic, vituperative letters, just this side of libel' to send to the firm's most hopeless debtors. Later he added the refinement of mysterious and threatening telegrams which were despatched for delivery to the victims at midnight. The ploy illuminates a harsh, ruthless side of his personality, the feeling that someone – anyone – had to pay for the suffering he underwent, for the fact that life seemed nothing but a senseless and cruel farce. Clearly he had a natural talent for violent, abusive language; but no writer really likes to acknowledge such a talent in his youth, and for many years he resisted the evidence of these dunning letters of his.

7

Almost in spite of himself, however, Henry enjoyed his time at the tailor-shop. These were the years of his real education, after the disappointments of school and college. One of his finest pieces of writing is the descriptive essay *The Tailor Shop*, which conveys wonderfully the club-like atmosphere that could overtake the place when the *raconteurs* among the visiting cloth salesman got going with their stories and jokes. One of Henry's favourites among these was a man he calls Fred Pattee whose skill in using irony to sabotage the defeats and futilities of everyday life he greatly admired. Pattee was a literate and cultured man who had acquired a taste for Heine and Schubert without losing his respect for the humour and mystery of the fart, and from characters like this he learnt that there was more to culture than just a refined accent and good manners.

He also derived pleasure and stimulation from the company of Chaimowitz, Bunchek and Rubin, who worked in the busheling room, and especially of Berg the cutter, a sympathetic Jewish immigrant who graciously listened to the youth's accounts of his latest reading adventures – Nietzsche, Herbert Spencer, Grant Allen, Henri Bergson's *Creative Evolution* – and in return broadened Henry's horizon with tales from the ghettos of his native Poland and the folklore of the Jewish people. One of the busheling room workers was an opera fan who would sing selections from Pagliacci or *Boris Godunov* when in the mood. Miller, who combined in equal parts the gifts of enthusiasm and overstatement, recalled that this man had 'probably a greater voice than Caruso'. It was from these workers that he developed his taste for the passionate melancholy of Jewish music, and in particular the singing of the cantor Gerson Sirota.[23]

The tailor-shop was situated not far from the theatre district, and many of its customers were well-known figures from the world of acting. Henry's father developed drinking friendships with several of them, and was flattered by the company of a Brooklyn legend like Corse Payton – a man who rejoiced in the title 'America's Best Bad Actor' – the elegant matinée idol Julian L'Estrange and John Barrymore senior, already a well-known stage performer on the verge of a long and successful career in films. Henry shared his father's fascination with the famous and was proud of the fact that he had a nodding acquaintance with other contemporary 'names' who patronized the shop, even if they were not always customers of Henry Miller and Son. The dramatist, actor and producer David Belasco was one of Erwin's clients, but he allowed Henry to help him on and off with his trousers; another well-known patron was the artist Boardman Robinson, then a cartoonist for the Greenwich Village magazine *The Masses*.

Some customers were of practical use to Henry. Through a photographer named Pach who had connections with the Metropolitan Opera he was able to get free admittance to concerts there and at Carnegie Hall, and heard recitals by some of the greatest names among contemporary piano virtuosi, artists like Paderewski, Alfred Cortot, and Prokofiev. Though he still vaguely entertained hopes of becoming a concert pianist himself one day, literature was playing an increasingly important rôle in his life. He had read a couple of books *about* pianos, including Montagu O'Reilly's two curious titles *Pianos of Sympathy* and *Who Has Been Tampering with These Pianos?*, but was getting at least as much out of the serious works of some of his American contemporaries and near-contemporaries like Waldo Frank, Theodore Dreiser, Jack London and Frank Norris. Further, his horizon had been dramatically extended by his encounter with Emma Goldman to include the outstanding writers in modern European literature. Though he does not list it in *The Books In My Life*, he seems to have read her book *The Social Significance of Modern Drama*, published in Boston in 1914, and used it as a reference book and guide during this period of his life. Here he came across discussions of the work and thought of Ibsen, Strindberg, Sudermann, Hauptmann, Wedekind, Maeterlinck, Rostand, Brieux, Shaw, Galsworthy, Yeats, Tolstoy, Chekhov, Gorky and Andreyev.

The political and philosophical slant Goldman gave to her promotion of all literature communicated itself to Henry, and is perhaps one reason why literature and philosophy never became clearly distinct branches of letters for him. Above all, perhaps, it accounts for his enthusiasm for anarchism. On the recommendation of her writings and lectures (she lectured frequently in New York during this period) he discovered the idealism of Peter Kropotkin. Kropotkin's theory that a viable social order will emerge of its own accord if people are left alone to do as they wish, follow their nature and discover what truly pleases them is an expression of substantially the same kind of limitless faith in human nature that Miller was to promote throughout his writing life. He also read Bakunin and the Bostonian Benjamin J.Tucker, editor of the weekly *Liberty*, the most influential voice in individual anarchism in the United States at the time, was another source of inspiration. Along with the vaguely oriental mysticism of Madame Blavatsky to which Challacombe had introduced him, Henry's readings in anarchism were a decisive formative influence during these years.

Henry read indiscriminately and widely during his adolescence; even so, one suspects him of exaggerating his precocity. Excluding the field of sex, there is no area in which we are quite so free to lie as in boasting of our prowess as readers, and Henry took full advantage of the ultimate inscrutability of both the sex-life and the reading life in creating his myth of himself. The tendency is evident in an interview he gave late in life to a French journalist in which he not only claimed to have read the *Tao Te Ching* of Lao Tzu at the tender age of seventeen, but in doing so specifically asked his interviewer to be astonished: 'In Brooklyn, I ask you! It's incredible. Me reading Lao Tzu in the middle of that crazy family!'[24] The precocity is belied by the wistful regret expressed in *Sexus* that at thirty-three he had yet to encounter the book: 'Had I been intelligent enough to have read that most illustrious and most elliptical piece of ancient wisdom I would have been spared a great many woes.'[25] In fact he almost certainly did not read the *Tao Te Ching* until he was in Paris in his forties. This naked desire to impress inclines one to look sceptically at the claim made in a letter to a professor that in his boyhood he had read 'what other boys read, such as Sir Walter Scott, Dickens, Dumas, Victor Hugo, and American writers too, especially the poets, practically all of them, up to a certain period. Include Ambrose Bierce, Lafcadio Hearn, Frank Norris, Dreiser, Anderson, Ben Hecht, many, many others' and that 'while in my teens, I believe, I read Petronius, Rabelais, Pierre Louys, Rémy de Gourmont, Jules Laforgue, Maeterlink, Pierre Loti, to mention a few. Nearly all of them very important to me. As were the Greek tragedies, the Restoration dramatists, and the 19th century dramatists of most European countries.'[26]

Whether the claims are true or not, the definite impression that emerges from such listing is of someone who prefers quantity to quality. It is also hard to believe that the Greek tragedies and the Restoration dramatists can have meant much to someone who left college in disgust at eighteen because he was made to read Spenser's *Faerie Queene*. One is on safer ground with a name that does not figure on this list, that of Frank Harris, another of the tailor-shop's famous customers. The Greenwich Village notable and charlatan Guido Bruno, Harris' assistant on *Pearson's* magazine at the time, brought Harris along with him to the Millers' shop one day in 1916 so that Harris could pick something suitable for a yachting trip. He began to laugh when Henry senior suggested a material with broad stripes, saying that it would have been more appropriate for someone appearing in a minstrel show. Eventually, however, he found some-thing to his liking. While he was being fitted in the back room, where the staff were amazed to discover that he wore no underclothes, he entertained them with monologues on three of his favourite subjects – Jesus, Oscar Wilde and William Shakespeare. Harris was a famous writer at the time, the author of a much-praised book on Shakespeare, and in his capacity as editor of *Pearson's* an exciting and controversial figure who had taken a consistently anti-British line after the outbreak of the 1914–18 war, with the result that the magazine had twice been seized by the authorities. The combination of literature and rebellion was impressive and attractive to Henry, as was Harris' informal manner with the cutters. In *The Books In My Life* Miller lists fourteen titles of books by Harris, including *The Bomb*, Harris' 1908 novel based on the anarchist bomb outrage in the Chicago Haymarket, and the *Stories of Jesus the Christ*. The association between sexual boasting and an occasional messiah-complex in the writings of both men suggests that it was the bold versatility of Harris' personality rather than his literary skills that impressed Henry. A man who could interpret, as Harris did, the biblical words 'much shall be forgiven her for she loved much' as a clear indication that Jesus had 'surely been in the stews' was a man close to Miller's own heart.[27] Meeting Harris meant a lot to Henry, and he always fondly called it his 'first contact with a great writer'.[28] At the time, however, he was not quite sure what to make of him, and in a letter to a friend related that he had 'mixed feelings regarding him. Like him immensely but can't see his greatness. Am I near-sighted?'[29]

A more respectable literary influence was that of John Cowper Powys, the Welsh poet, novelist, essayist and lecturer. Powys settled in America in 1914, the same year as Harris, and quickly established a reputation as a touring lecturer. After the mysticism of Challacombe and Mills, the politicized literary preaching of Emma Goldman and the rascally polemic of Frank Harris, Powys had a more purely literary influence on Miller's development – although Powys too considered himself as much a philosopher as a writer. In 1916, Powys held a series of lectures on great Russian writers at the Hudson Theatre, 139 West 44th Street, just a dozen blocks north of the tailor-shop, where he spoke on Dostoevsky, Tolstoy, Turgenev, Chekhov, Gorky, Andreyev and Artzybashev. Henry heard the lectures, and was smitten. 'Do you know where I have had to run for any satisfaction for my disgust?' he wrote in 1916. 'To Russian authors. There is a grim reality about their writing that appeases me.'[30] Powys's lectures contributed to a cult of Russia and the 'Slavic soul' which was noticeable during this period, originating among the bohemians of Greenwich Village in a reverence for Nijinsky and Dostoevsky. Miller was not yet a Greenwich Villager, but he had seen Nijinsky dance, and was deeply impressed by the intensity of Russian artists, finding in them an exhilarating contrast to the drabness of American materialism. Besides promoting Dostoevsky, Powys wrote and spoke frequently about Rabelais and Walt Whitman, both of whom were great favourites of Miller's. 'All the authors I was then passionate about were the authors he was writing and lecturing about. He was like an oracle to me,' Miller recalled.[31]

Powys the lecturer had the same effect on Henry as Emma Goldman. Both created a delirium in him, though of a different kind:

Powys, needless to say, had his own select luminaries whom he raved about. I use the word 'raved' advisedly. I had never before heard anyone *rave* in public, particularly about authors, thinkers, philosophers. Emma Goldman, equally inspired on the platform, and often Sibylline in utterance, gave nevertheless the impression of radiating from an intellectual center. Warm and emotional though she was, the fire she gave off was an electrical one. Powys fulminated with the fire and smoke of the soul, or the depths which cradle the soul. Literature for him was like manna from above. He pierced the veil time and time again.[32]

On a technical level, Powys's baroque style of writing impressed him, and readers of Powys's *Autobiography* are bound to be struck by the similarities with the style Miller adopted for his writing after the 1940s, with its taste for inversion, exotic words, and occasional semi-biblical formulations. Powys also had elements of the same quantitative approach to the world of literature that Miller had. In 1916 he published a list of his *One Hundred Best Books*.

8

While hiding out at Pauline's and living off the money intended to see him through Cornell, Henry had made his first halting and unsuccessful attempts to write in the drab little kitchen of her flat. On returning from California he made a further attempt, perhaps hoping to get a Jack London story out of his experiences in the citrus groves; but this proved equally disheartening. In the beginning, perhaps, these earliest literary efforts were only tactical manoeuvres in the general attempt to withdraw from Pauline into a private world of 'spiritual conquests'. Presently, however, it must have occurred to Henry that he was getting so much from the world of books that he ought to think seriously about becoming a writer himself. It was an unusual but not unheard-of idea in the circles in which he moved. Bob Challacombe wrote verse, and Henry's childhood friend Stanley Borowski had grown up wanting to be a writer. Stanley had moved away from Brooklyn in his teens, but one way of passing the time at the tailor-shop which Henry discovered was to write long letters of literary appreciation and criticism of the books he was reading to Stanley, and this way they had managed to keep in touch. Coming from a Polish background, it must have seemed natural to Stanley to choose Joseph Conrad as his literary idol. Similarly the strong, lifelong attachment Henry felt for the poetry and personality of Walt Whitman may well have had its roots in a simple sense of identification based on the fact that Whitman was from

Brooklyn, and proud of it. Whitman was one of the handful of writers who exercised real, traceable influence on Miller's writing. Like Henry's other early heroes, he was a cross between a writer, a philosopher and a prophet, someone for whom the spiritual content of the work was more important than its aesthetic qualities. The aspects of his poetry that particularly appealed to Henry are obvious enough in the light of Henry's own performance as a published writer in later life – the emotional, 'plain man' stance; the aesthetic which insists that 'who touches the book touches the man'; the religious ecstasy; the rough, wild, emotional humanitarianism; the man with a powerful sense of the importance of his feminine sides; the challenging and notorious writer whose personal honesty gets him into trouble with the authorities; the writer who changes people's lives; and the fierce social critic, whose criticism is tempered by an equally fierce patriotism which insists on the superiority of the local, American greatness of the Wallabout Martyrs over the greatness of the heroes of remote antiquity. Sanctioning his enjoyment of Whitman as poet and thinker, Miller had the example of mentors like Benjamin Fay Mills, whose *Walt Whitman: the Man and his Message* he read; Emma Goldman, who idolized the poet and valued particularly his 'extraordinary sensitiveness to the nature of woman conditioned in the fact that he had considerable femininity in him'; and the enthusiasm for Whitman's verse of John Cowper Powys.

The first piece of writing that Henry produced with the conscious hope that it would be read by others was an essay on Nietzsche's *The Anti-Christ*, written during one of the long, idle days at the tailor-shop. The essay has not survived, nor has the journal he kept in which he noted down, besides the intimate details of his life with Pauline, his reactions to public events like the death of Jack London in 1916 ('the news of his death really pained me, so much so that I got out my dairy to register my thoughts about it'). By his own account, anyway, most of the writing he did at this period was in his own head. Going to work he would take the elevated line from Brooklyn across the bridge each day, get off at Delancey Street and walk the rest of the way to 5th Avenue and 31st Street, all the while planning the books and plays he was going to write when he got the time, when he had the talent, when he was ready, when the weather was better, when the pencil was sharper, when the pages were all numbered and after he'd cleaned his shoes. Some writers run into a block once they've said all they had to say, but Henry had the block even before he started. He described his troubles to a friend:

I have had the devil's own torments lately from imagining that I have something in me to give to the world. I can't quite believe that I am capable of writing anything worthwhile and yet, for the life of me, I can't repress the desire to put my thoughts on paper. Have had some notions of writing a play, but I have such outlandish stuff to dole out that I am almost afraid to begin. If there is one thing worse than having an artistic temperament, it is thinking you have one.[33]

He felt that in working in his father's business he was 'living in a narrow sphere'. Yet for someone who was 'only a tailor', his adolescent sense of isolated arrogance was healthily large. 'From using my own powers of observation, I am able to form some judgment of the masses that surround me and I can truthfully say that I loathe them throughgoughly (sic). Their own sheer stupidity will be the death of them,' was how he expressed it. In the same letter he claims that he is 'no longer capable of railing against the capitalists and the politicians as I did several years ago. What bothers me now is the fact that there is no material from which to make men nowadays.' Interestingly, he expressly observes that he does not believe that 'the system is responsible for everything', showing that he had in his early twenties the same cheering faith in the importance of the individual that invests practically all the best writing of his later years.

In 1916, when he wrote the above letter to Charles Keeler, a poet, author and later Founder and Managing Director of something called the Cosmic Society, Henry Miller and Son, Tailors and Importers, were going through one of their better spells. Keeler was a former customer, and Miller's letter mixes metaphysics with news of the goings-on in the shop. Besides the upturn in trade, Henry could report that his father was 'going through a sort of regeneration, having cut out the booze for the last eight or nine months'. In fact, they were doing so well that Henry had allowed Guido Bruno to swindle him out of $200. As this was the equivalent of eight times the monthly wage he had been getting at the Atlas Portland Cement Company, it indicates not only how well the firm was doing but that Henry's later references to the poverty of his early manhood, when he had to queue for a ticket at the Metropolitan 'usually on an empty stomach',[34] and try to write among the pots and pans of Pauline's kitchen 'with a little broken pencil' were just romantic fantasies, and certainly had no bearing on his failure to make an early start as a writer.[35]

9

By this time Henry had reached his full height of 5 feet 8 inches. His hair had turned darker, and much of it was already gone. He wore glasses, weighed just over 10 stone, had a 38 inch chest and a 32 inch waist and his hat and shoes were both size 7 to 7½. He was the boss's son and he dressed correctly in suit, shirt and tie, the suit being often a good quality hand-me-down from his father. He kept busy, had many friends, frequently rode his bike, went to the theatre, the opera, the concert hall, read a lot, played the piano, played chess, listened to gramophone records, tried to write, and slept with a woman he didn't love. The campaign of 'spiritual conquests' had not worked: when he closed the piano lid, packed away the books and the chessmen and lifted his head, Pauline was still there. Her lodger, Tex the tramdriver, whom Miller called the 'star-boarder' because he had a regular job and paid his rent promptly, was a pleasant enough man, but he was not a reader or a talker, and Henry could not use him to ease the burden of life with Pauline. Accordingly he took a step he was to take over and again in his life, and persuaded one of his friends to move in with them.

Joe O'Reagan had had a genuinely hard upbringing. He had been raised in an orphanage and then travelled the world with the American army. Henry met him shortly after he was discharged at a lakeside village in New Jersey where the Millers were on holiday. Another friend of Henry's named Bill Woodruff was staying with them for a few days. Woodruff and O'Reagan were workmates and at Woodruff's invitation O'Reagan came out to visit them. Henry's private opinion of Woodruff was that he was something of a weed, but O'Reagan impressed him at once as a tough, manly, athletic young man. He had had little formal education, but was intelligent and a good *raconteur*. Being shy and oversensitive with girls himself, Henry always admired men who were not, and he thrilled to Joe's tales of army life and of sexual adventures with Japanese whores, soon making an idol of him. By the time Joe moved in at Pauline's, he and Henry had become close friends.

O'Reagan saw his role in the household rather differently from the motorman Tex, and as soon as he moved in he set about trying to seduce Pauline while Henry was out at work. She was reduced to tears by his advances and reported them to Henry. Henry found it difficult to care and even defended Joe. He had begun suffering occasionally from impotence as a consequence of his disinterest in Pauline, and may even have half-hoped that Joe would take her off his hands for good. Probably as a result of Pauline's upset, Joe soon left on his travels again; but he would return to play an oddly similar role in relations between Miller and women on two future occasions.

Eventually, sometime in 1915, the death-knell of the relationship between Henry and Pauline was sounded. Henry was at a wedding with William Dewar when Dewar introduced him to a young woman named Beatrice Sylvas Wickens. Beatrice, with her dark hair and dark

40

eyes, had the distinctly non-Germanic type of looks that Miller was to fall for again and again in his life. She was a professional musician and, according to Dewar, a 'brilliant concert pianist', while Henry, for all his practising, was 'no Franz Liszt' although he 'did play well in a popular sort of way'. She was a cultured, strong-minded woman, just twenty-three years old, a type of whom his mother could approve. Their mutual interest in music gave them something to talk about, and before they parted Henry asked Beatrice if she would be willing to give him piano lessons.

CHAPTER THREE

1916–1920
Beatrice

1

Many years later, when Miller began writing about his relationship with Beatrice Wickens, he pointed out the nagging shame she felt about her mother and a fear she had that 'one day she would behave just like her'. The mother was 'a bad sort', 'no good' and so on, though Miller never goes on to describe the background to this characterization. It appears that Beatrice, born in 1892, was the daughter of an unmarried woman named Catherine Scherer, and that she was raised as the child of her sister, Elizabeth Scherer, and her husband Frederick P. Sylvas, a shoemaker, at a house on Arbordale Avenue, Rochester, NY. She was educated at a convent school in Montreal, finishing her education at a music conservatory there when her talent as a pianist became evident.

On completing her education she went to live with her real mother, Catherine, who by this time had married a grocery clerk named Frank Wickens and moved into a house at 441 9th Street in Brooklyn. Beatrice kept both family names and called herself Beatrice Sylvas Wickens. She gave her occupation in the 1915 census as 'concert pianist' and apparently supplemented her income by giving piano lessons while she tried to establish her career.

Besides her appearance, her musical ability and the fact that she was some fifteen years younger than Pauline, Beatrice was also interested in literature. At the Fulton Street wedding where they met they had discussed Dreiser's controversial novel *Sister Carrie*, published in 1900. Miller had already developed the habit of identifying people he met with characters from books, and in Beatrice Wickens he thought he detected something of Carrie Meeber's excited and romantic expectations of life in the big city.

The relationship developed from the professional to the personal, and soon Miller was calling on Beatrice socially. They went to the cinema and the theatre together, to concerts and operas at Carnegie Hall, the Metropolitan Opera House, and to the Brooklyn Academy of Music on Lafayette Street. Reopened in 1908 after a fire, the Academy boasted an opera house, theatre, lecture hall and ballroom, and attracted performers of the stature of Horowitz, Rachmaninov and Toscanini. At last, it seemed, Miller had found in Beatrice that spiritual companionship which had been sorely missing with Pauline.

The courtship of the young and respectable Beatrice did, however, present him with difficulties which he had not known with Pauline. Where the older woman had taken the sexual initiative with the young man, Miller now found himself having to play the conventional pursuer's rôle, biding his time, showing respect for Beatrice 'as a person', as a way of winning her confidence. He continued, anyway, to provide for his sexual needs by sleeping with Pauline while submitting to Beatrice's 'testing' of him. Beatrice also introduced him to a rival for her affections, a man named James Haley, but any hopes she may have had that this would make Miller jealous backfired. At a dinner the three of them ate together in a French restaurant, Miller took a great liking to Haley, finding him decent, honest, respectable, kind, considerate – all the qualities he secretly suspected himself of not possessing – and privately thought Haley was more her type. Miller was much more jealous of her stepfather, Frank Wickens, and the way Beatrice would sit on his lap in a flimsy dress, talking to him in a low, caressing voice. It seemed to him that she enjoyed something perverse and incestuous with Wickens, something which made it very difficult to 'bring her out into any clear, open sexual relationship'.[1]

During this brief interlude in 1916, when he was seeing both Beatrice and Pauline, Miller discovered for himself the guilty erotic excitement enjoyed by the faithless in love. Soon enough Pauline began to suspect that he had found someone else as Miller began avoiding her, lying to her about having to work late at the tailor-shop or go out looking for his father, and her suspicions were confirmed when he took her with him to the Decatur Street house one day and introduced her to Beatrice, pointedly explaining to her that this was his piano teacher. He hoped that the meeting would be enough to persuade Pauline of the hopelessness of her case and let him off the hook, though no doubt he also found the situation exciting. However, the only result of the meeting was that Pauline, with the pitiful foolishness of the true lover, made her rival, rather than her betrayer, the object of her hatred.

Miller was sensitive, but only to a degree. He had that vanity characteristic of a certain kind of sensitive person who cannot bear to see their own sensitivity compromised by inflicting hurt on another. Even now, when he realized that nothing he could do would ever persuade Pauline to set him free, he was unable to tell her the simple, brutal truth that he preferred someone else. Instead, he resorted to his old trick and told her that he was leaving New York. This time his story was that he was on his way to Juneau, Alaska, to try his luck as a goldminer. The Chula Vista experience had toughened him emotionally, and on this occasion he felt under no obligation to go through the charade of actually making the trip. He simply moved the last of his belongings out of the flat on Macon Street, returned to his parents' house and – for the time being at least – dropped out of Pauline's life.

2

When Miller felt that he had done enough, through evenings at the opera and the concert hall, to establish his cultural credentials, he introduced Beatrice to another side of his personality and began taking her down the road to Keith's vaudeville theatre on 9th Street. At Keith's, he recalled, they used to 'sit during the dark acts masturbating each other'.[2]

Beatrice's stepfather died shortly after she and Henry met, and once they had become lovers their only slight problem at 9th Street was the presence in the house of her mother. Out of deference to her, the couple frequently resorted to those 'hallway and radiator affairs' which Miller describes so graphically in both *Sexus* and *The World of Sex*. Later on, he developed the habit of bidding the mother goodnight and then sneaking back to spend the night with Beatrice in her room.

Miller's initial experiences with Pauline had caused him tremendous feelings of guilt, but by the time the relationship ended he had become convinced that sex was nothing to feel guilty about. Beatrice had not had the benefits of his experience, and in observing the conventions of shyness and shame during their courtship she merely irritated Miller. Ever mindful of the disaster with Cora Seward, he was determined not to let romanticism dictate the course of this new relationship with a 'decent' woman, and he watched with scant sympathy as Beatrice struggled with her own sense of guilt:

If I took a seat in the corner and listened to her attentively she might stop half way through a sonata and come over to me of her own accord, let me run my hand up her leg, and finally straddle me. With the orgasm she would sometimes have a weeping fit. Doing it in broad daylight always awakened her sense of guilt. (The way she voiced it was that it deteriorated her keyboard technique.) Anyway, the better the fuck the worse she felt afterwards.[3]

'My affair with her began on the sex note, not as love,' he wrote once,[4] and it was the erotic complexities of the relationship that continued to fascinate him. What he savoured in particular was the conflict in Beatrice between the 'Puritanism' bred in her by her convent upbringing and her genuinely sensual nature. 'Because she had a Puritanical attitude did not mean she was weak sexually – this only made our sex-life more exciting, more passionate,'[5] he wrote. Miller liked to promote this conflict by making advances to her in public places like telephone booths, theatre foyers, bars and railway stations. She would protest, but her protests were precisely what he enjoyed.

This focus on the erotic both made and marred their relationship. Whenever Beatrice burst into tears at what seemed to Henry particularly inopportune moments she would send him away, and shortly afterwards he would receive a letter from her saying she hoped never to see him again. 'You don't really care for *me* – all you're after is sex,' was always her complaint. Whether the charge was originally true or not, Miller felt that it soon became so by dint of her constant repetition. Yet he kept coming back to her, and she kept taking him back.

One difficulty in the relationship was that Beatrice was never able to reconcile herself to Henry's fondness for using coarse language while making love.[6] Indeed, he felt a strong, natural attraction to the use of violently expressive words in all human contexts. His admiration for the passionate oratory of Goldman and Powys was one illustration of this; another was his regular presence among the crowds in Union Square and Madison Square to hear the inflammatory speech-making of anarchists, IWW leaders and radicals like Carlo Tresca, Giovanitti, Jim Larkin and Bill Haywood.

Miller was genuinely attracted to the ideas voiced in Union Square on socialism, anarchism, syndicalism and trades unionism. His cowboy friend in Chula Vista, Bill Parr, had given him an introduction to these, and after coming across Emma Goldman he had begun to study for himself books written by political prophets of the era, like the socialist pacifist Eugene V. Debs. Yet what attracted him as much as the ideas themselves was the fear they inspired in the hearts of ordinary, non-political people. The destroyer in him thrilled to the political revolutionaries of the IWW not as social visionaries but as 'saboteurs of progress',[7] and to hail what the ordinary man feared strengthened a feeling in him of being different and superior which was already considerable.

His grandfather, Valentin, had become a union man during his ten years in London,[8] and one of Henry's earliest memories was of watching Nieting washing at the sink in cold water as he prepared to go down to Paul Kerl's beer-hall to listen to the Socialist speeches; but Henry's father was a boss tailor, and after Nieting's death socialism became a dirty word in the Miller household. The philosophical and religious searching generated by his friendship with Robert Challa-combe back in 1912 did bring him into fleeting contact with political solutions to social problems, and in among the theosophy, the esoteric buddhism and the meetings of Ethical Culture he attended, he carried on a brief flirtation with Christian Socialism. However, his need to find his own solutions was too great for any of these systematic philosophies to hold his attention for long.

Beatrice was no Greenwich Village feminist. She was a respectable young woman, and once she and Miller became lovers she firmly expected him to marry her. While still living at 9th Street she had to have an abortion, which must have strengthened her moral claims on him. He was still bound to certain conventional mores, and in December 1916, as he approached his twenty-fifth birthday, he was also feeling, like Beatrice, that he was 'getting to the stage now where I should like to start out in life with a companion, and perhaps have a home of my own, after a fashion.'[9]

It was at about the same time that Miller finally achieved, in an unexpected way, the longed-for liberation from the tailor-shop. His father's nine-month period of abstinence in 1916 turned into a permanent break with alcohol. The constant battles with Louise, the smashed crockery and her threats to run away, finally decided him. He lost most of his friends in the process, endured a brief period of religious fervour during which he read, on the recommendation of a priest, *The Stones of Venice*, the Ruskin book which was his sole encounter with the world of serious literature, but stuck to his decision, and to the great surprise of his family never touched strong drink again.

The result of this show of character in his father was to release Henry from any lingering obligation he might have felt to carry on in full-time work at West 31st Street, either as apprentice tailor or as his father's minder. He had never really mastered the skills of the trade, and though he could cut trousers the complexities of the jacket and the coat remained beyond him. Anyway, as the disaster with Guido Bruno had shown only too clearly, he was hardly more capable than his father of running the firm at a profit. Thus, in 1917, a lifetime of pressure on him to become a tailor was finally lifted, and the freedom to do as he pleased beckoned.

His first move was an entirely modest one: through the influence of one of his father's customers, a Vice-President of the Federal Reserve Bank, he started work in the Wall Street district as one of a team of clerks checking for errors in the bank's adding machines. It was dull work, but the pay was good. One morning, after he had been there a few weeks, he was summoned to the office of the personnel manager:

46

To my great surprise he told me he was discharging me. Why? I wanted to know. Wasn't my work satisfactory?

Oh, there was nothing wrong with my work, he hastened to assure me. It was my character.

'My character?' I exclaimed.

'Yes,' he said. 'We have been investigating your life, interrogating your friends and neighbours – we know quite a bit about you.'

And then he told me how they had discovered about me and the widow.

'We are not questioning your morals,' he went on, 'but we feel we can't trust you.'[10]

If Miller's account is accurate, one can only marvel at the Kafkaesque powers wielded by the personnel manager of a Wall Street bank in those days, and at his extensive use of them against one of the thirty clerks checking for mistakes in the adding machine room. An interesting aspect of the story is the way it reinforces the idea of the presence of a highly personal form of paranoia in Miller. He relates the personnel manager's doubts about him in a way that flatters him by portraying him as a dangerous and special man who must be made the object of extraordinary attention.

Henry's next job was another clerking position, this time in the Bureau of Economic and Industrial Research, where he encountered something called the 'Belgian' system of indexing. In later years he recalled this with an awed respect for its pretensions as something that was 'meant to restore order to this world of chaos'. It was definitely not for him, though – as he added firmly, 'one must be *converted* to it, otherwise it makes no appeal'.[11]

His outgoing personality picked up friendships easily, here as elsewhere, which were later to prove useful to him. At the Bureau he met an economist named Karl G. Karsten who later helped him with a job and housing when he needed both badly. As with most of Miller's friends from this period, Karsten was also unconsciously sitting for a part in *The Rosy Crucifixion*: in one of Miller's cruellest and funniest portraits, he is lampooned in *Plexus* as the statistical pendant 'Karen Lundgren' who organizes his entire life on the basis of a card-indexing system.

This job too was temporary, and by the time it was over the European war had arrived in America. Until Miller saw for himself its effects on France during his European tour of 1928, for him, as for most Americans, this war remained 'an adventure, so to speak. Something done with one hand tied behind the back.'[12] However, with the German resumption of a campaign of unrestricted submarine warfare the US was forced to reconsider its neutrality and in March 1917 finally joined the Allies.

A whole bureaucracy at once sprang up to deal with the paperwork, and Miller found himself employed as a clerk in the mail division of the War Department in Washington DC. After about a month he was laid off. Not anxious to return to New York quite so quickly, and perhaps under the influence of a friend, Raymond Swing, who had had considerable success as a journalist and was later to become a nationally known broadcaster, he briefly and unsuccessfully tried to find work on a Washington newspaper before returning home to Brooklyn.

On June 5th 1917 all American males between the ages of twenty-one and thirty years were required to register in their electoral district: failure to do so meant an automatic one year term in jail. Miller awoke one morning stunned by the realization that he, a single man in his mid-twenties, would be among the first to be conscripted and sent off to be killed once Selective Service was introduced. In great alarm he confided his fears to a friend who gave him the succinct advice: 'Get married, you silly bastard, and you'll be deferred.'[13]

Miller at once proposed to Beatrice. He was accepted, and on June 15th the couple were duly married. Beatrice chose to be given away by her foster parents, Fred and Elizabeth Sylvas of Rochester, with Catherine Wickens as her witness. Henry, having breached one family tradition in tailoring, had studiously honoured another: both his grandfathers, Heinrich and Valentin, had emigrated from Germany in flight from conscription some fifty years previously. A neighbour who saw the couple together shortly after the marriage wrote that Beatrice 'looked like the cat that swallowed the canary', while Henry resembled 'a dying calf'.[14] The opinion of the Decatur Street gossips generally was that the marriage was a mistake.

While Henry was not exactly one of the 'hyphenated Americans' whose loyalty Woodrow Wilson had called into question over the response to his war preparation programmes in 1916, the fact that he was of German extraction is bound to have played a large part in his attitude towards fighting a war against the country of his forefathers, and to have contributed to the slight anglophobia that pursued him throughout his life. In addition, two literary figures whom he much admired at this time, Frank Harris and the critic and essayist H.L. Mencken, produced some fiercely anti-English journalism during the war which made them unpopular with the authorities and – in consequence – popular with Henry. The real target of Wilson's thrust were the Irish-Americans, and another element in the creation of Henry's anglophobia was probably the influence of the Irish immigrant friends of his Brooklyn childhood, many of whom were from strongly Republican families.

That said, Miller's horror of going to war was above all an instinctive reaction. William Dewar, recalling the Xerxes days, said: 'Henry hated any kind of fight, and was never the hero of the exploits he recounted.'[15] Miller himself described how, on the lovelorn and lonely bike-rides of his adolescence, he would sometimes be roused from his reveries about Cora when passing by the barracks at Fort Hamilton, 'for whenever I espy military quarters, quarters where men are herded like cattle, I experience a feeling almost of nausea'.[16] Pacifism later became a cornerstone of his passionate belief in the rightness of a thoroughgoing egoism as a response to the problems of society.

In his written version of his life, Miller liked to stress the Dostoevskian dimensions of the marriage proposal he made to Beatrice, claiming: 'I got myself married overnight, to demonstrate to all and sundry that I didn't give a fuck one way or the other.'[17] The interpretation is lent credence by the fact that it was the best man, Dewar, who paid for the marriage licence, as well as for Miller's ritual shave and haircut on the big day.[18] Dewar's prognosis was no more hopeful than that of the Decatur Street gossips: 'Henry had bad judgment when it came to women' was his opinion, 'and Bea was one of his mistakes.'

Yet whether Miller's approach to the marriage was quite so devoid of ordinary grace as he later liked to make out is open to doubt. He was still, in his puzzled way, trying to conform to accepted standards of behaviour, though he had made one characteristically eccentric attempt to escape his fate at the last minute, conscription or no conscription. In one of his notebooks, under the heading 'Marital Struggles', he recalls a 'Jim Haley episode at Hermitage before marriage. Our friendship. Subsequent visit to Washington DC to be with him. Disillusionment followed by estrangement. Saying hello to him at Utica on way to Rochester for honeymoon. Bitterness, sorrow etc.'[19] The incident appears in expanded form in *Moloch*, an unpublished novel Miller wrote in the late 1920s based on the years of his marriage to Beatrice. Here the Miller character, Dion Moloch, visits a Jim Daley a week before the marriage with an offer to withdraw and leave Daley free to marry Blanche. Blanche turns Jim down and she and Dion Moloch go ahead and marry as planned. Dion Moloch later tells his wife that 'after I took you home that night, and you told me you had refused Jim your hand, I went back to the Claridge and went to bed with Jim.' In *Sexus*, another version of the story appears, minus its startling conclusion.[20]

The episode recalls another incident Miller often refers to in his writing, the night his father came home dead drunk with another man,

49

got into a furious argument with Louise about his right to bring friends home to stay the night and staggered off to bed arm in arm with his pal to clinch the point. The possibility that in so doing Henry senior revealed the presence of some long-thwarted homosexual desire is certainly present in the tale, but common sense suggests that behind it all was no more than the tired indifference to propriety that often accompanies heavy drinking. This may have been what happened with Dion Moloch and Jim Daley, though Moloch's phrase 'went to bed with Jim' could hardly be misinterpreted today. It would cast a pleasingly novel light on Henry Miller's mid-century status as an American virility symbol if he had indeed experimented with homo-sexuality; yet somehow it seems unlikely.

What the Jim Haley episode does clearly show is the extent to which Miller was still dominated by a helpless passivity when faced with important decisions. He knew that his marriage to Beatrice would not work, and yet, as with Cora and Pauline, he was quite incapable of saying and doing what he actually wanted to say and do. Like trains, events were always setting off around him while he still had one foot on the platform, and this was proving a serious problem. The need to find a way forward that could accommodate this weakness would become one of the major quests of his life.

3

After the wedding the couple moved into a brownstone house in the middle of the most respectable part of Brooklyn, at 244 6th Avenue, renting the basement and ground floor from their landlords, Mr and Mrs Butler, who occupied the top floor with their daughter Marion.

Henry didn't like the house: it was gloomy, the rent high and the furniture kept getting in his way. It reminded him of a doctor's office. In spite of fierce protests from Beatrice, he installed a big round mahogany table from the tailor-shop in the middle of the parlour. He thought that sitting at this table might help him to become a writer, just as he thought that sitting at a second desk he owned, with pigeonholes, might teach him how to become a responsible husband. Here he filled out life insurance and accident insurance forms because 'it's important, when you're married, to do things like that, so they told me'.[21] Feeling that 'the instalment plan had been invented expressly for guys like me' he also plunged as swiftly as possible into debt, ordering 'books, music albums, gramophones, porterhouse steaks and such like'.

For their regular income the couple were dependent on the money

Beatrice earned from her music lessons. Henry also gave lessons, mostly on the East Side, though he had by now practically given up playing for pleasure. He worked briefly as an editorial assistant on the Charles Williams mail-order catalogue, but lost the job when he was caught reading on the firm's time. His heart was no more in his work than in his marriage.

Generally speaking, there was little money coming into the house. Beatrice's career as a concert pianist never took off, and if she did give recitals, they were not considered sufficiently important for the *Brooklyn Eagle's* reviewers to notice them. The Millers put an advertisement for lodgers in the *New York Times* in the hope of supplementing their income, and had a series of tenants. One of these was a young student from Japan named Tori Takekuchi. Miller followed Tori's erotic adventures with American women with great interest, and expressed a passing interest in learning Japanese from him, though he more than half suspected that Tori's hilarity as he fired off a salvo of Japanese words at him was because they actually meant 'foreign fool', 'shit-heel', 'white bugger' or something similar. Many years later he wrote about Tori in *Sexus*, and was pleased to receive a letter from him in 1954. Tori mentioned how astonished his Japanese wife had been to read about her husband's adventures as a young man in America.

Another tenant was Harold Orvis Ross, a name which Henry always and incorrectly spelt Harold*e*, perhaps to distinguish him from the Harold Ross who later founded the *New Yorker*. Ross was a pianist from Blue Earth, Minnesota who had come to New York to study music. He was blessed with the gift of enthusiasm, a quality that attracted Miller more than anything else in a person, and could discuss at length Dreiser's new novel or the precise reasons for the greatness of Nijinsky. Harold could read French, which made him a cultured man in Henry's book, and they often went to concerts together. But like Beatrice, Ross did not have Miller's need to satisfy a vulgar side to his personality, and when Henry wanted to watch the bike races, or Jim Londos and Strangler Lewis wrestling or Jack Johnson going through his training routines he had to turn to old friends from the days before his marriage.

The couple had their first fight on a day when Miller wanted to go off to Coney Island, or Sodom-by-the-Sea as it was known to Brooklynites, with his friend Bennie Epstein. Beatrice had other plans,[22] but Henry went anyway, and the marriage seems to have established itself quite quickly thereafter on a permanent war footing. Miller could not take discipline. He had had enough of it from his mother, and was determined not to allow any sense of ownership to develop in his married life. His attitude towards his father began to change from this point on, and he saw him as the victim of his mother rather than as her oppressor. It seemed to him that responsibility had killed Henry senior's spirit, that he had been 'left to die in the bosom of the family', and he became desperately anxious to avoid his father's fate. In many other unfortunate ways he seems to have assumed that his own marriage would inevitably echo that of his parents. The criticisms he presently began to level at his wife were the same as those he later levelled at his mother: that she was bossy, snobbish and pretentious. And like Louise, Beatrice found that her husband's easy-going charm masked a disturbing irresponsibility and lack of ambition. Miller was snobbish too, in his own way: Beatrice was forever rearranging the furniture in the house and planning new budgets, and his artistic ambitions, bohemian leanings and fondness for dangerous figures like Emma Goldman and the IWW leaders were all seriously compromised by such shameless domesticity.

4

The bickering was practically continuous, and soon Miller was recalling with longing the quiet life he had known with Pauline. He found out by chance that she was working as an usherette in a Newark theatre called Keeney's, and surprised her there one day. She remonstrated with him briefly for the way in which he had deserted her, but was, as ever, willing to forgive him. He walked her home to her attic room after the show. George was dead, she told him, and she had a job as a live-in maid. She cried when Miller told her he had got married.

Consumed by guilt and pity for her, Miller immediately hatched one of those extraordinary plans to make everybody happy which were to become a feature of his life: he decided he would invite Pauline to come and live with himself and his wife in their house on 6th Avenue. There was plenty of space and she could have her own room. Though Beatrice was as unlikely to respond warmly to the plan as his mother had been to his idea of marrying Pauline he went ahead and suggested it to her anyway, stressing that there would be no question of any funny business. Naturally, Beatrice rejected the notion out of hand, something which allowed Henry to blame her for the fact that the night at Keeney's was the last occasion on which he and Pauline ever met. Some years later he heard from a friend who had seen her working in Abraham & Straus' department store on Fulton Street, but after that she fades out of his life for good.

Uniquely among the women he wrote about in his autobiographical books, whether she is called 'Carlotta' or just 'the Widow', Pauline is treated with sympathy and tenderness. Her indulgence of him, her lack of intellectual curiosity and her freedom from neurotic posturing made her an increasingly attractive memory as he grew older and more entrenched in his anti-intellectualism. Where Beatrice had reminded him of Dreiser's Carrie Meeber, Pauline was his own Jennie Gerhardt, the eponymous heroine of Dreiser's novel about a working-class girl who sacrifices herself for her lover's happiness. Jennie withdraws from the hero's life so that he may marry a woman of his own social class and regain the approval of his parents. For Miller to have seen a parallel there illustrates well his habit of interpreting the events of his life in such a way as to protect him from feeling too much blame or guilt for what happened around him. Pauline did not willingly sacrifice herself or his happiness; on the contrary, she clung to him as fiercely as she could. Her only crime was to have been fifteen years older than her lover, and in late old age Miller conceded that she would have made him a better wife than Beatrice. He suggests somewhere that she had TB as well as her son,[23] so she probably died long before her 'Harry' became a famous writer in the 1930s. In any case, she was a woman who was not much interested in the world of books, and even if she lived to a reasonable age it is unlikely she would have heard about his success.

5

After the death of her husband Frank, Catherine Wickens came to live with her daughter and son-in-law and also kept house for them. Henry liked her. She had a way of humming to herself as she went about the house which relaxed him and reminded him of Pauline, who had the same habit. Twice, in an essay written for private distribution called *The World of Sex* and in the unpublished novel *Moloch*, Miller makes the claim that he and Beatrice's mother were lovers. In *Moloch* Miller disguises the identities of the people involved by writing that the Beatrice figure was raised by a 'maiden aunt', and that she hardly knew her real mother. One year after the wedding, the Molochs, as one would have to call them, take a delayed honeymoon to see Blanche's parents in Delaware. Dion soon realizes that the 'middle-aged woman who greeted her daughter so affectionately was the talk of the town', and becomes fascinated by her sensuality, her way of spending hours putting on her make-up in front of the mirror and of humming as she goes about her housework. Dion gives in to his fascination and goes on to describe this as 'the strangest honeymoon he had ever spent. He had taken with him a bride, and he had discovered a succubus.'

This account has much in common with the version given in *The World of Sex*, written some twelve years later. In this, the mother visits the young couple for an extended stay, bringing with her a poodle, a bird in a cage and two suitcases. When she leaves, she invites them to return the compliment and pay her a visit. 'Make it a honeymoon trip', she says laughingly.[24]

They duly visit her at some unnamed address, and one morning while his wife is out and Henry is sitting in an armchair in his dressing-gown reading the paper, the mother calls to him from the bathtub and asks him to fetch her a towel. From that point on, as he puts it, 'the honeymoon was really under way. I was honeymooning it all over the place, first with the daughter, then with the mother.' Luckily for Henry, the father-in-law is 'a simple, easy-going fellow who accepted me immediately and made me feel at ease'. Henry's wife is less concerned for his ease. She begins to suspect something and the adventure ends abruptly when she insists that they return to Brooklyn.

With moral stunts such as this Miller terrorized God-fearing Americans of fifty years ago, and because of his insistence that what he was writing was autobiography the story has generally been accepted as true. Perhaps it is – betrayal, after all, became in time almost his pet crime. There are one or two minor details, however, that suggest it might all be the realization in fiction of something which was merely a possibility in real life. *Sexus*, which contains the most extensive account of Miller's life with Beatrice (called Maude), describes how Maude's Aunt Melanie comes to live with them after their marriage. The chaotic and relaxed sloppiness of her room enchants Henry: 'It was a room where Dementia was caged and imprisoned. Always the parrot in its cage, always a mangy poodle, always the same daguerreotypes, always the sewing machine, always the brass bedstead and the old-fashioned trunk.'[25] Everything about Melanie contrasts favourably with his wife's rigidity, her formality, her pretensions and inhibitions, and he gets on extremely well with her. Even so, their intercourse is of a much less dramatic sort than that described in the earlier accounts. He recalls with wistful pleasure 'the most wonderful moronic conversations with her sometimes when Maude was absent – usually in the kitchen with a bottle of beer between us and perhaps a little liverwurst and bit of Leiderkranz on the side.'[26]

Her mind had sunk down into the flesh and, if she was awkward and doddering in her movements, it was because she was thinking with this fleshy body and not her brain. Whatever sex there was in her seemed to have become

54

distributed throughout the body; it wasn't localised any more, neither between her legs nor elsewhere. She had no sense of shame. The hair on her cunt, if she happened to expose it at the breakfast table while serving us, was undifferentiated from her toenails or her belly button. I am sure that had I ever absentmindedly touched her cunt, while reaching for the coffee pot, she would have reacted no differently than if I had touched her arm. Often, when I was taking a bath, she would open the door unconcernedly and hang the towels on the rack over the tub, excusing herself in a weak, self-effacing way, but never making the slightest attempt to avert her eyes. Sometimes, on such occasions, she would stand and talk to me a few moments – about her pets or her bunions or the menu for the morrow – looking at me with absolute candour, never in the least embarrassed. Though she was old and had white hair her flesh was alive, almost revoltingly alive for one her age. Naturally now and then I got an erection lying there in the tub with her looking on and talking utter gibberish. Once or twice Maude had come upon us unawares. She was horrified, of course. 'You must be crazy', she said to Melanie. 'Oh dear', the latter replied, 'what a fuss you make! I'm sure Henry doesn't mind,' and she would smile that melancholy, wistful smile of the hypochondriac.[27]

Clearly, mother and aunt, with their stout suitcases, old-fashioned trunks, poodles, parrots, tubs and towels, were based on the same figure, and as fond as he was of older women in his youth one has to suspect that Catherine Wickens, at sixty, was a little too old even for the tastes of the monstrous 'Henry Miller'.

6

After a while, all the arguing and bad feeling in the house on 6th Avenue began giving Miller headaches. Instead of taking pills, he developed the habit of spending the evening at a burlesque show to laugh them away. 'Thank God, there were such glorious institutions in those days!' he once wrote. 'Had there not been, I might have committed suicide long ago.'[28]

He got more from these evenings, however, than just a cure for his headaches. The magic world of the theatre had a great influence on him. As a child, one of his favourite amusements had been the toy theatre built for him by an uncle,[29] a wonderfully elaborate piece of work with a variety of casts, footlights, pulleys, wings and backdrops which kept him enchanted right up until he was sixteen or seventeen. His experience of real theatre began early too, when his mother took him with her to see The Spooner Stock Company perform *Uncle Tom's Cabin*. They became regular companions on visits to neighbourhood theatres like The Spooner Stock, The Novelty on Driggs Avenue, The Amphion and Payton's Lee Avenue, owned by Henry senior's old drinking companion Corse Payton. Louise was especially fond of tear-jerkers like *The Old Homestead* and *Way Down East*, and through these Henry was exposed early to the sentimentality which was to become such a strong part of his make-up. However, he did not recall these earliest outings with much pleasure. Not until he saw *Wine, Woman and Song* did he become truly enchanted by the theatre.

Later, in his adolescence, he developed the habit of going to the theatre on Saturday evenings locally in the company of a youth named Robert Haase. Payton had inaugurated a '10-20-30 cent' scale of prices that had proved popular and meant that people could afford to go as often as they wanted. In the fifteen years of its existence between 1900 and 1915, Payton's Lee Avenue theatre alone had over 300 plays in its repertoire, mostly new productions fresh from Broadway, but also revivals of popular favourites like *Three Weeks*, *Florodora*, *Charley's Aunt*, *Two Orphans*, *For Her Children's Sake*, *In the Bishop's Carriage* and *The Rivals*.

From local theatres Miller graduated to the New York houses. His first experience of one of these was with his father, who took him to see Douglas Fairbanks in *The Gentleman from Mississippi*. Later, his German High School teacher, one of many who interested themselves in Miller and responded to his hunger for contacts with the world of culture, took him to a German-language performance of *Alt Heidelberg*. Henry also read many of the plays in the multi-volume *Harvard Classics*, which his parents gave him as a birthday present one year. From vaudeville and drama he moved on to the concert hall and the opera, the boxing ring, the wrestling ring and the lecture hall, always bringing to these experiences the same exuberantly uncritical relish. It was a widely eclectic but somehow very American education, and perhaps its most memorable hours were the ones spent at the burlesque halls.

He had his first and unforgettable experience of these at the Empire in Brooklyn. Aged fifteen, just into long trousers but not yet shaving regularly, he went along with an older boy named Harry Martin to see a show called *Krausemeyer's Alley*, featuring Sliding Billy Watson and a host of naked women:

From the moment the curtain rose I was trembling with excitement. Until then I had never seen a woman undressed in public. I had seen pictures of women in tights from childhood, thanks to Sweet Caporal cigarettes, in every packet of which there used to be a little playing card featuring one of the soubrettes of the day. But to see one of these creatures *in life* on the stage, in the full glare of a spotlight, no, that I had never dreamed of.[30]

The freedom from guilt, the brash and showy openness of these celebrations of human sexual life, appealed greatly to him, and he became a regular visitor at theatres featuring this type of entertainment, like The Columbia, The Olympic, Hyde and Beeman's, The Dewey, The Star, and The Gayety.

In terms of the atmosphere and style of Miller's best books, this adolescent experience of the burlesque is a much more persuasive influence than the Goethes, the Ibsens, the Aristophanes and all the tomes and classics of antiquity he was so proud of having read. The shows thrived on rough humour, reflecting with cheerful honesty the cruelties of everyday life. John Cowper Powys was also fond of burlesque, and in his *Autobiography* he gives a good outsider's description of this now-vanished form of entertainment. Calling it America's 'grand vent and outlet for the repressions of a puritanical public opinion', he noted that it was attended almost entirely by men:

There was very little plot in the burlesque show in my day and what plot there was was concerned with the knockabout adventures of a couple of clowns, one generally masquerading as a Jew and the other as an Irishman. Very often, no doubt, they *were* a Jew and an Irishman; but whatever they were, the brutality of their words and of their jests and gestures was simply astounding to me. Compared with these burlesque jokers, Charlie Chaplin was as refined as Charles Dickens(. . .) I remember what struck me as especially shocking was the sardonic and savage derision of tramps and hobos. I suppose the bulk of these audiences were travelling salesmen, what in England we call 'commercial travellers'. Anyway most of them, I take it, belonged to what Harry Lyon used to call the 'lower middle class'; and I suppose it did not jar on their nerves, as I am sure it would have jarred on the nerves of almost any aristocracy, to see tramps and beggars and cripples and imbeciles – all the derelicts, in fact, in the great struggle 'to make good' – held up to ferocious mockery. But to my mind – with sympathies fed by Sterne and Lamb and Scott and Dickens in whose works these innocents are treated as almost sacrosanct – to behold rags and crutches and the gibberings of idiocy *made sport of* was extremely startling. (. . .) What I beheld in these places was, in fact, all the basic instincts of the bourgeois nature allowed, for once in the history of the human race, unfettered expression.[31]

The last observation might almost be a programmatic description of Miller's aims in *Tropic of Cancer*. Powys also made the same connections higher up the cultural scale that Miller later made, between the burlesque and Rabelais, Joyce's *Ulysses*, the 'Satyricon', and even Nietzsche, whom Powys imagined '*forcing himself* to like this sort of farce, and calling it "brave Aristophanic truth"'. But what

57

astonished him most was not what pleased him most: like Miller, it was mainly the girls he came to see.

Miller became a connoisseur of the best of these dancers and performers, and the literary debt of the author of the *Tropics* to comedians like Eddie Foy, Bert Savoy and Willie Howard is considerable. They taught him much about the difficult art of entering the taboo areas of human experience, and the equally difficult art of getting back out of them again. Like a very different writer, Samuel Beckett, Miller discovered particular virtues in the techniques and timing of the burlesque comedians which he was later able to put to good literary use.

His greatest admiration was reserved for the skills of a man named Frank Fay. In writing about why he liked Fay he reveals much about his own approach to the art of communication:

Frank Fay impressed me as a man who could put on an act without the slightest preparation, a man who could hold the stage alone for ten or fifteen hours, if he chose. And who could vary the performance from day to day. To me he seemed possessed of inexhaustible wit, invention, intelligence. Like many another great comedian, he knew when and how to cross the borderline into the realm of the forbidden. He got away with murder, Frank Fay. He was irresistible, even to the censors, I imagine. Nothing, of course, can so rouse the sensibilities of an audience as an incursion into the realms of the perverse and the forbidden.[32]

Miller retained throughout his life the child's easy power to suspend disbelief, something which led to frequent descriptions of him as 'naive' and 'innocent'. It encouraged him to identify indiscriminately all performers, whether they be striptease dancers, musicians, lecturers, actors, playwrights or novelists, as autobiographical actors engaged in the act of self-revelation. The idea of a distance between performer and performance, between the reality and the illusion agreed upon, seemed not to appeal to him, creating an inability or unwillingness to accept the fact that great skill and seeming effortlessness can only be achieved by hard work and the gruelling banality of rehearsal and practice. This developed in him an aesthetic of spontaneity which, much more than the lack of formal higher education, was to hamper him in his attempts to become a writer.

7

Miller's ability to suspend disbelief absolutely remained equally strong in him all his life, and when applied to the books he read it turned their authors into a race of fabulous beings who inhabited their own dreamlike realm called Literature. Events and people were more glamorous there than in the tailor-shop, writing abusive letters to bad debtors or listening to the befuddled maunderings of one's drunken father. In the novels of the great Russians and the dramas of Strindberg he encountered the Supersouls. He read of their passion, the enormity of their mistakes, the greatness of their triumphs, with the same awestruck enthusiasm with which he had once read about the dashing Aguinaldo, the strange and pathetic Pinocchio, Henty's heroes and all the fairytale heroes and princes of his earliest reading. Books were not *about* life for Miller, they *were* life.

'I used to think then that all the tragic events of life were written down in books and that what went on outside was just diluted crap,'he wrote once.[33] For someone with this outlook on life, catastrophic disillusionment at some point or another was likely, and he had already been dabbling in intellectual areas that posed a serious threat to the life of illusions, notably in reading Nietzsche, whose attitude towards life, 'toward woman especially,' had become for him 'the antidote to the poison of Pauline'.[34] Miller felt the implications of godlessness in Nietzsche, but was making plans to deal with it in his own way. At a certain point he had begun the primitive search for a road that would enable him to make the journey from the real world to the world of fiction. If he could find this road and navigate it successfully it would enable him to turn himself into a character in a book, and abandon for all time the world of 'diluted crap' in exchange for one of 'tragic events'.

In 1919 the successful completion of this strange metamorphosis from human being into fictional character was a long way off. He had done some writing, but he had yet to broach the serious side of things and make a concerted attempt to find a publisher. Perhaps significantly, in view of his later development, one of his earliest submissions to a magazine was a sketch based on a 'mystical experience' he had had on entering a burlesque theatre one evening. The piece seemed to him 'wild, abortive, thoroughly incomprehensible',[35] but on the off-chance no one else would think so he had sent it along to Frances Hackett at the *New Republic*. Hackett did not publish it, but sent Miller a warm and encouraging letter of rejection which did much to cheer him up.

Lowering his sights somewhat, he found success in the pages of a monthly magazine called *The Black Cat: Clever Short Stories*, published in Salem, Massachusetts. The editor had the interesting idea of involving readers in the life of the paper by inviting them to send in literary criticisms of each others' short stories, so that by thinking about writing and how to achieve different effects they might become writers themselves. Miller took out a subscription to the magazine and got down to work. Written in a folksy style and punctuated with generalizations about men, women and love from the mouth of 'an old philosopher I once knew', his articles, although strictly juvenilia, show early signs of his natural talent for destructive criticism, and between May and October 1919 five of them were printed in *The Black Cat*. He received his first-ever paycheck for a piece of writing, two dollars and forty-three cents, which seemed to him 'like receiving a thousand dollars, I was made'.[36] He celebrated by tossing his borselino slouch hat high in the air, and watched a truck run it over when it landed in the gutter.

Success in the pages of *The Black Cat* was small beer for a man who believed that he had at least the potential to write as well as Dos Passos; but the important thing was that he got paid for his efforts. There was no question of capitalizing on his success, however. On September 30th, just a couple of days before his last contribution appeared in the October *Black Cat*, Beatrice gave birth to their daughter. She was christened Barbara, after Miller's grandmother.

With this, the responsibility Miller had been ducking ever since his marriage now claimed him. He had spent a lot of time playing at being a writer and not much time actually writing. Part of the problem, inevitable for such a passive man, was that he simply did not know what to write about. Life was not like a book. There was no discernible pattern or plot to any of it. Things happened to him, and he went along with them. Now it looked as if he wasn't cut out to be anybody special after all, but just an ordinary family man. As usual, he and Beatrice spent Christmas at home at Decatur Street with his parents. Then, early in 1920, he put on his suit and tie and went out looking for a permanent job.

CHAPTER FOUR

1920–1923
A proper job and the first book

1

In 1920 a first wave of Lost Generation writers from Greenwich Village set off on a literary reconnaissance trip to Paris. The Nineteenth Amendment gave the vote to women, and Prohibition was introduced. John Reed was on his way to Moscow to arrange for the newly-formed Communist Labour Party to be affiliated to the Comintern, and twenty-nine year old Henry Miller was applying for a post which he believed he could not fail to get, as a messenger boy delivering telegrams for the Western Union Telegraph Company.

He presented himself at the company's personnel office with several fat books on economics and metaphysics wedged under his arm. These were intended to reinforce the claim made on his application form to be the holder of a PhD from Columbia University. To his surprise, the switchboard operator who appeared to double as employment manager turned him down for the job, and he had to slink back home to Beatrice with the bad news.

The rejection was a turning point in Miller's life, a salutary warning to him that it was time to stop playing games. Why, after all, should a healthy, white, literate, native-born American with a PhD from Columbia University and an interest in metaphysics be applying for a job as a messenger boy or 'mutt' as they were disparagingly known? The experience brought home to him the fact that he had achieved nothing in the ten years since leaving school. His feelings of being a 'special' and 'different' person, tolerable among friends and relatives as an adolescent foible, were becoming impossible to sustain. Of his old schoolfriends William Dewar was now a successful attorney, while Jimmy Pasta, a mere 'wop', was the rising local political star of the Bushwick section of Brooklyn. Along with another former pupil named Charles McMichael, Pasta was even running a scheme to help unemployed graduates of PS85 to find jobs. He had always been Henry's great rival at school, both on the running track and in the classroom, and his doings were regularly reported in the Bushwick local paper and in the pages of the *Brooklyn Daily Eagle*. Henry senior would sometimes torment his son by reading aloud, without comment, these accounts of Pasta's latest triumphs.

Miller slept little that night. The following day he rose early, made his way to the Western Union office on Park Place and asked to see the President, Newcomb Carlton. Mr Carlton was away. So was the Vice-President; but Miller, clean-shaven, wearing his best suit, and fuelled by an irresistible combination of anger and humiliation, pressed on until he obtained an interview with the Vice-President's secretary. Here he pleaded his case so eloquently that presently he was sent along to another office for a meeting with Jim Nathan, the general manager of the company. Again he went through his paces. Fortunately – at least for him – he arrived at a time when elements in the company were trying to cut down on the number of Jews employed by Western Union. J.C. Willever, the Executive Vice-President, perhaps one of those post-war superpatriots who believed that the Russian Revolution was actually masterminded by New York Jews, was urging Nathan to do something about the problem of a switchboard operator named Sam Sattenstein who was, Willever believed, taking advantage of the inefficiency of the real employment manager to play the rôle himself and fill the ranks of messengers with fellow Jews. Miller, as an American-born WASP, profited by the subsequent dreary manoeuvring and was eventually promised the job of employment manager after a trial period of several months as an ordinary messenger had given him the opportunity to learn at street level about the way the company worked. He was also apparently expected to function as a company spy, submitting confidential reports on his fellow workers to his bosses from time to time.

He served his apprenticeship at $17 a week, survived being sacked twice, once allegedly when caught reading James Joyce in Central Park with a batch of undelivered telegrams in his pocket[1] and was in due course given the job of employment manager. Sattenstein, the man who had turned him down in the first place, was kept on as his right-hand man. The two got on well together in spite of the bad start to their relationship – Sattenstein is the Hymie Laubscher of *Tropic of Capricorn* with whom Miller discusses, among other personal matters, Mrs Sattenstein's problems with her ovaries.

2

Miller's main task at Western Union was to see to the smooth running of the company's twenty-two hundred strong messenger service. He interviewed applicants, hired and fired them, offered them vocational guidance and acted as a kind of counsellor. He was also responsible for the tailoring of the drab olive uniforms and for administering discipline, either firing miscreants or taking them off commission and putting them back on salary.[2] He worked long hours, from eight in the morning to six at night, dividing his time between the company's four main hiring offices at Fulton Street, Park Place, the main Flatiron Building at Fifth Avenue and 22nd Street, and Vesey Street. He was paid $240 a month and given a company pass which entitled him to free rides on all subways, elevated and streetcar lines of the city of Greater New York.

Once installed, Miller set about building a team. A man named Harry Garvey handed out application blanks to the hopeful and kept an eye out for any dismissed former employees who came back looking for work under another name. Sattenstein continued at the switchboard and was responsible for dispatching messengers between offices to cover for sickness or absenteeism or undermanning. Miller's friend Joe O'Reagan, recently returned from the Philippines, was taken on as his chief assistant, promoted over another assistant named Joe Ramos. The company detective he worked with was a man named Richard Carey, and after Miller had shut up the office for the day he would accompany Carey on his rounds of inspection of some of the company's hundred offices, carrying out spot checks and looking for evidence of fraud. A typical trick they might hope to uncover was one in which telegraph operators carried out their own editing on long-winded messages and pocketed the difference in cost.[3]

It was unusual for someone as young as Miller to have landed such a post, and he was proud of his achievement. He put up a sign on his desk reading 'Do Not Abandon Hope All Ye Who Enter Here'[4] and threw himself into the work, satisfied that he had finally found a job worthy of his talent, his energy and his desire to do something meaningful. The power he exercised over individual destinies thrilled and dizzied him, and quite quickly came to terrify him. There were about six million unemployed adults in the United States in 1921, many of them war veterans, and every day about a hundred of them passed through his office hoping to be taken on. Pandemonium was routine and *Tropic of Capricorn* contains some vivid descriptions of the work:

Before I could take my hat off I had to answer a dozen telephone calls. There were three telephones on my desk and they all rang at once. They were bawling the piss out of me before I had even sat down to work. . . . If by a miracle I succeeded in a day of filling all the vacancies, the next morning would find the situation exactly the same – or worse.[5]

The hiring instructions that he received changed with bewildering rapidity. One week there might be three hundred vacancies to fill instead of the mere five there had been the previous week, and the message would be passed down to him that he was now free to employ last week's taboo groups, 'niggers, Jews, paralytics, cripples, ex-convicts, whores, maniacs, perverts, idiots, any fucking bastard who could stand on two legs and hold a telegram in his hand'.[6] About one fifth of the workforce was regular, and the remaining four hundred or so who were taken on each month came from this catholic grouping of outcasts. Inevitably crises arose, as some poor analphabetic immigrant cracked up in the middle of New York and had to be brought in and relieved of his telegrams. One man went missing for two days and nights in the middle of a bitter cold winter spell and was found wandering with a fistful of undelivered messages in his hand. When Henry opened his coat to see if he had any more messages in his inside pocket he discovered that the man was naked underneath his suit. Others started out for Staten Island and ended up on the wrong side of the water at Canarsie in Brooklyn. Some worked for an hour and quit, tossing the messages in the nearest bin or down the sewer. And whenever they quit they wanted their pay immediately, which was impossible, because the book-keeping system was so complicated that no one could work out what a messenger had earned until at least ten days later. From a report which Henry produced for his superiors entitled 'Proposed Solution to the Messenger Problem', it emerges that over a given six-month period the average length of service in the messenger force was no more than five days.

In the beginning Miller approached his duties idealistically and formally. He invited every applicant to sit down with him and gave him a full account of the obligations of his job. The 'Proposed Solution' report shows that he took the company's problems very seriously and had reasonable solutions to offer, especially to the problem of the enormous turnover in the work-force. The main causes of this seemed to be the lack of opportunity for advancement within the firm; the stigma due to the uniform and the general conditions of work; and the misguided policy of employing former messengers as clerks and supervisors who then adopted an attitude of 'unbearable arrogance and unnecessary harshness' towards their former colleagues. Henry proposed a wage of between $25 and $30 per week; a more enlightened way of using former messengers in clerical posts; and the hiring of old men and boys of a low mentality which would 'probably stabilize the force by ensuring long terms of service', though problems of morale, efficiency and increased operating costs would have to be met in that case. Above all, he tried to impress on his superiors the need for a great change in the company's attitude towards the boys: 'as a policy of business, not as a matter of sentimental humanitarianism,' he urged, 'the Company must make the boy feel that he is more than a mere cog in the wheel. He must be made to feel that the Company is concerned in his welfare.' He suggested that each messenger receive a weekly bulletin containing an inspirational article, news of appointments to positions and suggestions as to how the service might be improved. An optimum term of three months of service was proposed, after which the Company would actively try to help the boy to a better position.

After a while, however, Henry realized that the only possible way to get his own job done was to scrap the rule book and improvise. In particular this meant ignoring the company's policies on race, and he took on Jews as well as any light-skinned blacks and Indians who could conceivably pass as white. He developed a soft spot for Hindus in particular, and became great friends with one named Haridas Muznudar whom he eventually made his assistant. At the other end of the scale were the ex-prisoners on parole whom he took a chance on after being approached with a plea on their behalf by a former warder from Sing-Sing named Molloy. By Miller's own account not one of the ex-convicts ever let him down.

The period of almost five years Miller spent with the firm were instructive, in many ways his first taste of real life after the self-indulgent and self-protective drifting of his first thirty years. They inspired him to some of his finest writing in *Tropic of Capricorn*, where he turned the experience of working for the 'Cosmodemonic Telegraph Company' into a metaphor for the brutalizing delirium of twentieth century big-city business life. No straightforward account of the job can hope to compete with Miller's hallucinated version in *Tropic of Capricorn*, but the prosaic memories of a fellow employee named Max Kantor who worked with him briefly in the early 1920s suggest the conscientious manager of the 'Proposed Solution' rather than the demonic social worker of *Tropic of Capricorn*, and Kantor doubted whether the staff of the personnel department really were the erotomaniacs of Henry's version. He recalled him as 'no Don Juan, just an ordinary fellow, well-spoken but given to strong, foul language. There was absolutely nothing distinctive about him that I could see.' He was 'polite and easy to get along with'. Another contemporary, Mike Rivise, found him 'a weird person. I worked with him, had fun with him, enjoyed listening to his surreal stories.' Rivise worked in the Traffic and Delivery Department, and Henry probably treated him with the caution he deserved as the brother of his own immediate superior, Benjamin Rivise. Mike Rivise wrote a memoir called *Inside Western Union*, published in 1951, which again gives a very different and much cosier and duller picture of life at Western Union than *Tropic of Capricorn*. Where Miller the visionary saw a grotesque and insane Moloch, Rivise the good company man saw only a well-oiled machine. He found Henry's fulminations against the firm 'as unreasonable as his gripe against the world'.

3

At home the relationship between Henry and Beatrice continued to decline. He resented the fact that she had taken over the finances of the family completely by this time, and sent him off to work on Monday morning with just his car-fare and his lunch-money in his pocket. In turn she resented the way he treated their home as a clubhouse for himself and his friends, the irregular hours he kept and the fact that he was so irresponsible with money. Though he had become a wage-slave, Henry was becoming increasingly and almost aggressively bo-hemian in his ways. Kantor recalled that he 'dressed like a Green-wich Villager'.

The disastrous temperamental differences between the couple meant that they never became friends, and that they tended to disapprove of each other's friends. Only Harold Ross and a Norwegian named Ostergren were able to bridge the gap between them. Otherwise Beatrice's friends bored Henry, and his friends terrified her. His willingness to discuss problems of an intimate or personal nature in an open and relaxed way with relative strangers was one of his most unusual characteristics, and for someone as reserved and conventional as Beatrice one of the most disturbing.

She was especially dismayed when, after making the acquaintance of a youth named Emil Conason, he began taking a keen interest in psychological theory. Conason was a medical student at Columbia University who was writing a paper on the IQs of people who applied for various jobs, among them Western Union messengers. He wrote to Miller asking his permission to test them, and the two soon became great friends. Conason brought the poison of Freud into the house-hold, and Beatrice listened in silent horror as the two sat at the kitchen table talking openly and dispassionately about sex. She felt increas-ingly that her husband was a man with 'no sense of decency, no respect for me or for anything'.[7] For Henry, his talks with Conason were exactly the kind of verbal free-for-alls that he needed. Conason liked to put him down by calling him 'Mr Narcissus', to which Miller's feeble response would be 'it's the Jew in him that's talking now'.[8] He was the only one permitted to say this; Beatrice could call the pianist Leo Ornstein 'nothing but a flashy kike', but if she ever attacked Conason, Henry would accuse her of 'ill-disguised anti-semitism'. His only real worry with Conason was that his friend would ruin the conversation by being too analytical and adopting the psychologist's posture of understanding everything.

Upsetting to Beatrice in another way was the gang Henry called the 'Three Musketeers', consisting of himself, Sam Sattenstein and Joe Ramos. They were his vulgar crowd, his bicycling, boxing, wrestling, vaudeville and burlesque gang, and Beatrice distrusted their influence just as much as Emil Conason's. The problem of vulgarity continued to be a major source of contention between the couple. Miller identified it as the battleground on which his mother had broken his father's spirit and was determined not to yield to Beatrice's ideas of good taste. His insistence on having the large round table right in the middle of the parlour where it resembled, even to his own eyes, 'a mastodon in the centre of a dentist's office',[9] was a declaration of independence echoing one his father had made years before, one which left a lasting impression upon him:

One day my father buys, or rather exchanges for some misfits, three of the lousiest potboilers imaginable from a wandering Jew. My father did not think them so atrocious, however. He was drunk at the time, and if later his taste ever improved or clarified, he never admitted any change of heart. He bought them and he brought them home and what's more despite my mother's outcries, because even she could see that they were just punk, he insisted that they be hung in the parlour. To hang them there three other pictures had first to be taken down, and he told her which ones were to come down. He had begun to rule the roost. It was comical. Guests came, looked at the pictures, shook their heads, argued with him, derided him, made jokes about the pictures. The story leaked out of how he bought them, but no matter what anyone said he would not have the pictures removed. They were all 'Night Scenes' – a device which made it easy for the artist to get through quickly as he simply smeared a lot of black paint over three-quarters of the picture. They were lurid nights, touched by streaks of lightning. Nights on the meadows, among the frightened sheep, and the grass very green, atrociously green. Altogether frightful, absurd, grotesque pictures. But now I think that perhaps this was my father's revenge. His side of the family was too common. Very good. Then why not put up on the walls a commoner's taste? A vulgar, cheap taste? Do you not think so? I think it was a masterful stroke, and I must say that these three pictures have puzzled me all my life.[10]

After a while Miller even risked repeating the domestic upset with Pauline Chouteau, and perhaps even did so from the same motives, by inviting Joe O'Reagan to come and live with them. O'Reagan duly rose to the challenge by trying to seduce Beatrice, and Miller duly forgave him.

Despite all this Miller regretted the failure of the marriage. Of his first fictional alter ego, Dion Moloch, he wrote that 'His life with Blanche was so absolutely different from anything he had visualized', and Moloch meditates wistfully on the fact that five of his friends had married Jewish women and they were 'all getting along famously. No divorces. No plate throwing.' And why was this? Because these couples talked to each other – 'about books, politics, the marriage question, chess problems, the 101 things the ordinary Gentile usually takes to the saloon'. He admired these women because 'they refused to mould themselves into ornaments for hubby to stick in his nose'.

Beatrice did not mould herself into an ornament for Henry's nose either; but neither did she talk about the 101 things with him. She had picked up enough of Conason's vocabulary to accuse him of being 'hypersexed', but unless the visitor were the commercial artist, Emil Schnellock, she did not participate in the conversation. In particular, she resented being asked to provide meals for a gang of men whom she could only regard as leading her husband ever more hopelessly astray.

Some time towards the end of 1921 she had had enough, and left to stay with her foster parents in Rochester, taking Barbara with her. Ten days later she wrote to Henry. An exchange of letters and gifts followed. Shortly afterwards Henry joined them in the house on Arbordale Avenue on what was to be a trip of reconciliation. He was thrilled to see Barbara walking, and he and Beatrice spent three good days together before he had to return to New York.

During the separation Henry spent much of his time at Joe O'Reagan's apartment near Fort Greene Park at 260 Cumberland Avenue where there was an artistic, cosmopolitan atmosphere and he could easily pick up a discussion on the Maja, Hindu monkey gods, the Nordic race, the importance of Gandhi, the poetry of Tagore or whatever. After two months, however, Beatrice and Barbara returned to the house on 6th Avenue and the Millers resolved to try again.

The arguments continued. One was over a typically terrifying suggestion from Henry that he wished to spare their daughter Barbara the futility of his own experience of school by educating her himself. Far from being floored by Beatrice's challenge to explain how he would go about this, he responded with an impassioned thirty-minute account of his proposals:

Pacing back and forth, head down I found myself up against the hall door just as her words penetrated my consciousness. And at that very moment my eyes came to rest on a small knot in the panel of the door. How would I begin? Where? 'Why there! Anywhere!' I bellowed. And pointed to the knot in the wood I launched into a brilliant and devastating monologue that literally swept her off her feet. I must have carried on for a full half hour, hardly knowing what I was saying but swept along by a torrent of ideas long pent up. What gave it paprika, so to speak, was the exasperation and disgust which welled up with the recollection of my experiences at school. I began with that little knot of wood, how it came about, what it meant, and thence found myself treading, or rushing, through a veritable labyrinth of knowledge, instinct, wisdom, intuition and experience.[11]

It seemed that all his thinking, his reading, his discussions, and his insatiable desire to challenge every received social truth only widened the gap betweem them.

4

Though he claimed to be a writer to his workmates at Western Union, Miller's literary ambitions had been in deep hibernation since the birth of his daughter and the start of full-time work. Curiously enough, it was Beatrice who reawakened them, quite by chance, by slipping into his pocket as he boarded the train back to New York from Rochester a copy of Knut Hamsun's novel *Hunger*. It electrified him:

That it should have been *this* book given me by *this* person has never seemed to me other than a remarkable coincidence and in keeping with my strange literary destiny. For it was during the period of this marriage that I conceived the idea of becoming a writer and eventually made a few abortive attempts to put the thought to the test. Some years later (in Paris), when I realized what a miserable failure I was, as a writer, I made a fresh start; the result was the *Tropic of Cancer*, a romance of hunger and desperation similar in many respects to *Hunger*.[12]

Hamsun's apparently autobiographical account of his obsessed struggle to become a writer revived in all its original purity Miller's own buried dream. He was thirty; not old, perhaps, but an age at which youthful ambitions are in the balance, and the immediate result of the encounter with *Hunger* was the realization that it was time to make a serious attempt to go the full length of a novel or give up the whole idea for good. The main problem was what to write about, and for his first effort he adopted a suggestion made by the Vice-President, J.C. Willever, who had frequently urged him to write a book about the messenger service. Willever's idea was that an inspirational book would be good publicity for the company, and suggested that Miller use Horatio Alger as his literary model. Alger was an American literary phenomenon, the author of about 130 books for boys, as well as popular biographies of statesmen, in which the American dream always came true and the poor-but-honest, hard-working boy finally achieved success. Henry was attracted by the specific nature of Willever's suggestion, and had actually read half-a-dozen of Alger's books, including *Brave and Bold, Strive and Succeed, Fame and Fortune, Luck and Luck*, and *Striving Upward*; but when it came to the point the models he chose for his own book were a couple of recent successes, Theodore Dreiser's 1919 study of actual persons, *Twelve Men*, and Sherwood Anderson's similarly structured series of fictional portraits, *Winesburg, Ohio*.

He had not had a holiday since joining the company in 1920, and early in 1922 put in a claim for a full allowance of three weeks. He proposed to devote the entire time to writing, and in preparation for the task made out a list of sixty-eight 'bizarre messengers' from which he had selected a short list of twelve to describe. His first day was March 20th, and he wrote to the point of exhaustion. In the evening he went along to an off-Broadway dance hall called Wilsons, which had a string of red lanterns outside that were lit up, even in summer, and signs that advertised '30 Lovely Ladies. Dime a Dance.' He bought a book of tickets and spent the evening dancing with the 'taxi' girls, as the professional dance-partners were known. Each day for the next three weeks followed the same pattern, and by the time he returned to work on Monday April 10th he had produced a seventy-five thousand-word manuscript.

Clipped Wings was not a success. One reason for its failure was the bewildering mixture of influences he had brought to bear on the creation of the book. He made some attempt to set Western Union in a historical perspective by drawing parallels between the messenger boys and the aboriginal bearers of 'message sticks', quoting for the purpose from Spencer and Gillen's *Native Tribes of Southeastern Australia*, but above all he had wanted to impress on a literary level. A conscious mix of Ezra Pound, Vachel Lindsay, Otto Weininger, Walt Whitman, Freud, Madame Blavatsky, Darwin, Edith Wharton, Booth Tarkington, Knut Hamsun, Robert Frost, Ernest Poole, Carl Sandburg, Henry Adams, Willa Cather, Horatio Alger and James Joyce with Somerset Maugham, Anderson, Dreiser, Nietzsche, Dostoevsky and Stringberg, though it might produce an interesting personality, is unlikely to produce a coherent work of art during a three-week holiday; indeed, until Miller discovered the trick of turning his undisciplined personality into the work of art itself, his problem of finding the level at which he could write successfully continued to frustrate him. Preoccupied with a need to impress both himself and his potential readers with his ability, he wrote in the false tones of the Menckenian gentleman, ironic, beer-loving and aloofly civilised, conveying only disdain for the normality which he believed he was trying to honour. Not even his friends liked the novel, yet having gone to the trouble of writing it the least he could do was try to get it published. He submitted it to Boni and Liveright, a newly-established Washington Square publisher who had achieved much success with John Reed's *10 Days That Shook The World* the previous year; but they saw no evidence of another great American rebel in *Clipped Wings* and sent the manuscript back.

There are traces of the novel in the brief portraits of Western Union messengers that crop up in both *Tropic of Capricorn* and *The Rosy Crucifixion*, but as an independent project its life was miserably short. 'It was a crushing defeat, but it put iron in my backbone and sulphur in my blood. I knew at least what it was to fail,'[13] was how Miller later viewed the experience. The aesthetic of spontaneity which he had acquired from the burlesque halls had proved a great deal more difficult to put into practice than he thought. The zen-like sureness of touch required takes time, patience and endless, educated repetition if it is to succeed and if it is not to end up yet another exercise in mere self-expression. Henry was a long way from this kind of mastery in 1922.

5

The Millers were leading almost separate lives by now, and while Beatrice stayed at home with Barbara, Henry did more or less as he pleased, going off to the burlesque when he got his headaches, to dance at Wilsons or the Arcadia or the Orpheum, to hear Paul Whiteman at Roseland, or to play chess and hang out with the bohemians at the Cafe Royal on Second Avenue.

He was spending much of this time in Emil Schnellock's company, either at his studio or on long rambling walks through Prospect Park discussing their favourite writers. Schnellock was especially fond of D.H. Lawrence, whose *Women In Love* had, in 1922, just survived the efforts of Justice John Ford of the New York Supreme Court to ban it. Lawrence later came to mean a lot to Miller, and the atmosphere of rebellion, sex and fame associated with his writing impressed Henry even then; but the appreciation of Lawrence as a writer, thinker and prophet did not develop for another ten years. Hamsun, with his 'whisper of the blood' and his fiercely anti-industrial stance, was the great subjectivist for him. After *Hunger* he devoured Hamsun's other novels as they became available in translation in the wake of his Nobel Prize in 1920, and remained for some years literally obsessed by the characters in *Victoria, Pan* and *Mysteries*. One of the great disappointments of 1923 was the reply he received from Norway to a fan letter he had addressed to Hamsun. It was essentially a long and absurd plea to Henry to contact another of Hamsun's admirers in New York named Boyle and to try to work out a scheme for improving the sales of his books in America. Miller was crestfallen, but re-read the novels and again wept over his favourite passages, and Hamsun's star went on shining with the same lustre as before.

Hamsun could even bestow the gift of tongues on him: at about this time he was attending a course of literary lectures held at the Rand School of Social Science, a philanthropic institution for working-class people on East 15th Street, and after one lecture he stood up to make some point and, in the grip of the same spell of eloquence which had overtaken him when relating to Beatrice his ideas on education, suddenly found himself delivering a long and impassioned speech on literature. Afterwards he could recall nothing of this *raptus* save that it had started with Waldo Frank and reached its climax with the description of a famous scene from *Hunger* in which the narrator is invited by his landlord to watch through the keyhole as the landlady, his wife, makes passionate love with one of the lodgers. Henry's knowledge and obvious love of literature so impressed the rest of the class that he was asked if he would be willing to run the literary society for the school, but he turned the offer down, aware of the fact that his fluency that evening was a freak occurrence. 'I loathe public speaking,' he once confessed. 'On my feet I am a jackass, especially if there are more than three people around.'[14] With strangers or in a crowd he was unsure of himself. Schnellock chided him with this once:

'Let anybody come here and speak faultless English, refer to his travels or his yacht, and what do you do? You stand there like an oaf, you shut up like a clam.'

To this he retorted vehemently: 'Why, God damn you, don't you know what that means? *That's totem and taboo!*'[15]

More typical than the evening at the Rand was the occasion when Miller had accepted, on behalf of Western Union, an invitation from a New York State Commission investigating job opportunities for backward children to address a class, only to duck the engagement in terror at the last moment. 'When the morning came, I was so frightened I didn't show up. They waited for me an hour, I understand.'[16]

Miller's interest in water-colour painting developed as a result of his association with Schnellock, and the long evenings spent at his studio. He liked to watch Schnellock at work, and though he had nothing but disdain for the world of commercial art which provided Emil with his living, he admired his technical ability, while the linguist in him relished the names of the different colours like 'gamboge' and 'cerulean blue'.

Another reason he was attracted to Schnellock was that Emil had been to Paris. It was particularly exciting for Henry to think that an old school friend of *his*, 'just a Brooklyn boy', as Emil always described himself, should have done this wonderful thing. To Miller, who never quite stopped thinking of himself as 'only a tailor', Paris and Europe were remote goals, exotic places where other people went. He used to spend hours at the studio poring over Schnellock's map of the city and getting him to talk about his experiences there.

Often the two played chess together. Miller enjoyed the game, its lore and its heroes, and was a great admirer of the prodigious Paul Morphy, but he lacked the patience to develop his game, and seemed to hold the opinion that an opponent who did not adopt his own reckless style of play was in some curious way cheating. Schnellock recalled 'the good-natured scorn and contempt' with which Henry would observe him adding to his hoard of captured pawns.

Emil was a bachelor, and Henry would often join him on informal double dates with the women whom Emil invited up to his studio. Schnellock relied on chivalry and romance, while Miller, his adolescent shyness distinctly a thing of the past, tended to use a more direct approach, asking the girls if they were any good at farting, and if so would they care to demonstrate; or somehow persuading them to turn somersaults on the studio floor. A favourite trick was to examine the texture of a skirt with his fingertips, assuring the woman with a disarming smile that his interest was purely professional, this was just the tailor in him coming out. Or he might bring up the subject of the burlesque – he always found that this helped him to 'establish a more intimate footing without wasting a deal of valuable time'.[17]

Schnellock's memoir, *Just A Brooklyn Boy*, captures well the sense of chaotic vitality that Miller exuded during this period:

I remember that he wore then a tight-fitting overcoat and an army shirt. Frequently a worn suit would be replaced by one of imported cloth from his father's shop. . . . The steel-rimmed spectacles which he wore were set very close to his eyes; the whole eye-structure seemed to come out to meet them, creating a bland, Chinese flatness about the contours. His eyes, though a cold blue, more often suggested the warmth of quick interest, of lively response –

until his gaze followed his thoughts outside the room. Then he gave the illusion of being completely out of the body, a man rapt to another world. These trances came upon him now and then, often at the most unusual, unexpected moments. Suddenly he was 'gone' . . .

His body was well-developed but gave a deceptive appearance of frailty; it matched his intense, quick, volatile nature. It suited him, so to speak, and made you feel that he was one with himself. He kept in good shape without any ritual of callisthenics. The days of athleticism were over, though I believe he still used a racing wheel now and then. But he was always agile and would remain so always. When he chose to he could caper like a goat.

One day when he, Randolph Scott and I reached the street, after sampling some apricot brandy, he bounded to the top of a coupé in two leaps; the first carried him easily to the tonneau, the second to the top of the car which was slippery with rain. There he slithered, pumping his arms and jerking his knees, until he caught his balance. He was in a fever of ecstasy and gave quite a performance before he leapt to the sidewalk.[18]

Schnellock's honest and warm memoir makes no attempt to disguise the hard, unfeeling side of his friend, the 'viciousness, the monstrous cruelty' which enabled him later to produce such harsh portraits of people who had thought themselves his friends.[19] Even Schnellock, however, shows the blindness with which a charismatic friend can afflict us. To illustrate Henry's almost superhuman generosity he related that as a gesture of thanks for giving him $8 once Henry turned up on his doorstep bearing an armful of brand new clothes for him from his father's shop, including flannel trousers, knickerbockers, sports coats and an overcoat, 'all the finest imported material and just my size. They must have been worth a pretty sum!'[20] Indeed they must, but the generosity was presumably Henry senior's rather then Henry junior's. Small wonder the tailor-shop was permanently on the verge of bankruptcy.

6

Miller described this period of his life as one of ceaseless promiscuity in *The World of Sex*, recalling how 'every friend or acquaintance my wife had was destined to betray her' and that 'even when I took the baby out in the perambulator she kept her eye on me':

Often I would leave the house, innocent like, with the baby carriage, to keep an appointment with one of her friends. Sometimes I'd park the carriage outside an apartment house and take her friend inside, under the stairs, for a quickie. Or, if there was a gathering at the house, I would go off with one of her friends to buy food or drink, and on the way I'd stand her up against a fence and do what I could.[21]

As with the thundering list of books read, it is hardly possible to know in the end if there is any substance to these claims. Two of Henry's closest friends at the time, William Dewar and Emil Conason, have suggested that 'much of Henry's conquests were exaggerations',[22] and with a connoisseur's sense for such things Dewar adds that he was 'a cocksman, but no Lothario', revealing that 'he went to bed with two of my ex-wives but he was impotent both times'. In one of Miller's notebooks, however, he reminds himself to write about bringing: 'Peggy Dewar to Park Place, in rear. Tailor-shop. Stores. Tin pressing table. Intercourse there and on revolving chair.'[23]

Undoubtedly there were affairs. In his notes he mentions Anna Watenschutz, the teacher from Eastern District High who had taken him to see *Alt Heidelberg* and who in 1909 encouraged him to try for the scholarship to Cornell. They went together a few times to meetings of the Symphony Society, or met at the Woman's University Club, where he kept her amused with stories of his affairs and his marital failure. She was a feminist, and Miller was fascinated by her habit of smoking in public and the short skirts she wore.[24]

Another girlfriend was Gladys Miller, who read Nietzsche, Homer and the Odes of Pindar, and was working as a waitress while trying to become a writer. Her job was her downfall, for the permanent smell of food and grease on her hands was enough to put Henry off. Too much diluted crap, not enough literature. Her boarding-house world also depressed him, evoking memories of the melancholy poverty he associated with Pauline Chouteau. Beatrice, anyway, intercepted their letters and the affair fizzled out.

He carried on briefly with his secretary at Western Union, a mulatto woman named Camilla Fedrant who was not only beautiful but intelligent, with a deportment 'far superior to that of the American white woman, even the well-educated ones'.[25] They dined together in Greenwich Village after work sometimes, or went to the jazz clubs in Harlem. The attachment had its romantic side – Miller wrote a love poem for Fedrant, and she presented him with a copy of Ernest Dowson's distraught *Cynara* – and it had its realistic side – it was she who lent him $100 in 1922 to pay for an abortion for Beatrice. In the end, the general manager found out that Camilla was of mixed blood and she was forced to quit the job.

Eve Warrington was another light-skinned black woman with whom he went out for a while. Schnellock recalled meeting her:

He introduced me to one girl whose skin had the deep tone of languorous

75

days at the seashore. She had delicate features, shapely hands. I was always disturbed, however, by two things – the violent colours she wore (one turban seemed made of a cockatoo's plumage) and the way diners would stare at us when we entered a restaurant. When I mentioned this to Henry he said: 'Why, do you mean to tell me you didn't know she was a negress?'[26]

Miller's promiscuity was only one expression of the fact that by 1923 his enthusiasm for his job was gone and he was becoming seriously bored. The marriage to Beatrice had turned into a fiasco, and yet knowing this he remained paralysed. As in the past, he needed to be dragged to freedom by some outside force.

On previous occasions this force had always been provided by a woman. What freed him from Cora was falling in love with Pauline, and what freed him from Pauline was falling for Beatrice. The meaningless promiscuity of the Western Union years, however enjoyable it may have been, was anodyne for both the dullness of the marriage and the job, but it was also a declaration of the desire to fall in love again. Other men become alcoholics or worship golf. Miller's drug was falling in love, and after seven years with Beatrice he needed another shot.

The dark suit, white shirt and tie of the keen-to-please young father of 1920 had given way by 1923 to an aspiring author who dressed like a bohemian and didn't even like to go home anymore. Even when he had no one to go out with, he preferred to stay out on his own rather than go home to what he called the 'living death' of his marriage.

One evening in the late summer of 1923 he climbed the stairs to Wilson's dance-hall, bought some tickets and went in. A sign on the wall read 'No Indecent Dancing'. He began looking over the taxi-girls who danced with the customers, like the girl in the Rogers and Hart song, *Ten Cents A Dance*, looking for their dream man among the plumbers and sailors and bow-legged tailors, the fancies and rough guys who tore at their gowns. He danced with one and talked literature with her – Strindberg and Pirandello. As he sat out a dance, another girl approached and asked if he would like to dance: the talk about Pirandello had made her curious about him. He appeared embarrassed and confused, but said yes and went off to buy more tickets. The girl later said she thought he looked 'like an ordinary businessman. Rather sedate, perhaps a teacher.'

Miller's first impression of her was of something powerful but imprecise, like the hallucination of a *fin-de-siècle* poet, or the painting of a pre-Raphaelite madonna:

I notice her coming towards me; she is coming with sails spread, the large full face beautifully balanced on the long, columnar neck. I see a woman perhaps eighteen, perhaps thirty, with blue-black hair and a large white face, a full white face in which the eyes shine brilliantly. She has on a tailored blue suit of duveteen. I remember distinctly now the fulness of her body, and that her hair was fine and straight, parted on the side, like a man's. I remember the smile she gave me – knowing, mysterious, fugitive – a smile that sprang up suddenly, like a puff of wind.

The whole being was concentrated in the face. I could have taken just the head and walked home with it; I could have put it beside me at night, on a pillow, and made love to it. The mouth and the eyes, when they opened up, the whole being glowed from them. There was an illumination which came from some unknown source, from a centre hidden deep in the earth. I could think of nothing but the face, the strange, womb-like quality of the smile, the engulfing immediacy of it. The smile was so painfully swift and fleeting that it was like the flash of a knife. This smile, this face, was borne aloft on a long white neck, the sturdy, swan-like neck of the medium – and of the lost and the damned.[27]

When he returned with his tickets they danced together for the rest of the evening, talking about themselves, about Strindberg, Hamsun, Dostoevsky. He waited for her down in the street when she finished work at 2 am and as he walked her home she put her head on his shoulder and invited him to kiss her. This was June Edith Smith, the woman who was to take his life of 'diluted crap' and fill it with enough 'tragic events' to keep him writing for the next forty years.

CHAPTER FIVE

1923–1924
'America on foot, winged and sexed'

1

Apart from Miller himself, June Smith is the most heavily mythologized of all the characters he wrote about. Through Miller's numerous portrayals of her she has become a legend in her own right among his readers, and the most banal facts about her have interest simply because there are so few. According to the family's Naturalization Record in the County Clerk's Office, Brooklyn, her father, Wilhelm Smerth, was born in 1878 in Galicia in Austria. He met and married her mother, Francis Budd, in Buckovina, which was then a part of Austria, and the couple had five children, Maria Augusta, Herman, June, Sigmund and Edward, all born between 1896 and 1905. June, the second daughter and the third child, was born on January 28th 1902.

In 1907 Wilhelm Smerth emigrated with his family to the United States, leaving Hamburg on the *Batavia* on June 15th 1907 and arriving at Ellis Island on July 10th. Like so many immigrants before him, he got no further than New York City, and found work in the clothing industry as a presser. They bought a house at 1441 38th Street, Brooklyn, and Americanized the family name to Smith. In 1917 Wilhelm signed a sworn declaration that he was neither an anarchist nor a polygamist, and renounced forever his allegiance to Charles, Emperor of Austria and Apostolic King of Hungary. On January 23rd 1923 he took the Oath of Allegiance that made American citizens of the family.

June, a precocious and romantic girl with ambitions to be an actress, went a step further than her brothers and sisters and changed her name to Julia. Later, when she started at the dance hall, she changed her second name from Smith to Mansfield, by which she was generally known. Most of her acquaintances assumed that this was in honour of Katherine Mansfield the writer, whose early death from TB in 1923 had made her a cult figure among Greenwich Villagers, and this may well have been the case at the time, although June later preferred the macabre explanation that the name 'Mansfield' was the nearest

English equivalent she could find to a word meaning 'cemetery', since Smerth means 'death' in Polish.

Miller was clear from the start that in June he had met a symbol, a woman who could never be a mere human being for him. She was an ikon, his own personal Cleo, an unreal sex-goddess who had climbed down from the magic world of the stage, walked straight into his life and appropriated it. If Western Union became for him a symbol of the meaninglessness of modern, urban American life and the madness of the American dream, then June symbolized the other side of that same dream – alluring, frightening, febrile and seductive. The tailor's son, none too tall, short-sighted and thin on top, saw walking towards him that evening at Wilson's: 'America on foot, winged and sexed . . . the emery wheel of hope and disillusionment. Whatever made America made her, bone, blood, muscle, eyeball, gait, rhythm; poise; confidence; brass and hollow gut.'[1] What chance did Beatrice have against America on foot?

2

Miller slept little after that first night at Wilson's and reported for work next morning 'looking like a somnambulist'. He got through the day, but in the evening fell asleep fully dressed after supper and spent the night on the couch. Awaking early on Saturday he found himself in the grip of a full-scale obsession 'to have her at any cost'. He worked a half-day at Western Union and spent most of the morning writing a long letter to June which he had delivered to her home by special messenger. He also sent her a copy of Sherwood Anderson's *Winesburg, Ohio*, which he had promised her, and a bunch of flowers.

At noon he left the office and returned to 6th Avenue. His emotional excitement would not let him settle, and he left the house again and spent the rest of the afternoon walking fiercely in the park. Taxi-girls were not supposed to date men they met at work, but most of them did if they liked the man, and June had given him her phone number. At five o'clock he called her. She was not home. Nor had she left him any message. Miller rang home, told Beatrice he would not be back for supper, and boarding a passing trolley rode aimlessly around for a couple of hours before returning to the dance hall.

The hours during which he was falling in love with June are vividly described on the opening pages of *Sexus*, the first volume of *The Rosy Crucifixion*. Twenty years later he could still write about them as though it had all happened yesterday, marvellously conveying all the ecstatic strangeness of suddenly falling in love, the intensity of mood, the uncertainty, the inexpressible happiness and the terrible, banal frustrations involved. June was not at Wilson's when he walked into the dance hall with his tickets that Saturday night. It made no difference, though; he was now ridden by his obsession, and on Sunday he went out to visit her at 15th Avenue, Brooklyn, where the family was living. He rehearsed his doorstep speech as he went:

Here I am, take me – or stab me to death. Stab the heart, stab the brain, stab the lungs, the kidneys, the viscera, the eyes, the ears. If only one organ be left alive you are doomed – doomed to be mine forever, in this world and the next and all the worlds to come. I am a desperado of love, a scalper, a slayer. I'm insatiable. I eat hair, dirty wax, blood clots, anything and everything you call yours. Show me your father, with his kites, his race horses, his free passes for the opera: I will eat them all, swallow them alive. Where is the chair you sit in, where is your favourite comb, your toothbrush, your nail file? Trot them out that I may devour them at one gulp.[2]

Although, in its way, every bit as romantic, this mood was a far cry from the lonely bike rides of his adolescence, and the forlorn walks along Devoe Street hoping to catch a glimpse of Cora at her window. But alas, June was not there to have her chairs eaten when he arrived; Henry was greeted by a member of her family who brusquely parried his questions and then shut the door in his face.

He laid siege to her heart. 'He virtually camped outside my parents house for three days and nights waiting to meet me again,' June recalled.[3] And when he wasn't camped outside her house he was writing letters to her. Years of practice at the tailor-shop and in literary correspondence with Stanley Borowski and Emil Schnellock had turned Miller into a powerfully personal letter-writer, and in the kitchen at 6th Avenue, with Beatrice upstairs in bed and Barbara asleep, he poured out his heart to the elusive and mysterious June in a torrent of long love-letters.

She answered none of them. Miller's wild passion puzzled and even alarmed her. She read the letters aloud to her mother, who shared her unease about the writer. During that first meeting at Wilson's, Miller had impressed upon June his real ambition, telling her that he 'wanted more than anything to become a writer'. Bearing this in mind, June strongly suspected that Henry might only be 'experimenting' with her 'for the sake of writing a story'.[4] Yet she was also fascinated and flattered, and as a connoisseur of the Greenwich Village arty scene she wondered whether the writer of such wild letters might be a 'dope-fiend', and perhaps half-hoped that he was.

Finally she took pity on him. A few days later, back at the dance hall,

Miller found a note waiting for him: would he meet her at Times Square at midnight the following day, in front of the drug-store? And would he please stop writing to her at home.

This time she showed up, and at her suggestion they took a cab to a Village speakeasy called Jimmy Kelly's, a haunt of criminals and literati who found excitement in the company of criminals. They spent too much money that evening, and Miller had to wire the night manager at Western Union to send him enough to cover their bill. Afterwards they rode back to 15th Avenue in a taxi.

Miller's account in *Sexus* relates that they became lovers during the course of this taxi ride. It was apparently a successful encounter in which June had several orgasms before slumping back exhausted into the seat. However, in the notes from which he wrote up his account of these first days with June, he refers only to 'terrific battle in taxi', while a later note recalls her 'surrender at Marder's'. Perhaps the only person who really knows what happened that night would be the taxi-driver. When and wherever it happened, it was clear to Miller from the start that he had at last found a woman who satisfied him sexually. June, ten years his junior, turned out to be as bold, open and daring in her erotic behaviour as Beatrice was shy and shamed.

The taxi-driver might have had another reason for remembering his fare that night: as June was putting on make-up in her mirror she suddenly froze in alarm, announced that they were being followed and ordered him to speed up. Miller tried to find out what was going on, but June only hissed something about gangsters, and urged the driver on. Finally they arrived safely at her house. The incident taught Henry that June could satisfy another, perhaps even more important need in his life than the sexual, and that was the need for his days to resemble more closely the incident-filled days of characters in the novels he read, and his relationships to mirror more closely the fantastical and dramatic associations in which the heroes of books became embroiled.

As they parted company that night June fell to her knees in front of him in the street, and cried out that she was 'falling in love with the strangest man on earth. You frighten me, you're so gentle. Hold me tight . . . believe in me always . . . I feel almost as if I were with a god'.[5] These shamelessly novelistic turns of phrase set the tone for the whole of their gloriously turbulent relationship. From the start, the two identified in themselves and each other characters from their favourite novels and plays. June's god was Dostoevsky, and most of her parts were based on heroines like Fanny in *Crime and Punishment*, until Henry expanded her repertoire by introducing her to Strindberg's galaxy of perverted heroines. Miss Julie became a particular favourite, as did the wicked Henriette of *Crime and Crime*. Miller's personal obsession with characters from Knut Hamsun's novels led him to liken her also to the eponymous heroine of *Victoria*, and himself to the hero of that novel, Johannes the peasant boy, who loves the high-born Victoria, and dreams of one day becoming a famous writer in order to be worthy of her. Hamsun's *Pan* was another rich source of mythological inspiration which enabled him to cast himself as the hunter Glahn to June's erotic but remote and enigmatic Edvarda. Thus Dostoevsky, Strindberg and Hamsun defined the atmosphere and often even the conduct of this love affair to such good effect that Anais Nin, who met them both later in Paris, observed that 'the more I read Dostoevsky the more I wonder about June and Henry and whether they are imitations. I recognize the same phrases, the same heightened language, almost the same actions. Are they literary ghosts? Do they have souls of their own?'[6]

It was just a game, perhaps more understandable in the twenty-two year old June than the thirty-two year old Miller; but it was a life-game, and the seriousness with which June played it was at once apparent to Henry. In a low, rather guttural, vaguely English-sounding voice which Miller found intensely erotic, she told him a succession of astonishing stories about her background – that she was the daughter of a rich Englishman and a Romanian gypsy mother who had died in childbirth. Or that she had been born in Sherwood Forest, in England, and abandoned by her mother. Another tale was that her parents had worked in a circus, her mother as a trapeze artist and her father as a magician. June was a regular customer at a popular Greenwich Village restaurant called Romany Marie's, and many of her stories sound as if she might have lifted them from the legendary Marie herself, who liked to entertain customers with accounts of how she had been 'born in an Inn on the fringe of a great forest in Moldavia. My mother kept the inn. She met my father in the depths of the forest. He had a red kerchief about his neck. He was wild-eyed, he was full of song.' To confuse the picture further, June also claimed that she was a graduate of Wellesley College for young ladies.

It was with tales like this that June first enchanted then bewildered and finally maddened Henry, without ever ceasing to fascinate him. Later she ridiculed the idea that she had ever made such claims, admitting only that she had circulated a rumour about being a graduate of Wellesley as a way of ensuring that her customers at the dance hall did not make the mistake of regarding her an uneducated pushover. As for her parents, she said she had told Henry what was effectively the truth, that her mother was a witch and her father bedridden and dying of cancer. Perhaps what she was ridiculing was the notion that anyone would ever have taken seriously these stories of hers. Few ordinary people would have done – but Henry was no ordinary person. Like Alice's White Queen, he could easily believe as many as six impossible things before breakfast simply because he wanted to, because it was more fun that way. An instinct for the fantastic was one of his strongest waspons in the fight against disillusionment and existential boredom which had become a major theme of his life by now. June was a taxi-girl, and respectable women like Beatrice and Louise looked on taxi-girls as different only in kind from whores. Loving June was thus another hammer-blow to the detested image of 'Little Henry' and a necessary crack in the shell of respectability in which he was confined.

Professionally speaking, too, Henry must have realized that June was right about him, that he wanted an involvement with her in order to write about her. The author had found his character. Yet the meeting had come about only because the character herself had been in search of an author. In her account of that first meeting at Wilson's, June recalled that as Henry danced by with another girl that Thursday evening in 1923, the flying name she picked up which made her decide to approach him for a dance was 'Pirandello'.

3

One evening in the kitchen Miller summoned up the courage to tell Beatrice about June. She sobbed uncontrollably as he tried with banal and reserved tenderness to comfort her, and once she had recovered, she put up a fight, of sorts. Emil Schnellock was her favourite among Henry's friends, probably because he was the most successful and responsible of them. Miller himself treated him as his mentor at this time, often addressing letters to him as Pop, Papa, Poof and even Poop among other humorous variations on a word meaning father. Both Beatrice and Henry's own father tried to persuade Emil to use his influence on Henry, and Emil recalled:

visits, too, of a more serious nature. His first wife, the mother of his only child, came one day to ask whether 'all was hopeless'. Another time his father called on me to ask if I knew of any way to make Henry take a more sensible attitude. Often his friends came to discuss 'the case' with me.[7]

But having made the break, there was no way back for Miller. Personal problems seem to have been discussed with friends as simple theoretical instances that merely happened to involve him. His strategy was to admit the guilt for everything and just carry on doing what he wanted to do anyway. 'To be with him, however, one would never suspect what trouble was brewing all about him. A trail of disasters seemed to follow in his wake, but he was always innocent and starry-eyed, always mystified that things should go wrong, always ready to assume the blame for any unpleasantness, any mishap, any tragic happening,'[8] was how Schnellock recalled Henry's reactions to trouble.

For those closest to him, however, the charm of cheerful openness was no substitute for intimacy. Miller's love of discussion did not extend to discussion of his behaviour in personal matters, for to permit this would have implied a willingness to be corrected which he was not prepared to concede. In vain Beatrice tried to appeal to his sense of guilt as she saw him preparing to go out for the evening. Are you off to meet your little whore? she would ask. To which Miller would reply that yes, he was off to meet his little whore.

He was tremendously proud of June, and when Western Union unexpectedly paid out a bonus of $350 to the employment managers he treated a group including Sam Sattenstein, Joe Ramos and Bill Dewar to a night out which culminated in a visit to Wilson's to be introduced to his new love. He was so drunk by the time they got there that he almost fell off the balcony watching her dance. Afterwards she honoured him in front of his friends by handing him a red rose.

Most of Henry's friends were aware that the marriage to Beatrice had been a mistake, and for his sake were pleased that he had found a new woman. However, the general opinion was that it would be a mistake for him to marry again. Conason the medical student, whose pronouncements on sex, love and marriage had the special authority of Freud behind them, informed Henry that he was congenitally incapable of fidelity, to which Henry retorted that the only trouble was that he had never yet met a *real* woman. He was thinking of an image of blindingly satisfying femininity, like Ayesha, whom he had come across at the age of fourteen in Rider Haggard's *She*. Now, he insisted, he had found her, and he was determined to marry her, come what may. When Miller introduced her to Conason he found himself jealous of what he described as June's 'overtures' to his friend, and for the first time realized the difficulties it can cause a man to be in love with a beautiful woman. He calmed himself with the thought she was after all a professional flirt, and that the signals she gave to other men were dummies. Not that, after the aching stability of the relationships with

Pauline and Beatrice, jealousy was without its thrills. He realized that in this new relationship he might no longer be the loved one, spoiled and endlessly indulged, but the lover, the insecure partner who takes the longest and most violent emotional journeys, the one who lives most intensely and who in the end gets the most enjoyment out of life.

4

Patterns of behaviour repeat themselves. Henry and Beatrice still went out together, and one evening, after a visit to the Palace Theatre just over the road from Wilson's, Miller casually suggested a visit to the dance hall 'in hopes of having her meet June'.[9] His motives must have been much the same as those which induced him to set up the meeting between Pauline and Beatrice seven years previously – to afford himself the curious pleasure of introducing sexual rivals to each other, and to precipitate a situation from which he might somehow emerge a free man. Beatrice, however, declined the opportunity to meet June. Perhaps, if she had simply gone along with Henry's game that night, and greeted June at Wilson's with a tolerant smile, the glamour of the illicit romance might have suffered and the absence of a hopelessly unhappy wife deprived the adventure of much of its desperate excitement for Henry and June. She did not, though, and the unhappy situation dragged on, with Miller writing increasingly desperate letters to June, including one in which he spoke of committing suicide if the situation were not resolved soon. He was still unwilling or unable to act when faced with a major decision, and his wretchedness only confirmed what literature had always told him about real love – that it was a fatal disease.

Suddenly June went off to spend a few days in the country with a group of friends that included some men. Henry was wracked with jealousy and inundated her with letters and telegrams signed 'Glahn the Hunter'. He treasured the replies he received from 'Victoria' and 'Edvarda'. Generally speaking, however, as a letter-writer she was a disappointment to him. He recalled that the first time he received a letter from her he was shocked by how child-like it was. It seemed at odds with her extraordinary and chaotic verbal talent which enabled her to 'say things at random, intricate, flamelike, or slide off into a parenthetical limbo peppered with fireworks – admirable linguistic feats which a practiced writer might struggle for hours to achieve.'[10]

Time passed and no solution to the problem appeared. One possibility had already failed to materialize: the Millers had just been

85

visited by Harold Ross, the music student who had briefly been their lodger back in 1920. After his return to Blue Ridge, Harold and Henry had kept up a voluminous correspondence, and Henry discovered that Harold and Beatrice had also been writing to one another privately. Knowing that they were fond of one another, and with their shared interest in music, he hoped and believed that Ross might take Beatrice off his hands, as he had once hoped Jim Haley would. But Henry's psychological insights were often dictated by what he hoped would happen, not by what was likely to happen, and Harold returned to Blue Ridge alone.

One afternoon, as he lay on his back in Prospect Park contemplating the sky, Miller unburdened himself to his oldest friend Stanley Borowski. Stanley heard him out, and made a vague promise to try to help him if he could.

'I had a wonderful night and day with June at the Rockaways,' Miller wrote to Emil Schnellock on August 16th 1923. 'See her again tonight, perhaps to take her to "Trilby". We are getting on famously and fatuously.' Beatrice, meanwhile, decided that she needed to go away to the country for a while to think the situation over, and on August 23rd she left, taking little Barbara with her. To make quite sure they had gone, Henry even rode part of the way on the train with them before returning to New York.

His first day of freedom was spoiled by a terrible earache, and he spent much of the time in agony in a doctor's waiting room; but the following night he and June spent together on 6th Avenue, sleeping on the couch in the parlour. On the morning of the 25th, he dressed and went out to buy some bacon. A few minutes later he returned, rang the bell, and June, wearing a bathrobe, let him in. They started to cook the bacon. A few moments later the door was opened and Beatrice walked in, accompanied by the landlord's daughter Marion. They found the room in disarray and the couch had evidently been used as a bed. Beatrice ordered Henry and June out of the house. Twenty minutes later they were gone, and the marriage was over. Henry always liked to think that it was Stanley who had kept his promise to help free him by tipping off Beatrice, but his indiscretion was such that she scarcely needed to be tipped off by anyone. In fact, she had been staying in secret with the Butlers up on the third floor for two nights before catching him in the act.

The lovers camped for a few days at Emil Schnellock's studio until they could find a place of their own. Much as he had wanted it to happen, the unpleasant manner in which the marriage ended gave Henry a shock, and he was deeply grateful to Schnellock for the calm and helpful way in which he received them. 'The atmosphere created by your radiant personality has done more to restore my spiritual ease than any influence I know,' he wrote to him a week after the event. In fact, the shock was so great that his first instinct was to retire and become a calm and peaceful old man. 'We have had our fling, you and I,' he told Emil. Now all he longed for were 'great steady reaches of tranquillity and peace. . . . let us look forward to "the still water" running deep'[11] – but it was only a passing mood. Later he wrote with candour of how he had 'always been able to detach myself from a strong attachment without the least emotion, often in what might appear to be the very height of a fine relationship. Never because of any unpleasantness, any disagreements etc. I have slipped out of a relationship whenever I had acquired what I needed.'[12] Whatever it was he had needed from Beatrice, he had acquired it. Later that day, she called him at his office and asked him to move his things out of the house as soon as possible. She told him she would be filing for divorce.

5

Emil Conason found them somewhere to stay. He had recently married, and he and his wife Celia had lodgings with a Dr Paul Luttinger at his house in the Bronx. Luttinger had a spare room Henry and June could use and they moved in.

The Luttinger household was chaotic. Besides his wife and three children and the Conasons, Luttinger's mother-in-law and sister-in-law also lived there, and he appeared to have advanced ideas on child-rearing that included allowing the youngest child Lionel to urinate on the floor. Still, primitive as it was, it was their first home together. They called it Oom Paul's, or Cockroach Hall, because it was infested with bugs.

At Cockroach Hall, Henry penetrated further into June's mysterious world, and soon discovered it to be a sad and vulnerable place. Freud's theories that dreams are essentially personal revelations based on past experiences were much discussed in the house, and one day Henry asked June to tell him something about her dreams. She replied that it was so long since she had last had a dream that she couldn't remember. Miller knowledgeably insisted that everyone dreams every night, and that if she simply made the effort her dreams would probably come back to her. A few days later, she remarked casually that she had begun dreaming again, and when Miller showed an interest she began describing the dreams to him. The cool, detached side of him was intrigued, and passing them off as his own he began discussing them with Emil Conason. Presently Conason began ridiculing them as being only too obviously fabrications and Miller backed down.

A few days later, leafing through a book in Dr Luttinger's library, Henry came across evidence that June had been taking sections of the dreams recorded in this book and passing them off as her own in a pitiful attempt to impress him. If he had begun to experience the special difficulties of a man in love with a beautiful woman, she now experienced the difficulties of a woman in love with a sharply intelligent man. She felt intellectually out of her depth much of the time with him, unable to contribute to the discussions he so loved about art, life and religion, yet having little patience with the ordinary friends he called 'lowbrows'. Her frail and pretentious personality was constantly in danger of exposure and ridicule, and the danger brought out a tender side in Miller:

There was something disturbing to her in the atmosphere created by the coming together of such strong individualities as composed the new ménage. She felt a challenge which she was not quite able to meet. Her passport was in order but her luggage excited suspicion. At the end of every encounter she had to reassemble her forces, but it was evident, even to herself, that her forces were becoming frayed and diminished. Alone in our little room – the cubicle – I would nurse her wounds and endeavour to arm her for the next encounter. I had to pretend, of course, that she had acquitted herself admirably. Often I would rehearse some of the statements she had made, altering them subtly or amplifying them in an unexpected way, in order to give her the clue she was searching for. I tried never to humiliate her by forcing her to ask a direct question. I knew just where the ice was thin and I skated about these dangerous zones with the adroitness and agility of a professional. In this way I patiently endeavoured to fill in those gaps which were distressingly blatant in one who was supposed to have graduated from such a venerable institution of learning as Wellesley.[13]

Miller had no such problems establishing himself within the group, and was greatly enjoying his new life. The only painful moments were the Sunday visits to Beatrice and Barbara. He missed his daughter bitterly and was heartbroken once when she asked him: 'Daddy, why don't you come home with us?' June also felt guilty and Miller tried to comfort her – and himself – with the unlikely suggestion that he might be granted custody of the child after the divorce. On an outing to Mineola one day, Beatrice told him the lawyer handling the divorce case for her had proposed to her, and that his was only one of three proposals of marriage she had received since their separation. Miller hoped briefly that the lawyer might succeed where Jim Haley and Harold Ross had failed, but the lawyer let him down too.

6

For the time being, Henry continued in his job at Western Union. The enthusiasm he had brought to the work back in 1920 had gone by now. He had become disillusioned about responsibility, feeling increasingly that it functioned mostly as a censor of experience, a shield against spontaneity. He had begun to feel in his own eyes humiliated by the pretensions of being an 'Employment Manager':

They wept, they knelt at my feet, they snatched my hand to kiss it. Oh, to what lengths did they not go? *And why?* In order to get a job, or in order to thank me for giving them one! As if I were God Almighty! As if I controlled their private destinies. And I, the last man on earth who wished to interfere with the destiny of another, the last man on earth who wished to stand either above or below another man, who wanted to look each man in the face and greet him as a brother, as an equal, I was obliged, or I *believed* that I was obliged, to play this rôle for almost five years.(. . .) And so every day I found myself averting my gaze. I was in turn humiliated and exasperated. Humiliated to think that anyone should regard me as his benefactor, exasperated to think that human beings could beg so ignominiously for such a thing as a job (. . .) a man can be robbed of his human dignity by being put in a position above his fellow men, by being asked to do what no man has the right to do, namely, give and take dispensations, judge and condemn, or accept thanks for a favour which is not a favour but a privilege that every human being is entitled to. I don't know which was worse to endure – their shameless entreaties or their unmerited gratitude. I only know that I was torn apart, that I wanted more than anything in the world to live my own life and never again take part in this cruel scheme of master and slave.[14]

This was Miller looking back on his feelings in 1950, some thirty years and a great deal of thinking after the event, and though there was a philosophical side to his disappointment with the job at Western Union the truth is perhaps as much that back in 1924 he was gloriously and shamelessly ergophobic. Moreover, he became convinced that his immediate superior, Benjamin Rivise, had taken a dislike to him and brought his brother Mike in from the Philadelphia office expressly to spy on him and provide the company with enough evidence of malingering and malpractice to get rid of him.

Whether he was right, or whether it was only a paranoid suspicion fuelled by memories of his own experiences as a boss's agent on joining the company, Mike Rivise's activities took much of the fun out of the job as far as he was concerned. It bored him, and he was no longer enthusiastic about the reforming schemes he had put forward during his early years. Rivise, taking his cue from Henry's report, was doing all he could to rid the messengers of their image as 'shiftless and worthless' people,[15] while Henry was growing more and more convinced that the shiftless and worthless misfits who could not or would not adapt to the system were the only honest people around.

Rivise pressed ahead, however, and in 1923 West Point cadets were brought in to drill the boys, and a campaign to bring a military efficiency to the force got under way. Rivise himself worked unpaid overtime on the drilling. Regular army orders were issued, and the messengers had mess and uniform inspection. Boys were encouraged to be responsible for ensuring that their uniform was complete, their face and hands clean, their hair neatly combed and shoes shined. They were to salute clients before and after delivering their telegrams. The school for trainees was restructured, athletics introduced and competitions set which offered prizes for the best talks on road-safety. There was even instruction in etiquette. Discipline on the force was tightened, and a manual produced with sixty-six rules of conduct. Some of these had several subdivisions, such as Rule Nine, which included an entire page on the care of the feet: messengers were to 'wash the feet daily and put on fresh hose every morning if possible'. Another rule covered procedures in the event of rain and puddles: 'If your shoes get wet inside, take them off and dry them.'[16] The idea was the then peculiarly American one of turning the company into a way of life, and Miller detested it. The big shake-up in his personal life had destroyed the last strained shreds of respectability in him, and now any drive towards increased efficiency seemed like a personal insult.

His suspicions that some of his colleagues were out to get him were strengthened when he was abruptly moved from his old office at Park Place into the headquarters at the Flatiron Building on Fifth Avenue and 22nd Street and put into an office just a few floors below J.C. Willever himself:

No shenanigans now, as in the old messenger bureau with the dressing booths in the rear and the zinc-covered table where now and then I had knocked off a fugitive piece of tail. I was in an airless cage now, surrounded by infernal contraptions that buzzed and rang and gleamed every time a client put in a call for a messenger. In a space just big enough for a double desk and a chair on either side (for the applicants), I had to sweat and shout at the top of my lungs to make myself heard.[17]

All this sweating and shouting caused him to lose his voice three times in the course of as many months, which in turn meant visits to the doctor and sick leave. Miller, a fiendish man when he thought he had an enemy, liked to revenge himself on Rivise by continuing to address him in a hoarse whisper long after he had recovered his voice, obliging Rivise to cross the room in order to pick up some invariably quite banal piece of information.

As winter passed and the divorce proceedings moved slowly along, Miller was transferred again. This time he was put at the top of an old building in which his desk stood in the middle of a vast, empty floor where the messengers did their drilling in the evenings. He had been rationalized, and now worked with just one assistant, a former boxer who had been promoted from the cloakroom. His interest in the job deteriorated still further. 'I made no effort to keep the files in order, nor did I investigate references, nor did I conduct any correspondence. Half the time I didn't bother to answer the telephone.'[18] There was a gymnasium adjoining the drill-hall, and when downhearted or bored he was in the habit of strapping on a pair of roller skates and taking a spin there with some of the younger messengers. His assistant, a denizen of the vast world of normal people, thought his boss was mad.

7

The break with Beatrice was a decisive first step for Miller on his road to becoming a famous writer. The second step, to leave the security of a full-time job, was one he hesitated to take for some time. An obvious consideration was that, after the divorce, he would have two families to support. Furthermore there was no unemployment benefit in those days, and to opt out of the system once and for all involved a greater risk in 1924 than it would today. Yet there was something even stronger than anxiety at the prospect of a life in economic uncertainty which deterred him. Beneath his friendly, easy-going exterior, beneath the easy familiarity with which he discussed the works of great writers, Miller entertained serious doubts about his own ability to contribute in the field of literature.

This was the other side of the boast he borrowed from Emil Schnellock and later proudly adopted as his own, that he was 'just a Brooklyn boy' and it seems possible that the men he chose as his literary heroes also intimidated him. In the autumn of 1923 he attended a lecture by John Cowper Powys on Conrad, during which he heard Powys hinting at 'the deep mystery underlying the throes of authorship,' yet these hints did not bring him any closer to becoming a publishable writer. For a working-class boy from Brooklyn, growing up in a family with no literary tradition, Powys cuts a curious figure as a literary hero. He was an upper-class, not to say aristocratic figure, and for all the interest Miller had in what Powys was saying in his books and lectures, it was as much the man's aristocratic style which attracted the distinctly unaristocratic Miller.

Among the surviving letters that document this early period of Miller's life, the fifteen written to Emil Schnellock during the 1920s indicate that he was experimenting with a variety of literary personae at this time, and that his favourite impersonation of the first part of the decade was an arrogant, learned, rather flippant pedant. The problem for an aspiring writer from a non-literary background is, in the first instance, how to *perceive* literature. The world of letters was a curiously class-structured one in which the basic image of a 'real' or important writer was that of a highly- and, preferably, classically-educated man writing in an 'educated' style. There was a refinement about the received idea of literature, a sort of *salon* atmosphere, which Miller feared would never be willing to accommodate a rude voice such as his. His awareness of the existence of the problem emerges in an attack on Henry James contained in a letter to Emil Schnellock of November 5th 1923:

All great men write to order: Caesar, Balzac, Wells, Shaw, Barrie, Strindberg and the one-and-only Dostoievski included. The Jamesian method of approach was to pace up and down the room in a scarlet, brocaded, velveteen nightgown with a pungent cigarette dangling artistically between two silken fingers, the while he dictated from an overfed mind to an undernourished slave. To write a novel of a hundred thousand words Henry James found the most convenient way was to pour out about two hundred and fifty thousand. (. . .) Let us stop for a few moments and contemplate what it means to squeeze out, weed out, eradicate, eliminate and subjugate a hundred and fifty thousand superfluous words. What precious offal, what divine excrescences must have been contained in these unique Jamesian 'droppings'. Take the four walls of your cubby hole: then imagine, if you will, what it would look like, if on it we attempted to inscribe the pure didactic monstrosities of Henry James's artificial distillations, lucubrations and menstruations. Ask yourself whether you do not prefer the blatant phallic desecrations on the screaming red walls of the buried city of Pompeii. Or, if that is not enough of a contrast, choose the urinal in the Houston Street Burlesque Theatre. Take a characteristic bit of lyric poetry after the manner of Carl Sandburg, done by an inferior genius – such an inscription for instance as this: 'Your Mag has bleeding tits' or 'Suck this big, juicy prick'. . . . How pale and anaemic the following from the pen of Henry James must seem to your sound, substantial intellect.

He goes on to quote a few lines of what seem to him particularly precious examples of James's writing. The odd thing is that, obscenities aside, Miller's style is as artificial in its own way as James's, and he apes what he believes himself to be mocking.

These early letters, often quite openly exercises in descriptive writing with only a salutation at the top to define them as letters (the James letter is addressed to 'Amiel: Copies to Ross, Stanley and posterity) seem like the work of a fat man in a three-piece suit, and show few traces of the pronounced Brooklyn accent with which Henry himself spoke. He always prefers the florid and esoteric to the simple. A typical sentence in one letter reads: 'In the vast desert wastes of that great American novelist's tomes (Theodore Dreiser, I mean) the dull aridity is more than alleviated by the striking verdure of his opalescent oases.'

No doubt inspired by his meeting with June, in the winter of 1923-24 he set about a revision of *Clipped Wings*. To the earlier influences of Dreiser and Anderson he added that of Somerset Maugham's *On a Chinese Screen*, and when it was done he showed the result to J.C. Willever, the Executive Vice-President of Western Union who had suggested the theme to him in the first place. In doing so he destroyed the last surviving goodwill and status he might have enjoyed at the company as a 'writer'. The book remained unpublishable juvenilia, and he knew it. His honest appreciation of his failure led him to still greater self-doubt, and a further reluctance to let go of the umbilical cord connecting him to the rest of the world via Western Union.

8

Henry and June did not stay long with the Luttingers. Late in 1923 they moved with the Conasons to an apartment at 524 Riverside Drive in Manhattan which belonged to a friend of Beatrice's named Harold Hickerson. Hickerson was head piano teacher at the New York Conservatory of Musical Art and a sometime collaborator with the playwright Maxwell Anderson, so culture was well-provided for in the new apartment. Comfort was less important, and the Millers and the Conasons shared adjoining cubby-holes with what Celia Conason recalls as 'a connecting sink', while Hickerson and his wife Ruth had the main part of the flat. The rooms were 'like closets'.

In December 1923 Henry and Beatrice went along to the civil and supreme court buildings in Brooklyn for the hearing for their divorce. Miller usually refers to it in his writing as 'the divorce trial':

Everything had been agreed upon beforehand. I had only to raise my hand, swear a silly oath, admit my guilt and take the punishment. The judge looked like a scarecrow fitted with a pair of lunar binoculars; his black wings flapped lugubriously in the hushed silence of the room. He seemed to be slightly annoyed by my serene complacency; it did not bolster the illusion of his importance, which was absolutely nil. I could make no distinction between him and the cuspidor. The brass rail, the Bible, the cuspidor, the American flag, the blotter on his desk, the thugs in uniform who preserved order and decorum, the knowledge that was tucked away in his brain cells, the musty books in his study, the philosophy that underlay the whole structure of the law, the eyeglasses that he wore, his BVDs, his person and his personality, the whole ensemble was a senseless collaboration in the name of a blind machine about which I didn't give a fuck in the dark. All I wanted was to know that I was definitely free to put my head in the noose again.[19]

On December 19th 1923 Judge Harry Lewis granted Beatrice a divorce and gave her custody of Barbara. Henry had been making a voluntary contribution of $30 per week towards their upkeep and Judge Lewis made the order permanent. Miller's fictional account of the proceedings in *Sexus*, stressing his insouciant manner and the way in which his insolent offer to pay double the amount ordered by the court flabbergasts Judge Lewis, is at odds with the perfunctory 'Yes sirs' and 'No sirs' of the official record of the proceedings.

For a while June continued to work at Wilson's. At her request Miller would sometimes meet her at two in the morning to walk her home. This tended to leave him exhausted for his eight o'clock start at Western Union the following morning, but the discovery of the catastrophic extent of June's insecurity had touched new chords in him, and he was prepared to suffer if it would help her. The only area in which she was free from self-doubt was sex. Her sexual beauty was her strength, and she used her strength where it had most effect, among men.

Harold Hickerson shared Miller's tender regard for June's frailties, but his wife Ruth was distinctly unsisterly, and scoffed openly when June came home one day with the news that she had left Wilson's and been accepted in Lee Simonson's Theatre Guild. She had a part in the Guild's Christmas production of Shaw's *St Joan*, and was soon coming home from rehearsals with stories of how the other actors in the play were all in love with her. One, named Ian Maclaren, had a 'mad infatuation' for her, and she tormented Miller with her stories of 'seclusion in his room, of buying him make-up, magazines etc. Catering to his little whims. Wrestling with him on the floor.' Recalling the episode in his biographical notes Miller concludes tersely, 'Remarks of other members of the cast. My jealousy', and wonders just who the 'infatuated' one was.

He wrote later that his wife 'played a number of rôles with the Theatre Guild group',[20] and included in *Sexus* a scene that takes place outside the theatre on the evening of her debut: 'I looked at the announcements over and over, thrilled to see her name in bold clear letters.'[21] However, Walter Prichard Easton's *Theatre Guild – The First Ten Years 1919-1929* which includes a record of all plays performed by the Guild during this period, as well as cast lists for each of them, contains no reference to June performing in any of their productions. An actor named Ian Maclaren played the part of Peter Cauchon, Bishop of Beauvais in the December 1923 production of *St Joan*, which confirms that June did have some contact with the Guild, but she almost certainly never got to perform with them. Here as elsewhere, it is interesting to note points at which Miller the autobiographical reinventer of his life is most active; was he, in fiction, giving to June the little moment of fame and success as an actress that he knew she longed for in real life, but never achieved?

'In her presence the room vibrated,' Miller wrote of June. 'She had her own wavelength: it was short, powerful, disruptive'[22] – and it constantly precipitated dramatic scenes. After a quarrel one evening at Riverside Drive, she wrapped her belongings up in a brown paper parcel and ran out into the street. Miller did not follow, and it was left to Harold Hickerson to chase after her and bring her back. This was the first of many such gestures from June, and it is impossible to tell how far they were mere Dostoevskian melodramatics and how far she was genuinely unbalanced. Her periodic incarcerations in psychiatric hospitals later in life suggest that, if being disturbed had once been a game to make herself seem interesting, the game finally got out of hand and became the reality.

On February 28th 1924 June's father died and for a few days she went to stay with her family at 76th Street in Bensonhurst. June claimed later that she became the family breadwinner after Wilhelm's death, but as her three brothers were all still living at home with their mother at the time and all in full-time employment, one as a manager at a food store, another as a salesman and the third as a clerk in a grocery store, the claim is unlikely to be true.

When she returned, she was keener than ever to get married, and

Henry, with his self-confessed 'infatuation for the marriage state',[23] agreed. Shortly after his divorce from Beatrice became final at the end of March the couple took the train over to New Jersey and got married at Hoboken on Sunday, June 1st, at 11.30 am. The certificate and record of the marriage contains two slight inaccuracies in the personal details. Twenty-two years old at the time of the ceremony, June gave her age as twenty-one, and her place of birth as St Johns (*sic*), Vermont. A clerical eccentricity suggests that she had been married once before, and Henry twice. They celebrated the occasion at Emil Schnellock's studio, and afterwards all went out to see Cleo dance at the Houston Street Burlesque. No rings were exchanged.

9

For all her fascination for weird people and artists, June had a normal, domestic side to her, and she was keen to get a home of their own. Henry was not so enthusiastic. A chaotic, bohemian home-life was what he had been longing for all through the enforced respectability of his days with Beatrice; but being easy-going in such matters he went along with June's wishes. She had set their sights on a place on Brooklyn Heights, and towards the close of their first day of looking they fell in love with an apartment they were shown at 91 Remsen Street. At $90 a month the rent was twice what they could afford to pay, and Miller's first thought was to pass it up. Yet he knew that life with June was going to be a corrective to what he had identified as a cautious, Germanic side to his nature, and that if he really wanted chaos and adventure he must let her reckless and impulsive nature take the lead. So he agreed, and they moved in. It was a comfortable apartment in a high-class neighbourhood:

The floors were of inlaid wood, the wall panels of rich walnut; there were rose silk tapestries and bookcases roomy enough to be converted into sleeping bunks. We occupied the front half of the first floor, looking out onto the most sedate, aristocratic section in all Brooklyn. Our neighbours all had limousines, butlers, expensive dogs and cats whose meals made our mouths water. Ours was the only house on the block that had been broken up into apartments.[24]

The rooms were sparsely furnished, with subdued lighting, and a low divan in the middle of the living room gave it an oriental atmosphere. They called it their 'Japanese love-nest'. Of their old friends only Emil Schnellock was given the new address.

They had some of their happiest and most private days there.

96

During the day Miller went through the motions at work, and if June was working late at the theatre he would spend the evening playing chess and talking at Emil Schnellock's studio. He became more domesticated, and often prepared his own evening meals. He found that he enjoyed domestication, that the acquisition of such skills made a man feel less and not more dependent on his woman. If he did not feel like cooking, he might eat out at a little French-Italian restaurant on the corner, afterwards strolling the streets, maybe calling in at the Montague Street Library before returning home to read and play the gramophone. Scriabin was one of his favourite composers at this time.

It was June, as it had been Pauline, who had taken the sexual initiative in their relationship. It was she who had asked Miller for a dance that first night at Wilson's, making him blush with her directness and her beauty, and she who put her head on his shoulder later that night and invited the first kiss,[25] and the pattern continued into their married life. June was sexually bold, erotic, with a strong streak of exhibitionism. She rarely wore underwear, and when she wore a brassiere she cut it so that the nipples showed through. She had a habit, most disturbing to Henry when he was trying to write at his desk, of swishing about the room with her dressing gown open. Even when washing the floors she wore sexy clothes. The situation was the complete reverse of what it had been with Beatrice. June shared Henry's delight in adventurous love-making, in the bushes, on the floor, in the hallway, all the daylight ways which apparently distressed Beatrice so much.

For Henry the only dark moments continued to be the weekend visits to 6th Avenue to deliver the $30 alimony and see Beatrice and Barbara; melancholy occasions on which they might go for a walk in the park together, take a few rides on the funfair or a row on the lake or fly the kite Miller had bought for the child. Beatrice now had sole charge of Barbara's education and distressed Miller with her ambitious plans. Where Miller the utopian dreamer had proposed educating Barbara himself to spare her the futilities of organized schooling, Beatrice now spoke of private schools and dancing and painting lessons, and of the money needed to pay for such tuition. He saw the horrible cycle of ambitious parenthood, which he felt was still blighting his own life, beginning again with his daughter; but he was powerless to do anything about it. As the judge at the divorce hearing plainly told him, he had 'forfeited the right to parenthood'. The weekend visits and outings often ended in tears and recriminations, and Miller would return morose and guilty to June.

In a number of other ways it was June who played what was traditionally the man's rôle in their relationship. It was she who came home with gifts for Henry, curious items that seem more suited to Henry James than Henry Miller, such as a silk bathrobe, a pair of Moroccan slippers and a cigarette holder which he only ever used in her presence. Having been financially independent of her family from an early age, June had managed the difficult art of meeting her responsibilities without compromising her personality, an art Henry had never managed to acquire during his years at the tailor-shop, or later at Western Union.

Knowing how obsessed he was by the idea of writing and aware, too, of his lack of self-confidence, June constantly encouraged Henry to leave his job and concentrate on writing full-time. She had complete confidence in her powers as a hustler and when Henry expressed anxiety about their future if he gave up the job, she assured him that he had nothing to worry about; she would make enough to be able to look after both of them, and pay the alimony.

Encouraged by her, his malingering at Western Union grew steadily worse. Finally, in September 1924, came a period when he stayed off work for three days running. Returning to the office on the fourth day he decided to jump before he was pushed, and gathering up his belongings from his desk he announced to Sam Sattenstein that he was leaving, would Sam please see that the message reached Mr Nathan? Sattenstein asked what he intended to do about his outstanding wages and Miller replied that he didn't care about money, the company could keep the money.

A few moments later, he was out in the street again. Fully aware of the symbolic importance of the occasion, on the way back to Remsen Street he bought records of a Beethoven Quartet, a bunch of flowers and a bottle of good wine to celebrate the great day with June. She was delighted with his news.

The freedom he contemplated as he strolled away from the office and up Broadway that September morning back in 1924 was a simple one. It was the freedom of the truant school boy, of the dog following its nose, not the elaborate philosophical freedom of the intellectual. The mood of vibrant, reckless, joyous optimism in which it was achieved reminds one of the opening scene of *The Wind in the Willows*, in which the Mole makes his escape from chores and routine:

Spring was moving in the air above and in the earth below and around him, penetrating even his dark and lowly little house with its spirit of divine discontent and longing. It was small wonder, then, that he suddenly flung down his brush on the floor, said 'Bother!' and 'O blow!' and also 'Hang spring-cleaning!' and bolted out of the house without even waiting to put on his coat.

Miller left his Western Union job in much the same spirit of 'divine discontent and longing'. Perhaps it wasn't John Stuart Mill, but it was real, concrete, personal, accessible freedom, not a theoretical hypothesis or an intellectual achievement. In the years to come Miller's dislike of any work that was not vocational became an obsession. 'I want to prevent as many men as possible from pretending that they have to do this or that because they must earn a living. *It is not true*,' he wrote in *Tropic of Capricorn*. As he walked away from the office that day he was whispering over and over to himself 'My own master absolute'.

10

As he reviews his life in *The Rosy Crucifixion*, Miller strives at times to minimise the amount of guilt and discomfort he both caused and suffered on account of his behaviour as a young man. In the case of his first wife, he does this by presenting her in *Sexus* as a penitent sinner who comes to realize that her ex-husband had been 'right' all along in his attitude towards life, sex and freedom, and she 'wrong'. *Sexus* contains detailed descriptions of sex-scenes with her that take place after their separation and divorce, including a ten-page orgy in which the two of them are joined by her cousin. In these descriptions, Miller is at pains to depict his former wife's abandonment and joy; indeed, it is she who has the bright idea of clearing the kitchen-table when her cousin arrives, so that the three of them can make the most of the possibilities afforded by the situation. Beatrice's sexual conversion is clearly one of the least documentary parts of his life-story, and one of the least believable moments in all of the trilogy's twelve hundred pages is her quiet observation, as she stands watching Henry with his head buried between Elsie's legs, that it is 'wonderful not to be jealous anymore'.[26]

Divorce was not the commonplace in Miller's day that it became in later, secular times. In 1920 only sixteen per cent of marriages in the United States ended this way, compared with forty-eight per cent in 1988. At a guess one would say that Miller felt considerable guilt in the wake of his two major gestures of rejection; and though the freedoms he grasped for in 1924 were real freedoms they also ushered him into a prison in which success as a writer was his only chance of escape. The ambition became a compulsion, failure literally unthinkable. And beyond this: in order to justify completely behaviour which, by the canons under which he had been raised, was monstrous, mere success would not be enough: the sacrifices and sufferings of his parents, his wives and his child demanded a religious response if he were to feel himself worthy of them, and thereby annihilate the guilt. Success as a writer would become ever more associated with the idea of a religious quest, in which art itself was the religion, and himself the Clown-Jesus at its centre. The achievement must ultimately be, at its highest level, a religious achievement.

CHAPTER SIX

1924–1926
The apprentice bohemian

1

There were no schools of creative writing back in those days, so Henry was unsure how to set about being a full-time writer. In the end he simply bought himself another large and symbolic desk from a Fulton Street department store and got down to it. He described his first efforts in a letter to Emil:

I have been working my guts out lately – I ought to be dried up but I'm not. Pounding the typewriter incessantly. Decided to make one grand stab at newspaper or magazine work. Things look quite bright. *Collier's* want to see about four of my articles and *Sat Eve Post* wants one. Just finished one on the 'Sargasso Sea' for *Sunday Tribune* – and have a proposition to write daily feature articles of 400 words for a Syndicate – NY *Journal* and Hearst Papers[1].

In the same letter of 1924 or early 1925, he refers to 'three assignments from one magazine (*Menorah Journal*)' and lists some celebrities from the world of entertainment whom he intends to interview – Minsky, Margie Pennetti, and Cleo, his favourite burlesque dancer.

In the months following his departure from Western Union, Henry produced a great quantity of journalistic ephemera on a wide range of topics with titles like 'The Houston Street Burleskers', 'Wrestlers', 'Cynara', 'Asphodel', 'Chewing Gum', 'Brooklyn's Back Yard', 'Waterfronts', 'Our America' and 'Diary of a Futurist'. They seemed unpromising themes for a man who intended to be America's Hamsun or Dostoevsky, and almost at once a doubt about Henry entered June's head. 'Peregrinations in search of material', his notes from the Remsen Street days recall, 'always with June regarding me dubiously.'

The blitz on journalism did not work out as well as he had hoped. The magazine editors he submitted his articles and essays to in 1924 and 1925 rejected him, apparently because they were unable to place him. 'They all comment on the versatility of my style,' he wrote proudly to Schnellock, though in fact he was being damned with faint praise. Some of the damning was not particularly faint either. Bruce

Barton, a former editor of the magazine *Every Week* who had become a best-selling author himself, read the 'Diary of a Futurist' which Henry showed him and advised him to try his hand at something else since 'it is quite obvious that writing is not your forte'.[2] Miller took his revenge some twenty years later in *Sexus*, where Barton is referred to as a 'nincompoop who had written a highly successful book about Jesus-the-carpenter'.[3]

At about this time Joe O'Reagan returned to New York with a lot of money earned on a chartered fishing boat in the Caribbean. When he heard about Henry's gamble in throwing up full-time employment in order to write he offered to share his money with the Millers, and Henry reciprocated by inviting him to move in with them. June was not keen on the idea but Henry insisted. His notes duly record Joe's 'infatuation with June. Again betraying my confidence, as years ago with Pauline. . . . My tolerance and affection for Joe, despite all. His fascinating weakness.' Like many rootless men O'Reagan needed periodically to enjoy a stable relationship by proxy, and by comparison with his life Henry's was indeed stable. Conversely, Henry derived a vicarious pleasure from Joe's adventurous life and his commitment to a thoroughgoing sexual promiscuity, even if this always involved him in attempts to seduce Henry's women. Above all, Joe was company, someone to talk to while June was out at work. Her connection with the Theatre Guild proved transitory, and she was now working at a club called Remo's, where the men paid a fortune for the drinks while the girls drank cold tea. She was still trying to keep alive her theatrical ambitions, however, and planned briefly to put on plays for the patrons at Remo's; but nothing came of it.

Often when June returned from work she found Henry had invited a whole crowd of friends to the flat. He was astonishingly gregarious, and picked up friends and acquaintances wherever he went. A recent acquaintance was Angus Bolton, the librarian at the local Montague Street Library who knew Paris well and excited Henry with his account of his visits to the *Cirque Medrano*, one of the great circuses of the world. Talking was absolutely Henry's favourite form of entertainment, and these sessions at the flat could last far into the night, ranging freely between – among other subjects – chess, books, behaviourism, architecture, Bertrand Russell, Shaw, the institution of marriage and sex. An absinthe orgy one night ended in a huge argument about the morality of three-in-a-bed sex. 'Henry would sleep all day. I would come home dead tired and he would talk half the night with his cronies. Unable to rest I went off one evening to the Hotel Bossert for a forty-eight hour rest,' June recalled later.[4]

'Beloved children have many names' runs the saying, and from being 'Little Henry', 'Sunny Jim', 'Yorkie' and 'Harry' he had become June's 'Val', after the middle name which he had always despised as cissy. The presence of O'Reagan in the household discouraged the development of too much intimacy between the Millers, however, and June soon realized that one of Henry's articles of faith was that a woman is for loving, but for friendship you need a man.

Joe's money, so freely shared with the Millers, went towards their keep for a while, but before long a pattern was established which was to repeat itself throughout their relationship – they scraped just enough to live off, but never enough to relax. Miller's auto-biographical notes on this period refer to an unending succession of money-making plans, sometimes grandiose, sometimes banal, which rarely came off, and during these years the dangerous air of farce was never far away. They were already in arrears with the rent, and although Miller was still struggling to make his alimony payments the kites he once bought for Barbara were now a thing of the past.

One day he fell into conversation with a candy store dealer on Second Avenue who persuaded him that there was a fortune to be made in selling imported candies from Europe, and offered to employ him as a salesman on a commission basis. To prove how much faith he had in the candies he gave the Millers a suitcaseful on credit to get them started. Henry, who just a few weeks previously had been a godlet hiring and firing the wretched of the earth, found it a humiliating and embarrassing business to be shuffling from table to table in smart Manhattan cafes and restaurants trying to sell sweets from a suitcase. His obvious discomfort in the rôle made him a target for bullies and teases, and after a week or two they agreed that June should take over the actual selling while Henry acted as her minder, carrying the sweets from club to club and waiting outside for her until she was finished. Swathed in Henry's fur-lined winter coat, which a Hindu messenger had bequeathed to him on returning to India, the pockets bulging with boxes of candy, June would sweep into action while Henry watched through the windows. It was wearying work, and some days they were spending sixteen hours on foot; but June, with her beauty and her flirtatious ways, was a gifted saleswoman, and they managed to make enough to live off. Henry hated himself for allowing her to do it, but June enjoyed the game. It had its risks, though, and one night she was nearly raped by the manager of the Lido and Trocadero in his office. Henry waited two hours outside on the pavement for her. He had already begun to suffer from the piles which turned out to be one of the less romantic continuities of his life, and spent the time wretchedly clinging to some railings in an effort to ease his discomfort.

This dispiriting venture lasted for three months in the winter of 1924. Before it was abandoned completely Beatrice was briefly involved as part of a project to increase the profits by selling their own home-baked sweets. The irony of a situation in which his ex-wife was baking sweets for his present wife to sell so that he could maintain his alimony payments to her did not escape Henry. What struck him equally forcibly was the difference in attitude revealed by the two women over the venture; Beatrice's haggling over prices, trade-marks and petty rights contrasted unfavourably with June's generosity of spirit and careless disdain for such details. They never paid Beatrice any money anyway, for by the time they got organized they were already tired of the whole business.

The next money-making idea was to sell subscriptions to a series of articles and prose poems written by Henry. Under the general title of 'Mezzotints', a name inspired by Whistler's impressionist paintings, he was to write one of these a week, to be printed on different coloured sheets of card and sold in editions of 500, signed by the author. By March 1925 he had produced thirty-five mezzotints on a by now familiarly catholic array of themes. There was a hymn to beer called 'Make Beer For Man', literary thoughts on 'Hamsun' and 'Bernard Shaw', a description of the atmosphere of a typical dance hall written in a jazzy, chopped-up stream-of-consciousness style, 'Cynara', based on Dowson's poem, 'Bike Race', and character sketches like 'June the Peripatetic' and 'Papa Moskowitz', as well as autobiographical fragments. 'Nigger', an account of an incident of police brutality he witnessed involving a black man, got him into trouble when a copy fell into the hands of the precinct lieutenant. The policeman called on them at the flat and during the course of the visit Henry became so abusive that only June's intercession prevented an unpleasant situation arising.[5]

Several of the mezzotints were about films. From the first public exhibition of a moving picture in 1896 at Koster and Bial's Music Hall, through the advent of the star system with the career of Florence Lawrence and the appearance of films like *Queen Elizabeth*, *Birth of a Nation*, *Intolerance* and *Battleship Potemkin*, the new medium had developed rapidly towards acceptance as an art form. One of Henry's earliest memories was of the first moving picture he ever saw, which featured a Chinaman walking on the Brooklyn Bridge, and as the art developed he had become a keen cinema-goer. Like the books he read, films became mirrors in which he could trace mythological reflections of himself and the events of his own life. His favourite actor at the time was the German Emil Jannings, to whom he bore a vague physical resemblance, and one mezzotint was an appreciation of Jannings's performance in *The Last Laugh*.

Some mezzotints were submitted for publication, and one entitled 'A Bowery Phoenix', based on a letter sent to Emil Schnellock in 1924, appeared in the February 1925 edition of Frank Harris's *Pearson's* magazine. The real aim, though, was to raise subscriptions, and Henry and Joe O'Reagan set about peddling them in the Greenwich Village cafes, speakeasies and restaurants. The change from sweets was a relief. 'For three solid months', he told Schnellock, 'I never thought a literary thought. I never had an idea – unless it was to tackle some stranger with a box of candy. (. . .) Now my business is after my own heart. I sell myself – my work.'[6] Yet again, however, he showed little real talent for direct selling, and once more June took over and put her hustling instincts to good use. At her suggestion Henry's name as writer was removed and 'June E. Mansfield' was credited as the author of the pieces, on the understanding that it would be easier for a woman than a man to get half-drunk people in bars, restaurants and clubs to part with their money for literature.

The suggestion was realistic and logical. It was also self-serving, for in essence what now happened was that June requisitioned Henry's talent and passed it off as her own, acquiring for herself a new and wholly false identity as a writer. Even her friends and acquaintances were not party to the deception. This was a psychologically pregnant development in their relationship in which it appeared that June, a character who had found her author in Henry, now moved to appropriate his place in the drama too. Henry, while appearing to relinquish the rôle, was able to observe this development and use it to add depth and mystery to the act of creating her in which he was continuously involved. Such narcissistic and competitive manoeuvring set a pattern that recurred throughout their relationship. Long after the marriage was over, the two remained locked in dispute about who was the creator in the relationship and who the created. 'I did not create him to abandon me, but to offer him to the world for posterity' was June's most explicit statement, made long after Henry's rise to fame, of the part she had played in his success.[7]

On a practical level June was quite correct in suggesting that she was a better hustler than Henry. She knew her Greenwich Village well. By 1920, after eight years of radical and altruistic socialism, it was becoming a commercially exploitable place. Entrepreneurs like Guido Bruno published a range of fraudulent 'little magazines' which sensationalized the life-style of Village artists and bohemians and the ideal of Free Love, and Bruno opened the Garrett at 58 Washington Square South so that uptowners and Brooklynites could come along and see the beasts in their natural habitat. Other clubs sprang up to cater to what were known as 'thrillagers', such as Don Dickerman's

Pirates's Den, Julius', the Pepper Pot at 148 West Fourth, the Samovar, the Club Gallant – where whisky cost $16 a bottle – Sam Schwarz's speakeasy on MacDougal Street and Nick's Jazz Joint at Waverley Place. An artificial class of person soon arose to exploit this artificial environment, professional bohemians like Doris the Dope, who coughed for a living and told sympathetic daytrippers that she had caught TB while posing nude for the artists; when she had made enough for the day she would stop coughing, change into her good clothes and head down to the Brevoort to drink with her friends. Another professional bohemian was Tiny Tim, a pale-faced, long-haired young man who sold 'soul candy' on the streets. He charged inflated prices for this which he justified by giving away, free with each package, a few lines of neatly printed verse or philosophical specu-lation which had earlier been rejected by some publisher. It was this 'tourist' market that June hoped to tap with Henry's mezzotints.

Some of the first subscriptions she obtained came from leads Henry had given her among his contacts at the Cafe Royal on Second Avenue, but most of her luck was of her own making. She was a highly-skilled, professional flirt, able to string her admirers along without ever losing control over them, and as Henry now discovered she kept a whole little ring of sexual satellites in orbit about her, a varied group that included a professor from the Sorbonne, a professional wrestler, a banker and a shoe manufacturer. She ran them well, took what they offered and gave in return nothing but her company and her flattering attention. Some, like the importunate one-legged war-veteran Hoblitzell, had to be handled with particular care; but most of them, like Baker the shoe-millionaire, seemed content to let her dictate the course of the relationship. In all her platonic whoring she was protected by the same strange innocence that kept her husband from serious harm:

Baker would get in touch with me whenever he came into town. He'd throw a party and ask me to bring along 6 or 8 girls to whom he'd give $50 apiece. There was no dirty stuff. Each time he would offer me $200 and each time I would refuse to take it. I never took money from anyone who offered it to me freely. If I was in need I asked for money outright with the feeling that I had already earned it in kind for having been an interested or sympathetic conversationalist or listener.[8]

Baker was typical of the type that were referred to contemptuously as 'Elks' by such Village mandarins as the novelist Maxwell Bodenheim. He had a large estate in Scarsdale and a private golf course, but he liked to come to the village sometimes to enjoy the rare privilege of being treated like a nobody by the bohemians. The status of businessmen was generally low in the Village. Of Aimee Cortez, the so-called 'Mayoress of the Village' who liked to express herself by dancing naked with a stuffed gorilla, it was said that she 'never extended her favours to sterile, uncreative men, and the idea of sleeping with a banker or a shopkeeper would have been as abhorrent to her as engaging in an affair with a daughter of Lesbos'.[9] Like June, she reserved her ultimate gifts for penniless artists and writers.

On the whole, Miller preferred not to know too much about these shadowy friends, the marvellous benefactors who bought unnaturally large quantities of mezzotints and who helped June in other ways too, usually with gifts of money. Occasionally, though, he became personally involved with them. One of June's most faithful admirers was a banker named Howell French. Like most of her men, he was married. June went to great lengths to keep her own marital status secret, and on one occasion entertained French at the Remsen Street apartment with a curious charade in which Celia Conason and Henry posed as man and wife and carried on artistic-sounding conversations with Emil Conason while June tried to melt French's heart with a story about a friend dying in hospital for want of money for an operation. Futurist paintings and 'Cockroach' poems adorned the walls. Miller drank too much that evening and in the morning had to parry French's suspicious queries about why he had stayed the night there in June's flat.

It was an odd state of affairs, but Miller trusted June not to betray him. Her powerful personality, her innocence, her image of herself as unattainable and her ability to talk for hours on end were usually all the protection she needed, although she held special tactics in reserve for occasions on which her lovers' patience ran out. In French's case, for example, it simply involved bringing the conversation round to the subject of his wife's pregnancy.

This was bohemian life, of course. It was taking the bourgeoisie for a ride, and for much of the time Miller enjoyed it greatly. His account of this side of his married life in *The Rosy Crucifixion* depicts it in this light; yet his earliest notes on the marriage reveal at times a very different man from the cheerful amoralist of the trilogy. There are repeated references to the growing unease he feels about June's hustling, his pleas to her to stop it, his self-detestation for his failure to control her. 'Misery over June's golddigging,' he writes, 'which constantly preys on my mind'. Yet he was also developing a healthy appreciation of the absurdities into which his ambitions had led him, and a growing understanding that the best way to deal with the riot of interests and tastes with which he was struggling as a writer might actually lie in the pursuit of what he called a 'purposeful, literary buffoonery'.[10] A letter to Schnellock of March 18th 1925 offers a remarkably clear-sighted analysis of himself and his situation at the time, as well as early evidence of his refusal to be cowed into personal insignificance by the bellowing self-importance of newspapers:

God knows, I'd like to keep my wife home at my side, where she belongs; I'd like to pay the alimony and send my kid to a decent school; I'd like to keep on living in nice clean airy rooms in a respectable neighbourhood; I'd like to eat regularly three times a day and not have my food go back on me; I'd even join a church, everything else being equal.

But when I took the newspaper along with me tonight, to glance at during my repast, I realized what a long way off all that is. I didn't look at the newspaper. I wrapped it up and carried it home again. Newspapers make me sick. What good are they to me? Do I want to know what the rest of the world is doing? There's nothing the matter with my imagination. I know they're buggering one another, bitching up the works, fighting, scrapping, be-devilling themselves and making of this vale of tears a bed of thorns. Thank you, I'd rather go home, pretend I'm an artist and write some more flapdoodle. I suppose, in the last analysis, it comes down to this: that I really want to escape reality. I suppose I want to dream clean sheets, good meals, happy endings and all the rest of it. And I suppose, further, that I'm one of those lily-livered pups who hasn't guts enough to go out and get a he-man's job and slave eight hours, maybe ten, for some guy who knows a little less than I do.[11]

2

One day in the spring of 1925, the landlord at Remsen Street came to Henry, who was still in bed, and told him that he wanted the Millers to leave, whether they could pay the rent or not. Officially they had broken house rules cooking on a gas stove in the bathroom and – although he had once again left on his travels – in sub-letting to Joe O'Reagan. Unofficially, Henry was clearly no longer the respectable young office-manager to whom he had rented the place a few months earlier.

They accepted the ultimatum and left, to live briefly at an address at Garden Place, round the corner from Remsen Street, until June got in an argument with their new landlady who detested the Syrians in the neighbourhood and disapproved of the way the Millers fraternized with them. She also half-suspected that June was a Syrian, and after an exchange of insults they were again given notice to leave. Miller's old Driggs Avenue friend Stanley Borowski came to their rescue and offered to put them up until Henry could find a job and save enough for them to get a place of their own. The couch in the parlour at 284 Sixth Street was a change from the comfort of Remsen Street:

Luckily it was summertime, for the only covering we had was a sheet and Stanley's winter overcoat. The place was clean, fortunately, even though poverty stricken. No two dishes were alike; the knives, forks and spoons, all odd pieces, had been collected from junk heaps. There were three rooms, one after another, all of them dark – the typical railroad flat. There was no hot water, no bath-tub, not even a shower. We bathed in turn at the kitchen sink.[12]

The search for work was never more than a good intention. The pleasure of waking up each morning with nothing particular to do, no job to go to, no appointment to keep, was still a wonderful thrill, and after breakfast Henry would drift off to make the rounds of the art galleries, cinemas, shows, bookshops and libraries, idling and talking to people, adding to his eccentric and eclectic education. June would go to see her friends in the Village and perhaps try to raise some money, and they would meet up again at Stanley's in time for an evening meal. 'Neither of us had the least intention of looking for work,' he recalled. 'We never even mentioned the subject to one another.'[13] When Stanley realized what was happening he evicted them with calm efficiency, waiting while they packed their suitcase and driving them to the subway station. Here he gave Henry a dime, shook his hand and said goodbye. Miller's oldest friendship was at an end.

The kind of life he was now embarked on left Henry greatly dependent on the goodwill of others for his survival. Indeed, the sense of utter helplessness and incompetence he exuded would in time turn him into a living test of the generosity and patience of others, a traveller repeatedly beaten and stripped as he walked the road between Jerusalem and Jericho. His experiences of the generosity of strangers and the loyalty of friends led him to exalt true friendship in almost religious terms, and though his first feeling after being evicted from Stanley's was one of self-pity it gave way in time to one of shame for the way in which he had abused his friend's generosity.

A few days later, walking in Sheridan Square, he ran into Karl G. Karsten whom he had known during his brief period at the Bureau of Economic and Industrial Research in 1916. Karsten had become a professional statistician, specializing in unemployment remedies. He invited the Millers to dinner, and when Henry, open as ever, explained the predicament they found themselves in, Karsten had an idea. He and his wife were in the process of building a summer shack out at Far Rockaway – why didn't Henry and June join them? In exchange for board and lodging, Miller would work as his secretary and general factotum, while June helped Mrs Karsten about the house. Miller had happy memories of Far Rockaway, where the family had spent holidays in his boyhood, and he agreed to the deal.

After a couple of nights acclimatising themselves in the small storeroom that was their living quarters behind the main building it was back, with a vengeance, to the days of the Belgian indexing system as Henry struggled to keep up with his new master's voice on the dictaphone:

I'll never forget that first day with the bloody dictaphone. I thought I would go mad. It was like operating a sewing machine, a switchboard and a victrola all at once. I had to use simultaneously hands, feet, ears and eyes. If I had been just a bit more versatile I could have swept out the room at the same time. Of course the first ten pages made absolutely no sense. I not only wrote the wrong things, I missed whole sentences and began others in the middle or near the end. I wish I had preserved a copy of that first day's work – it would have been something to put beside the cold-blooded nonsense of Gertrude Stein.[14]

The practical side of the work went little better. Karsten believed that a session of hard physical labour was the ideal tonic after strenuous mental exertion and when Henry was finished at the dictaphone he sent him up a ladder onto the roof with a pot of nails and a hammer to bang in some tiles. Sitting astride the ridgepole Henry took aim, missed the first nail by about two inches, dropped the tile, the hammer and the pot of nails which fell through the roof into the kitchen and broke a teapot. Karsten, a logician scarcely able to credit the existence of people like Miller, encouraged his assistant to keep trying in the belief that he was bound to get the hang of it in the end. But, as he soon found out, Henry was almost supernaturally obtuse where anything practical was concerned.

In the evenings the two men socialized in a strained way. One night they stayed up until two in the morning, repeating an adolescent experiment they had tried with a Ouija board during an excursion to Bear Mountain with Raymond Swing back in 1916. On this occasion Miller summoned a characteristically catholic bunch of shades, including Nostradamus, Jacob Boehme, Ignatius Loyola and the Marquis de Sade, while Karsten scribbled down their occult messages. He told Henry he was going to transfer them later to the dictaphone for Henry to transcribe, and that he would eventually file them. Miller assumed he was joking until one day he found himself at the dictaphone typing out a message from Paracelsus in Karsten's solemn voice: 'Eating well. Time hangs heavy. Coronary *divertissements* tomorrow.'

With the passing of summer all four returned to New York, and while the Karstens went off to spend the first night in a hotel the Millers were dispatched to the Karsten's town flat with instructions to make it fit for habitation. A summer of neglect had left it overrun with mice and bugs, and there was stale garbage and rotting food lying about among Karsten's graphs and files and boxes of used string and old boots. The place was in such a state that rather than clean it up Henry and June decided to make it worse, and got up early next morning to rearrange the rubbish before quitting the place. Contractual arrangements like these between friends whose social status has changed over the years rarely work out, and the incident marked the end of yet another friendship.

3

The attempt to hustle a living without money, quite apart from the attempt to become a great writer, had got off to a poor start. The exploitation of old friends as a way of life was not proving very successful either, and the Millers' next move was to rent another place of their own, a two-room apartment on Clinton Avenue, not far from Fort Greene Park in Williamsburg.

The trial by economic impotence continued. Henry was already, after six months, well behind with his alimony payments and it was time to approach the problem of money-making seriously. Between them, they hit upon the idea of opening a speakeasy in the Village. June found a small basement to rent at 106 Perry Street consisting of three small rooms, one of them a kitchen, and Miller borrowed the capital to get the business started from his Uncle Dave in Manhattan and from his mother, whom he wilfully misled about the purpose of the loan.

To save money, they gave up the Clinton Avenue address and moved into the Perry Street basement. June's circus of men – Marder, Rice, Roberto, Barron, an army of names that march in and out of Miller's notebooks and journals without rank, title, character or face – all turned up to help them decorate the place. The ice for the new ice-box – Miller's favourite toy – came from a man in Abingdon Square, and the wine and whisky from their local bootlegger. If they ran short they could follow the well-known practice of popping into the Jewish wine shops on Allen Street for a few bottles of sacramental wine. They installed a ping-pong table and a chess board, and Henry pinned some paintings done by little Barbara up on the walls. The password, which nobody ever remembered, was to be the old Xerxes Society motto *Fratres Semper.*

The opening night was a great success. Henry's old friends were there in force, including Bill Dewar, the Schnellock brothers, Joe O'Reagan and former colleagues from Western Union like Joe Ramos. Many of June's old flames emerged from retirement to wish the venture well. All told they made over $500 that first night, and it seemed as if they might at last have found the solution to their money problem. There was a lot of work involved though, and while June played the hostess Henry handled the day-to-day running of the place:

Ostensibly I'm the manager of this joint. I also wait on tables, fill short orders, empty the garbage can, run errands, make the beds, clean house and in general make myself as useful as possible.[15]

His main job was to keep the customers drinking:

. . . to see that no one is without a fresh glass. Now and then I sit down to have a little chat with someone. But what I enjoy most is waiting on the customers, running to and fro, lighting their cigars, making up short orders, uncorking the bottles, emptying the ash-trays, passing the time of the day with them and that sort of thing.[16]

There were unforeseen hazards to the job:

The smoke was unbearable, by midnight my eyes were like two burnt cinders. When we finally got to bed and pulled back the blankets the smell of beer, wine and tobacco was overpowering. In addition to smoke and liquor I thought I detected the odour of smelly feet.[17]

There were fortunes to be made in running a speakeasy for the right people. During one ten-month period of her career in the business, the glamourous Texas Guinan made $700,000 from her operations, but with an estimated 200,000 speakeasies in New York City by the mid-1920s, the competition was fierce. Henry and June were not quite as incompetent as the two men referred to in a *Brooklyn Daily Eagle* story who were arrested twenty-four hours after opening a speakeasy within seventy feet of the Federal Building and in full view of the office of Deputy Prohibition Administrator Inglesby, but they were pretty unprofessional in their approach, and after its promising start the Perry Street enterprise went into rapid decline. It never established itself as a fashionable place to go, and the literary types whom they had hoped to attract did not materialize. The artists and bohemians who strayed as far from the Village centre as Perry Street tended to go instead to John Squarcialupi's place at number 30. The group that

112

drank there included Malcolm Cowley, Matthew Josephson, Allen Tate and Hart Crane – exactly the kind the Millers would have liked to have seen in their basement. Instead, their place soon developed into a boys club in which Henry and his friends would engage in marathon ping-pong or chess sessions, to the annoyance of their few legitimate customers. With no customers, they began drinking up their own liquor. If Joe O'Reagan was there, and Emil Schnellock with his ukulele, they would have a singsong.

Members of one of the Village in-groups did use their speakeasy occasionally. This was the circle that formed round the millionaire poet Bob Clairmont and his money, and included at times Maxwell Bodenheim, the poet Eli Siegel – whose Buddhistic poem 'Hot Afternoons Have Been In Montana' was a favourite of Henry's – and a friend of June's named Hans Stengel. Miller's shyness prevented him from coming into contact with this group. His large but frail ego thrived best in a guaranteed Miller-friendly environment such as that provided by Schnellock and O'Reagan. He was even shy of Stengel, an illustrator and caricaturist on a Village magazine whose real claim to fame was that he was a friend of Mencken and Dreiser. Yet Miller felt drawn to him, in part at least because he was a fellow-German, and the two struck up a brief friendship.

Stengel was instrumental in introducing Miller to a newly-published book that had achieved enormous popularity among young American artists and intellectuals at this time, Oswald Spengler's *Decline of the West*. Spengler's analysis of history, specifically identifying eight world cultures with mysterious origins and finite life-spans of roughly a thousand years, provided Henry with an intellectually respectable version of Madame Blavatsky's 'secret doctrine' of the seven planes of existence, the sevenfold cycle through which everything moves, and the seven Root Races of mankind which had impressed him so much during the days of his friendship with Robert Challacombe. Still struggling with the image of history as an unstructured chaos which he had acquired in his childhood, the highly specific nature of these explanations appealed strongly to him. He also took comfort in Spengler's cool and authoritative pessimism; the assertion that what Spengler called Faustian or Western culture was moving from its autumn to its winter period accorded well with his own subjective impression of things as he drifted from failure to failure through a culture that seemed to have no place for him.

Miller's friendship with Stengel was brief. In a letter to Schnellock he mentioned a project for Knopf or Liveright to publish his collected mezzotints with illustrations by Stengel, but nothing came of it. In January 1928 the artist hanged himself in the bathroom at his own party in Clairmont's studio on West 4th Street, leaving behind not a note but a caricature of what he would look like when his body was found. As for Bodenheim, the decadent King of the Bohemians, he was more interested in June than Henry, which explains the occasional disparaging references to him in Miller's letters and literature of the period.

'Henry was never jealous,' June said later, though she tried her hardest to make him so. 'Playing Ross off against me deliberately,' Miller noted. 'Regarding me as a freak.' Given the importance she attached to her sexual power over others, June was perhaps puzzled and disappointed at her failure to affect Henry in this way, and may even have interpreted it as a sign that he did not love her enough to care. Miller was a sentimental man who cried easily at films, yet he was able to mask his strongest emotions, and was perhaps only protecting his pride by pretending not to be jealous. One night at Perry Street June's admirer Hoblitzell began abusing Hans Stengel, picking on him for his cropped hair and his German accent. Miller did not enjoy 'scenes', but like a good manager he offered to eject Hoblitzell. Stengel assured him that this was not necessary; but Hoblitzell, who was extremely drunk, then turned his attention to June and began shouting for her: 'Where is that bitch? I'll fuck her yet, by Christ!' At this, Miller fell into 'one of my few blind rages' and with the assistance of Joe O'Reagan got Hoblitzell outside. To make sure he never came back again the two of them drove him down the street, dancing in rings round him, pulling monkey faces, scratching their behinds and howling weirdly. Besides being drunk, Hoblitzell had a wooden leg, which made it more difficult for him to get away from them. Miller may have appeared immune to jealousy, but the strange ferocity of the attack on Hoblitzell suggests that it was also the expression of a great deal of pent-up humiliation, frustration, rage and indeed jealousy.

Another time, as Henry and June lay in bed in the Perry Street kitchen after having closed up for the night, Howell French came by and began banging on the window and pleading with June to let him in. 'June, it's me,' he kept saying, 'let me in'. They kept quiet. Presently a policeman came along, remonstrated with French and ended by beating him up. Miller lay listening in ecstasy to the banker's cries of pain and outrage. 'Getting a vicious thrill, because one of the lovers is trimmed,' he recalled in his notebooks – again, hardly the response of a man who was 'never jealous'.

The decline of the speakeasy continued. With the falling-off in trade Henry and June were soon unable to pay their bills or their graft. The bootlegger, the landlord, the grocer, the delicatessen and the ice-man were all dunning them. Worst of all, Beatrice was getting tough about the alimony payments. Henry had paid regularly for about a year after the divorce, but after leaving Western Union had made only sporadic contributions; by November 1925 he was over $650 in arrears. Beatrice complained to him that she was destitute, and had been forced to go back to giving piano lessons to make ends meet, but Henry could see no prospect of making the back payments. He told her that in any case he was thinking of leaving New York to make a fresh start in the West. She at once got in touch with her divorce lawyer, and at her request papers were prepared for Henry's arrest and imprisonment for failure to keep to the terms of the court order. A process server was employed to deliver the summons but failed to find Henry. A second attempt to persuade him to appear at the County Court House in December to 'show cause why he should not be punished' was no more successful. Beatrice was convinced that June was behind it all. Hers was the only name above the bell at the Perry Street address, and it was Beatrice's firm belief that Henry was hiding out there at June's instigation and was refusing to answer the door to her. In fact he really had left town – and was on his way not west, but to Florida.

4

Joe O'Reagan was the instigator of the plan, which was worked out during the course of a ukulele session in the kitchen at Perry Street one evening with Miller and Emil Schnellock. He mentioned that there was a property boom going on in Florida which they might be able to capitalize on if they acted quickly. The idea was that the three men would find work as waiters, dishwashers, bellhops or whatever, live cheaply and save their money until they had enough to invest in some real estate, and then send for June.

In Western Union days, Miller had called the gang consisting of Joe Ramos, Sam Sattenstein and himself 'the three musketeers'. O'Reagan, Schnellock and himself, as they prepared for the great trip, now formed a second edition of this gang. In time there would be third and fourth editions. Throughout his early manhood Miller can be seen striving to recreate the sodality of the Xerxes days, and the Florida trip had little to do with real estate booms and a lot more to do with running away from responsibilities to have an adventure with a couple of pals.

On a level personal to Miller, it also had a lot to do with Jack London, Maxim Gorky and Knut Hamsun. He wanted to know for himself what it was like to be Hamsun starving in the streets of

115

Kristiania, Gorky stumbling through the lower depths, Jack London striding out along the open road. June suspected this was the case. She was against the trip, and disappointed Henry by referring to the idea as 'a lark'. He refused to listen to her, however, and at 1 pm on Thanksgiving Eve 1925, in the middle of a fall of snow, he left New York.

Miller and O'Reagan travelled together, hitchhiking with $40 in their pockets. Emil Schnellock went ahead by train with the ukulele and the chess set. The arrangement was that they would meet up in Washington before continuing south to Miami. No sooner had he said goodbye to June at Perry Street than Miller's conscience began pricking him as he thought of her, 'deserted in that gloomy basement, a prey to the wolves and my good friends,'[18] but the lure of adventure overcame his 'deep heartache immediately on starting out and desire to turn back at once', and on they went.

One of their best lifts that first day was with a Pullman porter driving an open Packard. They debated the race question and sang songs together. The Prince of Wales's highly successful state visit of 1924 was also discussed, as well as the Prince's drinking habits: 'Yassuh,' said the driver, 'he kin hold his likker awright. He's a great boy.'

The Florida property boom of 1925, which is said to have exceeded any gold rush or business stampede in United States history, had peaked even as the trio sat talking about it in Perry Street. Long before they reached Miami they realized that they had come too late. The roads were jammed with cars going the other way, and once they reached Jacksonville the 'three musketeers' decided there was not much point in going on, and that they might as well stay there and look for work.

A descriptive essay not published until late in Miller's life, *Gliding into the Everglades* is a near-contemporary account of what happened to them during their stay in Jacksonville. A number of other would-be speculators were stranded in town, and competition for jobs was fierce. For every vacancy, even the meanest, there were ten applicants, and the man chosen was invariably a local. Migrant northerners were hated for selling their labour cheap and raising prices. Luckily for the three musketeers, the educational director of the YMCA where they were staying was able to give them a couple of days work nailing up posters advertising a new course that he was offering, and when that ran out Henry and Joe were taken on as newsboys for a local newspaper. This turned out to be an interesting ordeal for the former employment manager of Western Union:

I shall never forget the first time I yelled 'Paper – whatta you read!' I felt like

116

the centre of the universe. My voice stuck in my throat, and I blushed to the roots of my hair. Then, suddenly people began shoving money in my fist and pulling papers out of my hand, and I realized that I was just like all the rest of the newsies, even though I wore a slouch hat and kept a pipe stuck in the corner of my mouth.[19]

One evening, along with Joe O'Reagan and a man from Tennessee whom they fell in with, Henry went on a sort of sight-seeing tour of Jacksonville's brothels. 'What I am going to record may come as a shock,' he warned any potential readers of his account. It probably would not have done so, even had it been published in the 1920s, for the men had money for neither girls nor drink, and nothing happened. *Gliding Through the Everglades* is fun, and although not especially well written it provides an interesting picture of Miller's style at the time. He used full-scale phonetic dialogue to record the speech of some of the people he met on the trip, and was especially proud of his skill at written Irish: 'I'm not disbelievin' ye, mind ye' says an Irish priest, 'but yer'll haf ter git out now. There's been three of yez here this marnin'.' Another notable feature is that, whether by accident or design, some of the adventures described carry loud echoes of Hamsun's *Hunger*. Like the starving, homeless hero of that novel, Henry and Joe are advised by a friendly policeman that they can spend the night free in a communal doss-house. This turns out to be, like Hamsun's doss-house, almost supernaturally dark. And the incident in which they visit the house of a priest who is not at home when they call in search of alms is the replica of an incident in *Hunger*. Miller either lifted these episodes and adapted them for his own use, or actually played out a few scenes from Hamsun's book while he was in Jacksonville. It was as if he were rehearsing for the performance he knew he would be putting on in Paris in a few years time.

It was, as June had forecast, 'a lark', and when he had had enough of it Miller wired his father to send him $100 and took the train back to New York. He was too delicate to be a real bum. During their night in the doss-house, he and Joe got up to leave long before daybreak simply because they could no longer stand the smell of a hundred sweaty feet.

5

Returning to Perry Street Miller found that their landlord had repossessed the property, and that June had moved back home with her mother and brothers in Bensonhurst. As neither of them had any money they agreed to live apart for a while and Henry, at the age of

117

thirty-six, returned to Decatur Street to live with his mother and father. Here he tried to forestall his mother's sarcasm by churning out articles on a wide variety of themes such as 'Numismatics', 'Jazz', 'Stamps' and 'Vocabularies' in the vain hope of finding the key to commercial success. Louise's indifference and indeed downright hostility to his literary ambitions is one of the cornerstones of Henry's mythological account of his heroic struggle to become a writer, and the tales of how ashamed she was of him and of how, during this period, she would make him hide away in the clothes cupboard whenever anyone called, taking his typewriter, books and cigarettes with him, are heartbreaking. If he happened to be spotted in the house the fiction was that he was 'just visiting'.

Later he wrote about such humiliations amusingly, but always made it clear that he could never forgive his mother for treating him in such a fashion. Perhaps she did indeed have this kind of authority over him, though it seems strange that a man of thirty-six would allow himself to be treated like this by his mother, no matter how guilty she was able to make him feel about deserting his wife and child. On the other hand, there is the possibility that hiding in the cupboard was originally an idea of his own to prevent Beatrice finding out that he was back in town and serving a summons on him. Indeed, perhaps the whole of the inexplicable atmosphere of furtiveness which accompanies the descriptions of this period in *The Rosy Crucifixion* can be related to the fear – not specified in the trilogy – that a knock on the door might be the prelude to what would have been, for Miller, the greatest horror of all – a jail sentence. Certainly it provides a better explanation for the fact that he never answered the door at Perry Street than the one offered in *Sexus* – that June, as part of her mysterious game-playing, had forbidden him to do so because she did not want her boyfriends to know that she was married.

Henry and June talked on the phone every day, and met regularly to eat together in a restaurant, but June was becoming increasingly unhappy about the situation. She had developed a facial tic which distressed Henry, and there may well have been times now when she allowed herself to wonder about her husband. For someone as willing to fight hard to survive as she was, being married to an intelligent, healthy white man with an apparently bottomless willingness to let things simply happen to him must at times have seemed a cruel fate. During their separation she began to doubt his love and to question whether he really did want to live with her. Her mood frightened him, and he persuaded his mother to let them to spend the night together on the couch at Decatur Street sometimes.

Despite appearances to the contrary, Henry did have initiative, but it was of the kind that only manifests itself as a last resort. One day, in a similarly determined frame of mind to that in which he had set out for the offices of Western Union five years earlier, he visited the offices of Ronald Millar, the editor of *Liberty* magazine, with a number of manuscripts he had been working on. He took June along with him as his lucky charm, and the trick succeeded. Millar liked some of the stuff and commissioned Henry to write an article on 'Words' for the magazine.

For someone who once estimated the average man's vocabulary at 'well over 10,000' words and his own at '100,000 easily',[20] the subject offered plenty of scope. He decided to consult an expert, and arranged to interview Dr Frank Vizetelly, an author of innumerable books on correct grammar and punctuation and a member of the editorial board on Henry's favourite dictionary, Funk and Wagnell. Miller was always a little worried during these years that he might be turning into a bookworm, and his encounter with the bookish doctor was a pleasant relief to him in this respect: 'What a virile, magnetic individual, this man! Who would ever dream, meeting him in the street, that he was the editor of a dictionary?'[21]

After the interview, Miller went away and spent a month putting together an article at three times the commissioned length. When he had managed to cut it by about half, he submitted it to Ronald Millar. 'Remember, our readers are not college professors!' Millar had warned him. Again, however, Henry had struck the problem of level. He was both too good and too bad a writer, neither talented enough to be taken completely seriously nor bad enough to be dismissed out of hand. Millar and Vizetelly both praised him warmly, and Vizetelly even wrote a letter to his father telling him Henry was a genius. Both of them advised him to carry on writing, but Millar did not publish the article, explaining with attractive tact that it was 'too good' for the lay readership of his five-cent magazine. As an earnest of his good faith, however, he paid him the $250 fee, making it far and away Henry's biggest payday to date as a writer.

6

The money from *Liberty* would have been nearly enough to pay for a Ford automobile (without self-starter) had Henry been that way inclined. Instead he used it to put down a deposit on a furnished room in Hancock Street in Brooklyn, not far from Decatur Street, where he and June could live together again:

A quiet, respectable street: row after row of the same nondescript frame houses, all adorned with high stoop, awnings, grass plots and iron railings. The rent was modest; we were permitted to cook over gas-burners tucked away in an alcove next to an old-fashioned sink.[22]

Henry carried on trying to write while June got a job at another speakeasy called the Perroquet, on East 61st Street. Henry's literary portrait of her as a waitress seems to be a slight underestimation of her rôle in the various cafés and bars with which she was associated. The journalist and writer Waverley Root, then living in a flat in Jane Street, Greenwich Village, met her at the club and recalled her 'acting as a combination of hostess and mistress of ceremonies'.[23] Once again, however, the main source of income appears to have been June's male admirers. She came home one day and told Henry that a man named Schacht had promised to buy her a house.

The chronic shortage of money continued, and while they usually managed to scrape together enough to pay the rent, for their meals they often went round to Decatur Street to eat with Miller's family. The first time Louise was introduced to June she enquired dubiously whether they were really married or not. When June answered yes, she shook her head and muttered: 'Too bad, he's no good, he's a murderer.' June was shocked, but Henry and his father had grown used to Louise's habit of belittling the men in her life, and comparing them unfavourably with her own father, Valentin. She went on to commiserate with her daughter-in-law, telling her it was a disgrace that she should be slaving away for her husband all the time, and that June would be an old woman before Henry ever got any recognition as a writer. June, however, always stoutly defended Henry and his potential in front of Louise. 'Holidays and Sunday dinners at their house were a torture for both of us,' she recalled. Louise had a habit of talking to them through Lauretta, priming the girl to ask them questions she hesitated to ask herself.

At the suggestion of Emil Conason, Henry next tried his hand at the saucy story market, and sent one off under June's name to a magazine called *Snappy Stories* for which he was paid $50. Thereafter, for the next two months, he wrote one story a week at $50 each, all of them under June's name and, apart from that first one, all lightly disguised versions of stories which had appeared in earlier numbers of the magazine. Again this was an aspect of his struggle which, in retrospect, he was able to describe amusingly; yet at the time it was only yet another disillusioning, tiring and occasionally depressing mark of his failure.

The values superimposed on his nature by his upbringing were still strong enough to burst through in occasional bouts of shame over his own fecklessness and the casual and insecure way of life he felt he was inflicting on June, and early in 1926 he gave in to the promptings of security and applied for and got a job on a Long Island newspaper at $50 a week. June was not pleased, and reacted to the news with threats. Their life together struck her as artistic and adventurous, and she saw nothing shaming in taking money from people. She accused Miller of throwing away the chance she had created for him when she encouraged him to resign from Western Union; but the real reason for her anxiety was that she had developed an emotional attachment to having Henry where she could keep on eye on him. She had made him dependent on her, and would not now tolerate any show of independence from him. Later in life she even claimed to have had two abortions about which she never told Henry 'in order not to upset him'; whether this is true or not, it is evident that she thought of him increasingly as her charge, her child. When he returned from his first day at work she was demonstratively not at home to greet him. He discovered later she had been out with yet another man-friend, a young Spanish musician. Utterly dejected, and realizing the hopelessness of even trying to stabilize their life together, he gave up the job forthwith and hibernated for the rest of the winter with his favourite writers Elie Faure, Oswald Spengler, Dostoevsky and Hamsun.

In the summer of 1926 Joe O'Reagan re-entered their lives with another pipe-dream, this time involving a real estate boom in North Carolina. He wrote to the Millers urging them to join him, and holding out the promise of a good job for Henry as a public relations man in the south. June had no wish to leave New York, and after the previous 'boom' in Florida neither of them had much faith in O'Reagan's judgement, but Henry listened to no one but himself, and rather than let him go alone, June agreed to accompany him.

This time, instead of applying to one of her male friends to finance the trip, June went to a lesbian admirer who worked behind the Tansy perfume counter in a department store. Miller may have persuaded June that he was never jealous of her admirers, but he made no secret of the fact that he disapproved of them, and was relieved that on this occasion the $50 towards the expenses of the trip had come from a woman rather than a man. Had he been able to see into the future he might not have felt quite so relieved about June's change of tactic.

Miller, who often writes with a fine irony about his years as an ageing literary apprentice, relates that he excused the suddenness of

121

their departure from Hancock Street by telling the landlady that he had been commissioned to write a book:

'What sort of a book?' she asked, clutching my hand in farewell.
'About the Cherokee Indians,' I said, quickly closing the door behind us.[24]

Protective lying about his achievements and projects had become second nature to him by now.

The Millers set off hitchhiking for Asheville with $145 to keep them going, and by the time they reached Harper's Ferry June was tired, bored, disgusted by the whole trip and missing the Village. Arguing all the way, they rode on from Johnson City to Asheville, and there met up with O'Reagan. The property boom was over, of course. There was no job for Henry either.

O'Reagan had found them a ranger's shack up in the hills where they could live rent-free for a while. After just one night of the insects and the heat they decamped and moved back down to Asheville where they rented a room in town. Henry borrowed a typewriter from a local restaurant owner and pretended to try to write, but spent as much time talking literature with his new friend, who turned out to be a former schoolteacher. June, meanwhile, was making plans to get a concession to sell silk hosiery to the women of Asheville. When she had made enough money they would buy a car and tour the south, selling silk hosiery wherever they went. It was just another round in their life of ceaseless, baffled searching for a way of making money without getting trapped by a job, and like most of their schemes it came to nothing. All Henry cared about was becoming a writer, and all June really wanted was to get back to the Village as soon as possible. They were cheered up briefly by a visit from Emil and Celia Conason, hung on in Asheville for a few more weeks with the money running down and the debts piling up, and finally, in mid-September, decided to return to New York.

7

Back in New York, they stayed briefly with the Conasons in the Bronx before returning to Brooklyn Heights and renting another apartment on Remsen Street. Miller, now more than ever thoroughly disgusted with their 'precarious, shameful existence', became briefly involved in what seemed to him the ultimate humiliation – selling encyclopedias door-to-door. June, the true bohemian, found work at the Pepper Pot at 148 West 4th Street and continued to add admirers and sugar daddies to her string. The Pot accupied a basement that ran the length of an entire building and it had a weird ambience that June liked. The interior was dark, lit by flickering candles which illuminated the drawings that covered the walls, and a sculptor had been employed by the manager, a Mr Miller, to create figures from the melted wax which were strategically placed about the room. The floor above housed a conventional restaurant.

June had by now developed an ambivalent attitude towards Henry. She loved him very much, but his failure to become a writer, or even look like becoming one, or even put on a passable imitation of being one, was a serious disappointment to her. She had put him on a pedestal and then realized he had no idea how to conduct himself up there. By offering to keep him she had given him the chance he needed to realize his dreams, but instead of *Pan* or *Crime and Punishment* he wrote 'Make Beer for Men'. 'Bourgeois' was a term of abuse among her Village friends, and his disapproval of the way she exploited herself sexually struck her as bourgeois and shamefully illustrative of his lack of artistic arrogance. He was no spiritual aristocrat, no supersoul, no artist taking what was offered him from lesser mortals as his God-given right, but a folksy German boy who was too easily intimidated by his dour mother. With the people who mattered to her, the Village Faces, the Interesting People like Clairmont and his circle, he was jealous and tongue-tied. If strangers offered to help him it was out of pity, not admiration. He was a charming nobody.

His acceptance of her countless flirtations was another disappointment. This was largely a studied, pragmatic pose, but June mistook it for a genuine indifference towards her, and was puzzled and hurt. She was also beginning to suffer from jealousy herself − not of other women but of the men friends with whom Henry seemed to have such intimate relationships. His behaviour on at least three occasions − at 91 Remsen Street, and on the trips to Florida and North Carolina − suggested strongly that he valued Joe O'Reagan's happiness more than he did hers.

June quickly established herself on the Pepper Pot scene, and one evening, in the early winter of 1926 she met there someone sufficiently weird and unbalanced to impress her as a 'real' artist, not a lost boy with a magazine horizon like Henry. This was a sculptor, a young woman with long black hair, high cheekbones, and violet blue eyes who had come into the restaurant in search of a job wearing overalls, no stockings and worn-out shoes. Her odd appearance attracted attention, and people were staring at her and laughing. June, a soft-hearted woman who sympathized with outsiders and underdogs, began talking to her. Within minutes she was making the girl more or less the same promises she had made to Henry two years previously.

She told her that she 'wouldn't think of letting a person of her beauty and artistic talent work at such menial chores as washing dishes or waiting on tables. That I would wait on the tables and look after her, even loan her money.'[25]

When June came home from work that night she carried under her arm a grotesque puppet whom she called 'Count Bruga'. Henry got no points for never having heard the name before. 'It's Bodenheim, stupid,' she informed him, explaining that Bruga was the main character in Ben Hecht's latest novel in which he satirized his former friend. 'They say Hecht has simply crucified him.'[26] Bruga, reflecting Bodenheim's legendary decadence, had been given violet twisted silk hair beneath a black sombrero, violet eyelids, a Pulcinella nose, a black velvet jacket and a coffee-coloured shirt. June put the doll in a position of honour on the dresser, and to Miller's surprise began talking about it in a most extravagant way, claiming that it had 'more personality than a human being', and that there was genius in it because it was the work of a genius. Something about June's absurd enthusiasm for the thing, and the intense care with which she spoke the words when she referred to its creator as 'my friend' caused an unfamiliar unease to invade Miller's mind. If it was jealousy, then it was a new and unknown kind of jealousy.

CHAPTER SEVEN

1926–1927
The first triangle: Henry, June and Mara/Jean

1

Miller's egocentric personality made him peculiarly well-suited to champion one of the rights he defended most fiercely in later life – the right of the individual not to read a newspaper. In his ground-level account of the five years between 1923 and 1928 in *The Rosy Crucifixion* fragments of history in the making do occasionally flicker through the story – in a bar one day, for example, he overhears two men discussing the Scopes trial of 1925* – but of the concerns of the world at large he relates little. He was the historian of his life, not its sociologist, so the relationship which developed between his wife and Jean Kronski in late 1926 seems, in his account, like a freakish bolt from the blue; yet in many aspects it reflected a general process of changing sexual attitudes that began in Greenwich Village back in 1912, and ran with accelerating effect from about 1920 onwards. This process was closely bound up with the growing impact of Freud's theories on the standards and behaviour of young Americans in the years between 1912 and 1930.

2

A wealthy hostess named Mabel Dodge played an important part in this process of change. Her Wednesday evening salons at number 23 Fifth Avenue, beginning in 1912, marked the start of the modern history of Greenwich Village as a bohemian and cultural centre. At these evenings a wide range of taboo subjects were discussed – sex, birth control, labour relations, trade unionism and the need for a socialist revolution. The Village was a nice mixture of political and personal radicalism, with political radicalism the dominant strain. Malcolm Cowley, the historian of the public life of the Village where Miller was the chronicler of its private life, wrote that the 'Bohemians

---

*John T. Scopes was charged with violating Tennessee state law by teaching the theory of evolution in the classroom. His defence lawyer was the celebrated Clarence Darrow.

read Marx and all the radicals had a touch of the bohemian: it seemed that both types were fighting in the same cause.'[1] Villagers, he wrote, might get their heads broken in Union Square by the police before going along to the Liberal Club at 137 MacDougal Street to recite Swinburne in bloody bandages. Bill Haywood of the IWW, one of the orators who so impressed Miller at Union Square meetings, was a regular attender at Dodge's evenings, and Dodge's brief affair with the communist poet John Reed in 1913 symbolized the coexistence of political and personal radicalism among Village artists and intellectuals in this pre-war period.

The War and the Draft Law of 1917 split and polarised the two tendencies. Those whose rebellion was largely a personal reaction against the restrictions of puritan morality had little difficulty in coming to terms with Woodrow Wilson's world, while political radicals were forced to take issue with government policy in a way that left them exposed to Establishment responses. *The Masses*, a magazine founded in 1911 in the basement of the socialist Rand School, where Miller had once been invited to lead the literary classes, became, under the editorship of Max Eastman, the mouthpiece of the political radicals. John Reed covered the war from Europe for *The Masses*, and his experiences there and interviews with French soldiers convinced him that it was being fought to decide trading rights rather than in defence of liberty and democracy. He said as much in his despatches, each of which closed with the words: 'This is not our war'.

Inevitably, *The Masses* fell foul of the law and in trials in April and October 1918 its political teeth were pulled. The demise of *The Masses*, the Red Scares of 1917 and 1919 – which led to the infamous Palmer raids of 1920 in which 4000 suspected communist revolutionaries were jailed – and the death of Reed himself in Moscow in October 1920 effectively signalled the end of political radicalism in Greenwich Village. By 1923, the time Miller and June were frequenting its tea-houses and speakeasies, talk about revolution had given way to talk about psychoanalysis. Mabel Dodge was also an early enthusiast for the new theories of psychoanalysis, and so nicely embodies the changeover from political to personal concerns among Villagers' leaders.

The Freudian theory that fueled this switch from the political to the private made its advance against an entrenched puritanism associated with the Progressive Era of Theodore Roosevelt. The sexual morality of this institutionalized puritanism was prohibitive, joyless and often frightening. Male masturbation was a common target, a typical product of the era being a book published in 1900, *Natural History and Hygiene* by Dr J.H. Kellogg, which described for the worried parents of adolescent boys thirty-nine unmistakeable signs of masturbation. As late as 1912, around Union Square and in the upper reaches of the Bowery, New York had its dime museums for 'Men Only' which exhibited the horrible effects of masturbation, syphilis and other venereal diseases. In his youth Miller frequented these 'Men Only' museums with a horrified fascination, and the guilt which accompanied his sex-life with Pauline Chouteau – the diary entries each time they made love, the driven athleticism, the sea-bathing and early-morning bike rides –was probably typical of the response of most adolescents of the period to the fear-ridden sexual atmosphere of the time. The general belief among physicians until about 1912 was that excessive masturbation and intercourse were not only debilitating but downright dangerous. With early hair-loss as well as short-sightedness among Dr Kellogg's thirty-nine symptoms of self-abuse, the fact that Miller contrived to hold on to the idea that sex was a joy, no matter what the doctors said, was a real victory for his faith in the truth of his own perceptions.

The invention of the concept of adolescence was another weapon in the war against sex. To a society that regarded sex as a violent and uncivilizing phenomenon it seemed that an artificially extended childhood might serve to contain it during its most explosive phase. The idea was the creation of upper middle class parents in England and Germany. It was successfully imported to the United States, where it spread to the lower middle class. Some odd paradoxes resulted from this theory, and *The Rosy Crucifixion* contains several descriptions of Miller, aged twenty-two, larking about with his Xerxes friends like a boy of fourteen at the same time as he was having a sexual relationship with a woman fifteen years his senior.

In the dominant puritan ethic of the pre-war years, only grown men, whores and lower-class women were believed to experience sexual pleasure. The medical stereotype of the average decent woman became progressively purer and less realistic between 1870 and 1912, and in 1911 at least one practising physician believed the wholly passionless woman to be the norm.[2] Repression, modesty and innocence were the sexual equivalents of social gentility and refinement, and since many women believed there was a connection between sexual pleasure and conception, the repression of pleasure became also a means of female contraception.

Women read more books than men, and it was out of consideration for the sensibilities of women that the censorship of books in the last years of the nineteenth and early years of the twentieth century was pursued with such vigour. Mabel Dodge recalled how the Hearst editor Arthur Brisbane cut the word 'pervert' from one of her short

127

stories, explaining to her that it 'represents a thought which I do not want to put into the minds of millions of people, even for the sake of truth'.[3] His words echo those spoken by Anthony Comstock at Clark University just a few months before Freud's epochal lectures there in 1909: 'Once the reimagining faculties of the mind are linked to the sensual nature by an unclean thought, the forces for evil are set in motion which rend asunder every safeguard to virtue and truth.'[4] Comstock was the promoter of what was known as 'civilized morality', an ideal of conduct rather than a description of reality, in which sexual purity, chastity, monogamy and moral cleanliness were the goal. Theodore Roosevelt was an avid promoter of the ideal which, with its rigorous opposition to birth control, clearly implied that sex for pleasure was wrong.

Mental purity was as important as physical, and Comstock and his Society for the Suppression of Vice campaigned energetically in this cause, seizing books, magazines, photographs, playing cards, pills, powders and rubber articles. Comstock, who once boasted of having caused the suicides of fifteen booksellers and publishers,[5] knew little about literature. The banning in England of *Mrs Warren's Profession* by the Lord Chamberlain and the withdrawal by the New York Public Library from its shelves of *Man and Superman* in 1905 drew a sarcastic response from Shaw and a counterblast from Comstock. He railed against 'this Irish smut-dealer' and warned that if any attempts were made to stage his 'filthy productions', the law would deal severely with them. The result of this outburst was that *Mrs Warren's Profession* attracted huge attention when it opened in New York, and the producer of the play was duly summonsed. Surprisingly, the Society lost the case.

Yet there was still a long way to go. In 1916 the publisher of Theodore Dreiser's *The Genius* withdrew the novel under pressure from the Society, which complained about its 'obscenities on seventy-five pages and profanities on seventeen'. Six years later, in 1922, along with *Ulysses* and *Women in Love*, the book was still having trouble. Even the mantle of scientific respectability was no guarantee of protection: in 1913 a Boston neurologist was threatened with prosecution after publishing articles inspired by a psychoanalytic view of sex, and in 1917 many basic psychoanalytic texts were still housed in a guarded room of the New York Public Library, where they could be read in a cage only by those who had the special permission of the librarian.

As the Shaw decision showed, the climate was changing. The period between 1911 and 1917 covering the breakthrough of Freud's theories in the United States coincided with a social development that has been called 'the repeal of reticence'. In part this was the unforeseen consequence of the agitation of purity crusaders who, in attempting to stamp out prostitution, discovered the truth of Arthur Brisbane's perception – that the major result of any reference at all to sexual behaviour, whether approving or disapproving, is to arouse public curiosity about it. Public debate about sexual mores soon passed beyond the control of the puritans who had raised the issues, and discussion was in time followed by actual changes in sexual behaviour. Zealots for prohibition found that they too had failed to foresee one important result of their campaigning: in pre-prohibition days the saloon had been strictly out of bounds to women, but with the legal dismemberment of a whole drinking tradition women enthusiastically invaded the new speakeasies.

3

In view of the strain of living with a dishonest image of themselves, women had a particular interest in promoting the sexual revolution of the post-war period, and many of the most active campaigners in Greenwich Village were female. From the establishment of Mabel Dodge's salon in 1912 to the end of Marianne Moore's period as editor of *The Dial* in 1929, women played a major part in breaking down the literary and social taboos of the period. Margaret Anderson and her assistant on *The Little Review*, Jane Heap, were the first to print *Ulysses* anywhere in the world. The instalments they ran between 1918 and 1920 earned them a conviction for obscenity and a $100 fine. In 1915, Margaret Sanger's *Family Limitation* was prosecuted and found 'contrary not only to the law of the state, but to the law of God', for which Mrs Sanger was sent to jail. Emma Goldman agitated tirelessly for free love, contraception and the repeal of literary censorship. Other outstanding women of the period were Crystal Eastman, whose Woman's Peace Party opposed American entry into the war; Henrietta Rodman, who invented the feminist uniform of bobbed hair, meal-sack dress and sandals and campaigned for equal rights, female suffrage and dress reform; Neith Boyce, Susan Glaspell, Elizabeth Cady Stanton and Susan B. Anthony, who led the agitation which resulted in votes for women in 1920. As well as these 'responsible' women there were those like June, strong individualists who did not need the support of a movement or the authority of statistics in order to live the kind of life they wished to live. June was not in any meaningful sense of the word a feminist. Rather than

129

Henrietta Rodman's drab costume she preferred a tight-fitting red dress, a flowing black cape and bare legs, and was a shameless exploiter of the difference between the sexes. Yet the atmosphere of foment and change in norms and values affected the use she made of her freedom quite as much as it affected Henry's response to her behaviour.

Kinsey's figures appear to confirm the rise of a new set of sexual mores after the turn of the century. The answers to questions put by his researchers suggest that women born around 1900 were between two and three times as likely to have had sex before marriage as those born before 1900, and that about a quarter of all girls born between 1900 and 1909 were having premarital sex by the age of twenty.[6] Surveys of American magazines revealed that after 1918 tolerance of adultery, divorce and birth control increased rapidly, reaching a peak between 1925 and 1929, especially among intellectuals; by the mid 1920s even the stereotype of the passionless woman was quite dead.

As discussions of sexual behaviour gave way to practical experimentation, the Village experienced a wave of experiments with lifestyles. The value of marriage as an institution quickly became the subject of a long-lasting debate that survived Bertrand Russell's attack and John Cowper Powys's defence in 1930. For a time there was a fashion for men and women to live together without being married. It took the self-assurance of the well-educated and the wealthy to carry out such experiments with aplomb, and while Miller remained 'addicted to the marriage state',[7] June's working-class instincts insisted on marriage while the Bohemian in her decreed that the marriage be kept secret from her friends. The ideal of 'free love' which Emma Goldman promoted so keenly, and which made such an immediate appeal to Henry Miller, inevitably turned into a fashion for promiscuity; and when promiscuity became tame it was replaced by a fashion for homosexuality.

When the cult of homosexuality first became apparent in the Village, around 1926, it was associated with a number of clubs and bars like the Rainbow Inn, Trilby's and the Village Grove. Even before she met Jean Kronski, June had been aware that homosexuality was in fashion and had developed a curiosity about such places. In talking about them with Henry she displayed a mixture of fascination, contempt, amusement and disgust. Her indiscriminately flirtatious nature was challenged by the opening up of a new field, and one evening at a club called Jo's she was bitten on the breast by a lesbian. Jo's was typical of the clubs she frequented. Caroline Ware, who carried out an extensive sociological survey of the Village between 1920 and 1930, described the place thus:

130

Jo's was located in the basement of a tenement building. In the low, narrow room, cheap, brightly-coloured tables, rickety chairs, a few booths and an old piano were crowded as tight as they could be jammed. Liquor was not served, but it was assumed that the patrons would bring it, and order sandwiches and ginger ale. The place was usually crowded and always informal. Girls making a first visit to the place could be sure that the men beside whom they found themselves seated would assume that they were a party for the evening and night. If the girls were first at a table, they were sure to be joined. From time to time someone started to play the piano and people danced in the crowded aisles between the tables with whatever strangers they happened to be sitting beside. The proprietor stood by the door, greeting everybody, eyeing all newcomers and making announcements. Many of those present were young girls and boys with pale faces and circled eyes who drank heavily. The rest were a few middle-aged men who had obviously come for relaxation and to pick up a girl, and a number of older people, some with an artistic or literary past, who were known as habitués. A young Chinese communist came to pick up someone who could help him translate and criticize his work. Certain familiar figures who were always known to be trying to borrow money were cold-shouldered by everyone. A couple of young girls from the south who obviously came from substantial homes and a cultivated background were regularly present and conspicuous, dancing together and constantly drunk.

These people had two preoccupations – sex and drink. In the early years of the decade, free love and promiscuity had been a sufficient subject for talk and entertainment in most groups. By 1930, promiscuity was tame and homosexuality had become the expected thing. One girl who came nightly was the joke of the place because she was trying so hard to be a Lesbian, but when she got drunk she forgot and let the men dance with her. A favourite entertainer was a 'pansy' whose best stunt was a take-off on being a 'pansy'. To lend a touch of intellectuality and to give people a sense of activity, the proprietor set aside two nights each week for discussion or performance by regular patrons. These evenings, however, did not interrupt the group's major preoccupation, for the subjects chosen for discussion were such things as 'the social position of the gigolo' and 'what is sex appeal?' On the latter subject, the views of the Lesbians present were especially called for.[8]

Elsewhere in her study Caroline Ware observes: 'at each stage in the Village's history some one group was identified with the locality and offered easy contact to newcomers. In 1930 it was the pseudo-bohemians and especially the Lesbians, into whose group it was easily possible for strangers to find their way.'[9]

One effect of Freud's stratification of the psyche on the breakdown of contemporary sexual morality was the creation in some people of sexual confusion, based on the implication in his theory of the

131

unconscious that accurate self-perception is, at the deepest level, an impossibility. Thus, besides the real lesbians in the Village, and the women merely pretending to be lesbians, there were also women who were not even sure whether they were pretending to be lesbians or not. It was into this baffling atmosphere of semi-intellectualized sexual confusion that Henry Miller was plunged the night his wife came home, breathless with excitement over her discovery of the young Jean Kronski in her overalls and worn-out shoes.

4

Miller always claimed to have an 'absolute belief in June's integrity, loyalty, fidelity' in spite of the 'attitude of friends who misinterpret my attitude ... think it indifference'.[10] His occasional expressions of hostility towards men like Hoblitzell and French only partially compromise the claim, for there is a fine distinction between real sexual jealousy and the superficially similar response that is largely an expression of affronted pride. The crisis of violent jealousy into which June's relationship with Jean Kronski plunged Miller certainly contained elements of both these responses; for humiliating as it was to discover that his first serious rival for his wife's affections was a woman, it was perhaps even more painful for him to have to listen as June enthused about the artistic genius of her new friend. It was only too apparent that, after her slight mistake with Henry, June believed that she had finally discovered a 'real' artist in Jean.

In fact, Jean Kronski was not the girl's real name. June claimed later that it was she who 'named' her Jean, although it is by no means certain she was telling the truth: the mental breakdowns she suffered later in life did further damage to a hold on reality that was always fragile, and in old age June made several curious claims – for example, that it was she who had submitted her husband's resignation to Western Union, and without his knowledge – all of which tend to exaggerate the extent to which she had been responsible for the aura of myth surrounding Miller's life in the 1920s. In his notebooks on the triangular situation Miller consistently referred to his wife's friend as 'Jean Kronski', while in *The Rosy Crucifixion* the lesbian who became infatuated with his 'Mona' is 'Stasia'. Early drafts of the auto-biographical novels experiment with still other names for her. In another casual twist Miller used the name 'Thelma' in a passing reference in *The Time of the Assassins*, his long essay on Rimbaud. Alfred Perlès, an Austrian writer who met the girl in Paris and used her

132

as a character in his autobiographical novel *The Renegade* also called her 'Jean Kronski'.

If there was once a purpose to this exercise in obscurity, it is hardly possible to discern it now, and Jean Kronski has established itself firmly in the Miller legend as the real name of 'Stasia' in *The Rosy Crucifixion*. A great deal of circumstantial evidence suggests, however, that she was properly Martha Andrews, known to those outside the Millers' circle as Mara. The daughter of wealthy parents from Baltimore, Maryland, she had only recently arrived in New York with the intention of becoming an artist. Waverley Root knew her slightly at this time and described how she would visit him at his Jane Street flat in Greenwich Village. The room was tiny, and when Mara entered 'the place suddenly became crowded'. 'She outweighed and out-reached me,' he wrote.[11] Her physical appearance was striking and called forth contradictory responses. June said that she had the 'face of youth, neither male nor female'. Miller thought she looked like Rimbaud, while the sister of her close friend, Jean Bakewell, recalled her as 'very ugly' and looking 'like a bullfrog'.[12] Perlès found her 'an extremely lovely girl' and a 'veritable *morceau de roi*'. Cyril Connolly, who met her in Paris in 1928 through Jean Bakewell, whom he later married, noted especially 'her frankness and sincerity, her boy's clothes and rather talented unhappiness'.[13] In the course of her brief life, which ended in suicide in a Bank Street apartment in Greenwich Village in 1942, this enigmatic young woman crossed the Millers' paths for a few months in 1926 to devastating effect.

Miller felt the force of Mara's influence on the marriage some time before he actually met her. He had always bemoaned the fact that June had no friends of her own sex, and actively encouraged her to try to establish friendships with other women, and June had always insisted that she had no need of women friends. Now, when Miller began to complain about the intensity of her friendship with Mara Andrews, she would retort: 'You forced me to seek someone else.'[14] The repellent Bruga on the dresser became the symbol of her independence, and Henry's ridicule of her enthusiasm for the doll only strengthened her defence of Mara.

Miller began noticing changes in June which he attributed to her new friendship. One was the bizarre make-up she would put on each day before going out to work: coal dust and vaseline round her eyes, heavy mascara, crimson alizarin on her lips, a green layer of powder on her cheeks. This dramatic-sounding toilette may have been part of a fashion inspired by the heavy make-up used by vamps in the movies, and Miller complained that it made her look like a whore. June was unmoved – it was only another sign that beneath Henry's khaki shirt beat an irredeemably bourgeois heart. And the more extreme she became in her bohemianism, the more did the Germanic properness and primness and fussiness in him come to the fore. One draft description of her spoke of:

Clothes, towels, shoes, socks, worn to shreds in no time, or ruined by cigarette holes, by spillt (sic) wine or gravy or paint. Habit of doing what she likes, regardless of what she has on – because it would cramp her style. Allowing others to wear her things and ruin them for her: fur coat, beautiful slippers, evening wraps, mantillas, scarves, etc. Mislaying, losing, having things stolen: purses, bracelets, pendants, costly kerchiefs, gloves, money. (Finding 50 dollar bills floating around on floor, staircase, in clothes closet, etc, where they had fallen out of bag in which they were usually carried all crumpled up like used toilet paper. Hence super-cautiousness on my part in guarding own personal belongings which have special value for me. Dictionary, for instance, watching it each time Joan (*ie June*) uses it so that it will not be dropped on floor, or leaves wrinkled, or pages cut or torn.[15]

Once when he met her outside a restaurant she was wearing a hat which was covered with sawdust or plaster from the walls. When he pointed this out to her she expressed complete indifference.

Her rampant bohemianism led to increasingly violent arguments between them as Miller struggled to assert some control. Every morning they argued about the make-up and about her habit of going bare-legged in public. Some of their fiercest arguments concerned her way of leaving the house with a freshly-lit cigarette dangling from her lips. Since the Sullivan Ordinance of 1908 it had been illegal for women to smoke in public in New York City, and although this had been breached so many times that it was not a vital issue by 1927, Miller was conservative in his view of sexual rôles and was humiliated by June's behaviour. With neither money nor artistic success to boast of, his only status lay in his having a beautiful wife; but what use was a beautiful wife as status symbol when the husband had no control over her? It was not, anyway, so much the *fact* of her smoking a cigarette in the street as the *way* she smoked it that bothered him. As they walked together to the subway, the breakfast argument still darkening the air between them, she would puff away at it in a silent, vengeful fashion that seemed to him 'not only defiant but insulting'.[16] At times his rage was such that he had to struggle against the desire to tear it from her mouth and fling it in the gutter.

By the time Miller met Mara Andrews in person he had already heard more than enough about her. According to June, she was a Romanoff princess, an orphan who had been educated in a convent. She spoke several languages, played several instruments, and besides being a sculptress was a painter and a poet. She was an androgynous mystic of a genius who uttered strange Slavic imprecations when entering a room for the first time, wore amulets to ward off evil, smoked marijuana and walked through the streets in odd shoes carrying a douchebag, with *Alice in Wonderland* in one pocket of her overalls and the *Tao Te Ching* in the other. At each successive revelation concerning the fabulous Mara, Miller wagged his head 'like a Jew who has just been informed of a fresh calamity'. He was already beginning to get the idea: no wonder he was not romantic enough for his wife – he was neither a genius, nor a Romanoff, nor a bastard. June was a collector of gods, and his place in the pantheon had been taken. Suddenly everything was 'bourgeois'. Even his heterosexuality was bourgeois: Mara was 'the greatest living poet in America' simply because there was the same strong flavour of homosexuality in her work as in Whitman. The ability to 'pass beyond the limits of normality, in love and in art, was to achieve the insuperable', according to June.[17] Mara was a lesbian who happened to write poetry, ergo she was a great poet.

She was also clearly a confused adolescent who appealed strongly to June's instinct for lame ducks and outsiders, and at June's prompting she moved from her squalid apartment in Clarkson Street to one in Pierrepont Street, just north of Remsen Street. Thereafter the two women spent much of their time together, either roaming the Village or at Mara's or at Remsen Street.

Meeting her for the first time, Henry detested her. His jealousy was further aroused when he saw June treating Mara with the same almost religious awe as she had once treated him. Once, at Remsen Street, she washed Mara's feet for her. Henry's protests over such scenes were dismissed as bourgeois, prosaic, dull. His jealousy, now that she had finally managed to get him to display it openly, was 'unnecessary'.

One day June came home with a story about Mara having been committed to Bellevue mental hospital; if she agreed to look after her, the authorities would be willing to release her at once. Miller, though disposed to regard this as yet another of June's inventions, haplessly agreed to allow Mara to move in with them. Shortly after, all three moved into a basement apartment on Henry Street which had formerly been a laundry.

5

Deliberately or not, June was paying Henry back with a vengeance for foisting Joe O'Reagan on her during their first stay at Remsen Street, and for all the intensity with which he had insisted on maintaining friendships which dated back to his childhood. She and Mara lived like men. They frequented speakeasies, got drunk together and stayed away all night without explanation if they felt like it. On one such occasion, Miller prepared the first of a number of dramatic scenes for June when she returned. He took all his old love letters out of the wooden chest that June had bought especially to hold them, gathered up old photographs and manuscripts, annotated them and then scattered them about the bedroom. He wedged their marriage certificate under Count Bruga's arm and propped him up on the pillow on her bed. When the two came in that night, Mara, who in yet another breach in the privacy of the marriage had adopted June's habit of calling him Val, asked coolly: 'Is this another one of your gestures, Val?' June did not even bother to read his annotations, and treated it all as a joke. Henry, from being a 'god', had become 'Val the nut', a child-like eccentric who could be lied to with impunity.

Waverley Root, an occasional visitor to the basement flat, recalled it as 'six or seven large rooms, all of them empty, unless you count a few burlap bags thrown into one corner'. On meeting Henry there for the first time he got the impression that he 'seemed to relish the idea that he was living with two women at the same time', one of whom was 'pretty and delightfully feminine' while the other was 'built like a football player'. Later he realized that his impression was mistaken. The place quickly became a bohemian nightmare for Miller as June abandoned all attempts to play the part of the domesticated wife. The beds remained unmade all day, the sheets were never washed, nor the towels, nor his shirts. The sinks would regularly get blocked with the remains of their meals, so that the dishes had to be washed in the bath. The window-shades were always kept drawn and the windows themselves were never washed. Mara Andrews's sculpting left the floor strewn with plaster of Paris, along with her paints, books, cigarette ends and dirty cups and saucers. The place was permanently cold.[18]

June no longer cared to save her husband's face in front of his old friends. When one day George Wright, a former member of the Xerxes Society, turned up with his wife on a visit, June left the house at the first opportunity, and went up to Harlem with Mara and a male friend on another fund-raising trip. She did not return until 5 am the following day. Miller, who had once enjoyed June's exhibitionist boldness, haplessly recalled her thereupon 'mounting me despite proximity of Wright's wife'. At his insistence – and much against June's will – the couple were now sleeping in twin beds, still a novelty in the 1920s. This, after just three years of marriage, suggests perhaps that June was already becoming too much for him to handle. Later, when the marriage was definitely over, he reminisced with angry longing about her 'overwhelming sex'.

Though he felt himself 'licked, incapable of anything', Miller tried for a while to compete for June's attention with Mara. He bought two tickets to *Battleship Potemkin* and asked her to join him. She made an excuse. Only half-jokingly, he suggested that she establish a rota system, dividing her time evenly between himself and Mara. The situation was so completely foreign to him: previously, whether with his mother, Pauline or Beatrice, he had been the centre of attraction, the loved one. Soon he had to suffer the sight of the two women sleeping in the same bed next to his. This happened twice, and though he had often in all innocence slept with his own male friends in the past, his knowledge that Mara was a lesbian made the situation sinister and threatening. Beyond dreaming up what he called 'asinine plans' to drive Mara Andrews permanently insane and get her locked up, he could conceive of no remedy for it.

His depression increased. Endless lacerating discussions in the flat about lesbianism and perversion over what he graphically referred to as the 'gut table' sickened him. In part it seemed to him merely the foolish complication and intellectualization of something simple, yet he read the *Satyricon* and Aristophanes, as well as Auguste Forel on *The Sexual Question* in an effort to understand more about homosexuality. He read Otto Weininger too, encountering there for the first time the theory of sexual polarity which was to baffle and fascinate him throughout his life. He sometimes induced Emil Conason to join their discussions, and thereby found himself in something of a quandary. In this intensely Freudian era Conason's status as a psychiatrist was high, and Miller clearly wanted him somehow or other to prove to June and Mara that there was something in some absolute sense *wrong* with homosexuality; or that it was a curable condition brought on by such and such a set of factors. Yet his respect for independent thinking and subjective truth led him to resent it when Conason dismissed as irrelevant or unimportant any confession by Mara that did not fit in with his theories; or clung tenaciously to his own explanations and theories even when Mara disagreed with them on the basis of her own experiences. This was perhaps the first inkling Miller had that psychoanalysis might not be the magic key to the understanding of human beings that it had at first seemed. June, aware that it was really her who was under attack, one day found a psychologist of her own and returned triumphantly spouting what Miller described as 'a lot of gibberish about glandular disturbances'.

An actress herself, she was utterly convinced that Mara was only pretending to be a lesbian. Henry was not so convinced.

There were times during these troubled months when Miller's strong pragmatic streak began to show itself, and he and Mara, spending a lot of time at the flat, began getting to know one another better. She even wrote a poem about him, dedicated 'To HVM':

His pupils upheld his eyelids
   with
      spherical
        blue
           columns
Where he placed the gift of a
      TARANTULA
(with a tiny pink bow
around its neck and spectacles resting on its nose)
      This he pushed
        with
   a
   pin
From his sardonic heights,
    He pulled melted sand in
   hopes of making it hard, and
     wore nose rings in his tongue
     that he might lick the steel dust off
     chalk kettles where he kept his stew . . .
But come back to the shriveling surface:
Such a being has forgotten the fast-fading
   stars
IN SCIENCE AND CAT TRICKS
      Deck him in moon tears –
(the breath of a freshly turned tendril)
May dew bleach the copper hairs at his ear.
   HE CAN'T PRESS OUT HIS PEARL.
   WRINKLED WITH A SCRATCHING
   STEEL PEN.
Let him live to prove
   dissection
    doesn't
     sleep
       with
        sky.
His circus only flings sawdust

> To crack the dovetails of speed.
>> On a dried sucking night he may muse
>> and finger a cottonwad 'til it's gray
>> and the beyond of his eyes will seek
>> that of the lonesome unborn.

Mara's god was Rimbaud, and it was during one of their conversations together that Miller heard the poet's name for the first time. She was obsessed by him, and even claimed to be living her life in direct imitation of his. Rimbaud's genius, precocity and strange fate made him a natural candidate for Miller's pantheon, and later on he did become one of his greatest idols. At the time, he was too put off by the source of the recommendation to accept it. Mara also introduced him to the worlds of Japanese and Chinese art, and impressed him greatly when she began covering the walls of her room with bizarre paintings. He was beginning to want to paint himself, and asked Mara if she would give him lessons.

For June, sexual deviation was what guaranteed the quality of an artist's work, while for Henry, childishness was the hallmark of genius. After getting to know Mara, it often seemed to him that she had 'all the childish characteristics' necessary to be a genius. It was a dispiriting thought. The fact that neither her puppets nor her poetry impressed him was never quite enough to free him of the fear that Mara was the real artist, and he 'the Failure'.

6

The old life, the pre-June life, had almost faded now. All contact with Beatrice had ended over Henry's inability to pay his alimony and the profitless farce of the candy enterprise. There would have been little point in their keeping up the relationship anyway, since it had declined to the point of total mutual antipathy. On one of the last occasions on which he had visited her there had been a miserable scene as the two of them held little Barbara on the kitchen table, screaming with fear, while a doctor pierced her eardrums. The visit ended in a more violent argument than usual, and shortly afterwards Barbara was told that her father had gone abroad.

Once, while wandering in the street near the old home, he saw a group of children playing, and thought he recognized his own daughter among them. The presence of uncertainty reminded him of the crime of his desertion, and in a forlorn attempt to ease his conscience he toyed briefly but vainly with Strindbergian doubts about whether or not he really was the child's father:

139

How do I know it's my child? How do I know whether my wife was faithful to me? And what difference does it make now whether she was or not? I was the one who was unfaithful. Someone opened a door unexpectedly and there we were. That's infidelity. If I sit here and dream about all the women I'd like to sleep with that's alright. The law doesn't say anything about bad thoughts. Bad thoughts! What are bad thoughts? . . .[19]

With the coming of Christmas there was no question of calling in to spend even part of the day with Beatrice and Barbara. As usual Henry made arrangements with his mother and father to go to Decatur Street. He was at first surprised when June asked whether Mara might come along with them. Whether a real lesbian or only a determined disorderer of the senses, Mara always dressed the part. She rolled her own Bull Durham cigarettes when not smoking cigars and dressed like a man, freely helping herself from Henry's selection of ties to complete her outfits. She also had a thick, brass-studded belt which she sometimes wore as part of a cowboy outfit. To please June, and to alleviate the certain boredom of the occasion, he agreed to let her come with them on condition that she dress like a woman.

They took small gifts with them, including a carton of Camels for his father, and Louise murmured, as she did every year, that they shouldn't have bothered with presents; it was too extravagant of them. Sherry was handed round and familiar scenes were re-enacted. Louise, having established that Henry was once again out of work, looked with tragic sympathy at June, commiserating with her over her burden. Then she turned to Henry, as she did every year: 'You ought not to let her work like that. It isn't fair.' It was 'futile' to expect anything to come of his scribbling. And what about Lauretta? What was to become of her? Did he never think of her? Of course, Miller answered forlornly: 'Please don't go on, mother. Of course I think about these things. Of course. Of course! But... .' Louise made him squirm with her absolute certainty that he would never get anywhere.

Meanwhile Mara and Henry senior were getting along nicely talking about painters and painting. Miller's arrogant adolescent disapproval of his father was by now a thing of the past. Instructed by his own experience of disapproving and demanding women, it had turned into a fond sympathy for the old man's accepting and unpretentious nature. Miller listened in on the conversation, and when he heard it flagging fed it titbits about the Ruskin book his father had once read, and introduced the names of some of the artists he knew Henry senior was especially fond of – Winslow Homer, Ryder and Sisley.

By the middle of the afternoon, however, the party was dragging. Tired and hungover from a late night and exhausted by the strain of being on their best behaviour, June and Mara excused themselves from the table after dinner and curled up on the sofa for a nap. As they turned about to get comfortable a sudden twanging of springs announced that they had broken it. June began giggling, Lauretta went to fetch a blanket, Louise called for a hammer, and Henry senior went out into the back yard and returned with an armful of bricks. While the sofa was being propped up Lauretta turned on the radio to listen to an operetta. The sofa had been in the family's possession since Valentin Nieting's time.

With June and Mara asleep, Henry had to endure alone the ritual of fielding questions about Barbara and Beatrice, followed by melancholy recollections about what an intelligent and promising boy he had been. Later his father announced that he was trying to learn French. He got out his Berlitz primer and showed Henry some of the words he was having trouble pronouncing. Trying to reassure his father, Miller told him he ought not to let little things like that worry him, adding: 'You'll probably never get to France anyway.' It was the sort of remark his mother might have made, and the moment he said it he wished he could have bitten his tongue out. To ease the situation he suggested to his father that they take some air together. As they walked the streets his father, who was the local historian before him, told him all the news about old friends and neighbours: who was married, who was in jail, who was rich, who was poor, who was dead... .

When they returned, June and Mara had stirred and were drinking coffee with Louise. June was trying to convince Louise that her son was a genius, and Louise was doubting it, especially since June insisted that he would be a genius even if he never wrote a line. Professionally speaking, as far as Louise was concerned, Henry was finished. Nor could she ever really forgive him for having deserted Beatrice and Barbara.

The conversation turned to relatives. The family album was produced and for a while they looked through photographs of Henry's German relations. In general the evening passed off better than any of them had expected, and when the three returned to Henry Street they sat up a while, drinking and talking about the success of the visit. From observations on Henry senior's surprising interest in painting the conversation turned, not for the first time, to the subject of Paris.[20]

Such truces were only temporary. With the two girls spending so much time together, Miller was left to his own devices in the gloomy Henry Street apartment. One of these was an early draft of a novel he would work on over the next couple of years, *Crazy Cock*, his account of the triangular situation which had arisen. He discovered that writing about his predicament was therapeutic. If he could not defeat the combined efforts of the women in life, perhaps he could do so in fiction by giving the world a version of events which would clearly show how greatly he had been wronged. He carried the notes for the book around with him like a loaded gun, and sometimes took them along to the Pepper Pot. Miller let June read what he was writing about her, hoping that she would see the magnitude of her errors and get back in line. She fought back, criticising the psychology of 'Hildred', as Miller called her in the book, and tried hard to persuade Henry to make changes. Mara Andrews was more phlegmatic in her response, and observed only that all the suffering he was going through ought to make a better writer of him. At the time, her response seemed to him cruel, although later it became his own credo.

He had other diversions whilst they were out, one of which was tidying up the apartment. Naturally this enabled him to do a little rooting in drawers and bags as well. He discovered that Mara's father was in fact writing out checks for the rent they paid. Clearly she was from a well-to-do family, Romanoff or not. Both she and June were extremely casual with money and he continued to find screwed up dollar bills lying about on the floor and among the bedclothes.

His most interesting discovery, however, came one evening in January when they had gone out to see Mrs Fiske play in *Ghosts* at the Mansfield Theatre. In Mara's room he came across a series of love notes written to her by lesbian admirers – 'David', 'Lovely Jo', 'Michael darling'. He was shocked to find a note from Mara to June which concluded: 'You would be a rare, delicate pervert (pardon!) if all this chaos which surrounds you were removed. Please, don't you see what you contain?' Most shocking of all was the discovery of a note to Mara which June had signed 'desperate, my lover'. It seemed to him conclusive proof that his wife and her new idol had become lovers.

Even at his most wretched, Miller had always been able to observe a distance from his own feelings. This knack had stood him in good stead during the years of suffering with Pauline while longing for Cora, and it did not desert him now. It enabled him to turn his suspicions into a literary game, and he now found himself slipping into the rôle of a fictional character with whom he practised an almost mystical identification – Johan Nagel in Hamsun's recently-published *Mysteries*. Fictional Nagel and real Miller both turned their suffering into existential entertainment, carrying out secret campaigns of detective work with the aim of unmasking a suspected liar. On the trail of June, Miller began making unannounced trips to the Pepper Pot. If he did not find her there he would carry on to the Caravan, the Vagabondia, the Bamboo Forest, the Mad Hatter, all the known haunts of the Village homosexual crowd until he located her; then he would watch, note, observe, follow. In spite of the background reading he had done, Miller's response towards the phenomenon of male homosexuality remained that of society at large – a vague, amused contempt in the abstract and, in the flesh, a distinct unease at the thought that they might be taking an unorthodox interest in his person. He found himself among a crowd of them one evening at the Caravan:

They all had dirty mouths, the crooked, evil expression which, erroneously or not, the world associates with degeneracy. He wondered why he hadn't walked away from them at once. He rubbed his perspiring hands on his overcoat as though by doing so he was removing the danger of contamination which lurked in their grasps.[21]

Repeatedly he tried to get June to admit that she was having a homosexual relationship with Mara, while June steadfastly maintained that her love was platonic, and that Mara was a 'platonic lesbian' who was simply acting a part. Unimpressed, Miller tried brutal tactics. He humiliated June once by accosting Mara at the Pepper Pot and demanding to know, in front of a crowd of their friends, whether she was 'an invert or a pervert'. During the violent row that followed June burst out angrily: 'You make things so complex, so ugly! You do! You see things only in your narrow, masculine way; you make everything a matter of sex. And it isn't that at all . . . it's something rare and beautiful.'[22] On another occasion she revealed her jealousy of his close friendship with Joe O'Reagan. Henry, firmly believing that Mara was a practising lesbian, refused to accept that the comparison was legitimate.

Finally, as the three of them sat at the 'gut table' one evening, June and Mara went the whole way and suggested to him that his friendship with Joe O'Reagan was evidence of latent homosexuality. Miller became furious, used language which 'only the very lowest had recourse to'[23] and threatened without more ado to put on a red necktie and make the rounds of the clubs advertising himself, 'a homo to rent – by the week or month – moderate terms'. 'All along,' he complained bitterly, 'I thought I was a man.'[24] But with Freud and the whole theory of the unconscious against him how could he prove it?

The fact that June continued her heterosexual flirting with other men was not the comfort it might have been under the circumstances. During one of his vigils outside the Pepper Pot, he saw her leave at 4 am arm in arm with a man named Nat Pendleton. Pendleton, an Olympic wrestler with a silver medal from the 1920 Games in Antwerp, was six feet tall and weighed about 200 pounds. Henry prudently kept his distance as he trailed the couple for a while before returning to Henry Street. He had his notes and his route clear in his head, and when June came back it was an easy matter to trap her into lying about her movements that evening. The difficulty was that June's were not guilty lies, intended to cover up things of which she was ashamed, but lies to make herself and her life more exciting. Pendleton had lately been having some success in films as a 'heavy', and June may have hoped that he could help further her own acting career. However, she was apparently no more indulgent with him than with any of her other admirers, and felt no guilt at being caught out in a lie over what was merely a late night between bohemians. The result was that the goal of Henry's investigations – to shame her into not lying again – was impossible to achieve. After the night with Pendleton, however, he managed to extract from her a promise that she would change her ways and not stay out late any more.

She was not merely late the following night, she didn't come home at all. When she did return it was with a story about her mother being ill which Miller was easily able to disprove by telephoning Bensonhurst, needlessly pretending when he called to be a millionaire in the lumber trade named Johnson. Francis Smith said she had neither seen nor heard from June in months. Moreover, she flatly denied that her daughter was married. Again Miller confronted June. In some exasperation she admitted that she had lied. The real reason she had stayed out all night, she told him, was to punish him for his suspicions. On the same hopeless trail, Miller now arranged a meeting with one of her brothers. The brother confirmed that June was a born liar who had always wanted to be a famous actress. He advised Henry to follow Nietzsche's advice in dealing with her and use the whip. Henry already had reason to be grateful to Nietzsche, since Mara specifically blamed her periodic insanity on his philosophy, but in the end he was no more capable than Nietzsche of using whips on women.

8

Extraordinary scenes were everyday occurrences in the Henry Street

1 Henry at the age of 4

2 *Above*: Henry aged about 12, with his sister Lauretta, father Henry snr and mother Louise

3 *Left*: The house at 662 Driggs Avenue, Brooklyn, where the family lived until Henry was 9

5 *Right*: Henry aged 18, centre, with his father and a family friend

4 *Below*: The Xerxes Society in rowing gear. Henry is on the right of the middle row

6 *Left*: Henry snr and Lauretta on a family holiday at Lake Pocotapaug, Connecticut, circa 1905

7 *Above*: Henry Miller snr during his days as a boss tailor

8 The site of the tailor shop at 5 West 31st St where Henry worked between 1913–16. The essay 'The Tailor Shop' in *Black Spring* describes the period

9 The bar of the Wolcott Hotel, opposite the tailor shop. Henry snr spent much of his working day drinking here

10A *Right*: Henry with Beatrice and Barbara in 1920. Having joined Western Union he had become a suit-wearing man

10B *Centre*: Beatrice with Barbara, January 1920

11 *Below*: Café Lafayette, Greenwich Village, in the 1920s

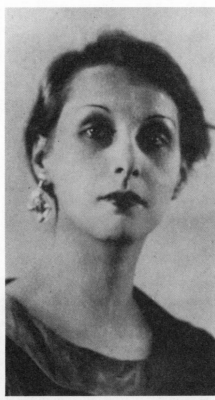

12 *Left*: Anais Nin, the muse of Miller's Paris years, in the garden of her house at Louveciennes, where Miller was a frequent visitor. She wrote an Introduction to *Tropic of Cancer*, and Miller dedicated *Black Spring* to her

13 *Right*: June Smith, Miller's second wife, photographed circa 1933 by Brassai. She was a dance-hall hostess when they met in 1923. Her talent as a professional flirt fascinated and bewildered Henry

14 Henry's Paris – the Gare du Nord metro station during the 1930s

15 *Top left*: Emil Schnellock, one of Miller's most regular correspondents

16 *Top right*: Alfred Perlès, a close friend in Paris during the 1930s

17 *Centre left*: Bern Porter, the publisher who compiled the first bibliography of Miller's works in 1945

18 *Bottom left*: Wambly Bald, 'Van Norden' of *Tropic of Cancer*

19 *Above*: Dr Emil Conason – Dr Kronski of *The Rosy Crucifixion* – with his wife Celia in the late 1920s

20 *Top left*: Madame Blavatsky

21 *Top right*: Dostoevsky was a god for both Henry and June. Miller identified with Prince Myshkin, hero of *The Idiot*

22 *Above*: Knut Hamsun, whose novel *Hunger* introduced Miller to the role of the starving would-be writer as narrator

23 *Right*: Walt Whitman, Miller's favourite American writer

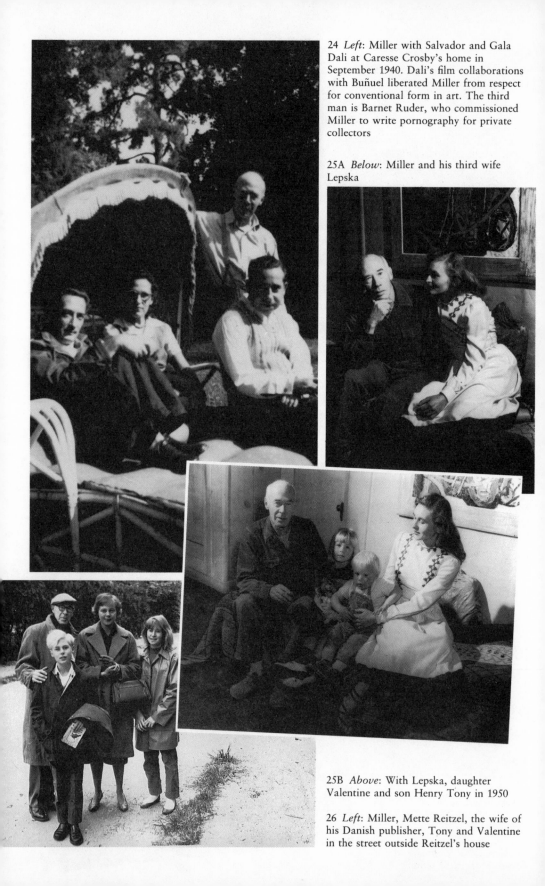

24 *Left*: Miller with Salvador and Gala Dali at Caresse Crosby's home in September 1940. Dali's film collaborations with Buñuel liberated Miller from respect for conventional form in art. The third man is Barnet Ruder, who commissioned Miller to write pornography for private collectors

25A *Below*: Miller and his third wife Lepska

25B *Above*: With Lepska, daughter Valentine and son Henry Tony in 1950

26 *Left*: Miller, Mette Reitzel, the wife of his Danish publisher, Tony and Valentine in the street outside Reitzel's house

basement flat. One evening a male friend of Mara's named Shelley gave her an exhibition of masturbation in her room. Henry didn't attend himself but sat in his own room listening to her hysterical laughter. Mara also described how Shelley would masturbate her while she sat writing poetry. Her revelations shocked even June, and when Mara began describing sexual orgies in which she and a prostitute had participated with Maxwell Bodenheim, and how she had given paid exhibitions of lesbianism with a prostitute for the benefit of a jaded rich man, June tried to shut her up. Miller encouraged her, however, praising her honesty. He briefly hoped that Shelley, who was clearly interested in Mara, might somehow manage to show her the sexual light and take her off his hands. June, realizing what was happening, barred Shelley from the house. She was the mistress, and both Henry and Mara were afraid of upsetting her. Shelley was a poet, and the fact that one of his poems contained a reference to 'that magnificent half-woman June' was further dispiriting proof to Henry of the reputation she was acquiring in the Village.

Miller contributed to the extraordinary scenes. One night when he had been out drinking until dawn at Hubert's cafeteria he came home to find Mara sleeping in his bed. In a fury he dragged her out by the hair, vomited, then urinated in the bath tub. In a second, less sophisticated account of the evening, he relates that he urinated on Mara and then slept in the bathtub.[25] This other version also trebles the amount of money spent on drink at Hubert's before the incident.

Often, in his desperate struggle to keep his place in the ménage, Miller resorted to gestures of violent infantility. Once he walked round and round in the outhouse until he collapsed from exhaustion. June pretended not to notice. An occasion on which he smashed up their few sticks of furniture and burnt them in the fireplace was dramatic enough to impress her, but a half-hearted suicide attempt was less successful: returning home to find June and Mara yet again sleeping in the same bed he chased them out into the night and then swallowed some pills given to him by Emil Conason. After willing his body to Conason and writing a suicide note to June he opened the windows and lay down naked on the bed. Presumably by prior arrangement, Conason sent a telegram in the morning to June at the Pepper Pot, telling her to return to Henry Street at once. June rushed home in a highly emotional state to find Henry lying in bed, perfectly well. The pills had been only a mild sleeping draught. Relieved, she hardly glanced at the suicide note he had written. Mara arrived home while they were still in bed together, and to Henry's outrage June let her into the room. Within moments, the girls were smoking cigarettes and planning to go out for a meal together. 'Could I ask you not to

145

smoke?' whispered Henry plaintively. After they had left he clambered up onto Mara's bed and wrote '*Et haec olim meminisse iuvabit*' (sic) on the toilet box above it. Virgil's suggestion – that even torments might one day provide happy memories – was the only consolation Henry could offer himself under the circumstances. That – and the faith that he might one day be able to turn it all into literature.

Henry and June seemed to encourage the melodrama in each other, and for all the emotional violence of their relationship there was also something unreal about their life together. Miller's desperate letters to his friends, for example, which he signed 'the Failure', were also being filed as carbon copies for the posterity he hoped would one day read them, and it is tempting to suspect that the composition of a good suicide note was the purpose of his suicide attempt, rather than its most pitiful detail. This is not to suggest that Miller was not deeply distressed; but he had the romantic's faculty of recovering quickly.

Earlier scenes from the marriage were replayed, but with the rôles reversed, and with Miller now in the part of the pathetic figure. Soon it was his turn to threaten to leave June, and after packing in front of an amused Mara he made his way to the Pepper Pot carrying his bag, a bunch of violets and a letter. June read the letter, thought it, like his suicide note, 'beautiful', and gave his proposed trip her maternal blessing: 'Alright, go for a little while. But let me know where you are.' Miller was devastated by her indifference, yet never connected it with his own indifference to her feelings the year before when he ran off to Florida with Joe and Emil and left her alone to face the creditors at Perry Street. Instead, he recalled the occasion when Mara, in response to his heartfelt pleadings, had finally hinted that she might agree to leave Henry Street. Then June had begged Henry to tell Mara she was welcome to stay, swearing she would do anything for him, 'only bring Mara back. Make her stay.' When Henry did so June's pitifully intense gratitude was further humiliation. She was terrified of losing her friend. In the flyleaf of a book she presented to Mara she dedicated it to 'my first and only real friend'.

Humiliation was the keynote of this period of Miller's life. One day a policeman brought June home to him and gave him some friendly advice, man to man: 'Well, if she wuz my wife... .' It was not necessary for him to finish. Mara had a similar brush with a policeman who found her walking down the street in overalls and smoking a cigarette and escorted her home to Henry Street. Miller reassured the man that it was quite all right, Mara was an artist, but the incident only added to his fears that he and his two uncontrollable women had now become figures of fun in the Village, suitable subjects to bring up in gossip sessions, along with Aimee Cortez and her stuffed gorilla or the

146

Baroness Elsa von Fretag von Loringhoven, the elderly poet who wore a coal-scuttle lid or sometimes a peach basket on her head and decorated her face with postage stamps.

The most humiliating experience of all, however, came as he was standing on the stairs outside the door to the apartment one evening and heard June reasure Mara: 'my love for Val is only like that of a mother's for a child, that's all.'[26] This, more than anything, brought home to him how he had sunk in her estimation in the three short years they had been together. Instead of becoming June's Raskolnikov, her Myshkin, he had become her Ridiculous Man.

9

From the day he left Western Union back in September 1924, Miller had been floundering. He was not a hustler like June. He had jumped down into the street, expecting it still to be filled with boys playing, having adventures and going back home at teatime. Instead he found a tough world in which, without June's help, he might not have held out at all. As his actual adventures show, from the Californian jaunt of 1913 to the Florida flight of 1925 and the night of the smelly feet, he was a man fond of his creature comforts. The sudden trips he made, to Florida, North Carolina, Philadelphia, Atlantic City or wherever, were as much desperate attempts to flee from insoluble practical and personal problems as they were expressions of wanderlust. Had June not absolutely forbidden him to, he might well have taken a proper job.

People have breakdowns all the time without going to doctors, and at the height of his wife's involvement with Mara Andrews, Miller seems to have had a sort of breakdown. He was plagued by vague ailments, piles and nervous vomiting, and became furious when the doctors found nothing wrong with him. The meaningless flights from New York; the pointlessly intense detective work on the trail of June, never quite knowing what he was looking for nor whether he was really looking for anything at all; his periodic nights of drunkenness; his blind furies and infantile rages all suggest that his life was slipping out of control, and by February 1927 he was about ready to admit defeat in the sex war. Tony Bring, his mouthpiece in *Crazy Cock*, put it very simply: 'Alone he could tackle the Bruga woman triumphantly. Alone he could subjugate his wife. But taken in combination they were invincible.'[27]

This time, instead of fleeing from the situation, he tried a different response and went to bed. There he remained for ten days, stirring only to go to the toilet. Twice a day, June would rub his bottom with cream to ease the pain from his haemorrhoids. Emil Conason was summoned to see what was the matter with him. Henry snarled that he didn't want any kikes tinkering with him, and Conason retorted that he was a lazy malingerer. Afterwards they played chess and argued about Hilaire Belloc's book on the Jews. Miller admired Belloc, but for Conason he was merely 'a scholar without wisdom'.

Conason was an invaluable friend to Miller. Too often in later years Henry had a tendency to cultivate sycophants among his friends. Conason, while supporting and encouraging him, never indulged him. He was especially hard on him about his sentimentality. Miller's own view was that sentimentality was practically an illness, and he would fly into 'a towering rage' if criticised for it: 'This dagger of sentimentality which people plunge into one another's breasts so heartlessly – how little it is understood! What has the sentimentalist to be ashamed of any more than the epileptic or the neurotic?'[28]

This ten-day sabbatical from life turned out to be of crucial importance for Miller in two respects. In the first place, it may have been the occasion on which he discovered for himself the tactic of responding to a difficult situation by simply giving up completely and just letting events flow on as they will. This fatalism, closer to the cheerful *wu-wei* of Chinese taoist philosophy than the grim stoicism of Icelandic saga heroes, became in time the deepest truth he knew about the art of living.

Secondly, while in bed he read a book which was most important in a practical sense to his own future as a writer. Beatrice, in giving him *Hunger* in 1922, had introduced him to a possible literary identity. The fact that in giving him the book she also indirectly hastened the end of their marriage always struck Miller as ironic. A similar irony lay in the fact that it was his second wife who gave him, for his Christmas present that year, a volume by Proust which suggested to him the literary setting in which he could place the character of the starving writer from *Hunger*. For in reading Proust, it occurred to him that the massive and detailed recall of the events of one's personal life, carried out in the form of a literary project, in the end creates its own synthesis and in so doing gives meaning to the life of the one recalling and recording. He also found, in Proust's obsessive fascination with Albertine, a reflection of his own concern with June. Yet the problem, which he recognized almost straight away, was how to write honestly about June unless she were a part of his past. It was a strange death she had arranged for herself; stranger still if he recalled her desire to be famous, and the mixture of fear and hope with which she had accused

Miller, in the first few days of their affair, of pursuing her only because he wanted to write a story about her.

Under the influence of Proust, Miller experimented with his own powers of recall while lying in bed. Beginning with his earliest memory, of sitting in a high chair reciting a German nursery rhyme, he realized to his astonishment: 'if I lie here long enough and think it all out patiently, I can string my whole life together, day for day'. These were persuasive revelations. In all probability it was at some point in that period between February 12th and 22nd that the idea of writing a working-class Proust, a Brooklyn Proust, occurred to him, and he had the first intimations of a lifelong involvement with an autobiographical project of his own, *The Rosy Crucifixion*.

That any such project would have much to do with women was at once obvious to him, and rehearsing his past during these ten days in bed Miller thought about the rôle they had played in his life:

Retracing the course of his life he could see that it was not a continuous drama, as was so often said, but a series of dramas, each clearly defined; the early ones involving Duty, God, Amelioration, and all those that came after . . . *women*. Not the chase, for that was a blind, instinctive affair, not more important than the food problem; no, it was rather the taming of them that produced the strife and discord. A distorted sense of their own importance led them to resist subjugation; they all had the cracked idea of wanting to be emancipated, which was simply another way of saying they wanted to wear the pants. They didn't want to wear wedding rings. Wifehood was the bunk and children a nuisance. Even the menstrual period was too much for them – a blow to their vanity, an unpleasant reminder of their femininity. If science interested them it was because science was an instrument, a weapon with which to combat nature.[29]

These ruminations, with their faint echo of Strindberg and Lawrence, show the extent of the bitterness he felt over his failure to dominate June, a bitterness which extended to embrace the whole tribe of 'modern' women who seemed not to know their place. They also show Miller's willingness to broadcast his prejudices, one of the most important aspects of his writing. *Crazy Cock* is filled with outbursts against women. He rails against modern mothers who 'have no breasts, or else they strangle them under brassieres'.[30] Wandering between speakeasies with friends like Conason, Dewar and Joe O'Reagan, he notices another distressing example of the modern woman's limitless boldness: places like the Perroquet, the Club New Yorker, the Côte d'Or, the Tree Club and Hubert's differ in only one striking respect from the saloons of pre-prohibition days:

149

The only innovation was the presence of the other sex. In the old days the female element kept to the back room. They weren't allowed to stand at the bar telling dirty stories or bragging about the number of men they slept with. Nor did they need to be dragged out with a boat hook when the place closed. No, in the old days the women of the streets sometimes conducted themselves like ladies, or at least they tried; the new age made it compulsive for the ladies to conduct themselves like whores.[31]

But, again like Strindberg, he never for a moment forgot how he loved both his torment and his tormentors.

10

During the 1920s the literary centre of gravity shifted from New York to Paris. The 1921 departures of Dos Passos, Cowley and Cummings, and the publication of Carl van Vechten's novel *Peter Whiffle* in 1922, marked the beginning of the large-scale migration. Though the most influential literary exiles – Pound, Eliot, Stein, Hemingway – were not associated with the Village, their achievements in Paris acted as a magnet on the young. Malcolm Cowley writes in *Exiles Return* of an evening drinking in 'an unfamiliar saloon – it was in the winter of 1925–26 – and finding that the back room was full of young writers and their wives just home from Paris. They were all telling stories about Hemingway, whose first book had just appeared, and they were talking in what I afterwards came to recognise as the Hemingway dialect – tough, matter-of-fact and confidential. In the middle of the evening one of them rose, took off his jacket and used it to show how he would dominate a bull.'[32] Miller read Hemingway. He read Eliot and Pound and Faulkner (but not Fitzgerald); he read all his contemporaries – Hecht, Bodenheim, Dos Passos, Dreiser, Anderson, e.e. cummings, Sinclair Lewis, Thornton Wilder, Willa Cather, James Branch Cabell, Elmer Rice, Amy Lowell, Paul Green, Carl van Vechten – and he felt intimidated and less confident than ever that there was a place for him. He was in any event much too busy trying to dominate his wife to find out how to dominate a bull. Dostoevsky and Hamsun remained the writers that spoke to him, with the added voices of Spengler, Faure, Van Gogh (the letters), Proust and Joyce, whose courage and linguistic artistry he greatly admired. D.H. Lawrence had still not entered this pantheon, in spite of Schnellock's enthusiasm, or perhaps precisely because of it – Miller was as obstinately determined at the age of thirty-six to discover the world for himself as he had been at the age of five.

As well as reading the work of his major contemporaries, Miller was nourishing a more esoteric side of his literary personality represented by writers like John Cowper Powys and Arthur Machen. He also discovered Gurdjieff, whose disciple A.E. Orage visited New York in 1924 and made a number of converts among Greenwich Villagers. Machen's *Hill of Dreams*, which he read in 1925, fuelled his attachment to a way of writing that appeared to observe a minimal distinction between imaginative fiction and straight autobiography. 'In my easy chair, in my sumptuous unearned grandeur,' he wrote to Schnellock, 'I am eaten by a secret rending desire to write such a book as this. I will not say it is the *greatest* book written in the English language (that for the idle critics) but I can say that it has bereft me of emotion.'[33] Miller's enthusiasm for the Celtic school of mysticism and eroticism represented by Machen and Powys is indicative of one of the real continuities of his life. The absorption in sex in the 1930s for a while obscured this religious side of his personality, but it re-emerged strongly as he moved into middle-age and beyond in the 1950s, forming part of a chain that would link the enthusiasms of his old age with his adolescent interest in Madam Blavatsky and the writings of her disciple A.P. Sinnett.

Literary centre of the universe or not, when Mara and June began to talk about the three of them going to Paris, Henry was not enthusiastic. Though he had learned to be civil to Mara, it was a cosmetic civility. He absolutely refused to share June with her. His failure as a man was compounded by his failure as a writer. At thirty-six the future he had gone so enthusiastically to meet with June had evaporated; yet a future that did not include his own success as a writer was an impossibility. He closed his eyes and imagined that it did not exist. It was not an easy task, since the girls were soon talking of nothing but their forthcoming trip to 'Paris. Godammed Paris. Eternally Paris.'[34]

For a while they worked at making puppets to sell around the Village as a way of raising money for the trip, hammering through the night as Miller tried to sleep his troubles away, never believing June would leave without him. With the coming of spring the girls' plans became ever more specific, and he had to work harder than ever not to believe in them.

One area at least – the past – was safe from the ravages of the future. The past stood still. Its inhabitants were known and dependable. Rambling the streets of Brooklyn one day he met one of them – his old rival from schooldays, Jimmy Pasta. The two went to a bar together and exchanged news. Pasta now had a good job as Chief Clerk of Parks in the borough of Queens, with responsibility for the one hundred non-specialized labourers working in the parks. Miller still bravely claimed to be a writer, but admitted that his financial situation was not good. Pasta, who never liked to see a good man unemployed, offered to use his influence to get Henry an office job in his department, though he warned him that he would have to put him down as a gardener to begin with.

June and Mara were not overimpressed by Henry's new job. However, on his first day home from work they made a fuss of him, decking the table with flowers and providing French wine. He enjoyed the work, and the other gardeners were kind to him, as the manual workers at Chula Vista had been, because he had soft hands and was unused to hard physical labour. At the end of the week, with his wage packet, he came home with a brassiere and a pair of stockings for June. The signs of packing and imminent departure were everywhere, and yet he dared not raise the subject for fear of hearing what he could not bear to hear. June and Mara went out that night to say goodbye to their friends, and when they returned Henry started a violent argument with June, rejecting all her attempts to caress him, refusing absolutely to caress her. In his rage he again choked on his own spittle.

In the morning, to set him up for his Saturday half-day at work, there was a bowl of strawberries on the table for his breakfast. And when he left June stood out in street, waving to him until he had turned the corner. When he returned the apartment was empty. June's note was the final humiliation. It read:

Dear Val, we sailed this morning on the *Rochambeau*. Didn't have the heart to tell you. Write care of American Express, Paris. Love.

CHAPTER EIGHT

1927–1930
Intimations of Europe

1

After a week or two of planting shrubs and weeding flowerbeds, Miller was moved indoors and started work on his real duties. One was to help Pasta write speeches for the Parks Commissioner, while his main responsibility was to edit the Parks Department's annual report.

Shortly after June's departure he moved back in with his parents on Decatur Street. Louise was pleased to see he had a proper job again, his first for three years. He began receiving letters from June and during the next few weeks made one or two half-hearted attempts to join her in Paris. He enquired about the possibility of working his passage over, and one evening in an Italian restaurant fell into conversation with an interior decorator who took him home, put his hand on his knee in the small hours of the morning and told him he knew of a way to raise the fare. Henry declined the offer. He missed June, but not that much.

Besides, the parting meant that he had his time and his thoughts to himself again. Being on his own gave him a necessary sense of detachment from the irruption of Mara Andrews into his life. He brooded much on the triangular situation, and one night in May remained behind in Pasta's office and began making notes on the history of his relationship with June, starting with his wild excitement at meeting her at the dance hall, and proceeding to outline subsequent events in eight chapters, concluding matters on the morning on which he was given strawberries for his breakfast, departed for work and returned to find June and Mara gone.

This document, in thirty-two typewritten pages, which he called *June*, became essential source material for the bulk of his later autobiographical writing, principally *Tropic of Capricorn* and *The Rosy Crucifixion*. The notes are telegrammatic, but referring back to them from the material in the published books reveals how strikingly close Miller stuck to the main outlines of his story. The focus is tight and obsessively trained on himself and June. No dates are given, the weather is never described, no world events are mentioned. In their

153

brevity and in the absence of excessive contemplation of his own thoughts and deeds they convey a rare sense of privacy and sponta- neity, and suggest that this was one of the few times when Miller wrote with the lights of his powerful self-consciousness turned off. He wrote June a long letter describing the divine afflatus, but realized he did not have her address in Vienna, where she was visiting some relatives, and so never sent it.

2

In June's absence, Miller again began frequenting the dance-halls and again met a literary taxi-girl. This one was from Texas, and she enjoyed their conversations so much that she would not charge him for the dances. Like June, she too received her copy of *Winesburg, Ohio*. Living on Decatur Street reawakened memories of the unattainable Cora Seward, and Miller again went for walks that took him past the house on Devoe Street from which she, now a married woman with a growing family, had long since moved. With such gestures he had already begun his obsessive lifelong concern with the 'unre-enterable' world of the past. Where he differed from other writers like Proust and Nabokov – writers with similar concerns, though with vastly different approaches – is that he never quite accepted the impossibility of a real return to this world.

Another distraction during June's absence was painting. Through his friendship with Emil Schnellock, and later at Henry Street as he and Mara struggled to find a *modus vivendi*, Miller's interest in drawing and water-colour painting was growing. Schnellock reminded him once, in a letter, of a drawing of June's 'rose-bush' he had done which hung on the wall at one of their apartments. But it was not until around 1926 or 1927 that he began painting himself, inspired in the first instance by some Turners that he had seen exhibited in a Brooklyn department store window. He was spending a lot of time with Joe O'Reagan at his Hicks Street apartment during June's absence. O'Reagan had a crush on Emil Conason's sister, and was a frequent visitor to the Conason's home. Celia Conason recalls how he and Henry would arrive to show off their latest 'Turners', which they had produced at Joe's flat by soaking the finished products in a sinkful of water and hanging them up on a line to dry. From Turner, Miller moved on to Chagall and George Grosz, and in the tenderness, mysticism and unashamed sentimentality of the one, and the violent, garish almost pornographic realism of the other, discovered a reflection of the contrasting extremes of his own personality. He soon began painting in a style which mixed elements of both, and which did not develop significantly over the years.

Miller usually played down his talent as an artist, but never quite ruled out the possibility that he might be, without realizing it, a 'great' painter, a hope easily encouraged by his firm belief in the child-like and unknowing nature of genius. Certainly he had preserved many of the qualities associated with childhood and youth, notably his sense of wonder, and the easy suspension of disbelief which led him, at the age of thirty-six, to sign some of his letters Hans Castorp after the hero of *The Magic Mountain*. This simplicity was essentially genuine; yet it was also conditioned by a fierce identification with Dostoevsky's Prince Myshkin, whose childlike directness in a world of sophisticates is both genuine and also a highly self-conscious philosophic response to life.

After some two months – long enough for Henry to ponder morosely the swiftness with which Lindberg was able to fly between New York and Paris in a mere thirty-three and a half hours – June returned. To Miller's great relief, she was alone, though the ubiquitous Count Bruga was still under her arm as she descended the gangplank from the *Berengaria*. Mara had rapidly grown tired of June's pretentious attempts to pass herself off as a writer and had run off to Morocco with an American sculptor and an Austrian writer with whom she had fallen – briefly and platonically – in love. The jaunt lasted only a few days, but Mara's desertion marked the end of the friendship between the two women. Clearly, it had always been much more intense on June's side than on Mara's. When June returned, Mara enrolled at the Colorassi, an art school on the rue de las Grande Chaumière which catered particularly for the needs of the numerous wealthy young Americans who were then flocking to Paris.

In amongst the pleasure Henry felt at seeing June again, and the hope that her return might give them the chance to save their marriage, he struggled with an unhappy realization that had come to him the night he sat outlining the story of their life together: that his detachment in the matter of his own unhappiness could only mean that, however distant, the end of their relationship was in sight. Loth to accept the fact, on his way to meet her off the boat he had stopped off at a jeweller's shop on Maiden Lane and bought the ring that had been missing from June's finger ever since the wedding.

3

The relative order that had settled over Miller's life in June's absence was soon disturbed. She found them a new apartment in Brooklyn

Heights and persuaded him to give up his job with Pasta and return to a life of full-time writing. Soon she had hustled up another patron, a man whom the Millers referred to as 'Pop' or 'Pop Roland'. His full name was Roland Freedman, and he earned a good living as a writer of jokes for Peter Arno's celebrated *New Yorker* cartoons. He was desperately in love with June, and hoped one day to marry her. He kept champagne on ice for her when she visited, and sent her love letters which she and Henry would read together and laugh over. 'The more passionate he became the funnier it seemed,' Miller wrote later. Though the letters always ended with kisses, 'the idea of June kissing Roland seemed preposterous to me always'.[1] Physically he was apparently an ugly man, and this, coupled with June's openness about the relationship, encouraged Miller to feel that he had no real reason to be jealous of him.

One day, June showed some of Henry's old mezzotints to Freedman, as usual passing them off as her own work, and so impressed him with her talent – as well as her beauty – that he offered to support her on a regular basis while she set to work to produce a full-length novel. As an extra incentive he also promised her that if she managed to finish a book he would provide her with enough money to enable her to make another trip to Europe. June agreed to this, and almost at once Miller set to work on the commission.

Moloch, also known as *This Gentile World*, was a 'medley of brutal realism, glorified sensuality and fantastic unreality'. Eighteen chapters and 384 pages long, it is substantially an account of Miller's rocky marriage to Beatrice ('Blanche') during his days as a personnel manager at Western Union ('the Great American Telegraph Company') which ends in his failure to leave her. *Moloch* tells its story in straightforward, chronological fashion, without the use of obscenity or explicit sex, giving much space to angry scenes of dissension between the eponymous hero and his wife Blanche, often in the presence of Moloch's friends. The focus of interest in the novel is intended to be the personality of the hero Dion Moloch which, striking as it is, never quite manages to live up to the promise of the name. Rather than dionysian scenes and four-letter words, the most striking quality of the novel is the breezy self-confidence with which Miller makes his hero an anti-semite. Its opening paragraph must be, on reflection, one of the least successful attempts ever made by a writer to enlist the interest and sympathy of his readers for his main character. Moloch, we are told, wears a suit of Bedford shipcord and a pale blue shirt with badly frayed cuffs and collar. He is an almost absurdly sane and healthy man, free from megalomania, *dementia praecox* 'or any of the other fashionable disorders of the twentieth century', and though he was often accused by his friends of being anti-semitic this does not count, since it was 'a prejudice and not a disease'.

In what appears to be a reflection of Miller's own street-prejudice, the anti-semitism or Jew-baiting of the main character is kept constantly before the reader's eyes. Moloch does quite a bit of wandering through the streets of Brooklyn in the course of the novel, 'depressed', as he puts it, 'by the melancholy transformation of the old neighbourhood, and furious with God's vermin'. The Wallabout Market, however, gives him an impression of permanence and durability, 'as though Peter Stuyvesant had laid his heavy hand upon it, and defied the dago and the sheeny to remove it'. Most of the staples of prejudice are tossed off: the Jews smell bad and throw rubbish in the street because they like dirt; the Jews condone deceit and make a supreme virtue out of cheating; the Jews take refuge in Karl Marx because they feel sorry for themselves, and so on. If Miller was not an anti-semite as a young man, then he gave a very good impersonation of one in *Moloch*.

Had Miller's parents been enlightened, educated people he might not have fallen so readily for the primitive prejudices of the gangs with whom he roamed the streets during his boyhood; but they were not. His mother in particular seems to have had a strong prejudice against Jews, and the move the Miller family made in 1900 from Williamsburg to Bushwick was in most respects the retreat of a respectable middle-class family from an area that was felt to be in social decline. Evidently the vocabulary, if not the actuality, of the anti-semitism of his childhood had pursued him into the years of his early manhood, to erect its inglorious monument in the pages of *Moloch*. Not until he finally broke away from the enclosed world of his childhood and began meeting more sophisticated people who were prepared to question his attitudes did he manage to overcome it completely.

What made it easier for him to do so was that his prejudice was riddled with large-scale inconsistencies, including his many close friendships with Jewish people like the Conasons and Abe and Esther Elkus, and most notably the fact of his own wife's Jewishness. Indeed, he once explicitly stated that he loved June precisely *because* she was Jewish: 'she represented another race, something wholly alien to me, something I did not know'.[2]

Miller's propensity for violent language and his strong desire to shock were what prompted him to take the idiotic step of actually making a feature out of his prejudice in his novel. The language of *Moloch* is linguistic head-butting, and the boast in the opening paragraph is in some ways the same head-on attempt to offend the sensibilities of the reader as the statement in the later *Tropic of Cancer* that the book is 'a gob of spit in the face of art' and an insult directed at 'you', the reader, whoever you are, and 'your dirty corpse', over which the narrator promises to dance. Miller specifically identifies the approach as one of provocation during a scene in which Moloch has been spouting off in a restaurant. A Dr Elfenbein rebukes him, saying: 'You might have some consideration for the guest you invited to your table.' Moloch finds the response 'a highly anaemic expression of one's injured feelings' and reveals that what he had been 'aching for' was 'a punch in the jaw'. Miller seemed to sense that there was something missing in him, a particular kind of insensitivity which made it difficult for him to know the difference between teasing and tormenting, and left him dependent on the signals of others for knowing when he had gone too far. One of the most striking observations he ever made about himself was the admission that 'I get frightened of myself sometimes (. . .) I don't know where the proper limits are',[3] and this unnerving state turned out to be both his greatest weakness and his greatest strength.

4

The use of himself and his friends and acquaintances as models for the characters in *Moloch* established a pattern that Miller followed for the rest of his literary career. It indicates the extent to which his work was, from the start, therapy rather than conscious art, a confessional record of events rather than an act of literary creation. In his later years he was little preoccupied with how his friends and acquaintances might react to their thinly-disguised portraiture in his writing, believing – usually correctly – that the prospect of a degree of fame was sufficient recompense for any offence he might give. At the start of his career, however, before the dispensation of fame was within his power, he was sensitive to the problem. When he was some two-thirds of the way through *Moloch*, June sat down one evening to read through what he had written thus far. She reacted with such dismay to the way in which he had portrayed his friend Conason that Miller was taken aback, and presently decided to write a letter on the subject to him. The letter is worth quoting at length, since it constitutes a rare statement of the aesthetic – if that is the right word – of a writer who used living models perhaps more ruthlessly than any other well-known writer this century:

She exclaims occasionally that I have done a striking picture of you, but that it is manifestly unfair, that I should have made you more human, etc. Her remarks shock me somewhat and yet I was not altogether unprepared for this reaction. I believe I set about consciously to distort you – possibly everyone we know who may appear in the pages of this book has been distorted. There is nothing remarkable or noteworthy about this.

But a graver question obtrudes: why, if I had to distort your character, why did I choose to distort in the direction of denigration? I am trying to ask myself that very honestly, very sincerely. I don't believe it is smartness which makes me answer immediately that it was because I felt that by doing so you became a more interesting personality. (. . .) There is a lot of ugliness in it. I make free confession of that. Your absurdities, the unlovely aspects, all these things have been heightened and exaggerated. Perhaps almost to the point of caricature. It made June wince and remark that 'you no longer would be a friend of mine if you saw what I had written' . . . Well, you know I intend having you read everything, that I desire your counsel, your criticism and guidance. Beyond and above that, and this is the really important thing – it never entered my head that you would take offence . . . even though I should say to you that I regarded you as such and such. I *don't* regard you as anything of the sort, of course. I'm assuming that at the outset. And I don't believe your friendship will go to smash on any such flimsy rocks. But I can understand people questioning my attitude, wondering about a friendship which could permit, or shall we say, provoke such a portrait.

He goes on to explain that, 'for reasons of expediency,' the novel is being written in June's name, and that Conason must not think that he has done the portrait at June's bidding. 'If you wanted to play a mean trick you could blurt out the truth,' he hints, and closes the letter with a surprising offer: 'Come over as soon as you find it convenient. I'll show you what's accomplished. If we have to do any retouching, you have but to command.' Conason may have taken him at his word, for in a second letter about the book Miller relates that he is 'endeavouring to make it what you expect it to be. Patiently rewriting from the very beginning, tearing down, building up, substituting, expanding, paring down the brashness. Up to page 150 now on the finished task.'

Perhaps Conason accepted the ugliness of the attitudes portrayed in *Moloch* as all part of the 'vein of harsh realism'[4] which Miller claimed to be exploring. Certainly, as he got older, Miller's taste was polarising sharply. He went with June to see a performance of Eugene O'Neill's *Strange Interlude* while he was revising *Moloch*. June, whose literary taste was not hampered by professional jealousy, enjoyed the play, but to Miller it was just 'subliminal nonsense. I'll go on record as saying that Eugene has a mediocre brain, even if he is the foremost dramatist in the USA.' He was 'amazed at the prodigious amount of labor he put in it. The man's a jackass for punishment.'[5]

5

There were interruptions to the work on the unfortunate *Moloch* project, such as the visit of a destitute Norwegian, Herr Mastrup, whom Conason sent along to Miller with the advice that for a good story about Hamsun or Ibsen his friend would be able to do something to help him. Though Miller was amused by his friend's presumption, he did provide Mastrup with a new suit, six top-quality new shirts, six cravats, a pair of underpants made by Bradley, Vorhies and Day 'for good crotch comfort' and a quarter for the carfare to Stamford. In exchange he was given the news that Ibsen was a vain old man who had a tiny mirror concealed in the crown of his top hat, that Knut Hamsun's brother was a Customs Officer, and that Kristiania, 'which I had always regarded as a gay old town (a sort of Paris of the Septentriones),' was simply Oslo under another name. However, by the spring of 1928 *Moloch* was almost finished, and at the end of April the Millers decided they needed a short holiday before Henry tackled the last chapters. They thought briefly of going to South Carolina and meeting up with the Conasons who were touring in Florida, but in the end decided on a more *outré* destination – Quebec. Miller set out hitchhiking, but got only as far as Montreal before being held up by a heavy thaw which made the road on to Quebec impassable. June travelled by rail to join him at Montreal, and they finished the journey together by train.

They booked in at an old-established and expensive hotel, the Chateau Frontenac, and set about spending money like 'drunken sailors'. 'It almost makes me weep,' Miller complained, 'I shall never get used to high living'. There was no Prohibition in Canada, and for a while they had the pleasure of wine with every meal; but though they enjoyed the vaudeville shows and a two-hour sightseeing drive round the snow-banked streets of Quebec in an open, horse-drawn *calèche*, they were big-city people, and were soon bored. There were no plays to see, no concerts, and the films were 'the very worst I have seen anywhere, worse than ye south'. In general Quebec reminded Miller of Grand Street, Williamsburg, 'only with French names on the window,' and well before their return to New York in mid-May their thoughts were on the much greater adventure that awaited them once the novel was finished: 'About Europe,' he wrote to the Conasons, '– no doubt any more. Next Fall will see us either in Spain or France.'[6]

6

Roland Freedman must have been an odd man. In return for supporting what he believed to be her attempts to become a writer, all he apparently demanded of June was the right to send her the passionate love letters which she and Miller laughed over. He must also have been an enviably credulous man to believe not merely that June was a single girl living at home with her invalid mother but that she could have written the fierce and aggressive *Moloch*, not to mention the mezzotint hymn to the joys of drinking known as 'Make Beer for Man', with its defiant final cry: 'Keep your libraries. Keep your penal institutions. Keep your insane asylums. Give me beer.' The secret of such credulity must have lain in what the writer Lionel Abel called June's 'almost frightening beauty, like Garbo's'.[7] It seems that at one point Freedman even provided June with the capital to open her own café on MacDougal Street, which she called the 'Roman Tavern'.

As part of their game-playing Henry would try to get June to admit that she and Freedman had been lovers at least on one or two occasions. Pressed like this she would eventually reply, like some dreamy sinner in a Hamsun novel: 'Ah no Val, it was more than that . . . too many times for me to remember . . . all Summer, or all Winter, I forgot which it was. Night after night.'[8] The chief difficulty in trying to get a clear picture of June is that almost all the information about her stems from Miller himself, whose deliberate reinvention of her as an enigmatic and mysterious person was so thorough that it is imprudent to believe too much of what he wrote. Can she really have said 'all Summer and all Winter, *I forgot which it was*?'; or was that something Miller invented later as part of his campaign to win the heart of the new woman he was then wooing by presenting himself to her as a pathetic lover, cruelly tormented by the capricious beloved? Or did June actually say it, but only to stop him pestering her? For when the game-playing was all over Miller was a realist who knew quite well that Pop Roland was only a poor fool, pathetically enamoured of an unattainable young woman who allowed him, for a price, and at a distance, to indulge his fantasies of winning her love. To admit as much, however, would have spoiled the fun. Miller liked to pretend that life was vastly more complicated and romantic than it really was. Poor Roland had no need to pretend, and took his own life in the early 1930s, apparently as a direct result of his ultimate failure to win June.

The trip to Europe at Roland's expense which the Millers embarked on late that summer lasted about six months. It is uniquely un-documented in Miller's life; as he wrote some thirty years later,[9] routinely doubling the duration of the adventure, there was 'almost a year of it. No diary notes, no notebook sketches,' a circumstance worthy of note in a life characterized by an almost pathological mania for documentation.

161

The sampling of the Canadian Frenchness of Quebec was intended to give them a taste for the real thing, although Miller had been disappointed by the sort of French the Canadians spoke, which he identified as 'the lingo of Louis XIV. It's flat, monotonous, *American* in tone and feeling.' He therefore made his own preparations for reviving his schoolboy French, and on visits to his parents' house would take a French primer along with him and get his father to read out the English questions for him to answer in French. His father much enjoyed these sessions, and when Henry answered '*Oui, monsieur, je suis très content*', his father would smile with pleasure and say: 'Why even I can understand that; it's just like English, only they use different words.' Whereupon they would shake hands and say '*Comment allez-vous aujourd'hui?*' The success of these sessions did not, however, prepare him for the dismaying gap he found between phrase-book French and the swift-flowing real thing he found when he actually arrived in Europe.

They travelled on a French liner, the *Île de France*, arriving at Le Havre and taking the boat train to Paris and the Gare Saint-Lazare. Miller, at thirty-seven making his first trip abroad, was primed for ecstasies, and found the station itself an experience, with its glass roof and its mysteriously-named waiting room, *La Salle des Pas Perdus*. From here they went to their hotel, the Grand Hôtel de la France on the rue Bonaparte, close to the École des Beaux-Arts.

They stayed in Paris for several weeks, sightseeing and visiting some of the many people June had met during her trip there with Mara Andrews in 1927. Most of these were artists or would-be artists. Some were famous, like Marcel Duchamp and the Russian sculptor Ossip Zadkine, samples of whose work June had brought back to New York with her in 1927 with the intention of acting as his American sales agent. June introduced Miller to Zadkine at a party held in the sculptor's garden. Miller was awestruck at shaking hands with his first real European artist, and felt like a small boy in his presence.[10] June also introduced Henry to the man who later became one of his closest friends, Alfred Perlès. Perlès had taken an instinctive dislike to June on meeting her on her earlier visit. He thought her a *poseuse*, and later recalled that on the day he saw her walking down the street towards him with Miller in 1928 his first impulse was to cross over to the other side and avoid them. He did not, however, and the three of them spent what turned out to be a most enjoyable day picnicking on bread and cheese and wine in the Jardin du Luxembourg. Perlès found Miller a simple and genuine man, and listened with pleasure as he enthused about Dostoevsky, Spengler and how much he and June were looking forward to their tour of Europe.

162

June had managed to raise about $2000 for the trip. With the dollar strong against the French franc, it was enough to keep them for months, and to allow them to indulge in the wonderful luxury of a long and leisurely bicycling holiday through France. They bought two bicycles. June, a true Greenwich Village bohemian, did not know how to ride, and Henry had the pleasure of giving her lessons on the rue Visconti, a tiny street close to their hotel. As soon as she was competent they loaded their bikes onto the train to Fontainbleau to start the tour.

From Fontainebleau they meandered slowly southward, vaguely following a route mapped out for them by Zadkine which would take them to Marseilles and thence to their goal, the Italian border. Whenever they got tired or bored with a stretch of road they would take the train and then join up with the towpaths running by the canals. They ate primitive picnic meals with cheese and fruit, cold sausage, and wine, or else stopped at village cafés. One hot day, at a place called Tournon, between Vienne and La Voulte-sur-Rhône, Henry had an experience of suddenly forgetting who and where he was which reminded him of a similar experience in National City, during his adolescent flight west to California. But where the adolescent experience had been distressing and alienating the Tournon moment was the blissful trance of pure, unthinking happiness.

By the end of September they were enjoying the Roman ruins at Arles and looking forward to the bullfight at Nîmes the following day. By the time they reached Nice their money had run out, and for three weeks they were supported by an American negro who was working as a shoe-shine on the Boulevard des Anglais. When funds arrived which enabled them to continue their travels, they made a pilgrimage to Èzes-sur-Mer, where Nietzsche wrote *Thus Spake Zarathustra*, and then carried on by train to visit Munich, Vienna, Budapest, Prague and Czernowitz (now Cernauti).

The train taking them from Budapest was held up at the border by the Romanian authorities, and an uncle of June's in the Hussars collected them and drove them in a three-horse carriage to Cernauti,[11] where they stayed briefly before moving on to visit more of June's relatives in Vienna. These were poor people, and though the Millers protested that they could stay at a nearby hotel the family insisted that their American guests accept their hospitality. On their first night Henry and June were tormented by bugs, and the following day went out and bought quantities of insecticide with which they discreetly sprayed the room.Even so the torment continued and after several days they fled to a hotel. This stay in Vienna was the part of the trip Miller enjoyed the least:

That whole Vienna episode was a nightmare to me – I gave a little of it in the novel, I think (*Crazy Cock*) – the part about the Ferris Wheel, the Jew who talked about God continually, the woman in the café playing the zither with long nails, the whores under the gas lamps, creating for me that imaginary scene which I inserted in the novel. Vienna! The name is magic to me (no, I don't destroy magic!) and I wanted to be so happy there with June, with Vienna, with her women, her lovely boulevards, her *désuétude*, her softness. But everything turned out differently, as everything always does. I lived cooped up in a ghetto, in a vile little flat with bedbugs and everyone was dying of poverty, of misery, around us.[12]

Having met June's relatives in person, one result of the trip was that Henry could no longer convincingly entertain himself with speculation about who June really was and where she really came from. Where people were concerned, his threshold of boredom was low, and the collapse of her mystery made the continued success of their relationship less likely than ever.

One of the outstanding experiences of the European trip for Henry was the day he got caught short in a Parisian street and had to use the toilet of a small hotel they happened to be passing at the time. Up on the third floor, the toilet was in semi-darkness, and so small that he had to manoeuvre in order to sit down on it. Neatly cut squares of newspaper hung on a hook on the wall. Finishing his business he rose to leave, and suddenly discovered a view from the small, dirty window of one of the oldest quarters of Paris, 'so sweepingly soft and intoxicating it brought tears to my eyes'. He fell into a trance there, and once he had recovered he hurried down to tell June about it, and encouraged her to go and see the view for herself. This experience of his, mingling the smells of the toilet with a sensation of ecstatic reverence for his ancient and grimy surroundings, sounded the keynote of the long love-affair with Paris on which he was about to embark. Indeed, it may have been the moment at which he actually fell in love with the city.

By the time the Millers returned to New York early in 1929, a world of new possibilities had been opened up to Henry. By contrast with the boringly rational and all-too-obviously man-made Manhattan grid, the European cities he had visited seemed wonderfully haphazard structures that grew like natural chaos out of history. The trip gave him the beginnings of a whole new set of perspectives on his own country, a frame of reference from which he would go on to attack the worst excesses of American society, notably the worship of success, the blind mania for progress, the promotion of a work ethic as though it were a religion, and that mania for personal cleanliness and hygiene so relentlessly promoted by the New York advertising industry as part of its campaign to market the fatuous idea of the 'life-style', in which it deliberately created a sense of shame in people over the fact that human beings sweat and are smelly and then made a fortune out of selling them the solutions to these invented problems, encouraging a definition of self-worth in terms of one's success as a consumer of this packaged 'life-style'.

Unfortunately, June did not share Henry's love of French toilets. Indeed, she was ominously averse to the smell of them – yet another small sign that they were drifting apart at an accelerating rate.

7

Back in New York after their six months away, the Millers moved into yet another apartment, this time on Clinton Avenue in Brooklyn. Here Miller set to work on a novel based on his notes from 1927, on the theme of a husband being cuckolded by his wife with another woman, and the bewilderment this causes him. The subject looked to have some potential for commercial success. Lesbianism was not only the most talked-about sexual fashion among Greenwich Villagers in 1929, it was also a much discussed literary topic since the tribulations of Radclyffe Hall's account of a lesbian love-affair, *The Well of Loneliness*. After being withdrawn under pressure by its publisher in London, the book had been attacked in New York in 1929 by the Society for the Suppression of Vice. Under the personal supervision of Charles Sumner, Society members carried out a raid on the offices of the publisher, Boni and Liveright, and confiscated remaining copies of the sixth edition. They then marched into the book department at Macy's and cleared the novel from its shelves. Miller had read the book, and may have entertained hopes of a scandalous success of his own with a novel on a related theme.

Yet even as he worked on *Crazy Cock*, literary fashion was moving on. In 1926, he had been well abreast of contemporary sentiment in a letter he wrote to the *New Republic*, passionately defending Dreiser's use of what a critic had called his 'cheap, trite and tawdry' language in *An American Tragedy*. But the debate that raged in the pages of the magazine in the winter of 1929 over Thornton Wilder was another matter. It was started by a working-class communist writer named Michael Gold who published an article attacking the revered Wilder on the extra-literary grounds that his writing was culpably non-political. Malcolm Cowley recalled that the attack 'was the occasion for scores and then hundreds of letters to the editor, some carefully reasoned, some violent and almost hysterical. The burden of them was that reviewers should confine themselves to the style and pattern of a book, taking its subject matter for granted.'[13]

When the violence of the initial reaction died down, however, the observable effect of Gold's attack was that he had made many grudging converts to his point of view. Along with events like the trial and execution of Sacco and Vanzetti in August 1927, the bitter and violent Gastonia strike of textile workers in North Carolina in the autumn of 1929 – the first major labour battle conducted by a Communist union – and the Wall Street Crash of October 29th, the net result was to lead to a consensus of opinion among American writers that the misery of the working class placed them under a moral obligation to produce a utilitarian literature that would fight for the cause of social progress. The self-indulgence and the horseplay characteristic of the art world during the 1920s continued for a few months yet, but serious days were definitely on the way by 1929.

Few things are more difficult for a struggling writer to respond to than a call from the literary trendsetters for him to make yet another change of direction while he is still trying to make sense of the old route. The prospect of having to restructure his idea of literature to make it useful, social and, above all, not about himself if he wished to be successful can only have appalled Miller. If the Crash had any noticeable effect on him it was to confirm him in his belief that he would have to remain absolutely indifferent to the vagaries of 'The Economy' if he ever hoped to get anything done at all.

So he carried on with *Crazy Cock*, loyal to his intentions, struggling to quell the feeling that he might be wasting his time, that even if the book turned out to be good, it would not arouse much interest. He also had to contend with the knowledge that June was reading what he wrote over his shoulder. She was the one who had reacted with disquiet to the portrayal of Conason in *Moloch*, and the realization that her husband's style was naturally caricatural. Now, as she read through *Crazy Cock*, she found that he was distorting her character in the same way as he had distorted Conason's, 'in the direction of denigration,' and she took exception to it. Miller's wholly personal difficulty was that, in the writing of the book, he was trying to take the consequences of the realization he had had while making notes for it during June's absence in Paris in 1927 – that he was no longer really in love with her. Her interest in his writing, so vital for his self-confidence, had always been slightly proprietorial. Now it was becoming directly inhibiting.

Progress on the book throughout 1929 was halting, and when June suggested to him, early in February 1930, that he should return to

Europe to try to get it finished, he jumped at the chance. She persuaded him that she would be able to keep him with money obtained from Roland Freedman, and promised that she would join him there as soon as she could. It was a cold, snowy day when the subject came up, and Miller's first response was to suggest that he should head for somewhere warm like Spain rather than France. June was his manager, however, and she insisted on Paris.

He left in the middle of the month, taking with him two suitcases and a trunk containing a selection of suits made by his father. The day of his actual departure acquired such symbolic significance for him later that it suffers from an embarrassment of often contradictory detail. What seems certain is that Emil Schnellock saw him off at the docks and gave him $10 to keep himself during the ten days he would be on board ship until he arrived in London. There he was to remain until June wired him the money to continue his journey to France. The time of the unorthodox hero was nigh. Rin Tin Tin was about to start work on his first barking picture and, within a few short months of arriving in France, Henry Miller too would be raising his rough, wild voice.

CHAPTER NINE

1930–1931
Paris on foot

1

While he waited to hear from June, Miller spent a week in London, staying at the Melvin Private Hotel in Gower Street, just off Tottenham Court Road, and seeing some of the sights. He was much impressed by the grimy majesty of the Thames and the Albert Docks, 'a symphony of fog and mist pierced by the music of giant cranes wheeling in tons of axle grease,' and enjoyed a pilgrimage to the Tate Gallery to see the Turners. Generally speaking, however, he was not enthusiastic about the city. His hotel room was too cold and London as a whole too dark. 'You said the gloom was rich,' he wrote to Emil Schnellock. 'It was. You could cut it with an axe.'[1] Charing Cross struck him as just another 42nd Street back in 1895, and he much preferred wandering in Whitechapel and Limehouse. His slight anglophobia, the legacy of his Brooklyn boyhood and the 1914–18 war, was not lessened by brief personal contact with the English on their home ground. On March 4th he crossed the Channel to France.

2

He rented a room at the Hôtel Saint-Germain on rue Bonaparte and at once began making a thorough exploration of Paris on foot. At the end of each day he would set down his impressions of the city and its street-life in a series of letters addressed to Emil Schnellock which were frequently twenty or thirty pages long. Like his 'Bowery Phoenix' mezzotint, these were really literary productions rather than personal communications. Inspired by Paul Morand's book on New York, Miller's idea was that these letters would be collected and published as a highly personal guide-book to Paris. He had an excellent eye for detail and arresting trivia, and the letters convey a vivid sense of the sights and smells of Parisian street life. After initial difficulties his French also improved, and he was able to busk his way through conversations with café waiters, hotel porters, old lady lavatory attendants, delivery men and street traders, with whom he had simple but interesting discussions on such matters as the relative merits of the French and American system of toilet plumbing. His regular visits to the cinema also helped him to improve his French, as did the careful scrutiny of the advertisements in the Métro. Wandering about the streets in the daytime, often carrying a book like Arthur B. Maurice's *The Paris of the Novelists* under his arm, forever stopping to take notes, he was frequently mistaken for a student and developed a little clown's routine by way of response, taking off his borsalino, pointing to his few remaining hairs and saying: *'Terminées, les études!'*

During his first few weeks in Paris he was very much alone. Letter-writing alleviated his loneliness, and it was during this period of his life that he changed from being a man given to writing letters into a man prodigiously given to writing letters. He hungered for letters in return, though few of his correspondents in New York could match him for length and flow. Emil Schnellock, whom he still occasionally addressed as 'Pop', wrote poor letters, never much more than three pages. Emil Conason and Joe O'Reagan were hardly any better, and: 'The one letter I look forward to most of all does not come,' he complained sadly to Schnellock. June regularly wired money to him at the American Express office on rue Scribe, however, and a visit there soon became a regular feature of his daily routine.

In April he moved from rue Bonaparte to the Hôtel Central on rue de Maine. His enthusiasm for the cinema led him to discover the world of *avant-garde* film, and he frequented the city's three leading centres of the art – the *Vieux Colombier*, the *Studio des Ursulines* and *Studio 28*, where he saw the Dali-Bunuel collaboration, *Un Chien Andalou*. However, he took good care not to get too rarefied in his tastes, and the afternoon of April 14th was spent watching the Six Day Bike Race at the *Vél d'Hiv*, where he was the only man cheering on the American rider Sam Horan, and 'nearly had a fist fight with two wops'[2] who were supporting an Italian. An article he wrote about the race was accepted and published by the Paris *Herald*, which also took an article about the *Cirque Medrano*, where he spent many pleasant evenings. He began looking out for a permanent source of income, and in May discussed with a sculptor named Fred Kann the possibility of their jointly opening an art school for their fellow Americans in Paris. Miller had to bluff Kann, since 'he doesn't know my true situation. When he finds out I think it will be all up – as he is strong on *references*. We would have to show the American Consul who we are! *(Who am I?)*'[3] Like the get-rich-quick schemes with June, this idea came to nothing.

169

After about two months on his own, Miller began taking an active interest in the prostitutes he had observed on his promenadings: '. . . everywhere: back of the Gare de Lyon, around the Bastille, *Closerie des Lilas*, Champs-Elysées'. Predictably, he fell in love with the first whore he picked up, a Madame Germaine Deaugard who accosted him one Sunday afternoon on the Boulevard Beaumarchais. As they sat talking in a café he confessed to her that he did not have enough money to pay for her. On hearing that he was a writer, however, and no doubt assuming that as an American his poverty was only temporary, she indicated that the twenty francs he was able to offer would be enough. Off they went to a five-franc hotel room on rue Amelot where Henry put on a two-franc preservative and had 'an awfully good time'.[4] Afterwards they dined together. Madame Deaugard was so taken with Miller that she began sending him postcards, and they made a date to meet again at the *Café l'Éléphant*. At her insistence, he turned up wearing his knickerbockers. She was so proud to be seen with an American that when he told her he was still broke she took him upstairs with her for nothing. 'I like this little factory kid,' he wrote to Schnellock. 'She seems like one whore who has heart.' There is an obvious callousness in stealing fucks from a whore when a fuck is all she has to sell, and when Paris of the early 1930s was still teeming with young American students, far from home, who were by many contemporary accounts quite liberal with their sexual favours and whom he could have had for nothing. Clearly the fact that he was actually being given freely something he should have been paying for had its appeal.

Madame Deaugard was one of the cheaper whores. A class above the five- and ten-franc girls, her full price was still only about forty-five francs (about $1.75). She was not in the same league as another girl who accosted Miller as he strolled down the Champs-Elysées one evening after a few glasses of wine. This one took him to a hotel room and for 150 francs gave an impression of enjoying herself which Henry found convincing up until the moment she began hawking his sperm up again with a bilious look on her face. The evening cost him 177 francs altogether, about a third of his monthly rent at the Hôtel Central. In the light of such prodigality the references which pepper his letters to Schnellock about 'living a dog's life' and a run of five dreadful days during which he found it 'very hard . . . to think of any other words but "desperate", "hungry", "prisoner" etc' have a melodramatic air. His life may have been uncomfortable, but his priorities were of his own choosing.

In May he moved hotels again, from the Central to the Alba, in the Italian and Russian Quarter behind avenue de Maine. Here he had only one room, without running water, but the rent was only 125 francs per month (about $5), and he was able to pay six weeks in advance.

At the end of May, June cabled to warn Henry she might arrive any day 'without funds'. He cabled back advising her not to come because: 'I can't seem to find a job here – much as I've tried.' One copy of *Moloch* was being read by Edward Titus for his Black Mannikin Press and another was with a publisher in Berlin. He was close to finishing a revision of *Crazy Cock* and hopeful that Schnellock would soon be able to submit his Paris letters to an American publisher for consideration. With more confidence than the situation actually warranted he therefore told June that he was 'firmly expecting to receive money through the books in a few months – I feel pretty sure I can demand a little "advance royalties". It is on these that I base all hopes of remaining here longer.'[5] He was also ambivalent about the prospect of being joined by June after having enjoyed complete individual freedom for four months.

His hopes that *Crazy Cock* might soon be good enough for publication received a setback at about this time. As he was sitting outside the American Express office one day, he met an old acquaintance from Western Union days, Jacobus Hendrik Dun. They spent the evening together and Henry gave Dun an account of his career as a great writer so far, ending with an outline of the plot of *Crazy Cock*. After listening to the story of 'two lesbians and a husband', Dun suggested that 'in a case like that it is always the husband who is to blame. There must have been something wrong with him.'[6] This seemed to Henry a disastrous misreading of his novel, and he rushed back to work on it in an attempt to make it quite clear who the hero was and who the villains.

In the late summer his poorly-husbanded resources ran out again, and he was asked to leave the Alba. He slept in the manager's office at a cinema for a few nights, and for a week or two lived at 54 rue Lafayette with an Indian pearl merchant named N.P. Nanavati whom he knew through his friendship with Haridas Maznudar, again from Western Union. Nanavati, while decent enough to put Henry up, obviously enjoyed having a white man for his flunkey, and made him work for his keep:

Life is very hard for me – very. I live with bedbugs and cockroaches. I sweep the dirty carpets, wash the dishes, eat stale bread without butter. Terrible life. Honest! Worse than Florida. Only a pair of flannel trousers and a tweed coat to cover my nakedness. I can't go any more bohemian than this.[7]

Terrible life it may have been, but it was better than a proper job; and the indignities he suffered were, like the painful experience of trying to sell newspapers in Florida, part of the making of him. Instead of breaking his spirit they brought him nearer to a realization of how to practise most effectively that 'purposeful literary buffoonery' which he was beginning to believe was his true vocation. The fictionalized account of his few days at Nanavati's in *Tropic of Cancer* are some of the funniest pages in the book.

4

That September June arrived for the first of four ultimately doomed attempts to find out what was going on in their marriage. Wambly Bald, who wrote the *La Vie de Bohème* column for the Paris *Tribune*, described for his American readers her characteristic manner of entering a hotel:

Her custom is to arrive at a hotel, tell the *patron* to pay the taxi bill, engage a room and then borrow money from the *patron*. The next move is to the telegraph office. 'Cable funds. Desperate. Ill'. She has half a dozen stock forms which invariably bring results.[8]

Tactics like this meant moving about a lot, and during her brief stay she and Henry lived in a succession of hotels, each of which they fled before the management could impound their baggage for non-payment of bills. To Henry's surprise June had arrived bringing nothing with her but evening dresses with slits up the side, informing him that Abe Elkus would be sending her other clothes on to her. One of the large circle of casual acquaintances Henry had picked up by this time, an engineer from Martinique named Stephen Blérald who was helping him with his French, gave her 150 francs to enable her to buy some new shoes.

Clearly June had come with expectations of a prolonged stay. As it turned out, Henry had lured her over on false premises and the visit lasted a mere three weeks. After seeing an *avant-garde* film, *La Souriante Madame Beudet* at *Studio 28*, he had written a fan letter to its director, Germaine Dulac, requesting an interview at which he hoped she might offer him a job. 'I would be proud to assist in the production of such films as she turns out,' he told Schnellock, and at the interview with her he gained the distinct impression that she favoured him. She treated him, in his own quaint phrase, 'like a brick', holding his hands and rolling her eyes at him as she spoke. Dulac was a lesbian, however, and Henry surmised that June might interest her

172

even more than he did. June was still hoping for success as an actress, and it was with an exaggerated impression of the amount of influence Henry had on Dulac that she travelled to Paris to discuss the prospects of her appearance in an English-language talking picture which Dulac and the Gaumont-Aubert Franco Film Company planned to start shooting in January 1931.

As so often before, nothing came of the plan, and June's visit turned into a holiday that was spoiled by lack of money. 'Poor June hasn't seen anything yet because of our circumstances,' he told Emil Schnellock. She made a brief attempt to raise money with Mara Andrews, who was still studying at the Colorassi. They called on Waverley Root, now a journalist on the *Tribune*, at his flat on rue de la Glacière where they tried to borrow from him. Root, who knew June of old, declined to help.

When, on October 18th, Henry saw June off at the station on the first leg of her return to New York, he had fifty francs in his pocket and she had ten. She told Wambly Bald that he could inform his *Tribune* readers that she intended to start work on a novel to be called *Happier Days* when she got back to New York. Henry had more faith in another fantasy: that she would get herself a well-paid job in the theatre so that she could rejoin him in Europe 'in a few months with sufficient to last a year or so'.[9] Her clothes had still not turned up by the time she left, but Henry told Elkus he would keep them in storage for her when they came. He intended to make use of her big cape himself when it arrived, because 'here you can wear any damned thing and get away with it'.

5

With June's departure he immediately set about looking for somewhere to live that was cheaper than the rue de Rennes hotel where they had been paying twenty-two francs a day (eighty-eight cents). He tramped the streets for three days in search of a room, a forty-year-old man competing with the thousands of impoverished students who were flocking back into the city for the winter term, also in search of somewhere cheap to stay. The gulf between his ambition to be a famous writer and the farcical reality of his achievement had never been greater, but his sense of humour never deserted him for long, and some of his letters to Schnellock still carried the signature 'The Cabinet Minister'. This was one of the aliases the narrator of Hamsun's *Hunger* acquired during his own wanderings through the streets of Kristiania in search of warmth, food, money and women, and Miller's appropriation of the signature shows the extent to which he identified with the hero of Hamsun's novel at this time.

In *Hunger*, the narrator turns up at a police station and reports that he is homeless for the night. Rather than have the desk sergeant believe him to be a common vagrant he airily passes himself off as a journalist on an important daily paper who happens to have had a little too much to drink and lost his house key. After an unpleasant and sleepless night he emerges from his cell in the morning to see the other vagrants queuing for their free breakfast tickets. Starving himself, he longs to join the queue but is trapped by his preposterous impersonation of the night before. As he is shown out of the station the sergeant politely asks whether he has spent a comfortable night, and with a despairing bray of laughter he answers that yes, he has slept very well indeed, he has slept *like a Cabinet Minister*. Though Miller did not have anything like this fanatical pride, in the juxtaposition of absurd pretension in front of others and savage honesty towards himself he recognised himself very clearly.

The writing had stopped with June's visit, but as soon as he had found a temporary room he began again, setting about a revision of *Crazy Cock* so violent that it was not far from actually destroying it:

Jesus, I'm getting a masochistic pleasure out of it. I wipe out whole pages – without even shedding a tear. Out with the balderdash, out with the slush and drivel, out with the apostrophes, the mythological mythies, the sly innuendoes, the vast and pompous learning (which I haven't got!) Out-out-damned fly-spots. Here I am, and I am only beginning to recognize it – a very plain, unvarnished soul, not learned, not wise, no great shakes any way you look at me – particularly '*comme artiste*'. What I must do, before blowing out my brains, is to write a few simple confessions in plain Milleresque language.[10]

He had given *Moloch* up for dead by this time. He liked to say later that Edward Titus had 'lost' the book, though this may only have been wishful thinking. In any case he had other carbon copies of it, and if that particular copy did get lost it was certainly not the kind of loss of which literary legends are made.

With *Moloch* abandoned and *Crazy Cock* committed to an ominously extensive process of revision, Miller now began thinking about returning to New York himself. The material obstacles that faced him in Paris were considerable, and he could see no satisfactory way of overcoming them. In the short space of time in which he had been there he had made many friends and become a convinced francophile. Once he had got rid of the plus-fours and the loud golf socks he became much less recognisably American, and he noticed with amusement that even the Americans sitting near him in the cafés took him for a Frenchman, and talked loudly and openly in his presence. One of his proudest moments in the city came when the proprietress of the *Café des Gourmets* told him, after his fifth glass of *vin ordinaire*: 'Monsieur, il me semble que vous êtes tout-à-fait Parisien maintenant.'[11]

He had established himself in a crowd of his own that included Alfred Perlès, the Hungarian Frank Dobo who worked for Opera Mundi, Europe's largest literary and news syndicate, the photographer George Brassai, a Hungarian painter named Tihanyi, a painter from Woodstock named John Nichols, as well as a number of journalists and employees on the Paris *Tribune* and the *Herald*, like Wambly Bald and Richard Thoma whom he had met through Perlès, and spent many happy hours sitting around drinking and talking at the *Rotonde*, the *Dôme*, the *Coupole* and the *Select*. All things considered, he may have felt that he had 'done' Paris, and enough was enough. In his romantic way he had paid the particular literary dues he had wanted to pay, dues that had as much to do with life-style as talent. He even believed he could see the outlines of his own myth shimmering, a little shabbily, perhaps, in the literary history of the future: 'When you read some day about how certain famous authors wrote their books,' he told Schnellock, 'you will know that I am in the same line – that my struggle with this has been as picaresque as any of them.'[12] He was satisfied that he had enough material already in his letters to Schnellock for his Paris book, and that with 'a few months of comparative security' he could get it finished.

By mid-November 1930 his mind was made up, and he was trying to raise $100 to pay for a return ticket to New York. The move to Paris had served to convince his parents – or his father, at least – of the deadly seriousness of their son's literary ambitions, and Henry applied to them confidently for half the sum; Elkus, Joe O'Reagan, Conason, June and Emil Schnellock were expected to provide the rest. His plan was to sail with the America-French line on Saturday December 7th, arriving back in New York just in time for Christmas.

And yet, when the time came, he did not go. He knew that logic and reason, common sense even, dictated that he should return home, but at the deepest level he was in revolt against the tyranny of all three. When an acquaintance named Richard Osborn offered to let him share, without payment, an apartment he had rented at 2 rue Auguste-Bartholdi, Miller thankfully abandoned common sense, moved in and continued his fascinated exploration of his own human weakness.

Osborn was an American lawyer from Bridgport, Connecticut, who worked in the legal department of the Paris branch of the National City Bank during the daytime and on leaving his office in the evening switched identities to become a bohemian. He liked to be thought of as a writer, but did little, complaining that what he did write was at once plagiarized. He was an unstable man, an incipient alcoholic who suffered bouts of paranoid schizophrenia. According to Alfred Perlès, he even boasted of his illness. American Paris had many such lonely neurotics who were attracted by Miller's affable, unneurotic personality and what Osborn once called his 'temperamental enthusiasm which amounted almost to a chronic state of intoxication'.[13] Friendship with him was a ticket to company, a way into the crowd.

From December 1930 to March 1931 Miller and Richard Osborn shared the seventh floor studio apartment. Each morning before he left for work, Osborn would leave Henry ten francs pocket money, and in return Henry would keep house and cook his evening meal. Like many of those who lived with Miller, including June, Osborn was struck by the apparent contradiction between the bohemian in him and his 'methodical German nature' which was silently outraged by what Osborn called 'my slovenly ways, my absent-minded nonchalance, my heedlessness' and kept the floor of their apartment scrupulously swept clean 'just to keep the mice away'.[14]

At Osborn's flat Miller was able to work in relative peace and quiet on his writing. He carried on with the revision of *Crazy Cock*, and had the first significant successes of his career with two articles written while living there. One was a fictionalized account of his relationship with Germaine Deaugard, the prostitute who had indulged him during his earliest days in Paris. In the story he called her 'Mademoiselle Claude', borrowing the name from another prostitute whom he and Osborn sometimes used and whom Miller, in his extraordinary way, corresponded with in French, addressing her c/o *La Coupole*. The other was an appreciation of *L'Âge d'Or*, the second cinematic collaboration between Luis Buñuel and Salvador Dali. Together, *Un Chien Andalou* and the ironically-titled *L'Âge d'Or* had a profoundly liberating effect on Miller's approach to the art of writing. Though he still laboured at the formally traditional *Crazy Cock*, he had become increasingly aware that disciplined writing was writing against the grain, and the violence and anarchy inherent in surrealism – superbly exemplified in these films – at once opened up a way out of the baffling strictures of literary othodoxy. Buñuel later described *L'Âge d'Or* as 'a militant film aimed at raping clear consciences', and its attack on the

Church, the Establishment and middle-class morality sent Miller into ecstasies. Its intended targets were less enthusiastic, and an alliance of *Jeunesse Catholique*, the *Ligue des Patriotes* and the *Ligue Antijuive* attacked *Studio 28*, the cinema where it was showing. The right-wing press mounted a campaign against the film, and the censor responded by placing a ban on any public showing which was to remain in force for the next twenty years. Miller's article was a passionate and emphatic defence of its creator. 'They call Buñuel everything,' he wrote. 'Traitor, anarchist, pervert, defamer, iconoclast. But lunatic they do not call him. It is true it is lunacy he portrays, but it is not his lunacy. This stinking chaos which for a brief hour or so amalgamates under his wand, this is the lunacy of civilization, the record of man's achievement after ten thousand years of refinement.' Both pieces, which appeared in Samuel Putnam's new magazine *New Review*, were prophetic of *Tropic of Cancer*, the former of its contents, the latter of its pervasive attitude.

Much of what Miller wrote was sent back to the United States where a small army of friends and supporters acted as unpaid literary agents for him. He received $25 for an article published in a short-lived Philadelphia magazine called *USA*, but hoped for greater rewards from his contact with a professional literary agent named Madeleine Boyd who despatched his various manuscripts from her office on East 49th Street and wrote reassuring notes to him saying that they were 'so good I think there is a chance of their being sold', then spoilt the effect by adding that she would return them to him 'when I finally do give up hope of selling them'.[15]

Another contact in New York was Leviticus Lyon, whom he had got to know when he went rent collecting with Abe Elkus among Elkus's black tenants in the Navy Yard area. He hoped Lyon might be able to open up a market among black people for his articles and books. Lyon was a useful man to know in other ways. He worked in the Customs and Excise Department, and Henry had always enjoyed looking through the large collection of confiscated pornographic material which Lyon took home with him from the job. Henry was interested in every aspect of human sexuality, and a keen student of all forms of pornography. While in Paris he read the four recently-published volumes of *My Life And Loves* written by his old favourite Frank Harris, and during the 1928 trip with June he had discovered Eve Adams's pornographic bookshop in Montparnasse and pur-chased a copy of *Fanny Hill* and a set of dirty postcards. While living with Osborn, he attended the live sex shows on rue Saint-Lazare which included exhibitions of lesbianism, sodomy and homosexuality. At a more innocent level he developed an erotic obsession with Marlene

Dietrich. He went to see *The Blue Angel* three times. 'Emil', he wrote to Schnellock, 'the thighs almost killed me. I studied them from every angle of the theatre. I dream about them at night.'

Miller was genuinely grateful to Osborn for the offer of free shelter during the winter of 1930–31; but the nature of their arrangement inevitably led to conflict. Osborn's memoir of the period implies that he believed that Miller secretly despised him, both for supporting him and for not supporting him in more style. Miller often looked emaciated, he noticed, but since he spent the ten francs pocket money on two packs of *Gauloises Bleues* each day instead of a square meal, Osborn felt no sympathy for him. The tensions which arose between beggar and almoner were similar to those which had spoiled Miller's friendship with Stanley Borowski in the mid-1920s when he and June camped at Borowski's house after being evicted from Remsen Street. They increased after Osborn picked up an eccentric Russian refugee named Sonya (Irene, according to Miller) on the Champs-Elysées one night and brought her back to live with them. She was a wild, dramatic, hard-drinking, pretentious woman who claimed to have a fortune locked away in banks in various European cities. She had the undisciplined ways of June and Mara, and soon after her arrival the floor was awash with orange peel, bottles, scissors, used condoms, pillows and wads of cotton wool soaked in menstrual blood. Her lack of hygiene terrified Miller, who found to his horror one day that he had used her towel, and gave her a fatherly lecture about the need to keep her things separate from theirs, and to wash the toilet seat each time she had used it. His revolt was genuine, yet he was fascinated and amused even more than he was horrified.

No one likes to be too shamelessly used, and during a party at number 2 one evening a pathetic flare-up occurred between Osborn and Henry. Miller, John Nichols, another painter friend named Frank Mechau and several others were eating and drinking – at Osborn's expense – when Osborn suddenly took it into his head to assert himself. Nichols, a gifted talker, was in the middle of a monologue which Osborn clumsily and irrelevantly interrupted in order to show him a letter an old friend had sent him. Miller, drunk, assertive and cantankerous, told him not to interrupt, he talked too much anyway. Osborn was furious, grabbed a hot poker and brandished it, demanding to know whose place it was anyway and telling Miller to go to hell. Miller took a deep breath then launched a verbal attack on him in front of the others, calling him a puerile tyrant, a childish exhibitionist, piling on the insults and in the end utterly crushing him.

Miller's attitude towards Osborn demonstrates the pragmatism of which he was capable when choosing his friends. He was aware of this tendency, and was very slightly uneasy about it. He later gave Osborn Schnellock's address in New York, then had to write to Schnellock to apologize for having 'inflicted' Osborn on him when his Paris friend turned up on Schnellock's doorstep. Miller confessed that he had nothing in common with Osborn, but pointed out that he could 'perhaps reach a few more levels – downward – than you'. Finally he advised him to look on Osborn as just 'one of my WU "nuts"'.[16] Elsewhere, and in public, he referred to him as 'my wise and goodhearted friend Osborn', and dedicated a book to him as the man who 'rescued me from starvation in Paris and set my feet in the right direction'. And when the Polish painter who owned the apartment returned from the Midi at the beginning of March to resume possession, obliging them all to move out, Henry wept.[17]

7

By the spring of 1931 Miller's status as a not-too-seriously-starving artist was well-established. He was a well-liked and popular member of the American community and he had little difficulty in finding people willing to feed him and give him a roof over his head for the night. He continued to earn occasional money for newspaper articles, and received 350 francs from the *Chicago Tribune* for an article entitled 'Paris in *Ut Mineur*'. He also made a small amount of money giving private lessons in English, but it seemed a waste to spend this on rent. He squatted for a while with Fred Kann at his studio near the *Montparnasse* cemetary, and often stayed overnight with John Nichols and his wife, and sat for them while they did portraits of him wearing the beard he grew that winter, which was dark red, but peppered with the tell-tale signs of advancing age. Nichols, like so many young Americans in Paris, had a private income, which made sponging off him a less personal business. Tex Carnahan and Frank Mechau could also be relied on to help him out, as could the young Brooklynites Albert Kotin and Dave Rosenberg. The contacts he had made through Alfred Perlès with the staff on the *Chicago Tribune* were especially useful to him, and a journalist named Louis Atlas often allowed him to share his hotel room on rue Monsieur-le-Prince.

Two other regular helpers during this period were Walter Lowenfels and his neighbour Michael Fraenkel. Fraenkel allowed him to sleep for a few weeks in his apartment at 18 Villa Seurat, a private *cul-de-sac* in the fourteenth arrondissement on the east side of the rue de la Tombe-Issoire. One of Miller's strengths during this period of need was his sound tactical sense. He always borrowed small sums of money, and worked to spread the responsibility for his welfare over as many people as possible so that he would not wear out a welcome in one home. After moving from the Villa Seurat he continued to eat with Fraenkel once a week as part of a system he had worked out for getting free meals. He drew up a list of households that were prepared to feed him, with the intention of eating at a different table every night for a fortnight. By way of payment he would amuse, provoke or flatter his hosts. His reasoning was similar to the reasoning June offered to excuse the prick-teasing hustling she engaged in to raise money in New York – that the money and favours received were no more than fair payment for being an intelligent listener and an interesting person – and show that by this time the scruples he had once felt about such behaviour, the 'shame over June's gold-digging' that he recorded in his notes in 1927, had vanished completely. One of the names on his list was Ned Calmer, a *New York Herald* journalist and writer who played Henry at his own game and in 1934 wrote a novel entitled *Always Summer* which contains a literary portrait of Miller under the name of 'Irving Brace'. At the end of the book Brace is knocked down and killed by a taxi.

His real stand-by during this uncertain summer was Alfred Perlès. Perlès, born in Vienna, was eight years younger than Miller, but he had had a better education and a more adventurous life. He had spent time in a mental hospital as a result of his experiences as a soldier during the 1914–18 war, and after the break-up of the Austrian Empire made his way to Paris where he had been living since 1920, supporting himself by his charm and his journalism while he tried to write novels.

Perlès was always willing to sneak Henry into his room at the Hôtel Central, and this became to all intents and purposes Miller's home address for the year. In August Perlès managed to get him a job working in the proof-reading room of the Paris *Tribune*. The pay was $12 a week, and for a couple of months Miller enjoyed again the awfulness of work. 'The very atmosphere of the place has gotten into my blood,' he wrote. 'I miss it on my night off. In the first place, it is a perfect maze of machinery. The air is fetid. And then there is the noise – a deafening noise, and the blinding lights.'[18] Even more than the mad chaos of the work he relished the company and conversation of his fellow-workers, who included a former bullfighter, now studying for a career as an opera singer, and a retired military man named Rush with a wooden leg and bad breath who wrote poetry.

With Perlès and Bald at the *Tribune*, Miller formed a Parisian edition of the 'three musketeers' to succeed Miller, Sattenstein and Ramos at Western Union, and the Miller, O'Reagan and Schnellock edition of the trip to Florida. The formation of this third gang, and the

180

talks and adventures they had together as they made their way home from work at night, came to form the core of *Tropic of Cancer*, the book that finally made Miller's name. Ever since his arrival in Paris he had been, without knowing it, assembling this novel – for it was an act of assemblage rather than of deliberate artistic creation. His rambles through the city streets, his experiences of Parisian hotels and casual acquaintances like Nanavati, his winter at rue Auguste-Bartholdi with Osborn and the Russian girl, encounters with whores and conversations with John Nichols, Ossip Zadkine, Walter Lowenfels and Michael Fraenkel, all featured in his notebooks and letters for many months before the sudden moment of realization that revealed their essential unity to him, showing him they all belonged together between the covers of a single book. His instincts were those of a film producer whose consciousness was actually a machine for assembling a cast, picking the locations and taking notes for the script of a major production. He himself was always going to be the star of his own film, but in Perlès and Bald, who became respectively 'Carl' and 'Van Norden' in *Tropic of Cancer*, he knew he had found his two most important co-stars.

Wambly Bald was a key figure in Miller's life. He was a brash young American of twenty-five who, through his regular *Tribune* gossip column, wielded a considerable amount of social power among the expatriate community of artists, students, and bohemians. His status lay in seducing as many women as possible, and boasting of it afterwards to his friends. Around 2 am, after the paper had been put to bed, Bald, Perlès and Miller would leave the *Tribune* offices on rue Lamartine and walk together back to their respective hotels, stopping off sometimes at the *Dôme*, the *Rotonde* or *Gillotte's* for an hour or two where Bald would regale them with accounts of his latest adventures. Miller listened to him with a mixture of fascination and contempt. Bald was fond of Miller, but reciprocated some of the contempt for a man who was fifteen years his senior and still living like a student. Richard Thoma has described an occasion on which he and Bald were walking along the street one day when they were approached by Miller. Soon, with every appearance of real need, Miller asked if Bald could lend him some money. With the obvious intention of humiliating him Bald offered him a derisory ten francs. Thoma blushed for him as Miller took the money, but his delicacy was unnecessary; Miller revenged himself amply when it came time to write about Bald in *Tropic of Cancer*.

Interviewed in later years, Bald confessed that the sheer cruelty of Miller's portrayal of him in the novel as what he called a 'hopeless, toothless, ranting sex-ridden fool' shocked him. He protested that the sexual boasting in which Van Norden indulges had been only to tease Miller, whom he regarded as 'just another puritanical guy who at a late age suddenly discovered sex with a big flounce and purpose the way Columbus discovered America'. To him Miller 'really was puritanical and actually winced when I kept bringing that up'. Bald implied that he invented much of what he told Miller about his adventures in order 'to get his awed, shocked reaction'. In one of the most famous scenes in *Tropic of Cancer*, Van Norden entertains Henry with an account of how once, in a desperate last attempt to find out what it was about sex that compelled his disgusted fascination, he had even trained a flashlight between a girls legs. Bald claimed that the story was untrue, a yarn invented merely to excite and shock Miller.[19] Bald would have obvious reasons for trying to discredit the *Tropic of Cancer* portrait, yet, as Miller showed during the years in New York with June, he was a credulous man and Bald's disclaimers deserve at least some credit.

Miller was in any case cavalier with reality: as far as he was concerned, Bald was his creation. Once he had appropriated and relabelled him Van Norden, he could do what he liked with him. The student of human types in him was amused and fascinated by Bald, the image of the dedicated lecher. One letter to Emil Schnellock contained a succinct description of his new friend's monomania:

Wambly Bald is a misanthropist, if this isn't too dignified a term to use in connection with such a sad figure. Everything is futile to him. Everything but cunt. On our way home we indulge in guessing games. 'Three guesses – what am I thinking about now?' Answer invariably and invariably correct: Cunt ... cunt ... cunt. Last night it was Ida's cunt. Night before, the Virgin Mary's. Very edifying pastime, as you can see.[20]

In his 'Notes on characters' written in 1928 in his 'June' notebook, Miller characterized his friend Dewar with the same three words: Cunt-Cunt-Cunt, and while it might please him to look down on such men, presumably he also experienced at least a touch of the jealousy men commonly feel for the unprincipled womaniser, and a grudging recognition of the ability of the Dewars and O'Reagans and Balds of the world to make things happen around them and to pile up any number of stupid, hilarious, memorable little incidents that help to pass the time. In another letter to Emil Schnellock, Miller described a typical outing with Bald which he later used as the basis for another famous scene in *Tropic of Cancer* in which two men and a whore search dully for a way for all three of them to realize, in the form of some comprehensible human activity, the ten-franc fee which has been placed on the table in the hotel bedroom. Bald, Perlès and Miller had gone to Les Halles so that Bald could pick up a whore. Bald, as usual, was the actor, Miller and Perlès the bystanders:

One with a red dress, transparent, frail little legs, but teats and ass well-proportioned. French to the core. Diseased. Brass. Ten francs – and Fred and I wait downstairs while Bald gives her a quick lay – on the edge of the bed, clothes on, no windows in the room, one towel for the two of them. She smoking while he jazzes her, calm, deliberate, uninterested. Go to it . . . take your ten francs worth. Customer at the door, waiting to get in the room while he's washing up. Door opens and customer watches. Timing him downstairs. Four and a half minutes.[21]

Miller once told Michael Fraenkel that 'hatred and vengeance' were the mainspring of *Tropic of Cancer*,[22] and Bald probably understood better than anyone that this apparently philosophical statement was every bit as relevant at the personal level. He had to live for the rest of his days with the caricature Miller created of him as a sex-obsessed moron, derided as one of the sights of the Overseas Press Club: 'See that guy there? He's Van Norden in Miller's book.' To Miller, Bald represented the kind of man he liked to think of as his polar opposite, someone who could never have carried a torch for a Cora Seward and would have found such behaviour ridiculous. Yet he was still weak enough to envy the brainless stud and the cold emotional efficiency of his way.

8

In a letter to Schnellock of August 24th 1931, Miller announced that he had finished *Crazy Cock*, and some two weeks before she returned to Paris in October 1931, readers of Bald's *La Vie de Bohème* column learnt that June Mansfield would soon be with them again, having finished the novel *Happier Days* that she had been working on in New York for the past year. Possibly the two announcements were connected, possibly *Happier Days* was *Crazy Cock* and June was still clinging to some mad agreement – like the one concerning *Moloch* – for a book written by Henry to be published under her name. The Greenwich Village writer Lionel Abel reported a number of con-versations with her in the early 1930s which suggested that this was the case, but the title of the work-in-progress she mentioned to Abel was *Tropic of Cancer*. This whole business of Miller writing his first two books under June's name is one of the most impenetrable and bizarre aspects of his mythological life.

None of these complications could alter the fact that *Crazy Cock* became the third unpublished book-length production before his success with *Tropic of Cancer*. A bad book, it provides a biographically interesting perspective on Miller's more successful attempts to depict himself, since it deals in some detail with the material used over the next thirty years in *Tropic of Capricorn* and *The Rosy Crucifixion*, concentrating especially on the humiliating experience of living with June and Mara Andrews in 1926–27.

'Tony Bring', as Miller calls himself in the book, is a pathetic character, bewildered by a world of cigarette-smoking women in speakeasies and lesbians shamelessly parading the streets of New York in boiler suits and big boots. His main preoccupation is how to gain control of independent women like June and Mara and keep control of them. Yet June, called 'Hildred' in the novel, is given persuasive lines with which to defend herself, in rejecting Henry's accusations that she and 'Vanya' are having a lesbian relationship. She complains that as a man he is incapable of understanding the qualitatively different kind of love that two women can feel for each other:

You make things so complex, so ugly! You do! You see things only in your narrow, masculine way; you make everything a matter of sex. And it isn't that at all . . . it's something rare and beautiful. The love of a man for a woman is a thing of appetites, entirely physical, transitory, an appeal to vanity. You can never understand me, however much you try. You will see in me only what you choose to see, what appeals to your ego. You do not love me for myself.[23]

By comparison with the later account of her personality in *The Rosy Crucifixion*, the *Crazy Cock* June is a more normal, believable character, a real woman rather than the dramatic, shadowy symbol she later became.

Tony Bring suffers more from guilt at having deserted his wife and small child than he does in his later incarnation as 'Val Miller'. In a scene typical of the oddly touching innocence of much of his writing, Miller describes Tony's visit to a whorehouse, where he blushes when a whore compliments him on his khaki shirt. When she touches him on the leg later, he again blushes violently. Tony Bring's reactions and the narrative ruminations on sex generally suggest that Wambly Bald was probably correct in detecting a hint of puritanism in Miller. Tony is distressed by the way 'women like to get themselves up as whores. Yes, at bottom they were all whores . . . every mother's daughter, even the angels.' At one point he becomes so disheartened by the direction modern life is taking that in a speakeasy one evening he expresses open regret about everything that has happened to him since leaving his wife and child, and longs for a return to family life with the conventional 'Paula'. He even quotes Dowson on being shown an old photo of his former wife, and feels 'his heart vibrating once again to the misty glamour of an old spell'. This sentimentality extends to the narrative style itself, and at times Miller uses inversions characteristic of women's popular fiction, such as: 'Close they lie, breathing each other's breath.'[24]

The self-portrait as Tony Bring, executed without irony or distance, shows the degree to which Miller had remained socially and sexually conventional throughout his years of bohemian life with June in New York. All change alarmed him, whether it was the radical reshaping of his boyhood neighbourhood by the arrival of Jewish immigrants or the change in the sexual behaviour of young women brought about by the war and the introduction of speakeasies. Later in life he misleadingly said of his failure to find a publisher for these first books of his that it was 'not because my work was larded with pornography but, as I am now convinced, because I had yet to discover my own identity'. In fact, there is nothing in either *Moloch* or *Crazy Cock* which could remotely be described as pornographic, and he was so little concerned to challenge the censor that he used his own typewriter to type out suspension dots in the manuscript where he believed the language might offend. This is not to suppose that the later Henry Miller was not present in the book. He was, but Tony Bring censored him.

Miller experimented with several different endings to *Crazy Cock*, but was never able to find a satisfactory one. His difficulty was that the dramatic love triangle he was proposing as the main area of interest for his readers had simply fizzled out in real life, and he had no talent for the kind of large-scale literary invention required to bring his book to a psychologically satisfactory conclusion. In desperation, he even wrote one ending in which Tony Bring cut Vanya's throat.

In view of the innocuous contents, the title remains a mystery. Perhaps it was only a commercial ploy intended to delude readers into believing that the book was full of exciting sex scenes. Yet it does carry echoes of Maxwell Bodenheim's 1924 commercial success, *Crazy Man*, with which it has certain thematic similarities. Bodenheim's book described the love-affair between a dance-hall girl and an artistic working man by the name of John Carley whose initials are intended to convey an identification with Jesus Christ. Carley falls in love with the girl, and his love gives her a sense of personal worth that has hitherto been lacking in her life.

Miller had worked hard on the book; but even as he announced its completion he knew that he had failed in his attempt to write a conventional novel. Worse still, as a self-portrait it was already woefully out-of-date. Walter Lowenfels read it and found it 'corny and purple writing, trash, pulpy'.[25] Michael Fraenkel described it as the queerest mixture of good and bad writing he had ever seen, and advised Miller to tear it up and forget about it. Miller did not; but on the day he finished *Crazy Cock* he hailed with obvious relief the commencement 'tomorrow' (August 25th 1931) of a new project which he was obviously looking forward to much more: 'the Paris book: first person, uncensored, formless – fuck everything!' – a fine, succinct description of *Tropic of Cancer*.[26]

9

Possibly June thought she might be able to persuade Henry to return to New York with her now that *Crazy Cock* was finished, but in the event all she managed to do before she left after her short stay was to get him to leave his job at the *Tribune*. As she had done in the Western Union days in 1924, she encouraged him in an extended bout of absenteeism lasting ten days, at the end of which his boss, Jules Frantz, gave the job to a new proof-reader in the belief that Henry had returned to America without telling anyone. Miller adapted the story for inclusion in *Tropic of Cancer* to make it seem as though he had been dismissed from his post. Soon he believed the story himself, and in 1935 he sent his ex-boss a pamphlet inscribed: 'To Jules Frantz, who fired me because I was a lousy newspaperman.'[27]

Frantz in fact retained few memories of Miller's first period of employment on the *Tribune*, and many years later apologized to one of Miller's prospective biographers that he could not be of greater assistance to him, saying: 'since half the personnel of the Chicatrib editorial and proof-reading staff considered themselves budding geniuses of one sort or another – writer, painter, opera singer, Casanova or what have you, Henry didn't make as much impression on the rest of us as he might have on others in a different *milieu*.'

June's departure, the loss of the job and liberty from the drudgery of *Crazy Cock* gave Henry the chance he needed to press ahead with the assembling of the fuck-everything book. He saw much of Alfred Perlès in these days, often sleeping in his bed at the Hôtel Central while Perlès was at work, and learnt many valuable lessons from him in how to give direction and edge to his literary buffoonery so that it would indeed be a *purposeful* buffoonery. This was the era of manifestos and of literary theorists like Gertrude Stein and Eugène Jolas, so one of the first things Perlès and Miller worked on together was a manifesto. Eugène Jolas, the editor of *transition*, had caused some comment with

186

the June 1929 issue of the magazine which proclaimed the 'Revolution of the Word' in a series of twelve ruthlessly formalistic propositions, of which the twelfth was: 'The plain reader be damned.' An American journalist and writer named Samuel Putnam, who had been working as Edward Titus's assistant on *This Quarter*, broke with Titus over his indifference to material that seemed old-fashioned in its straightforwardness. Titus, for example, dismissed the many stories submitted to the magazine by James T. Farrell as 'tripe', leaving Putnam with no option but to start his own magazine if he wanted to see this kind of realism in print. *New Review*, started in 1931, was a protest against a too-esoteric view of literature, and Putnam had been pleased by the examples of straightforward but refreshingly different writing submitted to the magazine by Miller. In 'L'Age d'Or' and 'Madamemoiselle Claude' Putnam saw healthy antidotes to the intellectualism of James Joyce and Gertrude Stein.

In further reaction to such writing and the progrommatic pomposities like that of Jolas, Miller and Perlès put together a manifesto in which they promoted their 'New Instinctivism'. They introduced it as: 'A proclamation of rebellion against the puerilities in the arts and literature, a manifesto of disgust, a gob of spit in the cuspidor of postwar conceits, a healthy crap in the cradle of still-born deities.' The new religion (Perlès and Miller announced the preparation of an Instinctivist Bible) was one of total subjectivity. It mixed nonsense, farce, the pseudo-science of Alfred Jarry's *pataphysique*, and the promotion of complete personal anarchy: 'Are you tired of your wife? Fuck her! Are you weary of politics? Don't vote! Are you disgusted with your job? Throw it up! Whatever you want to do, do.' The good Instinctivist was instinctively *against* admirals, but *for* rear-admirals; *against* prostitutes but *for* whores; *against* the photographing of hands – particularly poets' hands – but *for* the Church, since 'being for it does more harm than being against it'. He was also, instinctively, against the New Instinctivism.

The story goes that the busy Putnam put production of one issue of the *New Review* into Perlès's and Miller's hands, and that they at once threw out all the contributions Putnam had agreed to include and set about filling the issue with their own outrageous message to the world. Unfortunately for them, Putnam's wife found out what was happening and informed her husband, who obliged them to withdraw it, 'afraid of legal entanglements', and deprived them of their temporary editorial posts. The 'New Instinctivism', a long, funny and not overly-sensitive document, remained unpublished; but it provided an interesting harbinger of things to come, and gave Miller the gob of spit he needed for the face of art on the first page of *Tropic of Cancer*.

Christmas was approaching, and Miller's fortieth birthday. His health was good, and a description of him at this time by Wambly Bald depicts him as a young-old man of medium height, very slim, bald-headed, with a springy, youthful gait that made him look nineteen at a distance. He wore jauntily what Bald called a 'boy's cap', and the cigarette drooping from his mouth gave him 'an alert, snappy kid appearance'.[28]

Miller himself, approaching the birthday, did not feel much like a snappy kid. In spite of the youthful fun of New Instinctivism, he was beginning to feel the passage of time. In a Christmas greeting to Emil Conason he wrote that he was now 'almost forty years of age, a little balder, my gold tooth is more prominent, I have grown thinner, more aged, etc etc. No, I am not the man I used to be.' For the first time, the difference in age between himself and his wife was becoming a factor in their relationship. 'June is disappointed,' he wrote. 'She wants me to get younger, more pep, more romanticism.' She had found him 'too acquiescent, too phlegmatic, too cranky, querulous, critical etc etc'.[29] This was the familiar disappointed mood of Christmasses past, but the letter contains something else: a growing sense of self-certainty and self-confidence that seemed to embarrass him slightly. June's criticisms were hurtful precisely because Miller was beginning to feel proud of being 'acquiescent'. To him it seemed not a sign of dullness but a philosophical breakthrough, an 'answer' of the sort he had been looking for ever since schooldays, Challacombe and Mills, Chula Vista, the discovery of Madame Blavatsky, Elie Faure, Oswald Spengler and his other synthesist heroes.

Miller knew that Conason was his least indulgent critic, and before getting down to the revelation that he had had a philosophical breakthrough he carefully prepared his friend. He described himself with justification and pardonable pride as one of the few American expatriates who had genuinely embraced French culture rather than simply using it as a backdrop against which to carry on living an essentially American way of life. He had become acquainted not only with the historical greats of French literature but also with the works of lesser-known domestic favourites like Georges Duhamel, Jean Giono and Blaise Cendrars. His letters home to New York had been breathless, excited missives, always enthusiastic about every aspect of this new life he had made for himself; now, in a rare dropping of the mask to Conason, he conceded that Montparnasse was 'a sad place. Despite the lechery and the drunkenness these people are really unhappy.' Yet though he placed himself *in* this 'sad place', he insisted that he was definitely not *of* it. The great sense of detachment he felt from the life around him seemed to him to be moving him in the direction of almost religious egotism, one that placed at the pinnacle of individual aspiration in difficult and turbulent times the task of taking great care of oneself and one's contentment. This was the liberating realization. He told Conason that he had at last 'stopped looking. I am fixed, resolved, happy. I turn slowly with the wheel because I am at the hub.' These were plangent claims, and he was sufficiently shy about making them to add a throwaway invitation to Conason to 'trot out your philosophy now and ridicule me. I invite it.' For philosophy it was, and though great breakthroughs presently reveal themselves to be regular occurrences in Miller's life, the belief that he had actually found a mental attitude of lasting value to himself and others during his first eighteen months in Paris remains the most persuasive of these epiphanies.

11

In this mellow mood he even briefly began to feel that he might be 'sick of gathering experiences', and the fact that Wambly Bald's column of October 14th was entirely devoted to him and the romantic squalor of his daily life did not delight him as much as it might have done, since he was, by his own account, largely responsible for writing it himself. This was just one of many instances of the active interest he took in the creation and shaping of his own fame. He described himself for *Americans Abroad*, a directory put together in 1931 by Peter Neagoe, Samuel Putnam's assistant editor on the *New Review*, as not only a writer but a retired Six-Day Bike racer and concert pianist who had made his way through life with 'no schooling'. About the only true statements he made were that he had come to Paris to 'study vice' and that in his spare time he 'practiced sainthood'. These are fine ironies, but they would have been funnier and more impressive without the 'nature-child' lies about being an uneducated concert pianist and professional athlete. Even Perlès had received a distinctly exaggerated account of his friend's life in the pre-Parisian days. He had apparently 'been all over America, hitch-hiking, begging, scrounging his way over the length and breadth of that enormous continent', and had 'often spent the night on a park bench or in a local gaol'. Wherever Miller went, people had helped him along; often these helpers were 'mere tramps, not much better off than himself', and 'now and then it was a woman who took him in for a night, or for a fortnight'. All this before he married Beatrice, by which time he was, so he told Perlès, 'a past master in the art of living by his wits'.[30] Evidently the dividing line between fact and fiction, truth and lies, was getting finer all the time. Henry Miller was turning into 'Henry Miller', and the process of bibliomorphosis in which he had engaged was nearing its successful completion.

June had returned to New York, but he knew by now that he would not be following her for a long time. June, with her 'cockeyed idea of France and the French', would never move to Paris and, as he told Schnellock, he would rather 'go on living here even as a *garçon* in a bistro than live the routine life of New York in a swell apartment'. The situation would have been best served by plain speaking, but plain speaking has a tendency to take all the fun and drama out of life. In any case he was still very fond of June. What was missing from the marriage was something she could not possibly provide him with, what the love-addict craves most of all – the thrill of the first flush of a new affair.

CHAPTER TEN

1931–1933
The second triangle: Henry, June and Anais

1

Since arriving in Paris, Miller had had two or three pretend love-affairs. Besides the inverted romanticism of the affair with Madame Deaugard, he had briefly been the lover of a woman named Bertha Schrank while her husband Joseph, a successful writer of musicals, was out of the way in America. Mrs Schrank's main attraction for Henry was that she bore a physical resemblance to June. Apart from that they had little in common, and though they toyed briefly with the idea of running away together to Russia the affair soon foundered on its own tedium. Henry's only regret when it ended was that Bertha refused to let him have his love-letters back. He wanted to make use of them in his book.

The enthusiasm for the prostitute was a romantic joke, and the relationship with Bertha Schrank a physical matter. Until Miller met Anais Nin, no woman had seriously threatened June's place in his life. The meeting was arranged by their mutual friend, Richard Osborn, who was doing some legal work for Nin in connection with a publishing contract for a book she had written on D.H. Lawrence. Osborn had done a good job of promoting his talented friend to Anais, and she had seen Henry's appreciation of Bunuel in the *New Review*. More important, she had seen extracts from the assemblage of materials that had become, by late 1931, his work-in-progress, *Tropic of Cancer*. June had returned yet again to Paris as part of her continuing struggle to break the mysterious hold the city had established over her husband, and it was no doubt she who encouraged him, in the first instance, to cultivate the wealthy Nin as a good milk cow. When, in early December 1931, Osborn set up the meeting at Nin's house at Louveciennes, June was included in the invitation. For tactical reasons, however, she decided to remain behind and Henry went alone. It was a mistake from June's point of view, for she had not realized how ripe her husband was for another experiment in love.

The first meeting went off extremely well. Everything about Nin

191

impressed Miller. She had dark good looks similar to June's, but gave an impression of great physical frailty. She was an avid reader, and could discuss intelligently Henry's current literary heroes Dostoevsky and Proust. As regards her devotion to D.H. Lawrence and psycho-analysis, she was already ahead of him. The meal, which they shared with Osborn, was a great success. Nin liked what Miller said, but was struck even more by his relaxed personality and his obvious ability to savour the joys of the moment. He liked to advertise his happiness, and clearly did not subscribe to the conventional wisdom that it dies the moment one begins to talk about it. Nin was, by contrast, a fully-fledged neurotic who found his irrational and shameless contentment a revelation. The conclusion of this most successful evening was that he was invited back to celebrate New Year's Eve at Louveciennes.

2

Anais Nin's background was more exotic than anything June could have dreamed up for Henry's delectation. She was born in Paris in 1903, the daughter of Joaquin Nin y Castellanos, a Spanish composer and concert pianist, and Rose Culmell, a Danish singer. As a child she was close to her father, and travelled with him on his concert tours through Europe. His desertion of the family in 1913 was a great blow to her. The following year her mother settled with her and her two brothers in New York City where Anais began her practice of keeping a diary of her thoughts. In Cuba in 1923 she met and married Hugh Guiler, a wealthy young banker with whom she returned to Paris in 1925 when he was assigned to the First National Bank office there. Guiler's salary was paid in US dollars, which allowed them to live well in the fashionable parts of Paris, to run a car and keep a succession of Spanish maids. After the Wall Street Crash of 1929 they had to give up their apartment on Boulevard Souchet and moved to Louveciennes on the outskirts of the city. Here, in a rambling old house which had once belonged to the estate of Madame du Barry with a large and wild garden at the rear, she soon found that she had been incarcerated in a 'beautiful prison'. 'I mend socks, prune trees, can fruits, polish furniture,' she wrote in her diary, 'but while I am doing this I feel I am not living'.[1]

From this living death she was rescued by an interest in the novels of D.H. Lawrence. These appealed to her so much that she wrote her short book in appreciation of his work, singling out for particular praise *Lady Chatterley's Lover*. The publisher of the Paris edition of

Lawrence's book, Edward Titus, agreed to publish her *Passionate Appreciation*, and assigned his assistant Lawrence Drake to work as her editor on the manuscript.

Drake soon realized that Nin's marriage to Hugh Guiler had turned into some kind of genteel sexual disaster (she later confessed to Miller that, after seven years with Guiler, they still made frequent use of vaseline) and made a quick attempt to seduce her which she only partly repulsed, permitting him to ejaculate between her legs 'out of pity'. Afterwards she related the incident to her husband 'partially, leaving out my activity'. With the realization that she felt no guilt over the matter, a whole new world of possibilities opened up to her, one that provided a matchless cure for her boredom as well as giving her something to write about in her diary.

What Nin needed was someone worth being unfaithful for, and Henry fitted the bill on several counts. A part he could play most successfully in Paris, since it was only partly acting, was that of the noble savage, or, as far as nice ladies were concerned, 'a bit of rough'. His boast in *Americans Abroad* of having 'no education' was a part of this act, like the representation of himself as a rambling hobo and ex-gravedigger rather than someone who had lived, largely on his wife's earnings, in a succession of occasionally small but usually quite comfortable Brooklyn apartments. Nin was excited by the violence and the primitivism of the extracts from *Tropic of Cancer* which Osborn had shown her, and even before Henry arrived for that first meal together she was looking forward to an encounter between 'delicacy and violence'.

When Henry returned to June from Louveciennes that evening, she found his mood disturbing. Instead of joining her in the mockery of another rich sucker with artistic pretensions he was unnaturally quiet. June asked him how the evening had gone and he shrugged and said: 'Oh, so-so.' What was Nin like? She was like a bird. June asked him what kind of bird, but he declined to elaborate. She knew him sufficiently well to recognize that Anais had made a strong personal impact, and that evening they had the first in the short series of explosive rows that would mark the route to the end of their marriage. She would not give in without a fight, however, and made sure she accompanied him for the next meeting at Louveciennes on New Year's Eve.

She was determined to out-weird Nin that night, and dressed for the occasion in her red velvet dress with a hole in one sleeve and her velvet cape; she covered her hair, now shoulder-length and a colour described by Bald as 'a gold-kissed rust, almost red', with a battered slouch hat and wore, as usual, no stockings and a single cat's eye earring. Henry annoyed her by asking her, as they left the hotel, to be sure to watch her language at the Guilers. He was usually the one whose language was unpredictable; with prudes or with what June called holier-than-thou people he was liable to use the most shocking vocabulary, while he was propriety itself in the company of whores. As far as she knew, Nin did not seem to fit into either category.

The maid Emilia served up a soufflé of carrots, and Nin enjoyed the disorientated discomfiture of her working-class guests:

They were already hypnotized by the oddness of Louveciennes, the coloring, the strangeness of my dressing, my foreignness, the smell of jasmine, the open fires in which I burned not logs but tree roots, which look like monsters. The soufflé looked like an exotic dish, and they ate it as one eats caviar. They also ate purée of potatoes which had been made airy with a beaten egg. Henry, who is thoroughly bourgeois, began to feel uncomfortable, as if he had not been properly fed. His steak was real and juicy, but cut neatly round, and I am sure he did not recognize it. June was in ecstasy.[2]

June's enjoyment of the meal was spoiled by Anais's pet chow, Ruby, which sat beneath the table masturbating against her leg as she ate. June's powerful erotic signals were also picked up by Ruby's mistress, who developed in the course of the evening a quite fantastic infatuation with June. Nin invited her to visit again the following week on her own, and between New Year and June's departure in late January the two women spent a great deal of time together. On Nin's side at least these hours were a sort of tormented ecstasy, minutely recorded in her diary at the close of day. Yet despite the fervour in her account of her emotional turmoil, she never quite manages to convince us that the experience was part of an important and heroic search for her real self rather than merely another leg in the flight from the banality of everyday life.

June was partly to blame for the situation in wishing to be thought of as unusual, though one suspects that, of the three of them, she was the most clearly aware of the real extent to which they were all playing emotional games. As Henry had done, she allowed Anais's innocence to encourage her in her promotion of a weird image, hinting strongly to her of a life of unorthodox sexual practices with Mara Andrews, and of orgies of drug-taking in Village vice dens. Anais refused to play the bourgeois wet and countered with an aggressive intimacy, asking June point blank if she were a lesbian and getting an evasive answer which was actually a 'no', followed by a swift attempt to steer the conversation round to the subject of clothes.

Yet June continued for a few days to go along with the flirtation, almost as though sensing Nin's desire to play at Real People by taking over the position left vacant in the original New York triangle by the departure of Mara. Nin dreamt about June at night, and June revealed that she was so fond of Nin that, under other circumstances, she would like to have taken opium with her. They dressed for each other. June came to their meetings carrying the battle-scarred Count Bruga at Anais's special request. They flirted intensely with one another, went shopping hand in hand, and in general carried on like adolescent schoolgirls discovering sexuality for the first time. At one point June walked along with Anais's hand on her bare breast. They even exchanged a mouth kiss. 'Henry is uneasy. Hugo is sad,' Nin confided to her diary; yet in essence it was self-delusion, disguising a fierce skirmish between the two to see who was going to win the battle for Henry.

One sympathises with June in this situation. In the middle of this whirlwind courtship, in a moment of absolute good sense, she told Henry that 'Anais was just bored with her life, so she took us up,'[3] and bravely repeated the remark to Anais, hoping perhaps to put an end to the nonsense. Anais was enjoying herself too much, however. In her diary she dismissed the remark as 'crude' and 'the only ugly thing I have heard her say'.[4] Yet Henry later confessed to her that his first thoughts after meeting her were 'cruel, cold ideas of using you'.[5]

In the two or three weeks during which Nin and June were together, Anais gained insights into June that Henry had been avoiding for years in order to nourish his mythification of her. When the time came for June to return to the States, Anais accompanied her as she went round the offices of the various steamship agencies trying to arrange for a reduction on the fare for a third-class passage back to New York, and watched in fascination the persuasive, alluring way June smiled at the clerks, and the eager way they responded. At the agency where she eventually bought her ticket she made a date with the clerk to have a cocktail with him at six the following evening. Outside she told Nin that she had no intention of meeting the man, she had simply used him. Nin was briefly horrified by the dishonesty of the exchange, comparing June unfavorably in her mind with a prostitute who at least delivers the goods: 'June would never give her body. But she would beg as I would never beg, promise as I would not promise unless I were to give.'[6] She heard June boast of her sexual inviolability, and saw in her 'a woman accumulating huge debts which she never intended to pay'.[7]

This single experience was enough to show her that June was a cock-teaser rather than the nymphomaniac of Henry's imagination. She also satisfied herself that June's lesbianism was at best a confused and sad attempt to strike up an intimate friendship in one unused to making friends among her own sex, at worst a mere bohemian pose.

195

What it manifestly was not was the expression of a deeply contrary sexual nature. Yet the moment June was safely embarked for the States in January, Nin joined Henry in a literary orgy of speculation about her. June became an important symbol to them both, though what it was she symbolized they were never quite able to articulate; in any case, their fervid discussions and dissections of her soon became chiefly a means of establishing great intimacy between them in a very short space of time.

3

In January 1932 Henry travelled to Dijon to begin work as a *répétiteur* in English at the Lycée Carnot, a job arranged for him by Hugh Guiler through the Franco-American Exchange Program. He was only required to teach nine hours per week, in return for which he received no wages, but board and lodging. He had happy memories of Dijon from a visit there during the summer cycling tour of France with June in 1928, but Dijon in the winter turned out to be a dismal disappointment, reminding him of London in its dreary chill, and in the end he stayed only three weeks.

He enjoyed this brief experience of teaching boys. His predecessors as *répétiteurs* had bored them with unimaginative projects such as reading aloud from American newspapers, and he quickly attracted a lot of attention and interest in his classes because of his anarchically informal teaching methods. With great regularity, class discussions would turn to the subject of women, and as news of this spread his classes rapidly grew in size.

There was another American teaching at the school, Lawrence Clark Powell, with whom Henry became friendly much later in life. At the time he preferred the company of the young *maîtres d'internat*, or *pions* as they were known. His spoken French, which had been almost non-existent in Paris, improved dramatically through his contact with these young men, and he developed a particular fondness for the subjunctive and made a point of using it as often as possible. One evening he made a round of the local dance- halls with the *pions*, and became violently infatuated with one particular girl whom he was told was a whore. He tormented himself with fantasies of how easily she would give herself to the first man who asked for her, yet was too shy even to ask her to dance. The absurdity of his responses delighted and amused him: 'Only a week here and *voilà, une femme!* Always seeking something to worship. Always choosing those who may be had for the asking. What a spectacle!'[8]

196

Henry also developed an almost religious fondness for the night-watchman at the school, a slow-talking man with a fat belly, red cheeks and a cropped head of hair. He could fall into ecstasies watching this man make his hourly rounds of the school with his lantern and his bunch of keys. Henry idolized him as the Great Clod, a beast designed by God for eating, sleeping and drinking wine.

He seems to have had no specific reason for taking up this unpaid job at Dijon. Probably it was a combination of the desire to get away from June and the wish to get on with his new book. From the moment of his arrival he wrote lengthy letters almost daily to Anais Nin, so it is possible that he realized he was close to being in love with her, and wanted to go away and think about it for a while. Apart from the earliest letters they exchanged, he and Nin were soon on the literary equivalent of farting terms, and his letters to her from Dijon are among the best he wrote as he strove to amuse, impress and win her.

While at Dijon he was deeply engrossed in reading Proust and many of his letters to Nin refer to his reactions to the experience. He was still as convinced as ever that the important lesson of the act of reading was not to translate literature into life but to alchemise life into literature. His obsessive certainty that his life with June would be the great subject of his writing led him to develop the comparison with Proust's Albertine. He remained puzzled by the rumours that Proust was a homosexual who had disguised his lover as a female character but when Nin wrote back to confirm them he replied that he realized that, in the end, the sex of any 'real' Albertine was of no consequence: 'What we are enthralled by is the vast panorama of deceit, treachery, lying, jealousy. It's the phenomenon and not the creature who provokes it.'[9] He had clearly outgrown the stage of sweaty palms that had plagued Tony Bring in the presence of homosexuals.

In one of his earliest letters to Nin, Miller characterizes himself as someone who was 'aware, aware, aware'. This was Nin's problem too, reflected in the insistent mirror-gazing of the daily diary. It was this obsessive self-scrutiny which consititued the major bond between them. Where they differed was in the way in which Henry contrived somehow not to be crippled by this inordinate degree of self-consciousness, learning how to deal with it and even using it to his advantage. Thus it is reasonable to suppose that the serial sexual confessions contained in his early letters to Nin were calculated ploys aimed at presenting himself to her as an interesting sexual being and potential lover. He referred to the infatuation with Bertha Schrank, a married woman known also to Anais Nin, and wrote: 'But I must admit I loved her . . . for a while. I suppose I'll go on loving, one after the other, this way, but June always holding me, negating them all, proving to me how insignificant are the others. God, if she only realized how tremendous is my passion for her. She would never then be the least jealous.'[10] A romantic statement like this to a very attractive young married woman he had only just met was clearly a come-on, and a way of getting across the message that adultery held no terrors for him. In a letter of February 4th he also referred to some writing he had done on 'The Mansfield Woman', a deindividualization of June which Nin quickly aped and which presently became one of the most unattractive features of their correspondence.

As well as freely discussing his own sexual nature with Nin, he lent her a copy of *Crazy Cock* to read. Her reactions to the novel became the subject of several letters between them, in one of which she expressed special interest in Blanche's (Beatrice's) criticism of Tony's (Henry's) 'hypersexuality', which may have illustrated Henry's honesty as a confessional writer but was also an autobiographical author's cute way of boasting of his sexual prowess. The same might also be said of the letter in which Henry told her that her attempts to compare him to Casanova made him laugh: 'You don't know yet what men are like, pardon. I am fairly normal. It is true I swim in a perpetual sea of sex but the actual excursions are fairly limited.'[11]

On February 21st Henry wrote to tell her that he was returning to Paris. Perlès had managed to get him a permanent job on the *Tribune* as assistant finance editor, working an evening shift for 1200 francs (about $45) per week, and would be willing to share his hotel room with him until they were able to find an apartment of their own together. Nin had already shown her willingness to support the Millers financially: in January, at the height of her infatuation with June, she had given her 400 francs which she and Henry got rid of in one night. Henry now applied to her for enough to pay his fare back to Paris, his taxi to the station, his laundry and his newly-repaired shoes. He explained that the money she had already sent him had gone on meals out. The free meals offered by the school were not good enough.

4

Nin spent the first week in March posing for an artist friend of hers in Montparnasse, and on Friday the fourth she and Henry met at the *Rotonde*. Nin again forced herself into a triangular love situation with the Millers, puzzling and fascinating Henry with talk of her 'torment' at hearing about the influence of Mara Andrews on her beloved June. Henry's letters had done their work well, and her fascination with him was becoming increasingly erotic. She relished the contrast between the violence of his writing and the softness of his person, the 'soft voice, trailing off, soft gestures, soft, fine white hands'. Yet the courtship insistently hid behind literature, as though both needed constantly to remind themselves and each other of the fact that they were writers in order to justify and excuse the infidelities they contemplated. At one point during their meeting at the *Rotonde*, as Anais sat reading aloud to Henry from *her* notes on the effect *his* notes had had on her, he reached out and tried to take hold of her hand. She withdrew it. The following day she wrote to him in purple ink on silver paper: 'I will be the one woman you will never have.' On March 5th they met at the *Vikings*, on rue Vavin, where Henry made a declaration of love to her. Anais was still not quite ready to give in. Her resistance precipitated a sudden swoop into complete humility in which he berated himself for his presumptions: 'I'm a peasant, Anais. Only whores can appreciate me.'[12]

This feeling of class inferiority was real enough, and picks up the echo of his mother's snobbishness that had been sounding throughout his life. He had inherited this trait, and despised himself for it, for there is something both tragic and ridiculous in a snob with nothing to be snobbish about. Not all his wild fantasies about June's magnificence and her extraordinariness could prevent him from knowing that she was, in essence, a rough, working-class girl from a poor immigrant family in Bensonhurst. Nin, on the other hand, socially, materially and intellectually, was the refined one, the real princess, and her attitude to sex was as mind-perverted as any Victoria, any Edvarda, any Miss Julie. For all her respect for his talent and his determination, she saw him initially (and quite specifically, in her diary) as a Mellors figure to her Lady Chatterley, and she was amused by his social discomfiture and his ignorance of the fine wines and fancy food he tasted at her table. He complained frequently to Nin of June's 'vulgarity', yet was dogged by a sense of shame about his own vulgarity, his brashness, his Americanness. Even on the face of the cultured Perlès he believed he could read contempt when, for example, he asked for information about some intellectual giant of European culture whose name he happened to have come across in his reading and received the reply: 'Oh, he's not for *you*, Joey*.'[13] He told Anais later: 'Your background scared me.'

---

*Miller and Perlès often called each other 'Joey' as a way of reminding themselves that they were basically clowns.

His sincerity and his extraordinary truthfulness about his own weakness finally persuaded her to capitulate, and on the night of March 8th they climbed the stairs to his room at the Hôtel Central and became lovers. June's photograph observed them from the mantelpiece. Miller cried out how swift and unreal it all was. Afterwards he covered Nin's legs with her coat and asked her whether she had expected him to be more brutal.

5

The egocentric nature of both Miller and Nin inevitably leads to a cynical reading of their affair as the meeting of a pair of supersouls, heroically committed to a process of self-discovery in which the feelings of a couple of non-writing mere mortals like June and Hugh Guiler could hardly be expected to matter. But beneath the breezy Nietzschean way they joined together, their psychological problems became their shared interests. Nin in particular was utterly convinced of the value and truth of the psychoanalytic description of personality and was fascinated by the idea that her promiscuous longings were dictated by an unconscious desire to emulate her father's Don Juanism and so associate herself with him in some sort of incestuous relationship.

Possibly she passed this fascination with incest on to Henry who, shortly after meeting Nin, began making extensive notes of all he could recall of his own childhood, his earliest memories, his friends, his fears, ambitions and prejudices. These notes, which formed the genesis of his second published novel, *Black Spring*, were drawn up in simple, unadorned fashion and read like a lucid confession delivered from the psychoanalyst's couch. One of the keynotes of this confession is incest, the latent incest of his mother's cloying and possessive love for him, and the real incest of his Tante Carrie and her brother in a hayloft over the saloon at Maspeth which had resulted in the birth of his feeble-minded cousin George Insel. Yet the curious thing about these revelations is that they are not accompanied by any sense of horror, or pain, or catharsis. Miller cannot shock himself, the world was always just so. His memories of George Insel and the scandal surrounding his origins become finally just rich and interesting memories, pleasurable as all memories are, a piece of folk-history, not a family skeleton clattering up from the depths of his unconscious.

Nin's interest in incest, on the other hand, was the expression of a genuine neurosis which disturbed her whole sexual balance. A month after her affair with Henry began she went into analysis with a Dr

René Allendy to try to find out more about it. The analysis soon acquired strong erotic overtones, and before long the doctor and his patient were indulging in heavy petting sessions leaning up against his bookcase. Allendy became jealous of Henry and wearied of hearing Nin praise his masculinity. One day he surprised her by suggesting that her 'hundred-per-cent man'[14] of a lover was actually a latent homosexual[15] whose lack of a strong, protective instinct was what betrayed his real nature. Later Allendy abandoned his pretensions to reason entirely and promised her that if Henry ever harmed her, by writing about her or by using her letters, he would personally go after him with a whip.[16]

Nin's diary for the first year of her affair with Miller presents in general the picture of someone desperately trying to become something other than she was. Allendy's 'scientific' analysis of her behaviour lent a spurious dignity to her experimenting and excused her infidelity, and the use she made of psychoanalysis in general during this period serves to confirm many of the doubts expressed about the honesty of the method from the beginning, notably that it would be used to justify promiscuity under the guise of searching for an imagined real self. Nin's profound dissatisfaction with the self she was born with was symbolized by her decision later in the year to have her very slightly crooked nose surgically straightened.

Beside incest and psychoanalysis, two other interests which Nin quickened in Henry were for the novels of D.H. Lawrence and for astrology. He had resisted Lawrence since the early 1920s and Emil Schnellock's too-keen promotion of him during their walks in Prospect Park, but the recommendations of a desirable woman have a special authority, and he was soon deeply immersed in his works. In return Henry offered Anais his enthusiasm, and the encouragement he offered to every would-be writer he ever came across, regardless of whether they were talented or not. His religion of encouraging others led him in time to develop an enjoyably eccentric set of literary standards in which quality was rarely the decisive factor. Nin's diary was in its forty-second volume by the time he met her, and it was the sheer size of the enterprise that impressed him more than anything else. He once described it to a friend as containing 'over a million and a half *more* words than Proust's complete works', before adding almost parenthetically that it was 'infinitely more valuable to the world, I think'.[17]

After the beginning of the affair in March 1932, their greatest shared interest was always June, and the problem of how to deal with her. Henry's first reaction was that he had entered some kind of slightly problematic paradise from which he was determined not to be evicted: 'I'm not going to let her go,' he wrote to Nin, 'but I'm not going to let you go either. I don't care what sort of situation develops – only you must not betray me. I love June and I love you.'[18] He told Anais: 'If I were made to feel that I had to choose between her and what I call my art, I would choose her,' and yet he continued to direct fierce, personal complaints about his wife to Anais which could only encourage her in hopes of an eventual triumph. Often the nature of these complaints reveal that what Henry disliked most about June was her obstinate insistence on having her own mind, her own opinions, her own friends:

It is this that infuriates me about June – her going out to meet all sorts and rhapsodizing about the wrong ones. If you knew Bob McAlmon, for example, how would you feel, I wonder, if you heard June talk about him? It would make you retch. Why she even handed me a couple of his stories to read, thinking no doubt that I would find some good in them. Bob McAlmon is one of the vilest creatures alive. And then there is Bodenheim – you should see how he greets June! Well, if I saw you making such errors I would lose faith in you.[19]

In May, June cabled Henry that she missed him and would join him soon; in July, Henry, who had briefly become her 'Heinrich', wrote to reassure Anais that June had not yet returned, 'nor do I want to see her back'.[20] In August, a 100-word cable arrived from June in America which Henry at once forwarded to Anais with a message that she wouldn't actually be coming until October: 'This is just a preliminary barrage, as usual.' The possibility that such an extravagantly long cable was in any way an expression of June's unhappiness was firmly rejected – she did it to impress someone she was with: 'it certainly wasn't anguish that prompted it.'[21]

As June's plans to return to Paris in the autumn went forward, Henry became increasingly agitated. He knew from past experience that he would be unable to tell June to her face that the marriage was over, and he more or less pleaded with Anais to save him from her.

By this time Anais was becoming a little tired of hearing about June. Some of the letters Henry sent to her were wonderfully direct and erotic, leaving her in no doubt about the degree of sexual pleasure and happiness he was enjoying with her. Though not sexually aggressive in the way June had been, she had the same open fondness for lovemaking on floors, in chairs, in kitchens. Henry taught her to suck his penis until he came in her mouth, and though she wrote romantically about the experience in her diary – 'His kisses are wet like rain. I have swallowed his sperm. He has kissed the sperm off my lips. I have smelled my own honey on his mouth'[22] – she confessed to

Allendy that she did not much enjoy the experience, and did it only to please her lover. Under his tuition Nin was rapidly shedding her sexual innocence, and Miller had characteristically ambivalent feelings about this. He told her that he did not enjoy hearing her tell obscene stories because it did not suit her personality, and he disappointed her by refusing to introduce her to the more disreputable of his friends and acquaintances. But what she resented most of all as time went by was his habit of constantly comparing her to June. Once, after an especially enjoyable afternoon at Louveciennes, he praised her for being 'almost more sensual than June'.[23] His vacillation over June, his taking refuge in his weakness as 'honesty', brought her patience with him close to breaking point, and in some sharp letters in the early autumn she made it clear that she was willing to break with him rather than continue to allow him to play June off against her. 'Don't come and show me the immediacy of your *humaneness*,' she wrote. 'Behind your humaneness there is always a great evaluator.'[24]

Her strong stand paid off. At the end of September, a few days before June was expected, he wrote to reassure Anais that when his wife arrived 'I'll face the issue soundly, with a clear head, and a strong will. (. . .) I am a different being now than I was a year ago. She'll feel it. I won't tolerate any drama, nor any compromise.'[25]

6

In mid-October June arrived. She stayed for ten days at the Hôtel Princesse before contacting Henry at the apartment in Clichy which he was sharing with Alfred Perlès. When she did come to see him, a major disappointment was that she had not brought with her from New York his collected works of the 1920s. His disappointment was one of the few triumphs she was to know in the psychic war which now began in earnest between the two and which reached a tragi-comic climax some eight weeks later when the marriage was finally destroyed.

Henry at once rang Anais and in a grave, bewildered voice told her that June was in a 'decent mood, subdued and reasonable', and warned Anais that she wanted to come out to Louveciennes to see her. The following day she arrived and poured out her heart to Anais. Henry was a kind of Frankenstein, she told Nin. He was trying to create a monstrous image of her in his writing, simply in order to make his life seem exciting:

It is Henry who has made me complex, who has devitalized me, killed me. He has introduced literature, a fictitious personage from whom he could suffer

203

torments, whom he could hate; because he can only write when he whips himself by hatred.(. . .) It is he who seeks dramas and creates monstrosities. He does not want simplicity. He is an intellectual. He seeks simplicity and then begins to distort it, to invent monsters, pain etc. It is all false, false, false.[26]

Nin comforted her and played the rôle of benign mediator between two good, unhappy friends. 'I feel most human,' she told her diary, 'because my anxiety is protective, towards both of them.'[27] She encouraged June to continue believing in Henry, as a writer and a human being, and boasted that 'I am giving Henry and June to each other. I am the impersonal revealer.' When her guest left, after three hours, Anais found her infatuation finally over: June had bored her. She watched her leaving in a taxi and the sight of June's childlike face through the rain and the glass only aroused her pity. 'How can I rescue her?' she asked herself. Apparently it never occurred to her simply to tell June the truth.

During November and December, Henry and June engaged in a series of arguments, brutal, bruising sessions that could last until six in the morning. June tried everything to hold on to him, including tears and shivering fevers in the middle of the night. She realised that Henry and Anais were lovers, but as long as neither one would admit it she was condemned to the hellish uncertainty of her suspicions. After the visit to Louveciennes she came home and told Henry what Anais had said about him, that deep down he hated women such as herself and Anais who were exotic or intelligent, and could really only love servants. Henry, utterly besotted by Nin, duly cancelled out June's gesture by reporting the indiscretion back to Nin. Nin felt betrayed by June, and considered herself henceforth free of obligation towards her: 'My loyalty to June was from then on unnecessary. She had none.'[28]

With astonishing insensitivity Nin even turned up at the apartment in Clichy one night to participate in the argument, requisitioning it for her own purposes and engaging Henry in a 'brilliant interplay' – her own phrase – which reduced June to the rôle of dull spectator. Henry and June were drinking heavily, and after wandering out for some fresh air and to buy cigarettes Henry came back and went to bed. June sat with him for a while and tried to persuade him to drink something which would make him feel better. He refused to listen to her and in her humiliation she asked Anais to take over from her, while she retreated to the kitchen with Perlès, and asked over and over again: 'What are they doing in there?' A little later she threw herself at Perlès and began kissing him, then collapsed herself, vomiting and crying out: 'Val, Val, Anais, you are both too clever and cruel. Clever and cruel. I'm afraid of you both.' She told Anais to go away: 'Don't come near me – the smell – *you, you're* an aesthete – this is terrible, I'm so terribly sick, and tired – I want rest – won't you give me peace.'[29] Nin, who had drunk just one glass of white wine, wiped up the sick and slept the night on the bed, in her clothes, next to the drunken Millers.

Henry's reiterated grievance against June was that her presence made it impossible for him to work, either on *Tropic of Cancer* or on another book he was planning to write about D.H. Lawrence, as though the whole problem would be solved if she could only learn how to leave him alone to write. Rarely does the contempt for others latent in his personality emerge more clearly than in comments to Anais in his letter of October 21st: 'June . . . is making heroic efforts to be what I should like her to be – and I can't help but be touched by that.' Nevertheless his love for Anais is so great, he assures her, that when June visits her she is to feel 'free to do with her as you will – that's my gift to you'. He had, he said, 'treated her as if I were a psychoanalyst. Result is, she is content.'[30]

By the end of November he had managed to precipitate the break. 'Big blow-up – everything over at last, and a divorce in the offing,' he reported to Emil Schnellock. Remarkably, he had managed it thus far without incriminating Nin. June, however, remained in Paris, staying with friends in Montparnasse, and as long as she was still around the prospect of a relapse could never be discounted. Henry had effectively stopped writing and seemed to be declining into the same comatose impotence that had afflicted him back in 1923 when he was trying to leave Beatrice for June. On that occasion Stanley had come to his rescue – or so Henry believed – arranging the dramatic scene in which he was caught alone in the apartment with June. This time it was Alfred Perlès's turn to help. He suggested Henry take his manuscripts and disappear to London for a while until June had left. Henry agreed to the suggestion and between the two of them and Nin they managed to raise 1000 francs for the trip. They bought a return ticket at Cook's and changed the rest of the money into English pounds. As Henry was an American citizen no visa was necessary for the trip.

He was due to depart on December 18th. The night before he left June visited and found him sitting in the kitchen with his bags packed and his tourist folders about England spread out on the table before him. Sensing trouble, Perlès slipped away, leaving Henry to face June alone. They ate and drank their way through a 'bitter, nauseating conversation' that lasted several hours. Finally the truth emerged and June realized to the full the extent to which she had been betrayed by the two truth-seekers. She rose up and delivered a stream of invective on the subject of Anais which Henry listened to in humiliated silence. Always 'aware, aware, aware', he was even able to savour June's tirade in retrospect: 'the vilest threats and recriminations – so disgusting that I listened fascinatedly – awed by it.'[31]

The climax of the evening came when he handed over to June all the money Nin had given him to finance his flight to London. Miller told Anais that he broke down at this point, 'thinking of my betrayal of you,' but that fortunately for him June 'callously' interpreted his tears as a sign of weakness. His great terror was that June would go and reveal the whole story to Hugh Guiler. She did not, however, which suggests that for all her alleged infidelities, posturing and lying ('pathological lying', Henry called it, as distinct from his own 'creative lying'[32]) she had a distinct code of decency of her own. Her parting shot as she left him that night was: 'And now you have your last chapter for your book!'[33]

June remained in Paris, frightening, threatening and unpredictable, and a week later Miller made a second attempt to leave France and get out of her range, again with money provided by Nin and Perlès. The flight turned into a fiasco of a different kind as the immigration authorities in Newhaven who met him off the boat from Dieppe jailed him overnight as a potential vagrant (he only had 178 francs in his pocket) and grilled him for three-quarters of an hour the following morning. In the end they were convinced that he was mad, and because he was without visible means of support and could not provide the name of a guarantor in England, he was unceremoniously shipped back to Dieppe on the next boat. Miller was privately convinced that his treatment was connected with a diplomatic wrangle between the United States and Britain over the payment of outstanding War debts, and the experience sharpened his anglophobia, providing him with a useful theme for a later autobiographical improvisation, the short-story entitled *Via Dieppe–Newhaven*.

Back in France, he remained in hiding at Louveciennes for ten days until June, persuaded that he had fled the country, finally departed. She left a note in his apartment pencilled on a scrap of toilet paper: 'Will you get a divorce as soon as possible' which he duly dated and pasted into his Paris notebook, on page eighty-four, along with a receipt for 799 francs from Thomas Cook.

With this, June's active rôle in Miller's life was over. Aware that he had treated her in a cowardly and cruel fashion, he would sometimes burst out crying when he had been drinking and thinking about her. Nin was able to put his mind at rest. June was going to be all right, she assured him: one of her favourite astrologers had cast June's horoscope for her, and the prediction was that 'June will not be unhappy – in spite of Neptune – Venus and Sun make her strong, undefeated, imperishable'.[34] This was good news indeed, and confirmed Henry's growing faith in the usefulness of astrology. Unfortunately for June, the prediction was inaccurate.

CHAPTER ELEVEN

1933–1934
Tropic of Cancer and 'a half-dozen terrifying words'

1

The job on the *Tribune* as 'assistant finance editor' – the ostensible reason for Miller's precipitate return from Dijon – lasted less than six weeks. The newspaper was financially on its last legs, and as part of a rationalization process Henry was told in late March that as from April 15th his post would no longer exist. Briefly he had returned to the proof-reading room, noting the firming up of volatiles after yesterday's slump, the softness of pivotals, the rise in steel and the renewed stability in Abitibi; but the novelty wore off after a few days and he left, thus severing for all time his relationship with the world of proper jobs.

The drama of the involvement with Anais Nin and June had provided him with just the kind of stimulus he needed as a writer. At Putnam's suggestion he had sent off *Crazy Cock* to Pat Covici of Covici-Friede in New York; but he really only did so out of a sense of loyalty to the manuscript. The 'fuck everything' book, the book that had materialised from nowhere, out of his letters, his notes, his conversations, the films he saw and the novels he annotated, was the real thing. Between the decisive first reference to *Tropic of Cancer* on August 24th 1931 and its eventual publication in September 1934, it went through four more or less complete rewrites – the last as late as the summer of the year of publication. Such activity reflects in part the desire to improve the word-for-word quality of the prose; even more clearly it indicates the extent to which the book was a real attempt to capture the present moment. His life at the time was a flood of social, sexual and intellectual adventure through which he waded like some Yankee Heraclitus, struggling fiercely to scoop up as much as possible into the pages of his book.

Two factors enabled him, from the spring of 1932 onwards, to devote his full attention to *Tropic of Cancer*. One was the association with the wealthy Anais Nin, which meant an end to his worries about money; the other was the move to the apartment at 4 avenue Anatole-France in Clichy with his friend Alfred Perlès, the scene of those distressing encounters with June during her last visit to Paris. The acquisition of a permanent address meant an end to the amusing but time-consuming and occasionally distressing problem of finding somewhere to sleep at night which he had faced intermittently ever since his arrival in Paris.

Clichy was a working-class district on the outskirts of Paris with a strong local tradition of communism. Its inhabitants were mostly factory workers and shop assistants who lived, according to Perlès, 'in comparative comfort and without poetry'. Number 4 was a new building in a row of modern apartment houses. After many nights spent doubling up together in Perlès's room at the Hôtel Central they now had the luxury of separate bedrooms, along with a bathroom and a kitchen. The rent was less than 300 francs per month each, well below ordinary hotel rates. The only drawbacks were the boring view from the window of corrugated iron roofs, smoking factory chimneys, railway lines and petrol pumps, and the fact that on their way back home after a night out in town they had to pass through a rough district. Henry planned to repossess a heavy Mexican cane that he had brought with him from America and presented to one of his good samaritans. Perlès threatened to buy a knife.

For a while Wambly Bald lived next door to them, and Henry's Paris edition of the three musketeers all bought bicycles and took a regulation afternoon ride at four o'clock each day. Another of their shared enthusiasms was the cinema, and when the Tour de France was in progress they would combine pleasures and go along to the cinema every night to watch the latest newsreel reports of the race.

At this time Miller had a crush on a well-known dancer and actress called Mona Païva and pinned a picture of her to the wall above his washstand, as well as a photograph of Nin and two of June. He also put up some of his water-colours, and a large sheet of brown paper on which he built up a list of exotic and unusual words he wished to use in his writing.[1]

The fascination with Bald and his sexual obsessions soon paled. 'Cunt up to the ears' he may have been, but he was ultimately 'uninteresting as a human being – just a *character*'.[2] Miller had become a realist, but he clung tenaciously to his sentimentality as a souvenir of his adolescence. Bald was too young to understand this. He was too proud of his hardness and too proud of his lack of sentimentality. He referred to Henry as the man 'who stands for shit', and said of Miller's relationship with Anaïs Nin that 'he milked her, like he milked everyone he met'. This was close to *lèse-majesté*, and he was soon expelled from the gang; shortly afterwards he moved out of the district altogether. Miller was ruthless towards a friend fallen from favour, and crowed afterwards: 'Bald is paralysed. And now he has lost his best friend – Henry Val Miller, the one man he trusted implicitly.'[3]

Perlès, on the other hand, was every bit as enamoured of Anais as Miller was. He suffered torments at the casual way Miller treated her in front of him, and was particularly pained by an incident in which Miller dismissed him from the kitchen during one of her visits to Clichy so that he could have sex with her on one of the chairs. Miller liked to 'vulgarize' her a bit, as he put it. 'Oh Anais,' he would say, 'I don't know how you've learnt it, but you can fuck, you can fuck.'[4] Unlike Beatrice, she enjoyed his use of such words.

Anais was a frequent visitor to the apartment. Henry regarded her as 'my equal in every way',[5] and she was treated thus, staying up drinking and participating in the all-night talk sessions and tactical discussions on the assault on posterity. Sometimes she played the housewife, cooking and cleaning and doing the washing-up. Miller enjoyed her in these domestic moods, especially her way of singing as she went about the chores in what he described as 'a sort of inharmonic, monotonous Cuban wail'. Ever since the days of Pauline Chouteau he had interpreted such housewifely singing as a sign that his woman was sexually content.

As often as not it would be Henry himself who did the cooking and washing-up. Perlès recalled that 'he was always more German than Chinese in housekeeping matters'[6] and Nin, who had expected her first days and nights at Clichy to be 'sensational' and filled with Dostoevskian scenes was surprised to find 'a gentle German who could not bear to let the dishes go unwashed'. The distinctly unbohemian personal habits which disappointed June disappointed Anais also, and she soon lost her romantic illusions about his poverty: the stained hat and the hole in the coat he wore when he came to meet her one day struck her as 'willed poverty, calculated, intentional, out of disdain for the bourgeois who holds a purse carefully'.[7]

Miller's chaos, his wildness and bohemianism were more apparent in his writing discipline, or lack of it. He was a touch-typist, 'one of the fastest I had ever come across among writers,' according to Perlès, and on a good or a bad day he would still produce some twenty sides at the typewriter. Perlès exaggerates, however, in describing what came out as 'perfect sentences that required no subsequent polishing'.[8] Miller's first drafts now were of a much higher quality than the headlong rush at the dictionary of *Clipped Wings* back in 1923, but in the interests of simple comprehensibility he was always obliged to rework his 'spontaneous prose', much as he regretted the necessity for this. His remarkable willingness from this period onwards to promote fragments, notes and personal letters as documents worthy of publication might be simple egomania; but it may also reflect his search for an ultimate spontaneity and a presumed ultimate honesty in confessional writing – the notes from which he worked seemed to him to have 'a crude, raw flavour which is hard to recreate when I sit down for a final draft . . . they are written at maximum tempo, without a pause for mistakes. Often the language is poor, wrong words etc.'[9]

He chain-smoked *Gauloises bleues* while writing, often played music or burst out singing. In the afternoons he would put on his pyjamas and go to bed for a couple of hours. After a sleep he might rise and go for a long, aimless stroll, or take a ride on his bicycle. Never the careful writer with artistic problems à la Joyce, Beckett or Nabokov to solve, he could write quite happily in the presence of others, with a glass of wine beside his typewriter, turning round now and then to participate in the conversation. He was still, in a literal sense, playing at being a writer, and enjoying the paraphernalia of the rôle quite as much as the actual writing itself. When not working at the machine he would be 'fishing through dozens of opened books spread on the chairs, his bed and the floor, with coloured pencils in his hand to underline or copy certain passages. The walls of his room were virtually papered with tacked up pages torn out of books, his notes, quotations he would eventually use.' Wambly Bald, whose description this is, used to tease Miller about his 'literary larceny', to which Miller would laugh and reply that all writers were thieves: 'I steal something, twist it around in my own way and who's going to know the difference?'[10]

2

By July 30th 1932 the first draft of the 'fuck everything' book was complete and Henry wrote to tell Anais Nin that he had found a title for it: 'How do you like either of these – "Tropic of Cancer" or "I Sing the Equator"?'[11] A projected second volume was to be called 'Tropic of Capricorn' and a final volume simply 'God'. A literary agent named William Aspenwall Bradley had heard about Miller from a friend in the Franco-American Exchange Program, the body responsible for providing him with the job at Dijon, and wrote asking Henry to come and see him at his office on rue Saint-Louis-en-l'Ile. Henry went along, taking both the new book and *Crazy Cock* with him, and on August 8th Bradley wrote to tell him he had now read them both, and was especially keen to handle *Tropic of Cancer* which he found 'magnificent'. He asked Henry to visit him again to discuss possible publishers for the book.

The encounter with Bradley was Henry's first real break as a writer. After pursuing literary success for some ten years largely through the efforts of well-meaning amateurs like Joe O'Reagan, Emil Schnellock, A. E. Elkus, Leviticus Lyon and George Buzby, he now had the interest of a professional agent, a man whom Janet Flanner described in her *New Yorker* column 'Letter from Paris' as the 'leading agent and prophet here on transatlantic affairs'. At one time or another Bradley's clients included Gertrude Stein, John Dos Passos, Ezra Pound and Katherine Anne Porter. By September he had shown the manuscript to Jack Kahane of the Obelisk Press, and could report that Kahane shared his great enthusiasm.

Kahane was an Englishman from Manchester who had emigrated to Paris in the 1920s hoping to become a writer. He did manage a couple of meekly pornographic novels under the pen-name of Cecil Barr, but since 1930 his publishing activities as the Obelisk Press had been his main concern and his major source of income. He was proud to have published Joyce's *Haveth Childers Everywhere* and *Pomes Penyeach* and Richard Aldington's *Death of a Hero*, but his greatest financial coup had been to obtain from the dying Frank Harris in 1931 the rights to the four volumes of *My Life and Loves* which he published in his own edition in 1932. This move established his reputation as a man willing to take publishing risks, and he was especially glad to do so where literary quality could be married to the prospect of good sales figures, as was the case with *The Well of Loneliness* and Parker Tyler and Charles Henri Ford's *The Young and Evil*, which both profited from their scandalous reputations.

Whether at their suggestion or not, Henry had carried out by October 1932 a revision of the book that impressed both Bradley and Kahane, and Kahane provisionally scheduled *Tropic of Cancer* for publication at the end of February 1933. It was this date which Henry had in mind as he struggled in vain to impress the English customs officers during his abortive flight from June in the winter of 1932, that he was an as-good-as published writer. For a number of reasons, however, *Tropic of Cancer* had to wait for almost two more years before it was eventually published.

3

Throughout this period, Henry was seeing a great deal of both Michael Fraenkel, who had housed and fed him at the Villa Seurat for a few weeks in the summer of 1931, and Fraenkel's friend Walter

Lowenfels. Where Bald was an ultimately unsatisfactory version of his 'vulgar' New York friends Dewar and O'Reagan, Fraenkel and Lowenfels filled the conversational gap left by Emil Conason and Harold Hickerson. Lowenfels was a communist sympathiser, like Hickerson, while Fraenkel was an independent thinker and a philosopher. Both men were keen admirers of D.H. Lawrence and were among those students of psychoanalysis who preferred the subjective, hesitant theories of Jung to the dogma of Freud.

Fraenkel, the son of Lithuanian immigrants, had had a genuinely hard upbringing as a child-apprentice on the East Side, peddling candy to the sweat-shop workers in his spare time. As a young man he went into the encyclopedia-selling business, at which he had considerably more success then Henry, earning enough to retire to Paris in 1926, at the age of thirty, to become a writer. He had an intellectual obsession about death that he struggled to articulate in books like *Werther's Younger Brother*, published by his own company, Carrefour, in 1930, and in a later work called *Bastard Death: The Autobiography of an Idea*. Lowenfels was a promising poet who shared *This Quarter*'s Aldington Poetry Prize in 1931 with e.e. cummings, largely on the strength of his *Elegy for Apollinaire*. Together Fraenkel and Lowenfels had published a pamphlet entitled *Anonymous : the Need for Anonymity* which promoted the idealistic notion that writers should publish their works anonymously as a way of purifying their intentions of vulgar concerns about money and fame. In line with this idea *Werther's Younger Brother* was published anonymously.

It was Lowenfels who was instrumental in bringing Fraenkel and Miller together. He told Fraenkel that he had met someone who was 'not alive exactly, but certainly not dead. Alive in a kind of confused, old-fashioned way.' Fraenkel duly dropped him a note, Henry called and at once captivated Fraenkel:

He was a complete stranger to me, I didn't know a thing about him except for the few oblique remarks my friend Walter had dropped, and yet I felt perfectly at home and at ease with him the moment he entered the room and began to talk.[12]

Fraenkel presented Henry with a copy of *Werther's Younger Brother* when he left, and a few days later received a long letter containing phrases like 'made me jump to attention', 'great discovery', 'don't know where to begin', 'find myself thinking only in superlatives', 'applaud you humbly, sincerely' and so on. Miller's skill at judicious flattery was one of the keys to his survival during his worst periods of penury in Paris, and Fraenkel, delighted to hear what a great writer he was, gladly added his name to Henry's list of good places to eat. His pleasant apartment, his wealth and his publishing business

213

were additional factors in his favour; but beyond this simple pragmatism, Miller was genuinely delighted by Fraenkel as a person, regardless of what he really thought of his ideas. He knew that in this intense, articulate and distinctly eccentric 'weather prophet' he had found another main character to join Wambly Bald, Perlès and himself in his book.

Miller, Fraenkel and Lowenfels had many discussions loosely based on Fraenkel's 'death theories' in the early 1930s while Henry was carrying out his revisions of *Tropic of Cancer*. Henry enjoyed the apocalyptic level of the conversation in which statements like 'nothing can be written anymore because we are all dead' were commonplace, but he did not favour the overall seriousness of his companions' approach to solving the problems of human existence. The discussions they had with Miller usually involved their projecting serious ideas which he would then shoot down. What he valued most in Fraenkel as a person was his enthusiasm, a quality he prized highly and indiscriminately in people. 'Fraenkel', according to Miller, 'was the kind of person who believes one can win an argument. As for me, I played the game.' Both Lowenfels and Fraenkel patronised him slightly and addressed him as teachers address a brilliant but wayward pupil. He encouraged them in this attitude – in one of his letters to Lowenfels (he even corresponded with people he daily met in person) he wrote of 'your interest in my education', and suggested that 'if I mean as much to you as you do to me and if we are going to truly influence each other, for good or ill, then we ought more sedulously to exchange our notes after reading a book. Especially when the subject is one that the other fellow is hostile to.'[13]

Fraenkel liked to believe that these discussions about 'spiritual suicide' and the death theme were a major influence on Miller, and in later years was disposed to present himself as the *eminence grise* behind *Tropic of Cancer*; but in fact neither Miller nor Perlès, who participated often in the sessions, ever took him as seriously as he took himself. His work on a prophetic piece entitled *The Weather Paper* became the subject of a standing joke at avenue Anatole-France, where Miller and Perlès developed the habit of greeting each other with the heavily sarcastic query 'And how is the *weather* today?' Fraenkel's importance for the book and for Miller's thought was the opposite of what he supposed: his dreary and depressed metaphysics were what took the glamour *off* being an intellectual for Miller, and after years of trying to impress people with his abstruse reading habits and powers of logical thought, Henry began moving fairly swiftly in the opposite direction to Fraenkel, towards the Great Clod of Dijon, as his ideal and hero.

The period of Miller's association with Fraenkel and Lowenfels thus coincides with what was probably the one great turning point in his life – the final headlong rush through the barrier of intellectualism to discover the emptiness on the other side, and the pursuit and consistent cultivation thereafter of a religion of instinct, subjectivity and willed simplicity in an attempt to remain faithful to what he truly believed was his destiny : to practise his own form of class-solidarity and explicate as completely as possible in his writing his absolute ordinariness. In a letter to Emil Schnellock of October 14th 1932 he stated his position clearly : 'I feel good whenever an ordinary guy (rich or poor, educated or uneducated) gets a kick out of my pages. First I want to be read by the ordinary guys, and liked by them. Because I'm just the most ordinary guy in the world myself – a man living out of his solar plexus . . . I don't give a fuck about being *right* or *artistic* or *clear* – I only care about what I'm saying for the moment.'[14] Fraenkel saw with remarkable clarity what was so easily obscured by Miller's repeated insistence in later life that in writing *Tropic of Cancer* he had 'become himself', that in fact his whole aim in life, as a man and a writer, was not to 'become himself' at all, but on the contrary to *remain* himself.[15]

Yet Miller had too great a ballast of intelligence to become the quintessential Plain Man without the use of some kind of intellectual lever, and there are repeated references in his letters from the early and mid-1930s to 'China', a personal shorthand term he used to denote the admiration and sympathy he felt for the taoist philosophy of Lao-Tzu and Chuang Tzu. In the enigmas of the *Tao Te Ching* he found all his own inconsistencies and confusions hailed as essential aspects of a massive and diffuse philosophical world-picture which preached the interdependent relativity of all ideas and physical concepts, the absurdity of intellectual pedantry, the need for complete and cheerful fatalism and the inaccessibility of ultimate reality to words. Taoism had no rules and no dogma, and its only advice to would-be adherents was the injunction to discard wisdom and just flow along with things, with a full belly and an empty head.

From about this time onwards, Miller consciously worked to become the kind of person proposed by the *Tao Te Ching* as a Sage. The descriptions of himself which he liked best, 'the Happy Rock' and 'the Rock Bottom Man', were, like 'the Gread Clod', 'the Uncarved Block' and 'the True Man of Ancient Times', taoist terms denoting the man who has conquered his mind to regain his natural state. Whatever such a man does is always naturally right, as whatever a tree, a horse or a river does is right, since treeness, horseness and riverness are uncompromised by the corruption of thought. This is a daring vision, but its moral dangers are obvious, and Miller's breezy courage in going straight for it is what compounded the enigma of his reputation so violently during his lifetime, defining him as a saint to some and a psychopath to others.

His enthusiasm for China picked up a number of slender threads from his earliest childhood connected with that country and its people, commencing with the moving picture he had seen in a church hall in the 1890s of a pigtailed Chinaman walking across Brooklyn Bridge in the rain. It was an image that seemed shrouded in fascinating and slightly frightening mystery. The Chinese were the most feared of all immigrants into America. The infamous Exclusion Acts of the 1880s even set them apart from all others as their own class of prohibited being. To the respectable whites and superstitious blacks they were frightening figures, hatchet-men, dope-fiends, coolies, Fu Manchus and, as such, natural targets for the admiration of little Henry Miller, along with Aguinaldo and anyone else who could make his parents shudder. On trips with his father's shirts to the Chinese laundry, the strangeness of the proprietors, their shiny blue coats and the queer mixture of odours of exotic food and dirty clothes filled him with a frightened wonder. He knew, even then, that the Chinese thought that white people gave off a bad smell, and the knowledge pleased him. By 1933 he had revisited and penetrated these mysteries, and was a confirmed sinophile with an indiscriminate fondness for everything oriental. As well as the classic texts of taoism, he studied books on China and Chinese philosophy by scholarly popularisers like Herbert Giles and Richard Wilhelm. 'My clap-trap about China,' he called it in a letter to Walter Lowenfels, but 'China means a lot to me,' he wrote. 'Means everything.'[16]

4

Along with losses sustained in the 1929 Crash, Michael Fraenkel's publishing ventures had, by the end of 1932, seriously depleted the $100,000 he had brought with him to Paris in 1926, and he briefly returned to the bookselling business again to make up his losses. Within two years he had made $50,000 selling boatloads of re-maindered American books in the Philippines and in China. His business took him often to New York, where he got to know several of Henry's old friends, including Emil Schnellock and Harold Hickerson. Schnellock liked Fraenkel, but he did not have Henry's inhuman tolerance for people and by no means all of those whom Henry sent to him from Paris were equally to his taste. He did not like John Nichols the painter much, nor had he enjoyed Richard Osborn's visit.

216

By 1933 Osborn was back in the States, having been 'rescued' from the clutches of a French prostitute named Jeanne by Miller in an episode which Miller used to conclude *Tropic of Cancer*, and in May that year he took it upon himself to write a forty-two page letter to Henry giving him all the latest news about June, including the information that she was now being escorted around the Village by a man 'considerably your junior', and that she felt extreme bitterness towards Henry, especially at the prospect of being exposed in his book about her.

The news devastated Miller. He sat down, began drinking and wrote a long letter to Emil Schnellock which, with his peculiar honesty, he described as 'absolutely sincere, sincere as a man can be who is weeping and at the same time examining the carbons to see if they are inked enough'.[17] Becoming increasingly confused as the letter went on, he struggled to preserve the mad equation of his feelings for her which he best summed up by the claim '*I love her still but do not want her*'. He struggled fiercely with his sense of guilt about the sacrifices she had made for him and the hardships she had experienced in sharing his life with him in the 1920s: 'When I think of how I pushed her in the streets, cold bitter nights when we were selling the leaflets, or selling the candy, pushed her with love and vengeance and God knows what. I was mad, crazy. I loved her, and I was hungry. I was desperate. Nobody understood what I was, who I was. I wanted to be somebody.' His life without her was ghastly, he said, and while he offered to commit suicide if it would make her happy, the one thing he would not do was stop writing about her: 'I can't do that. That is my life.' He cursed her 'dirty little mean petty Jewish heart', 'her possessivity, her jealousy, her overwhelming sex and clawing beak'. She was his 'June Smith-Smerth-Mansfield-Miller-Cunt-Balls-Whore' whom he knew 'down to the roots of her insatiable cunt', and in the befuddled violence of his emotions she came to stand for an America he both loved and hated for 'what America did to me, through June, through B, through Muriel . . .'.

By the end of the letter his typing had gone to pieces completely as he raved against June and her 'five and cten tencet store athlete with his "considerably my junior" etc'. Osborn's pedantic formulation, not unthinkably a quite deliberate jab at Miller in return for the humiliations as well as the pleasures of the life the two shared at rue Auguste-Bartholdi in 1930, was what pained Henry the most. Twelve hours later he wrote a second letter to Schnellock deriding himself for his sentimental self-indulgence and confusion. Mindful of posterity's needs and the needs of his future biographers, he sent both the impassioned original and the cool and almost callous retraction in the same envelope. He called the episode 'last night's Sorrows of Werther'

217

and said that on reading his letter over he had laughed his head off. 'Never trust the author, trust the tale. If I say my heart is breaking, never believe me. It is just literature.' But such a sudden and complete disavowal was also 'just literature'.

Memories and news of June pursued him throughout that summer. Emil Conason's sister Betty came over for a few days in early June and they sat drinking Pernods and reminiscing under the awnings on the Place du Tertre on the Butte de Montmartre. Betty told him that June had visited Emil and wept bitterly over the break-up, and Henry ended the evening sick and drunk, not so much because of the Pernod as because of the hopelessness of his life.

Having long ago wandered beyond the moral pale by leaving Beatrice and Barbara, he had to devise his own ways of trying to balance the equations of pain and guilt that his chosen course in life threw up, and if two wrongs don't make a right then they might at least make the wrong feel less wrong. Instead of practising a romantic fidelity to Anais Nin, his new love and partner in crime, he openly threw himself ever deeper into casual sex with paid partners. As further insurance against the establishment of feelings of sexual loyalty he also sometimes paid for these women with money Nin had given him.

His favourite whore in the summer of 1933 was expensive, stout as one of Renoir's models, and her maternal hugeness was her chief attraction for Henry: 'I want this one – her huge rolling torso that's like a cradle for me, the massive limbs that inspire me just to touch. I like bending down beneath her when she's undressing, her foot resting on a chair. I look up at her crotch, dark, mysterious, *big*, and I'm in heaven.'[18] He told Emil Schnellock he was in love with everything about her – her face, her voice, her wonderful talent for listening – 'And then to think that it's so easy to go with someone you really desire strongly. Just a little dough.' The state control of French brothels meant that such encounters were also largely free of the fear of contracting disease.

Miller passed this information on to Emil Schnellock as further proof that his recovery from the distress caused by Osborn's letter was complete. 'You said you were touched by the letter about June. Christ, yes! I was *real* for a half-hour.' He went on to confess that the particular cause of the pain was 'the image of June beside someone else', persuasive evidence that he knew full well that this was the first and possibly only time in their marriage she had taken a lover who really was her lover in the physical sense. He even knew who the man considerably his junior was: Stratford Corbett of the NY Life Insurance Company, the man whom June later married.

The immersion in the world of casual sex and the determined confinement of the whole of sex within the simple parentheses 'Cunt' was one way of warding off guilt and pain over the way he had treated June; another was the insistent consignment of experience into the mirror universe of fiction – quickly, before the reality of the experience could do harm. Thus his distress over the news about June was 'very "Albertine". Very'[19] and he looked forward some day to describing his sensations 'in full'.

5

In early June, Miller and Nin spent a week together in Chamonix before Henry vacated the bed at the Hotel du Fin Bec for Hugh Guiler and returned to the flat at Clichy. He spent some time there being sociable and helpful to his Uncle Dave, who was having a holiday in Paris with his wife, before setting off again almost immediately in company with Alfred Perlès for a cycling holiday. They took the train to Orlèans and rode towards Tours. Strong headwinds for eighteen kilometres exhausted and depressed Henry. The Loire valley and the castles didn't interest him, their hotel room at Blois was filthy and Perlès irritated him by riding a mile ahead of him and complaining about his being irritated. In the end Miller gave up and finished the journey to Tours by bus. By the time Perlès arrived on his bike, Henry had already bought his ticket back to Paris. 'Fed up with travelling. Fed up with little provincial towns, and with nature especially,' he wrote to Anais when he got back. 'I'm a man of the big cities, sorry to say. I realize it now only too well.'[20] As much as anything else, the trip had reminded him uncomfortably of the cycling holiday with June in 1928, and without the opportunity to write he found he had deprived himself of the most important anodyne in his life.

His inhumanly hectic literary activity during this period reflects both the attempt to document as fully as possible the flavour of the rushing present in his writing as well as the need to be constantly escaping this present, with its lurking guilt and pain, into the sinless and empty future. Apart from the revisions of *Tropic of Cancer*, he was now also working on a second attempt to describe his life with June, *Tropic of Capricorn*, as well as a book referred to as *Self-Portrait* which later became *Black Spring*, and filling sundry notebooks with his dreams and his descriptions of the people and places he found interesting. In addition there was the flood of letters to Anais Nin which were also being written with one eye on publication. ('There is already on hand a 900-page book of letters,' he wrote to Schnellock in October 1932; and in August 1933 Nin was urging him to 'Please *date* your letters!'[21]) He also dealt extensively in a world of imaginary projects like *The Palace of Entrails* which, to judge by the tree-like

219

diagram depicting the intended scope of the book, was an attempt to produce an ultimate synthesis of all human knowledge so far, from Adam and Eve via astrology to the 'birth trauma' theories of the Austrian psychologist Otto Rank.

6

The same tree-like diagram – probably inspired by Miller's fondness for the image of Yggdrasil, the World Tree of Nordic mythology – was also used for his most serious unpublished project at this time, a study of D.H. Lawrence. This was undertaken at the suggestion of Kahane, who was still holding back publication of *Tropic of Cancer* and had advised Henry that such a study might establish him as a serious writer among the reading public before throwing the bomb of his own book at them. In spite of his conviction that *Tropic of Cancer* was 'magnificent, overwhelming', the work of a powerful, formidable writer beside which *Lady Chatterley's Lover* and *Ulysses* were 'lemonade'[22], Kahane was concerned that the book might be dismissed as mere pornography. After initially resisting the idea as beneath his dignity, Henry agreed to produce what was originally referred to as a 'brochure' on Lawrence. Shortly afterwards he boldly trebled Kahane's suggestion and announced that he would be producing a full-scale study containing definitive accounts not only of Lawrence but of Proust and Joyce as well. Walter Lowenfels became particularly involved in this project. His enthusiasm for Lawrence led to the publication of his *Elegy in the Manner of a Requiem in Memory of D.H. Lawrence* by Carrefour in late 1932, and as a friend of Samuel Beckett he recommended Beckett's short study of Proust to Miller which Miller read with considerable enthusiasm.

The Lawrence book, which remained on his agenda until the early 1940s before finally being abandoned, was in some ways the last expression of the terrible struggle Miller had been waging to overcome the inhibiting effect on his own writing of influences from well-known or successful novelists. Indeed, his first thought on beginning the book was to annihilate Lawrence. 'The sin of Lawrence is his own "idealism",' he wrote to Schnellock. 'He hated man in favour of some unknown and abstract being who will never be born.'[23] Against this inhuman idealism he proposed to set his own absolute acceptance of life as it is: 'I do loathe it sometimes – but it's the world, Emil, and it isn't our fault, nor even our business to right it.' However, the simple desire to escape from the shadow cast by Lawrence's reputation soon became a fascination with his ideas, and he reverted to his adolescent habit of copying out lengthy extracts from the books he was studying.

What finally converted him to Lawrence was his reading of the 'Fantasia of the Unconscious', the essay called 'The Crown' collected in *The Death of a Porcupine*, and 'Apocalypse'.

His enthusiasm spelt the death of the project; by about the middle of 1933, after having 'devoted the best part of the last eight months or so to a study of him,'[24] he had become so involved in Lawrence's universe that he confessed he had lost all track of where Lawrence's ideas ended and his own began.

'How? Why?' was Tennessee Williams's outraged reaction in later years on hearing of the alleged influence of Lawrence on Miller.[25] The explanation is that it was not principally Lawrence's art that interested Miller, but his ideas on the relationship between the sexes, and even more, Lawrence's fierce pride in his status as an artist. Lawrence's description of the novel as 'the one bright book of life' and the uncompromising pride which led him to insist on the inherent superiority of the novelist to the saint, the scientist, the philosopher or the poet were bound to strike a chord in one who believed, as Miller believed, that religion was a product of art rather than art the by-product of religion, and who had grown up looking on the artist as a higher type of human being, closer to the priest, the sage or the healer than the skilled tradesman. Certainly Lawrence's courage in trying to write honestly about sex moved Miller and excited an identification with his subject, as did his insistence on the need to recognise at the individual level the existence and importance of sexual polarity, but he had encountered the notion before reading Lawrence, in Otto Weininger's book *Sex and Character*.

Ultimately, however, their differences were greater than their similarities. The strange juxtaposition of sex and religion which invests most of Miller's writing from this time onwards apparently had its real origins in his discovery of the Bible. He does not specify the age at which this happened, but recalled the occasion in notes for an essay he hoped to include in *Black Spring* on the subject of French urinals:

Take the Bible out of the pulpit and put it in the toilet. (Gideon Society please note! Not in hotel rooms where it is flung out of the window or used for calculations and memoranda and toilet paper in a pinch.) I only began to read the Bible when I found its violence and obscenity, its great insane images. Then I read with gusto and relish, *con amore*. . . . From the pulpit, when I heard it expounded, it rolled off my back like water, had no meaning for me, no relation *to me personally*. But through sex I found its great meaning, and its great poetry . . .[26]

Lawrence's revolt against some of the moral hypocrisy surrounding sex and his conviction that 'the world is wrong, always was wrong,

221

always will be wrong' appealed to the anarchic subjectivist in Miller, but Henry recognised also that vulgarity was too important a part of what he had to express to allow it to be subsumed in any kind of exalted gospel of sex, and he had the honesty to recognize that his way of writing about sex and the language in which he did so would probably have disgusted Lawrence.[27]

Henry's ambitions were often larger than his mind, and part of his sympathetic foolishness was his willingness to undertake colossal projects with almost none of the requisite equipment. His whole personality rejected the self-discipline which might have enabled him to control the Lawrence book, and as he felt the material towering chaotically over him he loosed off a powerful defence of '*my* form and not what the jackasses call form', asserting that, anyway, there was very little form in Spengler's *Decline of the West* and equating 'any worthwhile artist' with 'any man who is above the usual considerations of form'.[28] In support of his claims he briefly proposed putting his Preface in the middle of the book, an unusual step, he admitted, but defensible in view of the fact that he had not begun to understand his subject until this point.

Finally, at about page 800, he laid the manuscript aside. In 1938 he declared the project dead, but in 1941 informed Anais Nin of his imminent retirement as a writer 'after the Lawrence book is finished'.[29] Indeed, he managed to sustain a degree of interest in it for the rest of his life by the Milleresque trick of presenting his failure to finish it as a success, since failure is every bit as true of human endeavour as success.

The closest the script came to publication was in the spring of 1934, when Nin took it with her to London to show Rebecca West. West thought it 'a completely silly book', but out of loyalty to Nin she showed it to several English publishers whose refusal to take it on seemed to her to their credit. She was especially contemptuous of Henry's 'delusion that Lawrence had been neglected in England and had been read and rewarded in America, which is not the case, as his sales were five times greater in England'.[30] Her judgement might have had more force had she not once declared Anais Nin 'the only real genius I have ever met in my life'. T.S. Eliot, in regretting the need to reject the material on behalf of Faber and Faber for commercial reasons, nevertheless thought the material 'interesting'. A fair description of the book might be Miller's own description of Lawrence's analysis of Whitman in his *Studies in Classic American Literature*, that it was 'a mixture of genius and twaddle'.

Perhaps it was thoughtless of Kahane to suggest the project, and perhaps Miller's willingness to undertake it reflects a fear that, yet again, closer than he had ever before been to the ultimate goal of publication and full status as a real writer, his dream would be denied him if he did not comply with the wishes of his publishers. But if the undertaking did end in confusion, at least it helped to keep his mind off June and any guilt that might possibly be on his trail.

7

On a practical level, Miller's affair with Anais Nin was conducted with remarkable ease. He was a frequent and welcome visitor to the Guiler's house at Louveciennes, and his overnight stays and extended visits of four or five days excited little suspicion from Anais's husband. Though not yet recognized by the world at large as such, both lovers thought of themselves as writers, and their common pursuit of the craft seemed to them an excuse to justify any behaviour. On one occasion when Anais, her mother, her husband and Henry were all together at the house Henry got up and said to Anais: 'I must talk to you a few minutes. I have corrected your manuscript.' Moments later, in Anais's bedroom downstairs, they were making passionate love. She had to bite her finger to prevent herself screaming. Afterwards she went upstairs, 'still throbbing,' and resumed her conversation with her mother. Henry reappeared a little later, 'looking like a saint, creamy voiced'.[31]

Henry liked Guiler, and Nin was touched to observe the humble way he sought to make Guiler like him, and how pleased he was when Guiler was kind to him. Nin seems to have regarded her husband with an affectionate and not entirely respectless contempt. It amused her to surprise him with some of the tricks she was learning from Henry, such as clasping her thighs around his midriff, but she was unfairly comparing a fresh erotic relationship with a seven-year-old marriage when she asked him one day why he didn't try coming twice – 'As Henry does,' she added in her diary. She also took her husband along to see live sex shows at an address personally recommended to her by Henry, 32 rue Blondel, where she noticed that a lesbian display had excited him almost as much as it had her. She whispered to him that she would not object if he wanted to go with one of the girls, but he knew his own mind better than this and declined the offer. As part of her concern for her own reputation and her husband's feelings, Nin's published diary account of the incident describes her escort that evening as Henry Miller.

'The place is an astrologic den, with violet blue lights and zodiacs on the wall, apricot-coloured dining room and peach blossom bedrooms, black painted bookcases, bowls filled with strange stones. The maids

223

are all half-wits,' was how Henry described Anais's house to Emil Schnellock. Louveciennes itself was less exotic. 'When I walk to the village I try not to look like a German. People pass you on the road and look right through you without a smile . . . You are among French peasants who hate your very guts, who cheat you with eyes open, sell you rancid meat. Lovely souls. Excellent neighbours.'[32]

From the start the degree of Henry's intellectual involvement with Anais was such that he had to choose between the two disciplines – astrology and psychoanalysis – in which her thinking and writing were steeped, and which she more or less insisted he take seriously. Astrology, with its esoteric rites of prediction and the pseudo-astronomical authority of its mathematics had, in the end, the greater impact on Miller. But it took some time before he was sufficiently convinced by the complexity and cosmological pretensions of the horoscope to accept it as the possible longed-for synthesis of all knowledge, his own version of a Unified Field theory which would make life less baffling without taking the fun out of it.

To begin with he had the healthy scepticism of the Brooklyn street kid. In September 1932, Nin wrote to tell him of a remarkable suggestion put to her by her psychoanalyst, that 'one person or one will cannot fight the predestinations' but that two wills in tandem against a planet's influence could alter its course. She told Henry that it was imperative for them to make the most of October and November, 'since the planets are going to separate us in December!'[33] Henry more than half-suspected that any problems of separation they might encounter in December would have as much to do with June's impending visit as the behaviour of the planets, and he dismissed talk of a combination to defeat destiny as 'claptrap'. 'The kingdom of heaven is within you,' he wrote. 'That's where I shake hands with Jesus Christ.' He assured her that when June came he expected to try to deal with the problem on his own, yet his curiosity was piqued, and when he sent a birthday card to his father the following week he enclosed a request for the *exact* date of his own birth. The same ambivalence was still in evidence in a letter of February 1933 in which he told Anais how well he felt, now that the 'crisis' was over: 'Saturn must have cast a cusp of melancholy over me. Taking wing again with Mercury and by Jupiter I'll have my fling.'[34]

He was also both amused and fascinated by his conversation with an acquaintance named Walter Freeman whose 'numerology bunkum' predicted a good year for him in 1933, involving some travel and, around October, the beginning of a new cycle and the end of his last nine-year cycle. Freeman also predicted the possibility of death, which Henry was to avoid at all costs. Miller's personal interpretation of the death warning was that it might actually be a misinterpreted reference to a coming rebirth, but 'I may run out to the American hospital just the same'.[35]

'Bunkum' the numerology may have been, but the death prophesy seems to have combined with Fraenkel's ceaseless insistence that everyone was dead anyway to convince him that there might be something in it all, and in December 1933 Henry duly made out a five-page will, telling Anais that 'a feeling of fatality hangs over me, which I can't shake off, a premonition of imminent death'.[36] He appointed her his testator and sole heir and thoughtfully included a list of his current debts, amounting to $3300. Later he was moved to draw up a list of dates and addresses intended to demonstrate the significance of the number six in his life, doing so with a thoroughness that suggests the referential ecstasy which was never far beneath the surface of his world. Among other things, Beatrice's address on 9th Street was included because nine is six upside down, his mother's birthday on June 13th because June is the sixth month, and his father's on October 23rd because twice three is six.

Though nothing could be more cerebral and less of 'the open street' than astrology, its basic idea that the cosmos takes specific account of the fortunes of each individual human being was impressive, flattering, comforting and synthetic. Once he did accept it – on his own terms – Henry continued to allow it to play what was at times a decisive rôle in his life. Sometimes he used it to give authority to his prophecies. One of his most striking forecasts in this field was his prediction in 1938 that, owing to the influence of Uranus and Pluto, 'by the year 2000 AD . . . the word communism will be an obsolete expression known only to philologists and etymologists'.[37]

He met several astrologers through Nin, including her cousin Eduardo Sanchez, and a Frenchman named Conrad Moricand who cast horoscopes for a living. Moricand knew, or had known, a number of famous artists and writers, including Max Jacob, Jean Cocteau, Blaise Cendrars and Modigliani, and soon Henry was meeting him once a week at his hotel on the rue Notre-Dame-de-Lorette to hear stories about them, and paying for lessons in how to cast the horoscope himself. Henry felt sorry for Moricand, 'an incurable dandy living the life of a beggar,' and persuaded his friends to commission horoscopes from the astrologer, taking the fee and the date of birth along with him. When he ran out of real people he took to inventing subjects as a way of providing Moricand with money without offending his pride. He met other illuminati through Moricand, including, on a couple of occasions, Aleister Crowley. After hearing Crowley boast one day of the ease with which he could read men's minds, Henry made a point of keeping quiet in his presence. 'I said nothing about my worries at all,' he told Anais. 'I wouldn't want that guy tampering with me. No sir!'[38] No one was numinous when it came to money, however, and Henry successfully applied to borrow from the Great Beast on more than one occasion.

Psychoanalysis received shorter shrift than astrology, for both professional and personal reasons. The psychoanalysts of whom Miller had close personal experience were the two whom Anais Nin used in 1932, the Frenchman René Allendy, who mixed orthodox Freudianism with alchemy, astrology and numerology, and his successor when Nin tired of him, the Freudian apostate Otto Rank. The timing of these analyses suggests that Nin, a lapsed Catholic, felt the need of confessional figures as she embarked on her adulterous affair with Miller. When Allendy became Henry's rival for Nin's favours, within the course of the year he managed to accuse him of being both a latent homosexual and a German spy.[39] Henry also perceived Rank as a rival, though out of respect for Nin he pretended serious interest in him for a while, and the ideas expressed in Rank's book *Art and Artist* inspired him to plan the writing of more than one nearly-book.

Face to face, however, it was a simple matter of an ego-battle. On March 6th 1933 he had a one-hour meeting with him. Afterwards he sent Anais a lengthy report of the interview in which the substance of their discussion is profoundly unclear beyond the simple fact that Henry refused to be cowed by Rank's reputation and his twenty years in Vienna with Freud:

What I needed was the high challenge, the acid test, and I got it. And where Rank stands after thirty years of struggle, diligence, research, exploration etc. etc. there I stood, equally firm, firmer I'm telling you, despite all the temperamental diffidences and all the questions and obscurities and contradictions in my soul. The triumph lay in the feel of the whole situation – there was no duel to vanquish, rather it was like some preliminary passage of arms where you test out each other's strength. And, if I may continue with that metaphor, I may say that I felt my wrist stronger, firmer, my aim more accurate, a deadly aim.[40]

As he did with Fraenkel's, he seems to have tested Rank's theories to the utmost by the talented way in which he disbelieved in them. 'I can meet the biggest now and swap blow for blow,' he told Schnellock.

Miller's most explicit and impressive statement of his rejection of the claims of psychoanalysis came in a letter he wrote to the painter Hilaire Hiler later in the year. In the winter of 1933, Hiler's financial

226

situation became so bad that he considered abandoning painting for psychoanalysis. Specifically, he intended to write a layman's introduction to Freud. Miller's long letter of November 23rd was in part an attempt to persuade him not to do this by analysing the weaknesses of the philosophy. He conceded that Freud was the artist type he was most attracted to, the determined outsider, ridiculed for his ideas, who in his fanatical desire to realize them preferred to invent a world of his own that conformed to them rather than accept an existing world that did not, creating 'a lie, a fiction, not the world as it is, but the world as it ought to be, as he desired it'. Freud was a great man, a man whom he admired as 'one of the finest examples of a sage in our time', yet his labours were ultimately of no use to anyone except himself. His work possessed, for Miller, 'a fictive value,' by which he intended to compliment Freud by placing him on a level with poets and great religious leaders, but also to imply that his ideas would have 'a short span of life'. Miller then proposed a striking theory based on what he called 'the unconscious desire of the physician to exploit disease' which led him to conclude that the practical results of Freud's work might be 'not only unimportant, but perhaps adverse, dangerous'.

Why Miller wrote with such clarity and passion on the subject of Freud and his theories is obvious, for the whole spirit of Freudian psychology was inimical to the existence of people like himself whom it would eventually kill off by its goal of enforced adjustment to a world which was fundamentally chaotic and insane. He understood, as only a highly suggestible man who was at the same time aware of his suggestibility could understand, that some people need only hear about a castration or an oedipal complex in order to acquire one themselves, and that the labels and definitions of Freudian theory, the insistence on realizing neuroses in words, can actually dignify idiotic worries with a reality which they might not otherwise achieve, and without which they might simply fade out of mind again:

It is inevitable that with the increasing sway of the analyst there will occur an increasing area of neurosis – it will become universal. Neurosis will take its legitimate place in the hierarchy of our diseases, just as tuberculosis, cancer etc. He will make a place, a niche for it, and the more he pretends to fight it the more strongly will it become entrenched . . . Neurosis is as definite and fixed a part of *our* life (modern, Western man) as the machine, the aeroplane, the skyscraper etc. This is the material, the psychic configuration that we want. And the moment we *want* another configuration we shall have it - just by wanting![41]

Much of the good sense in this is addled by less acute suggestions about the 'creative and anarchic' nature of Freud's contribution to humanity being 'in keeping with his temperament and his race', reminiscent of a remark that Rank's 'optimism' was characteristic of 'Germanic striving, the dynamic, aggressive, hopeful, wishful thing which always leads the German mind, in the end, into the bogs of hopeless mysticism', and recalling also an observation that Marie Bonaparte was 'a queer name for a psychologist' and that 'people can't have names like that and do serious work'.[42]

Despite such sudden swoops into absurdity, however, his rejection of psychoanalysis and the whole 'patient' mentality remains a sincere and, on the whole, impressive defence of the need to trust oneself, to insist on owing one's own life, and of his sincerely held belief that it is human weakness, or frailty, or neuroses, or whatever one chooses to call it, that makes life interesting. Love of its fantastical jargon was one of the things that excited Miller most about astrology, and the lexicographer in him likewise thrilled to the vocabulary of psychoanalysis, especially to words like 'enantiodromia'. The major failing of psychoanalytic theory in the end was that it was simply not as much fun as it sounded.

Miller fought hard to convert Nin to his point of view. In 1932 he told her that she ought to give up keeping her diary, that it was an 'outgrowth of loneliness', 'a sort of reinforced hedgehog position from behind which you survey your existence,'[43] and that *all* psychoanalysis was 'necrophilic'. She agreed with him to some extent, but enjoyed the excitement of her sessions with Allendy and Rank too much to give them up. Henry was jealous of the influence Rank had on her, and began to suspect, correctly, that the two had become lovers. Nothing, however, could spoil the great event of the autumn: the appearance, in September 1934, of *Tropic of Cancer*. At last he was a published writer.

8

Just over two years had passed since William Bradley's enthusiastic letter to Henry agreeing to handle the book for him, and the signing of a three-book deal with Kahane on November 28th 1932. Henry's interest in the financial details of the contract was minimal: 'I don't remember the exact terms any more,' he told Nin, 'but in substance I am to get 12½% up to 5000 and 15% over 5000 copies on the next two books, plus an advance of ½ the amount represented by the sales on the preceding books at time of acceptance. Is that clear?'[44] The indifference was partly temperamental, partly a recognition of the fact that the book would not be freely available for sale in the United States under existing American obscenity laws. Using the Hicklin rule, a judicial interpretation, formulated in 1868, of a British statute of 1857 which provided a legal definition of obscenity as anything with a 'tendency to deprave and corrupt those whose minds are open to such immoral influences, and into whose hands a publication of this sort may fall', Customs officers had, for over sixty years, been confiscating and destroying at their discretion any such books and magazines as seemed to meet this criterion. Since 1918, Joyce's *Ulysses* had been regularly seized and burnt, and although the ban on the book was lifted in 1934, this was not the liberal breakthrough it might have seemed to be. Judge Wolsey, in raising the ban, explained that the court was doing so because the sexual writing in the book was 'emetic, rather than aphrodisiac'. The erotic passages were found to be 'submerged in the book as a whole', which meant that they had 'little resultant effect'. Similar arguments could never have been used to defend Henry's book, and both he and Kahane knew it. French censorship laws of the time were not notably more liberal than those of the United States or other European countries, but a loophole meant that they did not cover material published in English – indeed, the existence of Kahane's Obelisk Press was entirely dependent on his exploitation of this loophole.

Thus the long delay in publishing the book was not due to the fear of prosecution – though Kahane believed passionately in *Tropic of Cancer*, and declared himself willing, if necessary, to go to prison with Henry for the sake of it – but rather to Kahane's own financial problems. What finally gave him the push he needed to schedule it for late 1934 was Anais Nin's gesture in underwriting the novel for 5000 francs in cash, money borrowed from Otto Rank.

Most of the revisions Henry carried out during the two year wait for publication involved work on its construction and its length (the original version was over three times as long as the published one), cutting down on the sentimentality, and putting in more action. 'Weeding out the useless shit. Putting in new shit,' was his informal description of the process to Schnellock.

What emerged from this process was a fictionalized and condensed account of the adventures that had befallen him since arriving in Paris in April 1930, 'for a reason I have not yet been able to fathom'. The novel has no formal plot and no structure, relying instead for its interest on the vivid, anarchic and irreverent personality of the narrator, 'Henry Miller', as he cheats, lies and charms his way to a subsistence living while in pursuit of his obsession to become a writer.

During the process 'Henry Miller' discovers, almost incidentally, that the experience of incessant insecurity, far from dispiriting him, has turned him into 'the happiest man alive'. The story closes with an adventure based on an episode involving himself and Richard Osborn in which he rescues his companion, 'Fillmore', from 'Ginette', a pregnant prostitute who has persuaded him that he is the father of her child and that he ought to marry her. Henry bundles Fillmore on board a boat-train bound for London, promising that he will visit Ginette later and hand over the 2000 francs with which Fillmore has entrusted him. About half of the money eventually goes to the girl. The other half is in his own pocket as he sits, in the final pages, on the banks of the Seine, meditating on his happiness and the bountiful nature of life, anticipating with relish the moment when he will rise and go off to squander the money.

Tropic of Cancer's outstanding quality is its relish of life and of human beings even in their most crude and unattractive states. In essence, it is a riotous statement of accord with a point of view put forward some two thousand years previously by Chuang Tzu:

> Master Tung-kuo asked Chuang Tzu, 'This thing called the Way – where does it exist?'
> Chaung Tzu said, 'There's no place it doesn't exist.'
> 'Come' said Master Tung-kuo, 'you must be more specific!'
> 'It is in the ant.'
> 'As low a thing as that?'
> 'It is in the panic grass.'
> 'But that's lower still!'
> 'It is in the tiles and shards.'
> 'How can it be so low?'
> 'It is in the piss and dung.'[45]

If the novel can usefully be said to have a recipe then *Tropic of Cancer* owed much to Hamsun's *Hunger*, much to Rabelais, much to the shamanistic Whitman who celebrated and sang himself, and announced to his readers that what they held in their hands was not so much a book as the result of an act of transubstantiation. It owed smaller debts to Rilke's *Notebook of Malte Laurids Brigge* and Céline's *Journey to the End of the Night*, which Miller read in 1932 in a manuscript version provided for him by Frank Dobo, and to the surrealism of Buñuel, Dali and even Lewis Carroll, from whom Miller learnt that elements like logic and chronology can be dispensed with in a novel provided one has the skill to replace them with a pervasive atmosphere that provides it with another kind of unity.

Like practically everything Miller was to write, *Tropic of Cancer* is hugely dependent for its success on a willingness to look *with* rather than *at* its narrator, and our willingness to do this has in turn much to do with extra-literary considerations, such as our age at the time we read the book, our mood, the changing climate of the times in which we live, how often we have read it before and so on. Reading it in the wrong mood, at the wrong age and in the wrong time, much of it is liable to seem dull, ugly, dispiriting and silly. At certain times, however, it can still work marvellously as a literary Feast of Fools, a liberating explosion of bad manners, bad thoughts and bad behaviour which make it the perfect antidote against a surfeit of righteousness, sanity and seriousness.

9

Miller and Perlès lived at Clichy for almost two years, until February 1934. Thereafter Miller lived at various hotels and squatted in various apartments while he put the finishing touches to *Tropic of Cancer* and stormed ahead with *Tropic of Capricorn* and *Black Spring*. In February 1934, he was staying at a residential hotel at 24 rue des Marroniers in Passy – 'all the swell shits live here!' – to be close to Nin who had moved, at Rank's insistence, to be closer to him during her analysis.

Henry had a quintessential Henry Miller experience shortly after moving to Passy. Deeply engrossed in his Lawrence book and not having read a newspaper for over a week, he took a stroll out on the evening of February 9th and found himself wandering through an attempted revolution:

I walked right into the middle of it – instinctively. Walked in and out again – in a hurry. . . . I was at Richelieu-Drouot, on the *Grands Boulevards*, hemmed in by police and soldiers. Had the queer sensation (so true when you are in danger) that I was a target. Saw the mob pressing me flat against the walls and the bullets mowing us down. Realized that I was in a net. Looked frantically about for an exit. Got home just as the thing broke loose.[46]

The immediate causes of the violence – world-wide economic recession, large-scale unemployment, two years of unstable left-wing governments and the rise of a fascist class which used the Stavisky corruption case to promote anti-semitism and to preach the corruption and inefficiency of democracy – were of little interest to Henry. He preferred the historico-cosmic response which gave him the chance to predict the 'Roman stage of dissolution – the mob and the tyrants' and the battle between *blood* and *money* as foreseen by Spengler. The eventual result of this long, drawn-out battle would be to throw up 'wonderful tyrants, wonderful sadists, degenerates, perverts etc' from the criminal underworld in the United States, and the rise of an 'army of wage-slaves gradually turned into robots who must be fed and amused – because they surrendered what inner life, what individuality they had, to the machine'. As for the middle class, they would be 'ground to dust between the millstones, disappear entirely, and with them the notion of "democracy" and "freedom" – *illusions*'.[47]

His reactions to the experience of real violence point up a central paradox in Miller's character; that all his violent longings expressed in violent words for the violent destruction of civilisation were at once set aside the moment he was faced with even the remote possibility of this actually happening. 'The crowd was ugly,' he wrote, and while they had caused much damage in their rioting the 'queer and perhaps fortunate thing was that the crowd lacked a leader'. Why fortunate? Perhaps because he knew instinctively that when violence manifests itself in the form of direct action, then the status of violent words is sharply reduced. He was a born agitator, an encourager, a whipper-up of emotions, but once the whipping-up had been done and things were starting to happen then he was off as fast as his legs could carry him to safety. He told Schnellock that gradually, as he walked through the empty streets that evening, 'it dawned on me that something *real* was about to happen' and reality, unless it were the reality of literature, remained a problematic, almost hypothetical condition for him.

By May he was living at the Grand Hôtel de la Havane on rue de Trévise, still moving enthusiastically between projects. An ex-whore named Bijoux read his palm one night and made a remarkably good job of it, predicting that he would live to be over eighty, suffer no accidents, enjoy great voyages and a great deal of luck and marry a beautiful young girl. In June, July and August he stayed frequently at Anais's mother's town flat at 18bis avenue de Versailles. There he proof-read *Tropic of Cancer* and worked on an introduction to the book with Anais. His general prejudice against mothers extended to include Mrs Nin, whom he described as 'an ardent Catholic – and a dumb shit too', and even her canaries: when he was left in charge of them once, he wrote that he was 'letting them die. They're a pain in the ass, chirping about nothing all day.' He hung some of his own paintings on the walls, between the ikons and the El Grecos, to brighten them up a bit.

Finally, in September 1934, Henry moved into number 18 Villa Seurat where he – or somebody – paid 700 francs per month inclusive for a studio flat previously occupied by Antonin Artaud. With the help of Anais Nin and other friends, he decorated the place before moving in, *orders for Cossery's "Men God Forgot"*

1. 7 Stairs Book Shop (Chicago) – Irish   – 10 copies   40%
2. Red Door Book Shop " – " (Paid)   – 10 "   " "

Outline of "Tropic of Capricorn"

note: "On the Ovarian Trolley"

Background – antecedents – philosophy of life – desire to live imaginatively (rather than seek "Truth") – against work (Jack Lawson's death) – desperate always – looking for work – a pastime. Western Union job (p. 19–50). Valeska key figure (Street Cleaner)

note: (See how "waybills" is translated in French version p. 27 top!) Mallory (Catholic Welfare League. Real names of goofy images mentioned! (Cases). Always broke – Swindling blind newspaper man for carfare. one we did get a bonus and Hymie took me to Delmonico's" (sic!)

note: p. 32: "Dave Olinski" (H. 40–41) note: The Horatio Alger first book! "Dave Olinski" (H. 40–41) Ulric – Friends – loads [them, all despise the other friends] "Just a Brooklyn Boy!" Kronski and my "euphorias! Hymie – "ovaries" cor. 6th ave + 9 St. Europe! (Talk of Paris descriptions) Book of the Hours – Same talk always (in the head!) fantasy on Hymie the bull-frog! (p. 55–57). Love for the old things. "Should have been a clown!" My irritating talk! (Persons not gotta) note: Valeska + her nigger. Blood. Borrowing money of her. Playing dirty tricks with child while B. gets abortion. Valeska told pud. Sense of desolation – wrong birth day + hour! "Always bragging behind", etc. (Born with crucifixion complex) A fanatic! note: Beyond crucifixion – becoming "gay" (p. 67–8) "Live like a rock!" O'Rourke + nocturnal rambles thru streets. "Whoever there too great x love..." (p. 72.) One man in me that had died! Walking around x in "center of chaos" there on telegraph rigmarole (Chaos) (H. 74–81)

Valeska + Lesbian midget (hermaphrodite) – Girl upstairs (no note: name) – sexual affair (p. 77) – "I wanted to be alone for a thousand years – in order to forget!" Note this ending!

End of Part I. (p. 78)

Pauline Janowski + Balzac. Telegram from "Monica" (Mona) Love letters. Her erudition. Egyptian corpse at Grand Central. "It's me, Mona." Death of Kronski's first wife – Yetta. Walk thru Prospect Park with him – His crazy talk! Jewess episode (Boudi) Des of our German funerals, by contrast.

had the plumbing done, the pillows cleaned and hung paintings on the wall. Anais provided towels and bedclothes and chipped cups and glasses from Louveciennes. The publication of *Tropic of Cancer* coincided nicely with the move, and Kahane ceremoniously delivered the first copy of the book to him on his doorstep on the day he moved in.

Villa Seurat, which was to become Miller's home for the next five years, had been built eight years earlier to meet the needs of painters and sculptors. Raoul Ubac and Chaim Soutine were two of the most well-known painters living there. Henry's landlord was Michael Fraenkel, and he knew the place well from his stay there with Fraenkel in 1931. The studio was large, with a skylight, a balcony and a built-in kitchen. He had his own bedroom and bathroom. Rebecca West, who visited the apartment several times as a friend of Anais Nin's, called it 'a particularly delightful flat which I greatly envied', and Miller noticed himself how everybody seemed to want to know him after news got out about his new apartment: 'the very mention of this street is sufficient to create longing and envy.'[48]

10

The winter of 1934 was a focal point for the whole of Henry's early and middle life. Publication at last, a permanent home, and on December 20th the arrival of his divorce papers on board the *Paris*, the boat on which he and June had sailed to Europe back in 1928. William Dewar's law firm handled this, acting with the firm of Salvador, Hernandez & Co, Mexico. 'Hooray!' was Henry's reaction.

In all the excitement of the publication of *Tropic of Cancer* and moving into the Villa Seurat, one thing Henry had not known was that the child Anais had given birth to in August was his. The girl was small, dark and stillborn. Three months premature, she was about a foot long and looked, in Nin's words, like a doll or a miniature Indian. The doctor told her afterwards that its hands and feet were exactly like hers, and its head a little larger than average. Nin knew that Henry was the father,[49] and also believed she knew well what sort of father he would be to the child. The published version of her diary does not reveal this, and the reader is left to make two incorrect assumptions: that the child was Hugh Guiler's and that the attack on fathers as congenitally irresponsible beings that accompanies the relevant diary entry is aimed at her own father, who deserted the Nin family when Anais was ten years old. The bitter passion of her attack suggests that she may even have taken steps to ensure that the child was born dead.

CHAPTER TWELVE

1935–1939
'Rome has to burn in order for a guy like me to sing'

1

Nin's attitude was that Henry's value to her and to others must be preserved by shielding him from responsibility and by allowing him to play his way through life. This strange mixture of the patronising and the maternal was inevitably finely balanced on the brink of contempt, and the result of her distressing experience of pregnancy and of keeping the abortion to herself pushed her briefly over the edge. That winter they had a major quarrel which almost led to the end of the affair.

Ever since completing the last revision of *Tropic of Cancer*, Miller had been planning a return trip to New York. Anais had left at the end of November on an 'official' trip as Mrs Guiler, leaving Henry with enough money to pay the rent at 18 Villa Seurat until he joined her in February, when Guiler would be away for three weeks on business. In the meantime Nin would be working for Otto Rank at his newly-opened clinic in New York.

Soon after they began corresponding, Henry realized that Anais had lied to him and that she was travelling alone. The knowledge threw him into a frenzy of jealousy made worse by her evident liking for New York and her references to the numerous attractive American men who had been trying to pick her up. He was violently jealous of her association with Rank, and wrote with heavy irony of 'the kind Otto' and his 'limousines and soft German words'.

Nin was ruthlessly impenitent. In her replies to his long and desperate letters she made it clear that she had lied to him deliberately because she needed to get away from him. In response, he abased himself before her. He offered to do anything for her, go anywhere with her. He begged her to leave Guiler and start a new life with him. Suddenly his tactic of hustling and sponging his way through life seemed much less smart. 'I made the great mistake of letting you mother me,' he wrote to her. She replied with pitying contempt that

235

she had left Paris 'because I want to stand on my own two feet, because you can't. You are weak, Henry.'[1] She rubbed it in by assuring him that she loved her 'little Henry' and would be cabling some money to him as soon as possible.

In the middle of all this Miller one day received a letter from her intended for Guiler. He made the assumption that her letter to him was now in Guiler's hands and began saying his prayers. He thought briefly of leaving town and going into hiding until Guiler had left for America, but decided against it and instead persuaded Perlès to move in with him to answer the door and provide him with moral support. For the next three days he did nothing but run up and down the terrace ladder every time there was a knock at the door. Finally Nin's cousin Eduardo arrived bearing the wrongly addressed envelope. '*Marvellous*,' was his reaction when he read the letter, 'there was not one word out of the way!!! I had imagined that *everything* was in that letter – that you had spilled the beans.'[2]

His elation rapidly turned to disappointment, however, at the very innocuousness of the letter. Secretly he had been hoping that the incident would be enough to break up the marriage and deliver Anais into his hands; but its tone of friendly neutrality was in dismaying contrast to the warmth of her letter to her husband. Shortly afterwards, Nin wrote a letter to Henry quoting Guiler's response to the incident: 'this error you have made proved to me there was nothing between you and Henry,'[3] at which point Miller began to suspect the truth, that the mix-up had been engineered by Nin to put her husband off the scent. In the end everybody was happy: Henry had enjoyed the intensity of the experience, and could continue to think of all women, be they whores, wives or princesses, as actresses; Anais had made a statement about her independence and had some fun playing at being June; and Guiler, stoically living out his life on the margins, could carry on banking happy in the knowledge that his wife was not having an affair with Henry Miller.

Nevertheless, Anais's taunts had had some effect on Henry. He decided not to wait until February, nor to give Anais the pleasure of paying his fare over to join her either. Instead he rolled up his sleeves and dashed off a dozen begging letters to friends in Paris and New York. 'I wanted to show you that I could do it on my own,' he wrote to Nin, suggesting that he had managed to miss her point by quite a wide margin.[4]

On January 3rd 1935 he was on his way. The third-class facilities on board the SS *Champlain* delighted him, especially the food which he found 'unbelievably good, stupendously bountiful, and exactly the same as first class'. He soon got in touch with the three most intelligent people on board – the cabin-boy, the barman and the steward – and two days out from France had already discussed 'everything under the sun' with them, apart from psychoanalysis', which he was pleased to discover that no one on board had heard of.[5]

2

He was in combative mood as the *Champlain* docked, and the first things he did on going ashore in New York was to have a fight with an Irish porter about his luggage. He had no need to worry, though; the desperation of his letters had persuaded Anais that he did indeed love her. When at the beginning of February Guiler left New York on business she and Henry moved together into a room at the Barbizon Plaza Hotel on 58th Street and Sixth Avenue which Nin used for seeing patients in connection with her work for Otto Rank.

Miller claimed on a number of occasions to have worked as an analyst for Rank during this trip, but there is no evidence to support this. What seems to have happened is that Anais let him see some of her own patients for a week or two that February, just long enough to confirm his belief that most of them were self-absorbed frauds who had read enough about psychoanalytic theory and acquired enough of the vocabulary to pass themselves off as sick. All they really wanted to do was talk about themselves, and with his repertoire of listener's tricks, including a steady gaze and a continual, almost sub-aural humming and grunting, he was the ideal man for the job.

Three weeks later, when Guiler returned to New York, Miller moved out of the hotel and into the Roger Williams Apartments at 28 East 31st Street and began socialising. Defying the Post Office ban on sexually explicit literature had become almost a liberal obligation for Americans returning from Europe, and the many copies of *Tropic of Cancer* already smuggled through the Customs had created considerable interest in Miller in New York literary circles. William Carlos Williams had obtained a copy through his friend Hilaire Hiler and loved the book, calling it 'a whore with her pants off for purity and candour', and Williams and Miller met twice at Hilaire Hiler's house on 12th Street. Though Miller never liked or understood poetry, he was a great admirer of doctors, particularly literary doctors. Williams was thus in the great tradition of Rabelais, and of Miller's more recent heroes like Céline and Duhamel, and they enjoyed each others company.

There was a slightly less successful meeting with e.e. cummings, whom Miller met at a party and with whom he had 'a friendly duel apropos nothing at all', and a completely disastrous encounter with Nathaniel West and James T. Farrell. They were going out to get drunk and Miller was in no mood to join them. 'West was OK,' he wrote later, 'but Farrell strikes me as a little louse, a gutter rat'. 'They treated me like a boy or something,' he recalled. His boyish ways and his tactic of acting helpless encouraged this patronising response. Kay Boyle, whom he admired as a writer, disappointed Miller by the way she talked down to him. He recalled her telling him about Lautréamont 'as though she was giving me a lesson in arithmetic'. Miller tried to compliment her once by telling her that she must have 'dagger-tipped' breasts to write the way she did, but she only wrote back and told him to stop 'exhibiting'.[6]

Miller and his friends did what they could to promote interest in his book in the States. As early as November 1934, Hiler had reported interest in a private edition of *Tropic of Cancer* from a Hollywood dealer, and Nin and Miller also enrolled William Dewar as their legal adviser in attempts to put out a pirate edition of the book in New York. Miller held out faint hopes of finding an American publisher brave enough to try to publish *Tropic of Cancer* legitimately, and had a brief meeting with a representative of Harcourt Brace and Co, at which he 'got a rather cold reception from the little prick'.[7] There was also some talk about getting Simon and Schuster to bring out a private *de luxe* edition. The most practical step he took was to contact Leviticus Lyon in the customs service for advice on how to ensure the safe passage of the book through the US mail from France.

The main achievement of his stay at the Roger Williams Apartments, just a few blocks east on the same street as the tailor-shop where his tortuous literary odyssey had begun, was to finish *Black Spring*, the collection of autobiographical pieces that would eventually become his second published work. 'The street itself has changed tremendously,' he wrote to Frank Dobo. 'I can't get over it. That's why going back and seeing the vast changes gives me a depressed feeling. Things are always changing for the worse.'[8] His mood wasn't improved by the fate of a piece entitled *Portrait of General Grant* which he wrote especially for the *New Yorker* and which they rejected. *Esquire* also turned him down: 'Said I didn't know how to write (sic!) So fuck them!'[9]

While in New York, Miller also saw several old friends and was dispirited by the experience. The only ones with whom he still felt he had something in common were Emil Schnellock and Emil Conason. New York itself disgusted him. He found it 'malign, vulgar, crass, stupid, empty, geometric, Jewish'. Every New Yorker was 'an incipient thug or gangster' and the city itself the 'living embodiment of Spengler's predictions'.[10]

Richard Osborn had a peculiar knack for finding Miller's achilles' heels when he wrote to him. He followed up his letter about June and the man 'considerably your junior' with one containing news of Miller's daughter Barbara, which Henry received not long before he left for New York. Osborn had seen her and reported that she was 'grown-up, a fine kid etc'. Miller wrote to Emil Conason, agonising over whether or not he ought to try to see her:

It will be a terrible moment. Once or twice here, sitting alone, suddenly when I heard some familiar tune, the whole scene crowded back, swarmed over me, engulfed me. And I burst into tears, not knowing what it was I was weeping about.[11]

What worried him most was what Beatrice might have told Barbara about him, though he insisted that he had no regrets: 'I'd do it all over again, if I had to. What I did was right – for me.' He knew that Beatrice had married again, but still feared that she might try to claim the unpaid alimony he owed her, and in the end his courage failed him. He spent his last night in the city 'starving to death' – Miller-language meaning that he was hungry enough to accept when an old friend offered him a sandwich and a cup of coffee during a visit – and left without seeing his daughter. Anais Nin and her husband had returned to Paris earlier in the summer.

3

Back at 18 Villa Seurat, Miller resumed a personal publicity campaign he had been running on behalf of himself and his book since the previous November, in the course of which he spent in postage enough to 'keep a fancy terrier'.[12] 'My publisher chides me for having given away so many complimentary copies,' he wrote,[13] explaining that had he not taken matters into his own hands like this the book would have been stillborn. To facilitate his campaign, shortly after returning from New York he made up a list of useful correspondents and contacts 'in order to solidly entrench myself, to be able to go it alone if needs be'.[14] His conduct of the campaign reveals a quite other side to the bone-idle, talented, sponging drifter portrayed in the book as 'Henry Miller', and shows instead a hard-headed, calculating man whom it is suddenly much easier to imagine spending four years at management level running one of the busiest Western Union offices in the United States.

Copies of *Tropic of Cancer* went to every influential writer and reviewer he could think of, including T.S. Eliot, Ezra Pound, Aldous

Huxley, Sherwood Anderson, Theodore Dreiser, H.L. Mencken, Emma Goldman, Havelock Ellis and Gertrude Stein, as well as French writers he admired like Céline and Blaise Cendrars and critics whom he thought might be useful. Besides writing literally hundreds of letters and giving away dozens of free copies, he personally visited Parisian bookshops large and small, chatting to the manager or owner and depositing with them a printed circular containing complimentary observations on the book from whichever famous name had had the courtesy to respond to his appeal for comment. The general tone of the quotes was one of enthusiasm, typified by Eliot's reference to it as 'a rather magnificent piece of work'. Some, like Aldous Huxley, were more circumspect. He found it 'a bit terrifying, but well-done', and compared it to 'certain kinds of folk music – Serbian, for example – which are pure unadulterated passion and engulf one completely in a way I can't stand for long'. Dos Passos would only say that the book was 'certainly interesting', but Pound hailed it as 'a dirty book worth reading' and 'a bawdy which will be very useful to put Wyndham and J.J. into their proper cubbyholes; cause Miller is sane and without kinks'.[15] The campaign was an unqualified success, and within a year of its publication the book had acquired a solid reputation as an underground classic.

In spite of the attention, however, Miller's faith in himself remained shaky. Adverse criticism could upset him violently, and when Robert McAlmon made slight fun of *Tropic of Cancer*, claiming to have 'blushed' at Miller's purity, Miller damned him as 'a con, a shit-heel, a pederast, a no good son of a bitch'.[16] Cyril Connolly's description of the book as 'the most important thing that has come out of American Paris in the ten years since Hemingway' mollified him considerably. Connolly's review was 'not only flattering, but highly intelligent and just'.[17]

He realized, however, that there was something freakish about the enthusiasm of the literary establishment. He had no interest in people like Pound and Huxley and Eliot whose writing bored him. Pound was 'full of shit – the Cantos are the worst crap I ever read. Everything borrowed or stolen. Dry, empty, artificial.' Eliot's poetry is described in similar terms in *Tropic of Cancer* – 'sterile, hybrid, dry as Boris' heart'. Boris was his fictional name for Michael Fraenkel, the man who probably more than anyone else had demonstrated to him by his own sad example the futility of following the intellectual route through life if one is not truly equipped to do so. Miller knew he was no intellectual, and he was keen to remain true to his roots, by which he meant his vulgar Brooklyn street-roots.

There was a sound commercial instinct at work in his thinking too. He wrote to Schnellock of his:

27 The cabin and studio at Anderson Creek, 1946

28 At Big Sur with Tony Miller

29 *Right*: Eve, Henry, Valentine and Tony in 1959, returning home after a four-month European tour

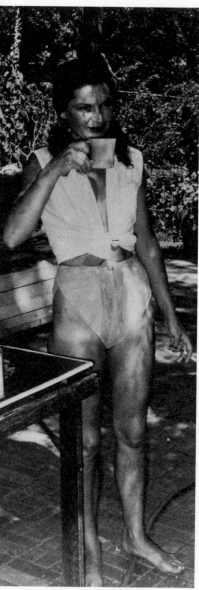

30 & 31 Eve Miller, Henry's fourth wife. Like Lepska, she was over thirty years younger than Henry

32 The house at Partington Ridge where Miller lived for 15 years

33 *Left*: In g-string, with sunhat

34 *Above*: Miller's friend Emil White made the little trolley which he used to haul groceries up to his home

35 *Left*: Miller in France, 1960, with his chauffeur and travelling companion Vincent Birge (r) and the French writer F-J Temple, an early biographer (l)

36 *Below*: Richard Aldington, Lawrence Durrell and Miller in France, 1959. It was the first time Miller and Durrell had met since 1939

37 *Bottom*: With Durrell at the Edinburgh Writer's Conference in August 1962. Miller was the star of the conference

38 *Left*: Miller and Emil White in California, 1962

39 *Below*: With his German girlfriend Renate Gerhardt in 1960

40 *Bottom*: In 1960–1 Miller and Birge toured Europe in the Fiat in search of a place for Miller to settle with Renate and their joint families

41 *Above*: Miller and his daughter Barbara at an exhibition of his paintings. For almost thirty years there had been no contact between father and daughter

42 *Left*: Miller and Lauretta in 1962. After his mother's death in 1956, Miller assumed responsibility for the care of his sister

43 *Bottom left*: Henry with Tony Miller

44 *Bottom right*: with Anais Nin, reunited at an exhibition of his watercolours

45 *Right*: Miller with the actress Brenda Venus. In his last years he resorted openly to emotional game-playing, and found willing partners in Brenda and other young women

46 *Below*: Brenda posing for *Playboy* magazine in July 1986

47 *Far right*: Miller never liked to disappoint his public, and willingly posed for arranged pictures like this one in 1972

48 *Right*: Miller at his last home in Pacific Palisades with his fifth wife Hoki Tokuda Miller and Puko, one of the many young Japanese girlfriends who shared the house with them at various times

49 *Right*: Miller beside his portrait by Aron Kalman in the mid 1960s

50 *Below*: At Big Sur wearing a Grecian outfit

51 *Bottom*: The graffiti wall at Pacific Palisades

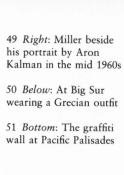

keen desire to hit various levels, and more particularly to make an appeal to the Hollywood and Broadway groups. . . . I seem to believe that among these lowbrows I will strike a more genuine level of appreciation. I have now the enthusiastic admiration of the English intellectuals – by some strange freak. But what good does that do me? I have very little in common with them. I feel that they like me for the wrong reasons. Maybe prejudice on my part – dunno.[18]

From the period of *Tropic of Cancer* onward, he began moving swiftly away from the pretentious intellectualism which had pursued him from his adolescence into adult life, and cultivated instead a wilful simplicity which he hoped would eventually kill off the adult in him. His definition of what constituted intellectuality was simple. He once had an argument with Henri Matisse about Joan Miró during which he called Miró's paintings 'highly intellectual'. Matisse disagreed, saying that Miró was just a peasant, to which Miller replied that he could not see 'how a peasant can get abstract in the way Miró does without being an intellectual'. Intellectuality was associated with a forced complexity that took the fun out of life, and Miller's exultant acceptance of life at its crudest and least exalted level in *Tropic of Cancer* was his flat rejection of its claims.

His aggressive way of expressing his opinions was always liable to get him into an argument where he came across someone with contrary views, and an exchange he had with the painter Hilaire Hiler over the film *The Informer* produced some clear statements of the sort of moral position that he found desirable. *The Informer*, which won five Oscars in 1935, including ones for its director John Ford and its leading actor Victor McLaglen, tells the story of a Dubliner, a man named Gypo Nolan, who betrays a comrade in the IRA to the police for money. Miller loved it and enthused about it in a letter to Hiler. 'Seeing that performance,' he wrote, 'I thought – there's the end of psychoanalysis. There's our man stalking the streets, doing as he wants and fuck everybody! That should have cured a lot of sad ruminants, eh wot?'[19] Hiler replied with a letter ridiculing Miller's enthusiasm, and Miller expanded on his views in a second letter:

When I said that the picture puts an end to psychoanalysis I meant that, for me, the moral lay in that 24 hours of lawlessness and freedom. Had I been the judge, and not society, he would have gone scot free. I would even have raised him to a high place, and thus shorn him of future menace.[20]

For Miller the beauty of the film lay in the main character's twenty-four hours of complete freedom from the prison of intellect, a liberty for which, even with the punishment afterwards, it was 'worth

241

betraying friend and country, worth losing the woman you love, worth death'. Anything a Gypo Nolan might do was all right, 'even if he fucked my grandmother,' simply because he was doing exactly what he wanted to do. He laid particular stress on the way that Nolan was forgiven by the minor characters in the film, 'if not avowedly, then silently,' because, as he saw it, they all envied him. He defended killing 'for need' against killing on moral grounds: 'I like the man who kills in a moment of weakness, because of fear, or greed, or this or that – but not the man who kills in cold blood because he is the spokesman of the law. Fuck these guys!'[21] The crucial fact for Miller was the perceived envy of the bystanders to the drama, the 'audience' at Gypo's performance, which throws interesting light on the extent to which Miller gambled on a degree of guilty collusion in his readers when presenting himself in such an amoral light in *Tropic of Cancer*. He knew exactly what he was doing in dispensing with idealism, and enjoyed the response of outraged or baffled idealists and intellectuals like Otto Rank, whose response to *Tropic of Cancer* was the uncomprehending question: 'Why do you insist on putting this book out first? Why don't you put your best foot forward?'

4

Hiler, whose father was a half-Indian Jew, was the first to take Henry seriously to task over the alleged anti-semitism in *Tropic of Cancer*, and Miller gave the point serious consideration:

You were the first one to bring that up, and perhaps your keen instincts were correct, perhaps I am what you say. I told you once quite frankly that I didn't like Jews, anymore than I did Irish folk, and Scotch even less and English still less. But that's an intellectual attitude. It's usually called an 'emotional prejudice'. Frankly there's never much emotion in it or behind it. If there were we'd get over it quickly. It's a pose more than anything else, and one to be gotten rid of, to be ashamed of, I suppose. I say that, and yet I must add that I'm not one to be concealing prejudices. Further, that I even believe in having prejudices, all kinds of prejudices. I think nothing is more false than this wishy-washy and untrue attitude of being open-minded, fair-minded, tolerant etc. When it comes to race-prejudice I know there are no legitimate foundations. One of the best books on this subject I ever read was called *Race Prejudice* by Jean Finot. Perhaps you know it. It is annihilating. There is no answer to his argument except the old instinctive one of blood which refuses to recognize instinct or logic or justice etc. When a man like Hilaire Belloc writes the perfectly sane, scholarly book which he has, called *The Jews*, and makes out a case against them, we all know that it is a case of rationalizing. But goddam it all, this thing exists, persists, endures, and however wipe it out? I don't think I made very much of that subject in my book, for the very good reason that it doesn't occupy me very much. The little of it that is there about corresponds to the part it plays in my life. And then you must remember too that I am a bit of a wag, and that I often have my tongue in my cheek. As far as human relationships go it would never occur to me to operate on a basis of anti-semitism. As a matter of fact my whole life is one long account of Jewish relationships – Jewish marriage, Jewish friends, Jewish bread, Jewish behaviour, d'you see? I must be very largely Jewish myself. How do I know what happened to my ancestors back in the days of the great plagues, in the days of the migrations etc? . . . Well here I ramble on about the Jews. It's funny the space we've allocated to this subject, both of us. It's supposed to be a minor thing and yet look how we dwell upon it. The fact is of course that today it is no small matter. It grows bigger and bigger each day and worse and worse, disgustingly so. And surely if ever my book were seized upon by some ardent Hitlerite or any other of that breed and palmed off as anti-semitic propaganda I would be the first to rush to arms in defence of the Jew. I would write by God the most virulent attack on the Gentile ever written. Notice I didn't say 'defence of the Jew', but that's characteristic of me, always the attack.[22]

The tone of this response is a far cry from the fatuous 'shocking' boasting about his anti-semitism in *Moloch* and shows the broadening effect on his mind of leaving Brooklyn for Paris. Many of his best friends in Paris were Jews or of Jewish extraction, including Alfred Perlès and Michael Fraenkel, and he was friendly with a number of refugee German Jews in Montparnasse, including Heinz Liepmann, author of a best-selling book called *Murder in Germany*, from whom he had heard first-hand accounts of how Liepmann had been beaten up by Nazi thugs.

As important as this personal contact was the fact that work on *Black Spring* had involved him in a full-scale re-examination of his past which led him to an understanding of what had saved him from genuinely going the way of his Brooklyn boyhood friends and his mother and becoming 'like every other Jew-hater'. This was the realization that 'the difference between me and other gentiles was more threatening than the difference between me and the Jews. And so, out of pure strategy, I suppose, I began to make allies of my Jewish acquaintances.'[23] Well before the outbreak of war in 1939 he had come to sympathize with the right of the Jews in America to resist full assimilation, and to identify at his own individual level with the need of minorities to retain their own identities.

Alfred Perlès recalled a brief holiday he and Miller took in Luxembourg. They visted a cafe in one small town, and as they rose to leave the proprietor thanked them for their custom and, inviting them to return, offered them his card. On it was written, in German, 'Café-free-of-Jews'. Miller rounded on the man, accused him of wallowing in his own shit and claimed to be a Jew himself, what was he going to do about that? The proprietor could only mutter that Miller did not *look* like a Jew, to which Miller replied that the proprietor did not *look* like an idiot but that he *was* one all the same. On their way out of town they reported to the local policeman that there was a riot going on in the Cafe-free-of-Jews and advised him to hurry down there before the proprietor killed someone.

'Remember too that I'm a bit of a wag,' he had warned Hiler, a caution reinforced by his comments in a letter to Frank Dobo that 'Hitler's latest speeches about the Bolsheviks and the Jews are simply amazing in their poverty of invention. Even a Jew-baiter like myself can't swallow such drivel.' Irony is a luxury that a real racist can never afford.[24]

5

The campaign to preserve and promote *Tropic of Cancer* occupied much of Miller's time after his return from New York, but he managed to work on *Tropic of Capricorn* and *The World of Lawrence*, as well as a number of short pieces like the comic essay entitled *Money and How It Gets That Way* and the portrait-story *Max*.

Max, a fictionalized account of Miller's brief relationship with Rudolf Bachman, an Austrian-Jewish refugee whom he and Nin tried to help in Paris, is one of his four or five best short pieces. The description in the opening paragraph of the protagonist as someone 'to whom you feel immediately attracted, not because you like them, but because you detest them' is a typically refreshing piece of honesty. *Max* also provides a fine example of Miller's narrative trick of attempting to present himself to his readers as a heartless monster only to be overruled by the good opinion of other characters in the account. *Max* ends with a movingly confused and misspelt love-letter from Max to Miller which makes it clear how much Henry has come to mean to him. It was the second time Miller had experimented with the device. His 1924 story 'Black and White' concluded with a similar 'letter to the narrator' which abruptly changed the piece from an almost documentary account of the difficulties of Hindu immigrants in America into a tragic love- story. The inspiration in both cases was one of Miller's all-time favourite pieces of writing, the heartbreaking love-letter from Victoria to Johannes with which Knut Hamsun concluded his novel *Victoria*.

In deciding to use his actual name for the character he was writing about in his books and short stories Miller took a short-cut to achieve the suspension of disbelief in his readers. We do not, without reason, assume that people will introduce themselves to us and proceed to tell lies. But the decision to use the same name for both author and main character in a book creates its own complications. Hamsun surmounted these in *Hunger* by giving his hero-narrator no name at all; but when a woman telephones the narrator in the middle of *Tropic of Cancer* and says 'Hallo! Are you Henry Miller?' and the narrator does not demur, then a statement is being made – this is not fiction, this actually happened.

The problematic nature of this statement is of special interest where those close enough to Miller to be written about by him had the opportunity to compare his published version with their own experience of the same events. Anais Nin discovered this when she read *Via Dieppe–Newhaven*, an account Miller wrote in 1937 of his attempt to flee from June to London back in 1932. Nin was baffled by the discrepancy between the account of the incident Henry gave to her in a letter at the time, with its description of a last, ugly scene between June and himself in which June more or less forced him to hand over the passage money, and what Nin called the 'hard, brassy' description of *Via Dieppe–Newhaven*, which depicted the couple sitting 'drinking merrily and in a fit of drunken sentimentality, Henry gives her money, etc'. When she put this to Henry he admitted categorically that the published account was 'fiction'. It was through experiences like this that Anais, who continued to be obsessed by Henry's relationship with June, began to realize that Miller himself practised the same self-mythification of which he accused June.

Orwell, on the other hand, reviewing the story in *Tribune*, found it a 'truthful and even moving piece of writing' and was fully committed to a position of sympathy for the narrator 'Henry Miller'. Rebecca West, who had known and disliked Miller since 1933, took the trouble of writing a long letter to Orwell denouncing Miller as a charlatan and liar, and expressing her 'wholehearted conviction that if he had an unpleasant experience with a policeman, or anybody else, it was probably because he had been very unpleasant to the policeman'.[25] Many readers, like West, remained unwilling to make the distinction between telling lies and writing the kind of fiction that Miller wrote.

Miller's habit of treating his letters as literature and publishing them was another example of the literary brinkmanship he practised. A letter to a friend is not a literary form at all, and the assumptions surrounding a letter are that it is spontaneous, truthful and private. Miller used these assumptions to create a strong sense of honesty and intimacy in his readers. *Aller Retour New York*, for example, was ostensibly a long letter to Alfred Perlès in which Miller described his recent trip to New York. The letter was never sent, however. Instead it was published, first in an edited version in the Freshman Issue of the *Havard Advocate* of September 1935, and later in a complete version, number 1 in the Obelisk Press 'Siana Series' ('Siana' being Anais backwards).

Much of *Aller Retour New York* was devoted to a favourite theme of Miller's – complaints about the treatment of the artist in the United States. He broached it again, once more in the form of a letter, in a 1935 publication entitled *What Are You Going To Do About Alf?* which was full of trumpeting and posturing about 'Art and Artists', but was actually, as he admitted later, merely 'a bit of a blague, intended solely to retrieve some dough'.[26]

In late January 1936, Henry and Anais returned to New York. Anais had the same ability as Henry to detach herself from emotional attachments whenever she had acquired what she needed, and on this second trip she wound up her personal and professional involvement with Otto Rank before heading off for Algiers. This second trip was only brief, and Miller was back in Paris by April.

Black Spring, for which he had originally contracted with Fraenkel's Carrefour, was published in June 1936 by Obelisk after Miller bought the rights back from Carrefour for $100. A collection of essays too varied to be described as novel, it contained some of his wildest surrealist writing. 'Into the Night Life' is too self-consciously strange to be really revealing; more successful is 'Walking Up And Down In China' which includes a delirious list of place names and personal names almost three pages long. 'Jabberwhorl Cronstadt' is a burlesque portrait of Walter Lowenfels, and 'The Tailor Shop' a vivid and amusing autobiographical account of the years spent working for his father on West 31st Street.

He dedicated the new book to Anais Nin, and kept working away at *Tropic of Capricorn*, or the 'June book' as he continued to think of it. This remained the central, stabilizing project in his life through the chaos of personal relationships and the jumble of minor publications, notes, nearly-projects and letters with which he filled his days. *Tropic of Capricorn* was now, almost ten years after he made his notes for it, slowly assuming the proportions of a major obsession: the quest for his former wife, and the opportunity to abandon himself wholly to the business of retrieving in written form as much as possible of the disappearing past.

During the 1936 trip to New York he had made useful contact with Frances Steloff of the Gotham Book Mart, and that October wrote to advise her of five works in preparation which she could list in her new catalogue: *Tropic of Capricorn* – an autobiographical novel in three volumes; *The World of Lawrence* – an uncritical study of D.H. Lawrence; *Letters to Emil* – being three volumes of correspondence dating from his arrival in Paris; *Scenario* – a readable film based on *The House of Incest*; and *Money And How It Gets That Way* – an extravaganza on gold. He did not mention what was in some ways, apart from *Tropic of Capricorn*, the most interesting project of all – the *Hamlet* letters.

The *Hamlet* correspondence was an idea conceived one afternoon in September 1935 while Miller, Fraenkel and Alfred Perlès sat drinking at the Café Zeyer, opposite the Alésia métro station. Fraenkel had for some time been wanting to write a book that would be exactly one thousand pages long, and as the three of them sat philosophizing over their *fines à l'eau* the idea of writing a joint book emerged. The theme would be an improvisation on Fraenkel's ideas of 'spiritual death' and 'soul death'. *Bastard Death*, which Fraenkel was then completing, was his own attempt to make a major statement of his theory, and he hoped to promote the book to reviewers as an articulation of the ideas that (he believed) invested and underlay *Tropic of Cancer*, without which, as he wrote to Orwell, 'the stark nakedness of the book would just simply frighten and depress'.[27] The projected correspondence might serve as a useful pendant to *Bastard Death*. After some discussion about the precise title under which they would write and publish the book, they settled on *Hamlet*.

The ensuing correspondence, which Alfred Perlès quickly dropped out of, lasted from November 1935 until October 1938. Fraenkel published a first, abridged volume of the letters on Carrefour in 1939, volume two in 1941 and a complete edition of volume one in 1943. Miller's contributions are among the best, most relaxed and amusingly provocative pieces he ever wrote. The form of the epistolary duel suited him well, dispelling the claustrophobia that the militant egoism of his solo writing sometimes produces in the reader. He was by now firmly convinced that 'China', his short-hand notation for those 'refreshing taoist principles which ... are the source and mainspring of my vitality',[28] was where he wanted to make his philosophical stand. At the time of writing he was engrossed in the *Chuang Tzu*, one of the 'bibles' of taoism, and the duel with Fraenkel provided him with a fine opportunity to recreate the debates that take place in the book between Chuang Tzu, the philosopher of 'free and easy, pathless wandering' and his opponent, Hui Tzu, 'intellectuality as opposed to imagination,' as Arthur Waley put it, the prophet of 'the hard and the white' who never strays from the path laid out for him by words and logic.

Miller's letters constitute a brilliantly unserious dance that is probably his best performance ever as the sage he longed to be and at times more than half believed himself to be. Fraenkel was an ideal foil, serious, passionate, but with something pedantic about him, the convinced rationalist and intellectual 'who believes one can win an argument'. The great fun of these letters is the way Miller time and again, to Fraenkel's consternation, derails the discussion from the subject of Hamlet on to anything else at all that happens to occupy his fancy at the time of writing. Miller never took the venture seriously, as he hardly took Fraenkel seriously as a philosopher. The exchange 'has an acrimonious tone now and then,' he wrote to Schnellock. 'He pans the shit out of me and I do the same for him. Hamlet gets lost in the rush – like father!'[29] The music-hall touch is appropriate. The letter of November 8th 1935, published later in a collection of essays entitled *The Cosmological Eye*, is a particularly funny piece of irritated derision that evokes perfectly the response of bored schoolboys being force-fed Shakespeare in a dusty classroom on a hot summer's day. The writing recalls *Saloonio*, Stephen Leacock's exercise in cultural ridicule on a similarly Shakespearian theme.

Michael Fraenkel was not really a gifted representative of the intellectual approach to life, at least not on the evidence of his writings, and it is hard to see why his idea that modern man is spiritually dead should have seemed so unusual to him. The titles he gave his books, *Werther's Younger Brother* and *Bastard Death: the autobiography of an idea*, are awkward and forced, and his style in *Bastard Death* is an uncertain attempt to blend poetry and prose and leaves his philosophical point obscure. A typical sentence reads: 'The light thins and shrinks, it walks over the hills, nostalgia rankling in it – the pain of distance, otherness.'

Fraenkel and Miller came to dislike one another in the course of their correspondence, although Miller wrote a preface to *Bastard Death*, and even acquired the distribution rights from Fraenkel for a *de luxe* edition of four hundred copies at 50 francs each that Carrefour published. 'I am to take the entire profits for the handling of the book,' he wrote to Frank Dobo, but, like most of the money-making schemes he thought up himself, it flopped. When Fraenkel left Paris in 1938 it was effectively the end of their relationship. He is remembered now only as a member of Henry Miller's Villa Seurat circle, and as 'Boris the weather prophet' in *Tropic of Cancer*. Yet he remained faithful to his analysis of twentieth-century man as a walking corpse, and retained the admiration of his friend Lowenfels, who wrote of how 'Henry went on to make a life career out of your death themes'. Hiroshima, when it came, did not surprise Fraenkel. He found it 'not enough. I expected it would be on a greater scale.'[30]

6

George Orwell, with whom Miller had a flurried relationship by letter in the late 1930s, was a better representative for an opposing point of view. He had reviewed *Tropic of Cancer* favourably in the *New English Weekly* on November 14th 1935, and while he did not believe it a great book, nor even a work of art, he thought it 'remarkable', and strongly advised people to read it if they could get hold of a copy. Miller was to him 'a discerning though hardboiled person giving his opinions about life', and the message of the book that 'if one stiffens oneself by the contemplation of ugliness, one ends by finding life not less but more worth living'.

Later, in reviewing *Black Spring* and comparing it unfavorably to *Tropic of Cancer*, he made the point that *Tropic of Cancer* was 'a kind of bridge across the frightful gulf which exists, in fiction, between the intellectual and the man-in-the-street,' an observation that goes some way towards explaining the 'enthusiastic appreciation of the English intellectuals' for *Tropic of Cancer* which so puzzled Miller. The novel was perceived as the work of a member of the general public, a representative but highly articulate working-class man of a type whom intellectuals and literary people of that era, from predominantly middle- or upper-class backgrounds, would not normally have come across.

Orwell remained consistent in his enthusiasm for the novel through-out the 1930s, and in 1939 wrote and published a long essay on Miller entitled *Inside the Whale*. In this he recorded his version of an experience common among those who read *Tropic of Cancer*: 'the peculiar relief that comes not so much from understanding as from *being understood*. He knows all about me, you feel, he wrote this specially for me.' At about the same time as he wrote this essay Orwell wrote in an 'Autobiographical Note' that what he saw during the fighting in Spain, and what he had seen of the inner workings of left-wing political parties, had given him a horror of politics. He described his political sentiments as 'definitely "left"', but maintained that a

249

writer 'can only remain honest if he keeps free of party labels'.[31] It was just this absolute freedom, in a decade in which political fashion dictated that every serious working writer and literary critic had a strong political opinion, that made Miller's cheerful and shameless egocentricity such a relief to Orwell. Orwell knew only too well the sort of dangers that can arise where writers identify themselves too closely with schools of political thought, the most sinister of these being the voluntary censorship of one's own thoughts in the name of a prevailing orthodoxy and righteousness. 'Ought I to say this? Is it pro-Fascist?' was how Orwell typified the condition in the 1930s. No such restrictions applied in Miller's mind.

In late December 1937, Orwell passed through Paris on his way to take part in the Spanish Civil War and spent an afternoon with Miller at Villa Seurat before catching the midnight express to the Spanish border. Miller did not try to dissuade him from continuing his journey; neither did he hide the fact that he thought it was extremely foolish of Orwell to do so *from a sense of obligation*. Had he been going out of curiosity, or from some selfish motive, that would have been another matter. Miller's pacifism was absolute and unconditional, and his ideal the absolute and unconditional egoism of the taoist philosopher Yang Chu. According to the *Lieh Tzu* 'even if he could have benefited the empire by pulling out one hair' Yang Chu would not have done so. Only a man so particular about his own well-being and contentment could be trusted to run a country without leading it into war.

The two men corresponded sporadically for another year or two without ever meeting again. In April 1938 Miller wrote to Orwell, who was then convalescing in hospital at Aylesford, and tried to persuade him to give up the attempt to influence the world and follow the way of inaction instead. He even offered to send him copies of the *Tao Te Ching* and the *Chuang Tzu*.

The distance between the two men was too great, however, and like most of Miller's original 'respectable' supporters Orwell presently found Miller's literary egoism too unsubtle and undifferentiated. Miller for his part responded to Orwell's defection and rather dismissive post-war reviews of his later books by damning him as just another stupid English idealist.

Their parting in 1937 was on friendly terms, however, and Miller gave Orwell a corduroy jacket to take to Spain with him. He had a harsh tongue and a harsh pen, but despite that, or perhaps because of that, he was a tolerant man. 'What enrages me about people today is their willingness to *die* for things – for any fucking thing!' he wrote to Emil Conason in 1934. But, as Perlès pointed out, Miller would have given Orwell the corduroy jacket even if he'd been going off to risk his life for the wrong side.

7

At about the same time as Miller and Orwell were making their tentative approaches to one another, Miller was cementing a friendship with another English writer. Lawrence Durrell, living on the Greek island of Corfu, had been given a copy of *Tropic of Cancer* in the summer of 1935 by an Englishman named Barclay Hudson. Durrell, a precocious twenty-three year old writer with a first novel already accepted for publication, responded with delight to the violent irreverence of Miller's novel, and in August 1935 wrote the author a fan letter in which he saluted *Tropic of Cancer* as 'the copy-book for my generation'.[32] 'I love its guts,' he told him. 'I love to see the canons of oblique and pretty emotion mopped up; to see every whim-wham and bagatelle of your contemporaries from Joyce to Eliot dunged under. God give us young men the guts to plant the daisies on top and finish the job.'

Miller had already had the experience of disliking and being bored by readers of his book who insistently tried to meet him in the *Dôme* and the *Rotonde*; and other than commercially he did not prize the enthusiasm of Eliot, Pound, Orwell, Connelly *et al*. The response from the young Durrell, however, was another matter. Miller told him in reply that he was not only the first Britisher but 'the first anybody who's hit the nail on the head'.

Within the first few exchanges of letters the terms of their lifelong literary relationship were established. Durrell made the point that the book lacked art, but did so without reneging in the slightest on his unconditional enthusiasm for what Miller had done. Miller's aggressive dismissal of literary intellectuals was perhaps in part conditioned by a suspicion that they did not regard him as a 'real' artist but rather as the circus chimpanzee who is applauded, not for riding his bicycle well but for riding it at all. In Durrell, however, he found someone intelligent and literate enough to refer knowledgeably to Ben Jonson and François Villon who yet admired him on his own terms. He trusted Durrell with his honesty, and long before they met had done him the honour of admitting that he knew 'scarcely anything of the Elizabethan literature. Practically nothing, I should say.'[33]

Durrell, born in India, had already opened his account with Lao Tzu, and appreciated not only the Rabelaisian side of Miller's book but also the sense Miller conveyed of being 'beyond damage somehow'

251

and exposing 'a bright, hard immunity to life'. Miller was, to him, the author of a great, original novel, a literary father-figure forty-five years old who was still struggling to make it, and who had not only survived years of failure intact but clearly strengthened by the experience. A rapport based on a common passion for a Chinese philosopher, a profound distrust of politicians, youthful irreverence and the enjoyable pursuit of literary success was rapidly established.

In August 1937, Durrell and his wife Nancy visited Europe for a few months, and at Villa Seurat met Miller for the first time. The degree of intimacy the two men had already established through their correspondence made the personal encounter quite painless. On a warm Sunday afternoon a meal was prepared in honour of the visitors in the ground floor studio of number 18 that was rented by an American art student named Betty Ryan. Durrell, Miller, Betty Ryan, a painter named Hans Reichel, a Chinese friend named Mr Chu, Alfred Perlès and Nancy Durrell ate fillet steak prepared by Nancy Durrell, and drank wine and talked far into the night of Corfu, Nijinksy, Lao Tzu, Hamsun, Krishnamurti and Madame Blavatsky.

The Durrells stayed in Paris for several weeks, Durrell delighted to have come across such amusing people, Miller equally delighted to have someone to accompany him on his repeated visits to the cinema to see Ronald Coleman as Conway and H.B. Warner as Chang in Frank Capra's film adaptation of James Hilton's novel *Lost Horizon*. *Lost Horizon* seemed to Miller 'the first *significant* film out of Hollywood', and most contemporary critics shared his enthusiasm – James Agate called it 'the best film I've seen for ages'. The few dissenting voices were of those who preferred to praise the film's lavish spectacular effects rather than its solemn metaphysics. It was precisely these, however, which appealed so strongly to Henry. Mixing the fruitful self-confidence and the arbitrary critical sensibilities of the auto-didact, he at once incorporated *Lost Horizon* into his codex of Oriental wisdom, along with the *Tao Te Ching* and the *Chuang Tzu*, and developed an obsession about the lost paradise of Shangri La which accompanied him for the rest of his life. In more corporeal mood he also took Durrell along to spectate at the Sphinx, a luxury brothel on the Boulevard Edgar-Quinet which was at that time the only building in Paris with air-conditioning. Miller had written the brothel's promotional brochure and received a small commission for every American he induced to visit the place. He also introduced Durrell to the method of painting Turners which he and Joe O'Reagan had discovered in New York back in 1927.

Miller was closely involved in the publication of three literary magazines at this time. He was a regular contributor to *Volontés*, edited by an admirer of his named Georges Pelorson, which published French translations of his *Open Letter to Surrealists Everywhere* and his enthusiastic appreciation of Balzac's novel *Seraphita*. He was also, grandly, European editor of the *The Phoenix*, a Woodstock magazine run by James P. Cooney which was dedicated to the promotion of D.H. Lawrence's work. Miller was soon busily trying to shift it in the direction of a Henry Miller Appreciation Society, and sent off 135 pages of fan letters he had received which he hoped Cooney would publish as a brochure. He also tried to persuade Cooney to publish a horoscope done for him by Moricand.

Lawrence Durrell arrived in Paris in time to participate in the launching of the third magazine, *The Booster*, under the editorship of Alfred Perlès. Since the demise of the *Chicago Tribune* in 1933 Perlès had been struggling to earn money while he worked on his own novels (the 'bit of a blague' appeal *What Are You Going To Do About Alf?* was Miller's effort to raise money on his behalf). An American businessman named Elmer Prather had started a country club and golf course for the amusement of Americans and Englishmen in Paris and employed Perlès as the club's subscriptions manager and editor of the club magazine *The Booster*. Perlès proved a charming but untalented manager, and was presently sacked by Prather, who softened the blow by allowing him to retain control of *The Booster* with permission to run it as a literary magazine.

Run it he did, right into the ground, with the help of his Fashion Editor (Henry Miller), Sports Editor ('Charles Norden', one of Durrell's *nom-de-plumes*), Oriental Department (Mr Chu), Department of Metaphysics and Metempsychosis (Michael Fraenkel), Literary Editors (Durrell, Miller and William Saroyan), Turf Editor (Patrick Evans), Society Editor (Anais Nin), sundry other editors in charge of dubious departments and Walter Lowenfels, son of a family of wealthy butter retailers, responsible for all Butter News.

The first issue appeared in September 1937 and caused no great sensation. The second issue did the trick. It contained a joke Eskimo folk tale, 'collected' by Durrell, about an old bachelor slowly ingested during the sexual act by a young woman who ejects his skeleton the following day. Shortly after the appearance of this story, Mr Prather withdrew the goodwill of the American Country Club from the venture, and with the goodwill went the magazine's revenue from advertising. The publishers scraped together enough money to put out a third issue, after which they yielded to pressure to change the name. As the *Dial* it appeared three more times, the second and best edition being the 'Special Peace and Dismemberment Number with Jitterbug-Shag Requiem', which came out just after Munich and the farce of 'peace in our time'. It contained among other things, a fragment from *Tropic of Capricorn*, which was nearing completion, an extract from Nin's novel, *The Winter of Artifice*, Durrell's *Hamlet, Prince of China*, originally a private letter to Miller on the subject of the Miller-Fraenkel *Hamlet* correspondence, a short story by Antonia White, a piece by Durrell's friend Dylan Thomas, and contributions from Perlès himself and Fraenkel. The final issue, a poetry special, appeared a few weeks before the outbreak of the war, by which time neither Perlès nor Miller were directly involved in its production.

After a trip to London, the Durrells returned to Greece in 1938. Heavily influenced by *Tropic of Cancer*, Durrell had written a novel, the *Black Book*, which he submitted to Faber for consideration. Faber were unwilling to risk publishing the work unless Durrell was willing to make cuts. Miller urged him not to do so, and volunteered to act as Durrell's agent in Paris. He spent long hours typing out extra copies of the manuscript with Anais Nin and boosting for its author in *The Booster*, where he described him as 'the most important – practically the only – English writer of our time,' and was responsible for its appearance in 1938 as one of Kahane's Obelisk Press books.

In late 1938, Durrell was back again in Paris. He and Miller crossed the Channel to spend Christmas and the New Year in London where he introduced Henry to some of his friends. There was a meeting with T.S. Eliot at Durrell's Notting Hill Gate flat at which the Paleface and the Redskin got on quite well together. Eliot was in a grave and composed mood, and suprised to discover that Miller did not use bad language in person. Eliot's admiration for *Tropic of Cancer* had been qualified by what he had seen of Miller's subsequent work, and he suspected that a cult was on the way; in 1937 he returned ten *Hamlet* letters which Miller had sent him for consideration for *The Criterion* with what Miller described as 'a mildly sarcastic letter about it being more suitable for my "admirers"'.[34]

A meeting with Dylan Thomas, once Durrell had persuaded the poet to leave a pub in which he was lurking and drinking, 'too frightened to move', was more relaxed. Thomas found Miller 'a dear mad mild man' and Miller hailed Thomas as 'a wonderful man. Very tender.' Thomas thought *Tropic of Cancer* 'the best modern fucking book', but did not consider it a 'universal life-and-death book'.

Miller was back in Paris by January 12th, pleased by the success of the trip to London which had done much to wipe out the humiliations of the Dieppe–Newhaven fiasco. Durrell returned to Greece, and Perlès, who had been with them in London, found work as a freelance correspondent for *Paris-Soir*, fell in love with an English girl and decided to remain there for the time being. He was lucky: an Austrian Jew living in Paris on a Czech passport without a regular job or a regular income, he would certainly have ended in the hands of the Gestapo after the Nazi invasion of France.

8

Perlès had remained one of Miller's closest friends all during the Villa Seurat period. Another friend whom he saw regularly was the American expatriate David Edgar, a shy, decent, neurotic man who painted water-colours in secret. Edgar, with his enthusiasm for Rudolf Steiner, Zen Buddhism and Madame Blavatsky, was largely responsible for reviving Henry's adolescent interest in unusual philosophies and religions. His talk supplemented the influence of the astrologer Moricand, and of Nin's reports of her adventures in the byways of psychoanalytic theory. The cultivation of interesting and semi-mystical ideas gave a focus to Henry's anti-intellectualism, and in reviving the interests of his adolescence gave him a powerful sense of the continuity of his own personality which was important for him.

For a long time the German painter Hans Reichel was a welcome visitor at Miller's Villa Seurat studio. Like Perlès and Edgar, he lived but a short walk away in the Impasse du Rouet. Miller genuinely admired his talent and his demonic personality, but found his alcoholism hard to take. Perlès recalls the frighteningly aggressive rages Reichel would fall into, made worse by Miller's insolent imperturbability or his tormenting. Henry enjoyed alcohol himself, and frequently got drunk on wine; but he confessed to Schnellock that one of his weaknesses was that he could not put up with drunkards, 'especially those who change suddenly when they get drunk'.[35] Reichel was such a drunkard, and Henry devised his own way of trying to cure his drinking: when the painter turned up at the Villa Seurat and demanded a drink Henry would set six glasses in front of him and fill them up. Then he would pull on his coat and say he was on his way out to buy some more, he would hurry back as quickly as he could. The sarcasm bit sometimes, but if it failed then Reichel would get angrier than ever. In the end, like Osborn, he was hospitalized for observation because of his dipsomania.

There were a number of Hungarians attached to the Villa Seurat circle at this time, including the photographer Brassai, Frank Dobo, and another painter, Michonze. In addition to these, number 18 was host to a vast floating population of what Perlès called 'cranks, nuts, drunks, writers, artists, bums, Montparnasse derelicts, vagabonds, psychopaths'.[36]

Miller was the undisputed leader of the group. Cecily Mackworth, who was introduced to the Villa Seurat circle through David Edgar, recalled that his friends played 'separate but essential' parts in his life. 'Quite a lot of them were younger than he was, so that one sometimes had the impression of a benevolent uncle, or perhaps one of those gurus who refuse to take themselves seriously and dispense wisdom in jokey, throw-away phrases.' 'Guru' is perhaps an anachronistic term to use for 1935; Miller was more like Ibsen's Dr Relling, a near-failure himself with a deep understanding of the need of those around him for a 'life-lie'. In most cases this was the longing to believe one was an artist, or a philosopher, or in some way an unusual person. Miller sowed this 'confidence trick' ceaselessly among his friends, and they loved him for it.

Mackworth also remembered Anais Nin 'lying on a sofa, looking like a lithe, beautiful cat', a striking contrast to Henry, 'bald, spectacled, already middle-aged . . . a general impression of untidiness . . . clothes rumpled, perhaps not very clean . . . an eager concentrated look, as if he was waiting for something to happen and wanted to be ready for it'. The something he was waiting for often turned out to be inspiration, and her description of his working practice once the great moment had arrived underlines the extent to which his writing was a social act:

When the writing moment came, it made no special difference. If there were visitors, they went on playing jazz on the gramophone, reading their poetry aloud to each other or doing whatever they happened to be doing at the time. Henry just moved over into the table in the corner and started to write. Once he began, he went on, apparently never feeling the need to take a walk or go to bed. He wrote on without fuss; pages of *Tropic of Capricorn* piled up beside him while the red wine in the bottle at his elbow sank lower and lower. After a time, someone – generally Alfred Perlès – would bring him a plate of food, to be forked messily into his mouth with one hand, while he went on typing with the other.[37]

Mackworth's memories are warm, as are those of Betty Ryan, the wealthy art student who had a ground floor studio at number 18. Other women who had briefer contact with Miller at this time, like the painter Buffie Johnson, found his charm resistible. Johnson recalls only a man who talked all the time and always about himself, and viewed with contempt his attempts to borrow money from her, a student barely out of her teens. The dislike was mutual.

By 1938, the Villa Seurat group was breaking up. Perlès and David Edgar were in London, Durrell was gone and Hans Reichel was locked up and drying out. Fraenkel had disappeared from the scene for good, and Lowenfels's Parisian adventure was over too. In their place, Richard Osborn – 'Crazy Osborn', as Miller called him – had returned from New York in a seriously disturbed state. He had no job, and hung around Henry's studio, lolling on the couch with his tongue sticking out and trying to chew the end off it or hacking at his hair with a pair of scissors. Sometimes he would take his penis out and insist that Henry examine it to reassure him that it was not syphilitic. His presence was so disturbing that in the end Miller began staying away from the house; even when he was at home he was afraid to use the typewriter for fear that Osborn would hear it and insist on coming in to talk to him.

Out of gratitude for what Osborn had done for him in the early days, and feeling perhaps a touch of guilt for the way in which he had exposed him as a mad, alcoholic clown in *Tropic of Cancer*, Henry was unwilling simply to reject his former flat-mate. Osborn was a misfit, an unhappy soul, the type of man who was attracted to Miller because of his popularity and his tolerant, confident personality. To Miller he was probably not much more than a stray dog which he had absent-mindedly patted on the head one day, and now found himself unable to get rid of. Wherever he was, it seemed, there were always one or two such men around. Of all the great mass of humanity that wandered in and out of his life in Paris during the 1930s, Durrell and Fred Perlès were the only two he called his real friends.

Then there was Anaïs Nin, his shadow wife and his shadow mother. From the start he had hoped that she would one day divorce Hugh Guiler and agree to marry him. But though she was not happy in her marriage it is hard to imagine that she ever seriously considered leaving her husband for Henry. 'I know literally thousands of people,' he wrote to her once, 'I know hundreds intimately.' But no one knows literally thousands of people, nor hundreds of people intimately. Nin realised soon enough that Henry's talent was to be intimate with a whole world; at a personal level he had little gift for intimacy. Moreover, his insistence on the liberty to do exactly as he pleased, and his dependence on a steady turnover of new faces and new relationships in his life to keep it interesting were bound to make any woman who married him feel always insecure and uncertain of her position. He continued to visit whores occassionally long after he fell in love with Nin, and did not resist the special fascination which the sexual betrayal of those closest to him offered. In a letter to Schnellock in 1935, he described with great relish an occasion on which he and

Perlès got drunk with Maggie, the girlfriend of their mutual friend Roger Klein, brushed aside her complaints that they were treating her like a whore, 'and while Fred is sucking her off I ram my prick down her throat'.[38] Klein was housing Perlès and feeding him at the time.

Yet had Miller been the most faithful lover in the world it would probably have made no difference to Anais's attitude. June was surely right when she told her, shortly after meeting her for the first time, that though Anais might envy the Millers their colourful life she was too attached to her wealth and the security of her marriage ever to consider abandoning them.

Henry and Anais had a second major row in 1937, again precipitated by Nin, in which she raged against Henry for what would nowadays be called his sexism. In one especially direct letter, written after she had seen a fragment of *Tropic of Capricorn*, she criticised him for depersonalizing women in his writing, reducing them 'to an aperture, to a biological sameness'. June, she told him, was the only person who had ever forced an admission of individual reality on him by the sheer strength of her personality. In Nin's telling phrase June had managed to 'distinguish herself from the sea you make'.[39] The sex-drenched world he uncovered in his writing was not, she informed him, the world of a god or a prophet, but the product of a diseased mind, an imagination in the process of disintegrating. She attacked his 'primitive attitude towards lesbianism' with its limited fascination at the 'did she or did she not' level. More damningly, she criticised his social personality as pathological rather than admirable:

You make the whole world the simple thing which we feel with acquaintances. We always say: we have a good time with certain people who don't mean much to us, but all of us agree that this 'good time' is not what nourishes our life, and those who have only this kind of ephemeral light contact with people, who have a continuous good time, soon find out they feel their life empty.[40]

The quarrel passed; but every such exchange lessened the possibility that she would ever decide to make a life with Henry.

9

His forty-sixth birthday found Miller in reflective mood. 'Incredible,' he wrote to Emil Schnellock, 'the years went fast – too fast. The men of my age seem old to me.' His mood was darkened by thoughts of his daughter Barbara. Twice now he had failed to take the opportunity to make contact with her when in New York. Recently Joe O'Reagan had written to tell him that Beatrice was 'in great poverty and half-dippy etc' and that Barbara was helping her mother out by giving music lessons. She was also doing some writing, and had apparently won contests 'for writing' in the papers. 'It's strange,' he mused, 'to think you have a grown-up daughter and no idea what she looks like, or even what her voice sounds like. The last especially – why I don't know.'[41] He had tried indirectly to get further news of Beatrice and Barbara from his Norwegian friend Ostergren, but received no reply to his letter.

On top of this he received a pathetic note from his father asking if he could help him by sending – in secret – a little pocket money. The long, slow decline of the firm of Henry Miller and Son had finally ended, and in spite of the financial assistance of Robert Berg, the cutter who had joined Henry senior as a partner in the early 1920s, by 1937 the firm had been wound up and Henry senior had hired himself out to another tailor on a commission basis. His father's health was breaking down too. His prostate gland had packed up and he was struggling to get used to wearing a belt and bag round his waist.

Louise found out about her husband's approach and hastily wrote to tell Henry that he was not to take his father's stories of poverty too seriously, the family were managing fine. Miller, who recognized in his father much of his own tendency to dramatize a plight, sent him $3 and arranged with Frances Steloff to forward the royalties from sales of his *Scenario* to his father, as well as telling his *Booster* connections in New York that if they felt they owed the magazine a 'token' payment they should send the money direct to his father. He also sent Louise and Lauretta a little money. Then, typically, he turned the whole episode into literature, writing and publishing in the form of an open letter to his father an account of his own poverty since deciding to devote his life to writing, the suffering he had endured and the decline that had come about in his ethical standards. It was in some ways an attempt to shift the blame for his father's plight on to a world that refused to recognise and reward, in him, a real artist, and as such the gesture shows that he occasionally felt keenly his failure to make money. 'And yet I feel somehow it's not always going to be this way,' he wrote to Schnellock. 'Only, when it comes, it will be too late as usual. They will all be dead, those whom I would want to repay or help.'[42]

The pathos would be affecting, were it not for the fact that he was earning money at the time. By the end of the decade, *Tropic of Cancer* alone had been reprinted five times and was the best-selling book on Kahane's list. Nin's diary notes that in March 1937, Miller received 3000 francs in royalties; and he told Frank Dobo that in 1938 he had earned 8000 francs (about $200) in royalties 'which I spent in ten minutes. A fact!'[43] He was earning money, but to husband it, to be sensible with it, would have spoiled the fun.

10

From the start, Miller had had a low opinion of Hitler and the goings-on in Germany since 1933. The rapid spread of race prejudice against the Jews only confirmed his opinion of human beings as little better than thinking animals, and of civilisation itself as mass-hallucination. He saw Hitler as an 'animated human foetus of the new human species which will bring the Machine Age to completion', and the Nazis as '*real* half-wits, you know, hardly a notch above the messenger boys'.[44] Yet he was hardly more impressed by communism: 'it doesn't matter whether there is Communism or Fascism – wherever there is a dictatorship there is purity,' he wrote to Leviticus Lyon. 'For me as an artist there is absolutely no difference between Communistic Russia and Hitler Germany. Both are purity-mongers, both are unliberal. Both are *collective* . . . If I am out of step with the times, OK. I *want* to be out of step with these times. I want to be alone, if necessary, rather than with these pigs.'[45] He had been predicting the outbreak of an apocalyptic war ever since 1933; and when in September 1938 he finally thought he saw it coming he was off like a whippet.

The French mobilization was the key that precipitated his flight. Utterly horrified by the apparent readiness of normal working people to don uniform and bear arms, and convinced that a German invasion was imminent, as soon as he had finished *Tropic of Capricorn* he headed for Bordeaux with the intention of taking a boat to America. He carried with him two *valises*, a cane and a typewriter. On the walls of his room at Villa Seurat he left three paintings by Reichel, some of his own water-colours and a few books he thought might do the Nazis good. Isolated at Bordeaux where 'I don't know a soul and never meant to be' he used his last contribution to the *Hamlet* correspondence to make his position on war quite clear:

War is not just war: it is a universe which each one explores to a different end. Myself, I am terrified of it. If this is cowardice, then I am the vilest coward of any man on earth. As long as I have two legs to run with I shall run from it, and if necessary, I shall crawl away on all fours, on my stomach even, wriggling through mud, anyway, anyhow, but out of it! Even if what I see about me now is Hell, it is Life just the same, and I prefer this life of hell to the gamble of war. I love life above truth, above honor, above friends, country,

God or anything. I want to keep alive until I have had enough. I want to die of my own desire, peacefully fulfilled, in bed if possible, and in my sleep.[46]

In Bordeaux he at once fell victim to his own lack of planning. After posting a letter to Kahane asking him to cable six of his friends to send money, he went along to the steamship lines to make enquiries about departure times. Only then did he discover that there were no boats at all leaving Bordeaux for America. The money arrived safely, however, including 3000 francs from Kahane and a sum of money from Durrell. This latter gift he returned, indicating the unusual esteem in which he held Durrell.

The prospect of war made him slightly hysterical, and he became convinced that his powerful intuitions were correct: Hitler would declare war at midnight on September 30th and Paris would be bombed. He wrote to Nin imploring her on no account to remain in Paris on that night. He even contemplated intervening personally to prevent the war, and toyed with the idea of approaching the American Ambassador in Paris to suggest the mobilization of every crippled war veteran in Europe who would then be flown in a fleet of planes to Germany to confront Hitler with their wounds. If he remained unimpressed they were to form a line along the Czech border and announce that Czechoslovakia would only be occupied, literally, over their dead bodies.

Unfortunately Chamberlain got to Hitler first, and though he had little faith in a pact made by 'two bandits armed to the teeth' Henry abandoned his plans to leave France, and after a brief sightseeing trip to Toulouse and to Lourdes, which reminded him of Coney Island, he returned to Villa Seurat. He was still furious at the way in which Hitler was inconveniencing his life. 'He's temperamental – and terribly earnest,' he wrote to Lawrence Durrell.[47] 'Somebody has to make him laugh or we're all lost.' The threat of war seemed to him a gross personal insult, and he swore to Anais that he was henceforth going to do his utmost to bring about not only the fall of Hitler but the castration of the entire German people. Anais accused him of being neurotic, but as he pointed out to her, neurosis was surely the only normal reaction to such an absurd and terrifying situation.

His return to Paris was merely a postponement of the inevitable. Back at Villa Seurat he prepared *Tropic of Capricorn* for publication. Originally scheduled for February, after a couple of hitches it eventually appeared in May 1939, with advance orders of one thousand copies. Written in a spirit of blind, violent defiance, the book was his own apocalypse. He called it his last fuck: 'fuck everybody and everything! . . . Breaking all connections, all ties. I want to become the monster I am.'[48] Formally it was a free-ranging account of his life at Western Union in the early 1920s, mixing descriptions of his unhappy marriage, his infidelities and friendships with a furious attempt to blow up civilisation by revealing the existence of a hidden world he referred to as 'the Land of Fuck':

This is all a figurative way of speaking about what is unmentionable. What is unmentionable is pure fuck and pure cunt; it must be mentioned only in *de luxe* editions, otherwise the world will fall apart. What holds the world together, as I have learned from bitter experience, is sexual intercourse. But *fuck*, the real thing, *cunt*, the real thing, seems to contain some unidentified element which is far more dangerous than glycerine.

Tropic of Capricorn was nominally the 'June book' he had been struggling to write for the past ten years. Rather than deriving from astrology, it took its title from Henry's pet name for one of June's breasts. 'Tropic of Cancer' was his name for the other, so that in a remarkably literal sense he completed in this book the act of revealing his second wife to the world. Yet her presence is pervasive rather than featured, and it is not until the closing pages that she makes her appearance as that vision of 'America on foot, winged and sexed' which transfixed Miller on the floor of Wilson's Dance Hall back in 1923. Biographically speaking it is probably Beatrice who plays the larger part, since what would appear to fuel the anger of the writing – particularly the 'Land of Fuck' section – is the sense of a man who has, at some point in his life, been made to feel low and disgusting for his refusal – or his inability – to collude in the treatment of sex as a dirty little secret. The pent-up anger that resulted produced a work of powerful and liberating violence.

Perhaps, instead of laying plans to make him laugh or to block up his advance with a pile of old soldiers, Miller should have sent Hitler a copy of *Tropic of Capricorn* – with any luck the book might have brought on the catharsis he was so obviously in need of and thus spared the world a great deal of trouble. By 1939, however, Henry had abandoned the idea of participating actively in the war and turned his thoughts instead to a new work, *Draco and the Ecliptic*, which he announced would be ready by 1942. *Draco and the Ecliptic* was a striking title but, as he proudly confessed to Lawrence Durrell, he had no idea what the book itself would be about. Like the *The Palace of Entrails*, it turned out to be another of his many nearly-projects.

Perhaps as a way of warding off the spectre of impending war, throughout 1939 Henry was plunging ever-deeper into esoteric philosophies and religions. He studied the life of the Tibetan Buddhist Milarepa, whom he thought 'a wonderful egg', and joined with

Durrell in appreciation of the taoist-inspired theories of an obscure English psychoanalyst named E. Graham Howe. During the early months of the year he was one of a group which used to meet every week on board a houseboat which Anais Nin had bought on the Seine, *La Belle Aurore*, to discuss articles in the *American Astrologer*. Conrad Moricand, whom Miller was supporting financially by this time, was busily trying to wish Hitler away by drawing up horoscopes which unmistakably pointed to his imminent death. It might be from from natural causes, or maybe somebody would assassinate him. Either way, he was definitely scheduled to fade out of the picture.

11

Some time in the winter of 1938–39, Miller had decided to take up Lawrence Durrell's invitation to visit him in Greece. Having received notice to quit from the landlady, on May 22nd he moved out of Villa Seurat and into a hotel near the Porte d'Orléans. Disposing of 8000 francs in ten minutes inevitably meant another hard round of fundraising activities. It was conducted amid the usual air of farce attendant on these occasions. First he tried to raise money on twenty first editions of *Tropic of Cancer* and fifteen of *Black Spring* through the Gotham Book Mart. Acting on instructions from them, he took the books to the offices of their French jobbers, who shipped them by mistake to the United States where they were promptly impounded by the Customs. Next he wrote an urgent note to Bessie Breuer telling her that he was leaving Seurat for good 'at the doctor's urgent request' and that twenty dollars or so would help him greatly: 'the doctor has taken everything – in fact, more than I had.'

There was *some* truth in this; for most of his adult life he had suffered from piles, and the student regime of life during the Clichy days with Perlès during which they sometimes ate oatmeal three times a day exacerbated the condition. His teeth also needed attention, and he spent 800 francs at an opticians in June on an examination and on two new pairs of glasses. A check for $200 from Frances Steloff helped to offset these expenses, however, and by the time he finally left Paris, early in June, he had about 3000 francs in his pocket. On one of his last nights before leaving the city he attended a performance of Jean-Louis Barrault's stage adaptation of *Hunger*, nicely rounding off his stay in Paris with the book that had had such an influence on how he had been living, writing and performing during his nine years as an expatriate.

He headed first for Rocamadour to take a last look at one of the most beautiful parts of France, the Dordogne. From a base at the Lion d'Or hotel in Rocamadour he visited the fortified city of Domme, and the heart-shaped medieval town of Sarlat: 'I could write ecstatically about it and probably will,' he told Nin.[49] Nothing could dampen his enthusiasm, and at the restaurant at the Cro-Magnon caves at Les Eyziès he ate a 20 franc meal that he was able to add to his list of the greatest meals he had ever eaten in his life.

He travelled on to Nice, sunbathed and swam, climbed in the hills and watched Edward Titus watering the plants in the garden at his villa. He went to the cinema and saw a documentary film about life in the Malayan jungle which included scenes of a cobra fighting an alligator and a tiger fighting a python. He was fascinated by these bizarre encounters, and by the realization that animals in situations like these do not fight to the death.

Later in June, armed with some astrological advice from Moricand, he went to the casino and watched the roulette for a while to see how he would have fared had he chosen to bet. He was aware that his situation was serious, and hung on to his remaining 900 francs.

In the evenings he read Nostradamus and was pleased to see that the predictions agreed more or less with his own instincts – Paris was going to be destroyed by night in an air-raid; the Germans would break through the Maginot Line and be heavily defeated at Poitiers. A French king would arise at Avignon, and France and Spain would form an alliance, leaving Italy and Germany to fight it out to the bitter end. 'Sounds right to me,' he concluded.

In July he travelled to Marseilles to catch the boat to Greece. Nin was on holiday in the area, and she and Henry spent his last night together at Aix-en-Provence. She would not leave Guiler. All the hopes Miller had sustained throughout the 1930s of their one day being able to make a life together were finally abandoned when he boarded the *Théophile Gautier* on July 14th and set sail for Greece.

CHAPTER THIRTEEN

1939–1944
Ancient Greeks and air-conditioned Americans

1

The Colossus of Maroussi, which Miller wrote during the spring and summer of 1940, describes in detail his five-month stay in Greece between his arrival at Piraeus on July 19th and his departure for America at the end of the year. He spent most of his time with the Durrells on Corfu and through them met a number of figures from the Greek literary world, including George Katsimbalis, the 'Colossus' immortalized in the title of his book, and the poet George Seferiades, who later won the Nobel Prize for Literature. He let his beard grow and was nicknamed 'the old man' by the locals who presumed he was Durrell's father. With his informal personality and his willingness to play the clown he became a great favourite. Shortly after arriving, he and Durrell went on a rough camping trip by the sea, and walking on his own on the beach one day Miller met the Mayor of a nearby village. They gestured to one another in sign language for a while, then Miller commenced a monologue in his own brand of *Lost Horizon* Chinese about his trips to China and his many visits among the pygmies of Africa. The Mayor responded with a handsome lie about a Chinese junk which ran aground some years ago on the very beach on which they were standing, obliging its four hundred crew members to live and sleep on the beach until the boat was repaired. The exchange was an excellent start to the visit.

From his base at the Durrells' home he travelled back and forth between Corfu and Athens several times, and with Katsimbalis as his guide visited Spetsai, Nauplia and Mycenae. On such occasions, walking among the ruins of an ancient civilisation, he would be overwhelmed with a feeling of incredulity that it was he, Henry Miller, who was seeing and doing these things. Greece was, like France, a well-established, self-confident, comfortable culture, and the sheer historical authority of its antiquity aroused feelings of slight shame in him at being 'merely' an American. Corrupted himself, he hated to see the imagined purity of his dream of Greece being corrupted by the spread of soda stands, ice-cream parlours and candy kiosks which he saw everywhere. The paradox was that, while he was busy revering Greece for its Greeks, the Greeks were busy revering him for being an American. What he hated above all was to be accosted by returned immigrants, like the former molasses thrower on the boardwalk at Coney Island whom he met at Mycenae one day. Such men liked nothing better than to fall in with him and tell him what a poor, dull and shabby land Greece was compared to bright and shining America.

They horrified him almost as much as the Englishmen he met in Greece. He believed himself to be a great expert on the English: H.G. Wells's handwriting, which he saw in the register of the Apollo Hotel at Delphi, struck him as fine, small and feminine, 'but then that is so characteristic of English handwriting that there is nothing unusual about it'.[1] His subjective honesty is always self-revealing: on another occasion, while signing the visitor's book at Phaestos, he found the name of an old friend. When he had recovered from his astonishment, he relates that his first thought was simply to cross the name out. He was fond of describing himself as the last man on earth, but on occasions like this his instincts were those of someone who wished he were the only one.

Durrell arranged for them to visit an astronomical observatory in Athens, and while they enjoyed the sight of the Pleiades and the Milky Way, whistling in astonishment and murmuring '*Rosicrucian*' to each other, Miller afterwards gracelessly referred to the telescope as a 'dull instrument', largely reflecting his distaste for its operators, fact-bound scientists whose capabilities and discoveries could not compare to the wonders revealed by the mathematics of a first-class astrologer like Conrad Moricand, Dane Rudhyar or Frederick Carter. The process of withdrawal from rationalism and the resumption of the religious interests of his adolescence, begun in Paris under the influence of David Edgar, continued apace in Greece. From Frances Steloff, herself a Theosophist, he had received a copy of *The Secret Doctrine*, and at Ghika's home at Hydra he and Katsimbalis, Seferiades, Aspasia and Madame Hadji-Kyriaco had long discussions over the whisky bottle that ranged from Tibet to Madam Blavatsky.

Even more significantly, during his time in Greece Miller had two outstanding mystical experiences of his own. The first was his meeting with an Armenian soothsayer in Athens who predicted that he would bring great joy to the world and eventually receive the greatest honours man could bestow upon man. There would be three trips to the orient, and from the last of these he would never return. Nor would he die either: Lao Tzu-like, he would simply vanish. Henry asked him to clarify this – did it mean he was immortal? The Armenian refused to elaborate, and only reiterated that Henry would never die. This prediction had a great effect on him.

The second experience took place at Phaestos, where Miller had travelled in a hired car to see the ruins. The imminence of war had greatly reduced the tourist trade on the island, and Miller was given a royal reception by the local guide. After presenting him with a flower and brushing his shoes for him the guide showed him round the ruins, served him a meal with wine afterwards and as he was leaving presented him with some more flowers. The whole business seemed miraculous to Henry.

These two encounters were the symbolic high-points of Miller's visit to Greece, and they lie at the heart of his conviction, as his holiday ended, that he had experienced a rebirth there from which he had emerged less a writer and more a sage. For a man whose first idol was Whitman, who believed that religion developed from art, such a promotion was logical. Yet a second rebirth, coming so soon after the first one in Paris with *Tropic of Cancer*, might seem like one rebirth too many. He was infatuated with Greece, but infatuation is a superficial ecstasy, whether the object is a woman or a country. Five months is not long enough to get to know a land and its people in any depth, but his visions provided him with at least an illusion of intimate insight into the spirit of Greece.

The details of the war, the rights and wrongs of fascism and communism and democracy, were of no interest to Henry. His only thought was of how to keep out of the way of them. The war caught up with him in December, however, and on the fifth of the month the American Minister to Greece ordered all United States citizens to leave the country before January 1st 1940. After that date all passports would be invalidated.

He took his farewell of the Durrells on December 27th and boarded the *Exochorda*, bound for Boston and New York. His mood was sour, and he visited it on an Americanized Greek with whom he found himself sharing a table. The man was not only pro-American, but learned and self-confident. His views commanded the respectful attention of everyone at the table save Henry, who devoted considerable effort into staring through his adversary when addressing him, looking away from him on being spoken to, declining to laugh when he jested and discussing him with others at table as though he were not personally present. He spoiled the atmosphere with great success, and the arrival at Boston in mid-January 1940 must have been a relief for all concerned.

2

Shortly after landing in America, Miller visited his parents and

Lauretta, an occasion described in *Reunion in Brooklyn*, one of his half-dozen best long stories. By this time his father was ill, dying of cancer. He had trouble walking and had become one of those old men who sit out in a chair on sunny days and watch people. Miller joined him sometimes and was amused to find himself mistaken for his father's brother. He loved it when his father asked him about his adventures, and put questions to him like: 'Now tell me, what is the Parthenon?'

The atmosphere at home remained unchanged, with his father slightly henpecked by both Louise and Lauretta, but lovingly nursed. Miller's hatred of his mother is strongly to the fore in his account of their meeting, and seems as wildly disproportionate as ever. He comes bearing a gift of $50 acquired from the sale of a manuscript to a collector only to hear what was to him the dreaded refrain – that he shouldn't have bothered, it was too much, he shouldn't deprive himself like that. The few letters from Louise Miller in the UCLA collection from the late 1930s to Henry in Paris sound a similar note as she thanks Henry for the small gifts of money he sometimes sent to the family. She apologises to him for the way in which his father fills his letters with complaints about how awful his life is, and how much he is suffering, and she tries to reassure him that they are managing well enough. This pathetic courage, the almost pious humility, the brave smile that is at times a little too brave, all irritated Miller. He was more like his father, apt to wring his hands and express himself like Job or Jeremiah when things were not going his way.

Perhaps the most striking moment at the reunion came as Henry was preparing to leave. Louise rushed up to him and in a tearful voice pointed out that he had a loose thread on his coat. Urgently she picked it off. This seemed to him only another demonstration of his mother's stupidity, her trivial mind and fussy nature, but a psychologist might have discovered a deeper and more touching significance in the gesture.

Miller closes his account of the reunion, which is really another elegy for his own lost boyhood and the inexorable nature of change, with a beautiful evocation of a transcendent moment. Walking away from the house, he happens to glance up and sees through a window a young girl reading a book at a table:

It was as if the girl, her pose, the glow of the room falling upon the book she was reading, the impressive silence in which the whole neighbourhood was enveloped, combined to produce a moment of such acuity that for an incalculably brief, almost meteoric flash I had the deep and quiet conviction that everything had been ordained, that there was justice in the world, and

268

that the image which I had caught and vainly tried to hold was the expression of the splendor and the holiness of life as it would always reveal itself to be in moments of utter stillness.

3

In 1939, New Directions, a publishing house founded by a wealthy young American admirer of Miller's named James Laughlin, published a collection of essays, extracts from published work and work-in-progress entitled *The Cosmological Eye*. After the three Paris publications, all of which had been met with a customs ban in the United States, this was his first book to be published in his home country. Among the essays included were Miller's 'boost' for Anais Nin, *Un Être Étoilique*, which presented her to an American public for the first time and started the long process of puffing her diaries that resulted in their commercial publication in the 1960s; the Buñuel article which had so impressed Nin herself back in 1931; an extract from the *Hamlet* letters; a brief 'Autobiographical Note'; and the section entitled 'The Tailor Shop' from *Black Spring*. A curiosity of the collection is the odd way in which the anthologised version of 'The Tailor Shop' was adapted to meet the censorship requirements of the United States authorities: the word 'fuck' was allowed to remain in two places, while a scene in which 'Henry' makes love to his wife was censored to read: 'I could stand her on her head and *I could drag her past the parson's house, as they say, any god-damn thing at all – she was simply delirious with joy.' In both versions the description ends with the sentence, pointedly italicised by Miller himself, ' *"And I hope God take me"* as the good master used to say, *"if I am lying in a single word I say."* '

Miller complained later that the selection in *The Cosmological Eye* had been made without his consent or connivance, and that he had not even been consulted about the title; but he was pleased by the possibilities of the essay collection. Like the letter, the form allowed him the freedom to broadcast his opinion on any subject that happened to interest him without need of further justification. In later years he published several essay collections with New Directions.

The slight reputation within the United States that he had acquired at the time of *Tropic of Cancer's* publication had grown considerably by the time of his return to New York in 1940 and the appearance of *The Cosmological Eye*. The response fell into fairly distinct groupings. One was that of the literary establishment already

*Omitting at this point 'blow into it, I could back-scuttle her'.

noted, including T.S. Eliot and Ezra Pound. Edmund Wilson's review of *Tropic of Cancer* in the *New Republic* of March 9th 1938 was the most sophisticated notice the book had received thus far. Describing the passages on the ecstasies of art or the impending doom of European civilization, he found them 'old-fashioned and rhetorical in a vein of late romantic fantasy reminiscent of *Les Chants de Maldoror*', yet he was struck by a youthful and even ingenuous quality which contrasted oddly with the cynicism of the story. He also commented on the 'strange amenity of temper and style which bathes the whole composition even when it is disgusting or tiresome'. Miller as a writer was 'not self-conscious and not amateurish and he has somehow managed to be low without being sordid'.

Yet he misunderstood the closing scene of the novel, in which 'Henry Miller' sits watching the Seine flow by with his pockets full of someone else's money. The whole seemed to Wilson to have a 'deadly ironic value' which was directed *at* the narrator and his 'vaporings on the banks of the Seine' to which he 'evidently attaches some importance'. Wilson was a civilized man, an Insider. Though he had in his youth been a connoisseur of the burlesque, and even written his own appreciation of the same Houston Street burlesque that Miller made the subject of one of his mezzotints, he was sufficiently orthodox to find it artistically inconceivable that a writer could extol amorality and still expect to enjoy his readers' sympathies. Miller put him right in his response, a Letter to the Editor which contains the key statement that he had 'painstakingly indicated throughout the book that the hero is myself. I don't use "heroes", incidentally, nor do I write novels. I am the hero, and the book is myself... .'

In the same letter he rebuked Wilson for claiming to be the first to pay serious attention to *Tropic of Cancer* and referred him to an earlier review by Professor Herbert West, in the Dartmouth Alumni Magazine in 1937. West was one of the first of a second distinct entity among Miller's earliest and most enthusiastic supporters, the academics and university professors. Their response to his writing and his personality had much in common with that of a third group comprising respectable businessmen, career diplomats and politicians who described themselves as 'collectors of erotica' and sought out original manuscripts of erotic and pornographic writing for which they paid high prices. Among this latter group was one of Miller's keenest admirers, a man named Huntington Cairns. To have won the heart and mind of Cairns was a particular and extraordinary triumph, for Cairns was none other than the Special Adviser to the US Treasury Department with responsibility for ruling on the difference between obscene books, which were to be intercepted by customs, and 'works of art' which might be allowed in. He was, in other words, the man personally responsible for forbidding the entry of Miller's book into his own country. In August 1936 the writer and his censor had met in Paris. Miller showed Cairns round the city and captivated him utterly, having mastered himself the trick performed years before by his favourite burlesque comedian Frank Fay, who could travel in the realms of the taboo with such skill that even the censors were charmed. Miller liked Cairns, realized fully the value of such an important ally, and flattered him shamelessly. In one letter he told him that he considered him one of only two friends he had in the whole of America.

West and Cairns relished *Tropic of Cancer* for what it was, an honest book, devoid of Lost Generation self-pity and sentimentality and at times hugely and sarcastically funny. Yet they were also suit-wearing men, Walter Mittys who derived vicarious enjoyment from Henry's performance as a middle-aged Huck Finn. He was their alter ego, their barbarian, their Redskin, breaking all the rules and getting away with it. They also had much of the naivety of the learned man, and believed implicitly in Miller's repeated assertions of his own incorruptibility, his artistic integrity and his total rejection of compromise. They made a god of him in a way that more sophisticated men like Wilson and Eliot did not. Cairns did not hesitate to tell Miller that when he was with him he felt that he was 'in the presence of a holy man,'[2] and a great deal of Miller's correspondence in years to come was with men who wanted to indulge in what Lawrence Durrell once called 'metaphoric barn-dancing' with him.[3] Miller enjoyed and encouraged these responses. The adoration of such men fostered his occasional tendency to megalomania, and it was to Cairns that Miller addressed one of his first authentic, heavy-duty biographical documents, a letter of April 30th 1939 on the subject of his life and career so far, 'which will be of interest to the biographers later'.

The early response to Miller does not seem to have split according to sex. Men and women made common cause against the censorship of sexual fiction, and there was no question of any kind of disapproving feminist analysis of Miller's literary 'attitude' towards women. Writing to Morton Czabel in 1939, the poet Louise Bogan actually praised Miller for the honesty of his sexual writing, notably in 'The Tailor Shop' in which the youthful 'Henry Miller' describes his seduction of a grieving widow. The counterpoint between the widow's anxious 'You'll always love me, won't you?' and the youth's 'Why did I wait so long, anyone could have her, she's a pushover' seemed to her to 'chart the difference between man's and woman's attitude to sexual intercourse very truthfully and clearly'.[4] She also found him amusing and clownish, 'very German and Til Eulenspiegel' and loved his

271

farcical account of the goings-on in *Hamlet*. In the correspondence of many other writers of the time can be found similar references to the phenomenon of Henry Miller, even if it was simply to observe, like Wallace Stevens, that 'the only definite impression I have of Miller is that he is prolix'.[5]

Perhaps his greatest admirers among the writers were the young. A whole generation of American authors who came to the fore in the 1950s had been weaned on the *Tropics* and *Black Spring* in the 1940s. The young loved him for being a rebel and made him their cause. As early as 1934, within three months of the publication of *Tropic of Cancer*, Miller wrote to Anais Nin that he had received a money order from 'a guy in Philadelphia whom I don't know and whose address wasn't stated'.[6] He was soon to discover that America was full of such guys from Philadelphia.

4

In the spring and early summer of 1940, Miller wrote three short works in New York. One was *The World of Sex*, which he wrote at the request of Huntington Cairns to elucidate his views on sex and which was privately printed in a limited edition. The second, written in May and June 1940, was *Quiet Days in Clichy*, a pendant to *Tropic of Cancer*, which is a brief, fictionalized account of the two happy years in which he shared a flat in Clichy with Alfred Perlès. It is largely a description of sexual encounters, in the burlesque style, with eccentric women and sensitive whores who say things like 'You're a brick' when Henry empties his pockets for them. This is one of Miller's most enjoyable books, a portrait of the author as pantomime clown on the razzle: if there's food he eats it, if there's a woman he makes a pass at her, if there's a policeman he knocks him down. If he gets upset, then it's fiercely, tearfully and briefly, and it all ends well with a meal. *Quiet Days in Clichy* also contains a stout piece of anti-anti-semitism in the form of a description of his encounter with the Luxembourg café proprietor and his 'Café-free-of-Jews'. *Mara-Marignan*, a subdivision of *Quiet Days in Clichy*, is in the same vein of burlesque promiscuous encounters, but ends on a note of existential doubt which is unique in Miller's writing. After yet another high-spirited romp he and 'Carl' sit down to eat. Suddenly Carl 'mumbled something to himself, then added, as if doing a sum – "It doesn't make sense."'

Miller's major project for the summer was to finish *The Colossus of Maroussi*, largely expanding on notes made in November at Hydra. He worked on this in the summer in New York and finished it in

272

August at Hampton Manor in Bowling Green, Virginia, the home of the writer Caresse Crosby whom he had met in Paris. The aloofly mad Salvador Dali and his wife were among his fellow guests. It was here he wrote the most inspired section of the Greek book, a passage called 'Boogie-Woogie Passacaglia'. This had nothing whatever to do with Greece, being instead a surreal paean to 'that great Negro race which alone keeps America from falling apart' as represented by Louis Armstrong, Count Basie and Duke Ellington. The piece later became a favourite among black jazz musicians in Chicago, although when Louis Armstrong was shown it he apparently failed to understand it.

In spite of a characteristic insistence on his freedom to occasionally use the word 'nigger', Miller was a great admirer of the black people in America. Rather as Orwell regarded the Proles, Miller saw in blacks the custodians of naturalness and sanity and of the secret of ordinary day-to-day happiness which too much material success and too much deodorant had destroyed in the whites. Carl van Vechten was the leading white exponent of this romantic view of black Americans at the time, and Miller sent him a dedicated transcript of the 'Passacaglia' section 'with much trepidation' for his comments. Van Vechten was one of several of his heroes from the 1920s whom Miller got to know personally in the 1940s, and it must have tasted sweet to find himself lionised by his own idols. H.L. Mencken was another former hero with whom he became friendly at this time.

Miller had a brief professional relationship in 1940 with an agent named John Slocum at Russell and Volkening. Slocum introduced him to Wyndham Lewis, another writer whom he came to admire greatly. Lewis was living at Long Island that summer, and Miller found him 'witty, charming and highly intelligent'. Lewis was an obvious candidate for Henry's pantheon of violently-talented enemies of the people like Knut Hamsun and Louis-Ferdinand Céline. He liked Miller personally but had little time for his writing.

Once he had finished the Greek book he placed it in John Slocum's hands and Slocum sent it off on what soon became a dreary round of rejections that would eventually include ten commercial publishers. In its mixture of cosmic meditation, knockabout humour, mysticism, unreliable history and strange authorial intrusions – such as the apology to Hans Reichel over some old and quite private misunder-standing – it was simply too baffling a product for most editors.

However, Slocum was able to report interest in the notion of a book on America which Miller had mentioned to him. The idea for this had occurred to him as early as 1935, after returning from his trip to New York, when he wrote to Hilaire Hiler about his plan for a book that would be like 'a loaded gun at the head of America'.[7] By 1938 he had the title, *America, the Air-Conditioned Nightmare*, and had noted down fifty chapter-headings. Doubleday, Doran, as the firm of Doubleday was then known, agreed to commission the book and advanced him $500 in August 1940, some of which went towards the purchase of a 1932 Buick. Anais Nin was living in New York by this time, and for a while Miller hoped that she might make the trip with him. She neither could nor would, however, and in the end he joined forces with a painter whom he had known in Paris named Abe Rattner. In October the two men set off to look for America, Rattner with his water-colours and Miller armed with his notebooks, which included a printer's dummy of *Leaves of Grass*, some Dostoevsky, Hamsun's *Mysteries*, a copy of Walter's *My Secret Life*, and *Leaves of Grass* itself.

5

With brief intervals of return to New York, Miller motored through America for almost exactly a year before producing his report on the state of the country. With a journalist's instincts, what he was actually looking for was not America itself but evidence of a healthy alternative America. Every sign of independence, every sign of rejection of the white man's society pleased him. In a black district of Washington one evening in November he was delighted to be refused entry to a café because of the colour of his skin, and writing to Anais Nin he expressed the hope that clubs and bars in Harlem would start barring white people too.[8]

From Washington they continued in an arc down to Richmond, headed south-west to Asheville, on to Atlanta, Georgia, then south-east to Jacksonville, scene of the ill-fated attempt to cash in on the Florida property boom with Joe O'Reagan and Emil Schnellock some fifteen years previously. From here they headed due east along the coast to Mobile, Alabama, following the old Spanish trail from St Augustine through desolate parts of Florida, fifty miles without even a petrol station, the only signs of life the hogs and cows wandering on the roads. The corpses of dead hogs littered the roads: 'the young pigs look ghastly,' he wrote to Anais, 'as if they were struck down naked'.

On Monday January 20th they arrived in New Orleans. They took a steamboat ride along the Mississippi, and spent some days visiting friends of Rattner's. One of these was an old doctor and water-colour painter named Dr Marion Souchon, whom Miller afterwards portrayed in his book of the trip. Another was a writer named Weeks

274

Hall, a wild, eccentric man who owned a dog which drank black coffee and had a full-sized bed to himself.

Rattner and Miller split up for a while after this, and Miller drove on to Natchez alone, stopping off on the way to see an ancient burial mound belonging to the Natchez Indians. He carried with him a map given to him by the Indian Bureau and made a point of visiting Indian townships and encampments and historical and holy sites, determined to see through the veneer of civilization which the white man had laid across the area. He observed the cynical way the Indians had been palmed off with the most arid and desolate lands.

While staying in Natchez Miller received a message that his father was not expected to live much longer. He made arrangements with a local garage to look after his car and took the ten-hour flight back to New York, arriving just two hours too late for a final meeting. Fortunately, he had broken his trip briefly in late November to return to New York for his parent's wedding anniversary. He had known for some time that his father was dying and visited and talked with him frequently during the summer of 1940. There was nothing outstanding between them and when he visited the grave at the Evergreen Cemetery his mood was mellow rather than grieving.

He remained in New York for four weeks after the funeral before resuming his trip, and this time decided to see something of the industrial north before turning south again to pick up his car. He travelled by train to Cleveland, Ohio, went on to Detroit, then westward to Chicago. The area depressed him, and so did the salesmen he kept meeting at his hotels. He was reading a book of Indian philosophy and trying to feel serene and above the riot, but the thought of the Ford plant festering on the landscape not ten miles out of Detroit made him feel more like Céline than Ramakrishna. The discovery of the Amish community in Pennsylvania and the Amaria in Iowa cheered him up a little, and he exulted in their rejection of the American way of life and their fidelity to their own past. 'No matter if the others are killed off,' he wrote in his notebook, 'the religious groups will recreate America.'[9] Followers of the Baha'i faith, whom he visited at Wilmette, Illinois, impressed him similarly, and he predicted the movement would increase in strength over the next hundred years. He noted and wrote constantly, feeling strongly that the angry mood of his 'celebration' of America was not at all what his commissioning editor at Doubleday, Doran was looking for from him, but unable to do anything about it. Not even the slums of Chicago's north side could cheer him up. Eventually he turned south and headed for Natchez to resume the journey by car.

Before setting off westward again he visited Jackson, where he spent three days with Eudora Welty and her mother. The visit was in connection with a curious enterprise Miller was involved in at this time which involved writing pornography professionally for a number of private collectors of erotica. Besides the Dalis, another house-guest at Caresse Crosby's house where Henry stayed in the summer of 1940 was a man named Barnet Ruder. Ruder operated as an agent for these collectors, and had soon persuaded Miller, Caresse Crosby and a painter named Virginia Admiral to write for him. Miller enrolled Nin, who in turn put several of her friends to work, including George Barker, Harvey Breit and Robert Duncan. His purpose in going to Jackson was to persuade Miss Welty, whom he had met in Paris, to join them, having previously written to her with an offer to put her in touch with an 'unfailing pornographic market' if she ever found herself in need of money.

Because of Henry's notoriety, the material allegedly written by him began circulating in typescript form and soon acquired an underground reputation of its own. Six copies of unsigned stories allegedly by Miller were donated anonymously to The Kinsey Institute for Sexual Research in Indiana as early as 1946, and carbon copies of the scripts circulated among collectors of erotica throughout the next forty years. Finally, in 1983, three years after Miller's death, the pieces were collected and published under the title *Opus Pistorum*, dog-latin for 'the work of a miller or grinder'. The six pieces are a series of pornographic fantasies which include sex with an ideally corrupted child, with a dwarf, incest, full-scale orgies, bestiality and ritual humiliations involving urine and bottles. To collectors and biographers who came across the typescripts of these stories in the course of their reseaches, Miller always denied having written them and, presumably because of the grossness of the fantasies, there have been persistent rumours to the effect that the pieces are in fact forgeries. The man who has concerned himself most with the question of their authenticity is the writer and folklorist Gerson Legman, a man with an encyclopedic knowledge of the history of sexual writing. He was offered the stories for sale by a collector as early as 1945, but declined to accept them as genuine, reasoning that Miller could not have written them for to have done so 'would represent traducing and travestying his own sincere work'. He remained so convinced of the forgery theory that, in an unpublished introduction he wrote for the 1983 Grove Press edition of *Opus Pistorum*, he made what amounted to a confession having written the material himself, with the assistance of another professional writer of pornography named Robert Sewall. Nor was he the only claimant. Another was the late Bernie Wolfe, a journalist, film writer and author of *Memoirs of a not altogether shy pornographer*, although better known for his *Really the Blues* collaboration with the jazz musician Mezz Mezzrow. Lupton Wilkinson has also been named as a possible author.

That hard-core pornography was written by Miller, Nin and their friends is not in dispute. The issue is whether Miller was responsible for these particular stories commercially published under his name. No original scripts exist, and the argument for forgery rests almost exclusively on the frequent appearance in the stories of sexual slang like 'jism', 'John Thursday' and '*bonne-bouche*', words which do not appear anywhere else in Miller's writings, published or unpublished. On the other hand there are numerous Miller trademarks in the writing: the cunt as a clam, the ejaculation as a roman candle going off, the presence of a distinct anglophobia, a passing reference to Dostoevsky and even to the chess champion Alekhine, as well as an eight-page section of 'France In My Pants' about American journalists in Paris which contains no sex at all and could have come straight from the pages of *Tropic of Cancer*. Moreover, the writing contains many examples of Miller's comic sexual surrealism, like the description of a navel big enough to keep a horsechestnut in, and of pubic hair so thick that you would need a lantern to get through it, as well as a recurrence of the famous 'torch' image from *Tropic of Cancer*. And one might think that it would take an unusually conscientious forger to come up with the little touch of narrative curiosity about whether or not the midget has a half-size toilet in her flat. Beyond this there is the evidence of George Barker, who succinctly dismisses Miller's denials as 'absolute balls' and confirms that the writing produced for private collectors in and around 1940 was of the grossest sort.[10]

The interest of *Opus Pistorum* really lies in the fact that Miller seems to have been uniquely ashamed of his involvement in the project.* The first occasion on which he denied responsibility for them was in 1950. He was by that time corresponding with a collector, J. Rives Childs, who mentioned in one letter that a mutual friend named George Howard had offered him some manuscripts 'by Henry Miller' for $60. He quoted from Howard's letter, including the punning French titles of the pieces, 'Sous les toits de Paris', 'Rue de Screw' and

---

*Copies of all six pieces have been a part of the Henry Miller Collection at UCLA since 1962. Miller took a keen interest in this collection and was aware of their presence. When Lawrence Clark Powell, the librarian in charge of the collection, asked him outright whether he had written them he did not say he had; but neither did he deny it.

'France in my pants' and the description of them as 'excellent Miller material'. Miller replied to Child's letter on July 21st 1950, categorically denying that he had anything to do with these: 'The titles of the three you mention *I* could never have invented! They are completely out of my "line". I abhor erotica – this sort – "smut for smut's sake" – as I suppose them to be. Now, it is possible that "they" invented these titles too – perhaps for pieces I have written – but I doubt it strongly.'[11]

Perhaps it was with some idea of lessening his shame by involving as many people in the enterprise as possible that Miller had written to Eudora Welty of the 'unfailing pornographic market', and telling her that he would be calling on her in Jackson. 'Not in this house,' was her mother's response. When Miller did arrive mother and daughter were equally nervous, and Miss Welty made sure that during the three days she ferried Miller about in her car she was always in the company of at least two chaperones. She had imagined that he would be something like the author of *Tropic of Capricorn*, but found instead 'the most boring businessman you can imagine'. She wrote that he never took his hat off once all the time he stayed with them, and on being taken to the same restaurant, the Rotisserie, for three nights running expressed his surprise that a town like Jackson could boast three such fine restaurants.[12]

Whether he broached the subject of the pornographic connection with her in person is doubtful. Like *Moloch*, the first of these two noisy skeletons rattling in his archives, the *Opus Pistorum* business suggests that Miller at times had to rely on the reactions of others to what he did to provide him with behavioural guidelines rather than on a response from within. The guarded hospitality of the Welty family probably made it clear to him that there was no point in his pursuing the matter any further. Soon enough anyway he was regretting his own involvement in the business. In a letter to Nin he described the work as 'devastating' and 'like getting rid of an incubus'. 'I don't want to do that work any more for anything,' he told her. 'I feel sorry you're involved.'[13]

7

After picking up his car again in Natchez he moved on to Santa Fe via Little Rock, and from there on to Albuquerque, where he became aware that he had a namesake travelling in the region. When he called in at the Albuquerque post office to collect his mail and the cheques that Nin was sending to him at regular intervals the clerk told him that all mail for Henry Miller had been forwarded to a man by that name in Colorado. The Buick needed urgent repairs, and to pay for them would leave him with just $8 in his pocket. His only hope was that the other Henry Miller would be honest enough to return the money orders to him if he opened the letters by mistake. As he ruefully admitted to Anais, however, it was surely a great temptation for the man. In the end he risked the repair and sent off another flurry of letters 'begging for help and explaining the situation'.

He was joined by Rattner again, and together they visited another Indian settlement at Albuquerque, at Isleta. The sight of the blue corn thrilled him, as did the primitive lifestyle of the Indians. 'People say they stink,' he wrote. 'I didn't notice it myself.'[14] What he enjoyed most was the time they were tricked by a six year old Indian girl who offered her services as a guide, rode around in the car with them for a while and finally admitted she wasn't taking them anywhere in particular, she just wanted the ride. That was real taoism, real free-and-easy wandering along trackless paths. Henry always made a point, even in Paris, of asking children the way. 'You might not get there,' he would say, 'but you'll have a more interesting time'. He had his hair trimmed by a Mexican barber in Albuquerque who complained about the arrogance of the whites, the way they never bothered to learn the local language. Stateless, rootless, a nation of one, Miller agreed wholeheartedly.

He stayed on in Albuquerque and worked on the America book for a few days before pushing on towards the Grand Canyon, where he spent another nine days writing before making the last leg of his coast-to-coast journey which brought him to Hollywood. There he remained, pleased by the climate, the palm trees and the scenery. Though he wrote to Nin in May 1941 of his plans to sell the Buick and return East he stayed on through the summer, meeting and being met by the likes of Aldous Huxley and Christopher Isherwood, the actress Miriam Hopkins, the astrologer Dane Rudhyar and old acquaintances from Paris like Richard Thoma and Hilaire Hiler. He also met the film magnate Joseph von Sternberg and his erotica collection (worth, to somebody or other, $100,000), John Steinbeck, whom he did not like especially, preferring the company of his friend Ed Ricketts, the original of 'Doc' in *Cannery Row*, Tennessee Williams, whom he met at Man Ray's house, and John Cage, who approached him with an offer to collaborate on a radio commission. He shook hands with Dos Passos, one of his early favourites among American novelists, and was lionized at the RKO studios. In short he found himself treated like an important man, and loved it.

By this time he had given up hope of finding a major commercial publisher for *The Colossus of Maroussi*, and accepted an offer from the Colt Press of San Francisco to do the book, so continuing his association with the small publishers of the world that had begun with the Obelisk Press and which would remain a characteristic of his literary career. His fears about the reception *The Air-Conditioned Nightmare* would meet with appeared to be justified when the *Atlantic Monthly* turned down the chance to publish an extract. Americans were going through a wave of patriotism, and though Henry abandoned his original, provocative title, he was afraid he might have wasted his time completely, that 'soon it will be treason to say anything against America'.[15] Later he told Durrell that it was 'a wasted year' and to Anais Nin he confessed that he had only scratched the surface of the country: 'the average American knows more about America than I ever will.' But it was a bold venture nonetheless, and perhaps only a real auto-didact would have had the necessary bravado to set off in search of the largest and most complex country in the world in a ten-year-old car, without even a cheque book in his pocket, and nearly succeed in finding it. *The Air-Conditioned Nightmare*, when it finally appeared in 1945, turned out to be a fine book. Perhaps it was more about Americans than America, but it displayed to the full Miller's fondness for grotesques, geniuses, oddballs, eccentrics and the dogged, indomitable nobodies who make up ninety-nine per cent of the population of any country. Along with Philip Wylie's *A Generation of Vipers*, it was widely regarded as a useful counterbalance to the complacency of American society.

In September he managed to drag himself away from Hollywood. With the money from the sale of *The Colossus of Maroussi*, a small Chicago edition of *The World of Sex*, some autographed copies of his books (in a pirate edition from Shanghai brought back by American sailors), some back royalties and what would appear to be the dodge of faking a notebook of his America trip out of extracts from his notebook proper – and then selling it – he had enough to finance the journey back to New York.

There he stayed during the winter and spring of 1942, working mainly on a first draft of *Sexus*. In the daily-record form of *Tropic of Cancer* he had managed to arrive almost completely in the present, but already with *Black Spring* and *Tropic of Capricorn* he had returned to his true home in the past. Evidently, seven years after their divorce and with the therapeutic *Tropics* behind him, Henry remained obsessed by the image of June and loyal to the committment he had made in 1928 to write a full-scale account of his life with her. *Sexus* was to be the story of the earliest days of their affair, beginning with an account of

the break-up of his marriage to Beatrice, his subsequent disenchant-
ment with life at Western Union, and his growing obsession to be a
writer. The conception was of a larger, more detailed work than
Tropic of Capricorn, something that would give the same impression
of a near-exact description of a life and a love affair as Proust had
achieved in *A la recherche du temps perdu* and which would attempt a
similarly minute recreation of the scenes and sights and smells of the
author's childhood and early manhood.

By now the affair with Nin was effectively over. His procrastination
in spending the entire summer away from her in Hollywood was
something she took as a personal insult. In July 1941 she told him that
if and when he did come back to New York, it would mean little to her:
'You allow two minor things – the book, your mother – to stand in the
way of returning to me.'[16] His attitude seemed to her tantamount to a
suggestion that 'the time has come to separate'. Henry, who never
overcame his desire not to be the guilty or wounding party at the end of
a relationship of which he had grown tired, protested that this was not
the case, that she was incorrect in thinking that his work was 'now
merely an excuse for doing whatever pleases you'.[17] Yet in essence she
was right. He had only just managed to start work on the project
which, for fifteen years now, had seemed to him his life's real work.
Relationships with strong-minded women like June and Anais,
stimulating as they were, proved ultimately too demanding of him,
both as a person and as a writer. The trip to Greece followed by the
long trek across America had loosened the ties that bound him to
Anais and liberated him to pursue his literary goal. It meant that he
was now, for the first time in his adult life, free from any strong
emotional attachments. Temperamentally he had never outgrown the
simple desire to be free to do whatever he liked, without need of
consideration for the wishes of others, and in many ways the situation
as he passed his fiftieth birthday seemed to be approaching the
ideal.

8

The summer of 1941 had been enough to persuade Miller that
California was where he wanted to settle. Purity is for other people,
and in Hollywood, among the dream-merchants and charlatans, the
rich, the famous, the ambitious, the pretentious, the poor and the
failed, he had discovered Americans who were more truly his
Americans than any Amish or Baha'i could ever be. In the summer of
1942 he returned to California, and took up an offer from a young

couple called the Neimans to share their small house in Beverley Glen in Hollywood.

Almost at once he began seriously looking for work in the film industry. For some time he was involved in a project to adapt for the screen *The Maurizius Case* by Jakob Wassermann, a novelist who was widely read and appreciated in the 1930s. Wassermann was one of a whole class of writers of whom Miller was becoming increasingly fond as his hostility towards intellectualism increased. Other favourites included Jean Giono, Georges Duhamel and the later Hamsun. Reading Giono's *Que ma joie demeure* and Duhamel's *Salavin* series, Henry was able to identify with characters who mixed an ecstatic acceptance of life with a rejection of material values, exhibiting along the way personally attractive failings and weaknesses that undermined them and prevented them from fully becoming either the gods they aspired to be or the monsters they feared secretly they might be.

Miller duly produced a treatment of the Wassermann novel, but was unable to raise any interest from the major studios. His collaborator, a Dr Friedman who had obtained the film rights to the book, paid him $100 in September for the work he had already done and gave him a promise of a percentage if the film were ever made; that was the last Miller heard of the project.

No matter; much of Miller's time was spent, as before, in enjoying the unique possibilities afforded by Hollywood. The puritan reactionary in him disapproved of the place and everything it stood for, and he frequently expressed the hope that the Japanese would bomb it flat; on the other hand he was fascinated by its vulgarity and the freakish behaviour of its inhabitants. In one of his notebooks he refers to tales he heard of movie-stars so fed up with the spread of syphilis and the frequency of blackmail that they had abandoned human intercourse completely in favour of elaborate sex machines. He was especially struck by the story of one man who had shot himself dead in front of a mirror while wearing some sort of masturbatory device on his penis.

He was also struck by the strangeness of meeting in person actors whom he had seen performing on the screen. They seemed 'like live ghosts' to him, and he derived great pleasure from the blurring of fantasy and reality that took place on such occasions. His meeting with an actor who had played a monk in *Lost Horizon* was an especially tantalizing experience which compounded his fascination with the film. He enjoyed the surreal cultural atmosphere of a place where, in the space of one week, he could meet Marlene Dietrich's daughter, receive admiring messages from Errol Flynn, dine with Stravinsky (whom he found too polite) and fall asleep during a lecture on music by Schoenberg.

Hollywood pleased him, but the wealthy people he met there did nothing to shake his belief that money and happiness were unconnected. He wrote to Nin that it was terrible to witness the disgust which people felt for the work they did, and that he would never compromise his integrity by writing commercial trash for the film studios. As Nin pointed out, however, there was nothing especially honest about writing pornographic trash for a dollar a page either.

In fact, he received several respectable offers of work while in Hollywood, including a chance to adapt Graham Greene's *Brighton Rock* for the screen. These offers he either turned down or were later withdrawn. He also found that his voluble insistence on being an uncompromising and suffering artist worked against him. The Hollywood crowd took him at his word, and treated him as the ikon of unassailable integrity he pretended to be, trapping him in the rôle. They looked up to him, from the depths of their own compromised and depraved lives of wealth and luxury, and loved him for not selling out. The Lone Ranger would never take his mask off when children were present, and Henry Miller felt much the same sense of obligation towards his fans. So there were no films and no film work. If the evidence of his single play, *Just Wild About Harry*, is anything to go by, the truth is probably that he was incapable of writing for films rather than unwilling to do so.

By November 1942 he had given up hope of making a million in Hollywood and applied for a job at a local probation office for ex-convicts. The comings and goings around the office during his interview reminded him forcibly of his Western Union days, and with a caseload of 750 men per officer the amount of work was about the same. Miller was initially turned down for the job because he lacked a college degree. Later they were prepared to reconsider his application, and as Christmas and his fifty-first birthday approached he was on the verge of returning to the world of useful citizenship.

Much as he might have enjoyed working in such an environment, however, Miller realized that a return to full employment would make it still more difficult to get *The Rosy Crucifixion* written. He therefore conducted another campaign of letter-writing and fund-raising which equalled in its scope the campaign of 1935 which had kept *Tropic of Cancer* alive during the early months of its existence. By the end of the year his efforts had begun to show results. He was offered review work (his first paid review was of a biography of Kierkegaard for the *New Republic*), his old admirer Cyril Connolly sent him a check for $80 for an extract from the America book which was published in *Horizon*, and each post bought fresh contributions to his round-robin appeal –

'An Open Letter to All and Sundry' – in the form of money, offers of accommodation, food, cigarettes, stamps and much else besides. An English edition of *The Colossus of Maroussi* sold out within thirty days and was due to be reprinted while negotiations were under way for a Greek version. The American edition was almost sold out too, and although Colt were having money trouble they were also planning a second printing. The greatest boost of all was a check for $200 from the National Institute of Arts and Letters which arrived in mid-January. The day was, as always, saved, 'Imagine having money in the bank,' he wrote to Anais. 'I can scarcely believe it.'

9

Miller's following soon began to show signs of becoming a cult. One of its most active promoters was a young man named Bern Porter, a research physicist at Berkeley at the time he became interested in Miller. He was also a small publisher and in the autumn of 1942 visited Miller at Beverley Glen with a request for material. Miller gave him the letters he had written to Schnellock from Paris to consider, and Porter eventually published a small selection of these as *Semblance of a Devoted Past*, illustrated with some of Henry's own water-colours. He also showed himself willing to publish ephemera like Miller's *Plight of the Creative Artist in the United States of America* and a new edition of Miller's 1935 appeal for money for Alfred Perlès, *What Are You Going To Do About Alf?*

These were works that promoted an image of Miller rather than displaying his literary talents and Henry was soon describing Porter as 'a most ardent disciple of mine' and a man who 'doesn't want to make money but put money in my pocket'.[18] Porter was clearly determined to play a part in his hero's immortalization, and quickly graduated from being his publisher to being his bibliographer. Henry participated actively in the work, helping Porter to track down the innumerable minor publications in which his essays had appeared – issues of the London *Modern Mystic*, for example, which had published 'The Wisdom of the Heart' and 'Seraphita' in 1939 – and nursing his reputation along by helping to create the apparatus of a writer's fame.

Another early promoter of the cult was a young friend of Porter's named George Leite, an Oakland taxi-driver. Together they published a primitive literary magazine called *Circle*. Miller contributed to *Circle* and persuaded friends like Anais Nin to do so too. The attention flattered him. 'I know they are making quite a cult of me,' he told

Anais, attributing it to his writing. He claimed to be unable to do anything about it, yet clearly he fostered it. Once he sent a note to young Leite urging him not to forget to read the life of a millionaire cattle king for no apparent reason other than that the man was called Henry Miller. Such behaviour was only a logical extension of the obsession with being famous which Miller had shown from his earliest manhood. In the early letters to Emil Schnellock this feature of his personality was sometimes relieved by a healthy self-irony; but by the time he reached Hollywood the ability or the desire to ridicule his own pretensions was largely gone.

10

A pattern that begins to emerge in Miller's life is the recurring sense of someone trying desperately hard to recapture a freshly-lost happiness, recover complete a beautiful vision, a better time, a better place, a better woman. The new country, like the new woman, was at first glance always better than the old one: Beatrice was better than Pauline, June better than Beatrice, Anais better than June. France was better than America, and Greece was better than France.

Greece was his new obsession, and henceforth he took a special interest in any Greek people he came across. He was especially pleased to meet Greek admirers of *The Colossus of Maroussi*, and became friendly with Melpomene Niarchos, then wife of the shipping millionaire Stavros Niarchos. Another admirer was a young woman named Sevasty Koutsaftis. Early in 1943 she became involved in a projected Greek translation of the book, and after reading it she wrote an enthusiastic letter of appreciation to Miller. The librarian friend who brought them together had told Henry how beautiful she was and predicted that he was sure to fall in love with her.

Fall in love with her he did, although he was pleased to find her not quite as beautiful as he had imagined she would be. She lived with her sister and mother, a woman who was about the same age as Henry, in a house in the Hollywood Hills, a six- or seven-mile walk from the Beverley Glen cabin, and Henry began courting her, 'assiduously, and always on foot'. Her name meant, in Greek, 'revered one', a fact to which Henry attached great significance[19] and which, along with her self-control which allowed heavy petting but not intercourse, duly enslaved him, to the disgust of the man with whom he was by then sharing the cabin at the Glen, John Dudley.

John Dudley, a painter whom Henry had met at Caresse Crosby's house in Bowling Green, was determined to do something about it, and one day when Henry had a date to meet Sevasty in a bar he went along with him and after a couple of drinks persuaded Miller to break the date. The situation recalls the conclusion of *Tropic of Cancer*, with Henry in the rôle of the love-sick fool, Fillmore, and Dudley playing Henry's old part as the hard-headed liberator. Shortly afterwards the affair came to an end. Miller was certainly very keen on Sevasty for the few months that the relationship lasted, and even wrote a dreadful poem in honour of her, 'O Lake of Light'.

The affair marked the start of a whole series of sometimes comic and sometimes tragic relationships with much younger women into which Miller plunged repeatedly and passionately, but without real conviction, over the next thirty years. Perhaps his experiences with June and Anais had used up his capacity for real love, leaving only the ability to indulge in game-playing simulations with women young enough not to know the difference, or not to care. After their break-up he and Sevasty met one day to discuss their reunion in the Beyond. 'I love you more than I will ever love anyone,' Sevasty told him. 'But I am not *in* love with you.'[20]

There were other affairs during this period, including one with a woman referred to only as 'Laure', and he had his share of propositions to deal with too, like that from a young woman so moved by the sections of *Sexus* that she was typing out for him that she burst into his room one day and declared herself. Though he did not want her, it was gratifying confirmation of the success of his struggle, as he wrote the book, to 'visualize on the faces of all my coming readers this expression of unreserved love and admiration'.[21]

11

Henry's life at the Glen, first with the Neimans and thereafter with John Dudley, had become oppressively social, and he found himself longing increasingly for solitude. While he was by no means rich he was by now financially established. The success of his occasional public appeals had a knock-on effect, and this period sees the full flowering of that unique reverse paranoia of his as the money, clothes, messages of support, offers of help and water-colour materials continued to pour in – and all because, as he wrote in 'An Open Letter To All And Sundry', of the refusal of the Supreme Court to restore 'a half-dozen terrifying words' to currency. He had also begun to establish a reputation as a painter of charming, child-like water-colours which he produced with great rapidity and was selling at exhibition and privately for anything between $30 and $100 each. In 1943 he earned $1400 from sales of his paintings alone – and when he ran out of his own paintings he was not averse to signing the nudes done by Margaret Neiman which were lying around the cabin and selling those too. One of his biggest fans was Arthur Freed of MGM who bought up an entire window of paintings at Bowinkels shop in Westwood village. Pleasing as the pictures undoubtedly were, much of the interest in Miller as a water-colourist was clearly due to his notoriety as a writer.

Back in August 1942 he had been dreaming of a retreat, and wrote longingly to Nin that if he had 'a little shack of my own in the hills here I think I would become a hermit'.[22] The visit from a painter named Janko Varda at Beverley Glen one day brought his dream a step nearer realization. Varda was another fan of the *Tropics* anxious to meet the author, and Miller liked him at once. Not only was he Greek, he was an extroverted, larger-than-life figure, the kind of Rabelaisian adventurer to whom Miller was always attracted. Varda urged him to return the visit when he left, and presently Miller took him up on the offer and went to see him at his home in Monterey.

Varda took him on a motoring tour along the rugged Big Sur coastline south of Monterey. Henry had earlier mentioned to Varda that one of his plans was to move to Mexico in pursuit of the simple and cheap life, and Varda mentioned that the same living conditions could be obtained at Big Sur. Specifically, there were a number of shacks at a place called Anderson Creek which had formerly housed the convicts who built the road along the coast. Now they were unused, and available for rent at $5 dollars a month.

They drove through the area and Miller fell in love at once with its rugged and desolate magnificence. Anderson Creek in winter, however, seemed almost like more solitude than he wanted. Nevertheless, on the drive home Varda introduced Henry to a friend of his named Lynda Sargent who lived nearby in a much more handsome house than the Anderson Creek shacks, with two bedrooms and guest quarters. This was a single-storey log-house that she rented, beautifully situated on a promontory, high above the sea. Henry told her how keen he was to get away from Beverley Glen for a while and she invited him to join her and live in one of the spare rooms. He accepted the offer and early in March 1943 moved in. Lynda Sargent had the reputation locally of being a highly-sexed woman, but the relationship between them was strictly platonic. Henry was amused by the image he had acquired through the *Tropics* as an oversexed monster, and in a letter to a friend about his chaste life with Miss Sargent wrote that the gossips on the

287

peninsula were sure to have heard the news, and to have made the obvious inference that the great Henry Miller must be impotent.

He lived at the Log House, as it was known locally, for some eight weeks, and was thrilled by his new home. He told Durrell that it was on the farthest rim of the western world, facing China, and resembled not only the Tibet of *Lost Horizon* but also the Greece of *The Colossus of Maroussi*. The area had an aura of mysticism, magic and strangeness about it, and when Lynda Sargent remarked, over the cherry pie one evening, that one of the odd characteristics of Big Sur was that no one ever died there Miller's thoughts at once returned to the prophesy made by the Armenian soothsayer in Greece. More and more, Big Sur was looking like the right place to mutate from 'Henry Miller' into 'Henry Tzu'.

In May 1944 the owner of the Log House sold it, and Miss Sargent and Henry both had to leave. She had good connections in the area, however, and helped Henry find a place of his own, a two-room, furnished log-cabin with inside plumbing and its own spring water at Partington Ridge. It belonged to a local man who was away on military service. Lynda Sargent contacted the owner and arranged for Henry to live there for $15 a month. By May 5th he had moved in.

Taking stock of his situation, he felt at last that he was ideally placed. He had a home of his own in the surroundings he had been dreaming of; a patron had approached him, anonymously, in the wake of his last public appeal and offered to pay him $200 a month and had even paid out the first instalment on time; and a small Miller-industry run by Bern Porter had been established. To cap it all, Henry was by now involved in one of the most surreal episodes of his entire surreal life, involving a woman whom he later referred to as his 'mail-order bride'.

The girl's name was June Lancaster. She lived in New York and met Henry through her boyfriend, an ex-seaman and aspiring writer named Harry Herkovitz. Herkovitz had fallen so completely under Miller's spell after reading the *Tropics* that he had found his own dancer named June and by 1944 was busy living out a carbon copy of Miller's life as a struggling writer. Anais Nin became involved in Herkovitz's infatuation with Miller's life and fiction in a distressing manner when Herkovitz turned up at her apartment on West 13th Street in New York one day to visit her. She discovered a 'violent, primitive and confused' man who claimed to be Henry's symbolic son, and in seeking her out he clearly expected to meet the mythical Anais whom Miller had described so persuasively to him during their meetings in California. In words that eerily resembled those she had heard Miller use to her, Herkovitz complained that he wanted to be a

288

writer, but that his June would not let him write. He followed up his visit with a love-letter to her, addressed to June, Anais, Sabina, Djuna, Alraune, Isolina (characters from Nin's *House of Incest* novel). A few days later his June, June Lancaster, came to see her in person, a pitiful girl aware that her lover was wilfully mythologizing her. Nin, who had much of Miller's direct self-confidence when solving other people's problems – with as little apparent grounds – told Miss Lancaster that her task in life was to restore Harry to reality. The two women embraced 'like sisters' and parted.

What June Lancaster had neglected to tell her 'sister' was that she and Henry Miller had been carrying on a love-affair by mail for some months in which, at his specific request, she had been addressing him as 'Dear Val', and signing herself 'June the Second'. Even before he had met her Henry wrote to inform Durrell that the new woman was 'almost like a copy of the first June. I am crazy about her.'

In May, after a great deal of wavering, June finally made up her mind to take the chance and join Henry in Big Sur. Henry had no car, and as there was no public transport serving the remote Big Sur area she travelled first to Monterey, arriving at the end of the month and staying with Janko Varda while word was sent to Henry. As they waited for Miller to arrive and claim his prize it occurred to Varda – an artist specializing in collage – to dress June Lancaster in exotic clothes and stand her on top of an upended barrel. Here she was to pose with her hands above her head in an attitude of supplication. When Henry eventually arrived he was not unnaturally stunned at the sight, and paused briefly in the doorway. Then, recovering his poise, he rushed forward and prostrated himself at the foot of the makeshift pedestal.

Within six weeks he was, predictably, utterly fed-up with his 'mail-order bride', and by mid-August she was on her way back to New York. In his haste to be rid of her he let her take his trunk and suitcase. Bern Porter contacted her later for her impressions of life with Henry and learnt of his fondness for cats, his intense dislike of vermin and insects, his exceeding generosity, the odd impression he gave, like an Icelandic shape-changer, of undergoing metamorphosis in the course of the day, his immaculate orderliness and the harassed look on his face when he discovered her one day using his threadbare and faded washcloth as a rag. She appeared to harbour no bitterness towards him, nor he towards her.

In October of that year Harry Herkovitz provided a coda to the whole episode, telephoning Anais Nin and informing her that he was waiting for her downstairs with a gun and was going to kill her. She rang the police who refused to intervene until she had actually been shot. Later in the day she called a friend who knew Herkovitz by sight to come round and see if he was there, but by then he had disappeared.

The failure of the affair with June the Second returned Miller to a state of isolation which he simultaneously relished and feared. He made some attempts to relieve it by conversing with his dog, Pascal, a stray which he had acquired. He tried to encourage Pascal to listen when he played music on his gramophone, but it was not easy, and if he tried to entertain him by dancing the animal just moaned in terror. Henry only possessed one record anyway, from the soundtrack of a film version of *Carmen*, and he would play this over and over, dancing to it and roaring like a bull. He was a city-dweller, a New Yorker, a Parisian, and it was hard to get used to his new, Tibetan life. On one occasion he did meet Robinson Jeffers, the community's other literary man, while out walking. He liked him, but Jeffers was no use as company. Henry found him 'very very shy. A trembling rock.'[23]

Relief from his boredom eventually came about in a curious way when he got word in September that his mother was about to undergo an operation for the removal of a cancer. He decided to travel to New York to see her. Louise made a quick recovery from the operation, however, and Henry turned the journey of filial support into a social trip. He stayed briefly in New York with Harry Herkovitz, then travelled out to New Haven where he stayed for a fortnight with a recent pen-friend, Wallace Fowlie, a teacher at Yale. Fowlie, already an admirer of the *Tropics* and an authority on Rimbaud, by now one of Miller's great favourites, was another of those respectable members of society who found the violence of Miller's language and the unpredictablity of his personality liberating and exciting.

Once news of his presence on the campus became known Miller was fêted by others at the university, and the President of Trumbull College even offered him $1000 to deliver one lecture. Miller declined the offer. The gesture left Fowlie speechless with admiration, although in retrospect it is hard to see why – a thousand dollars for a single lecture could hardly be called selling-out.

The real purpose of Miller's visit seems anyway not to have been to visit Fowlie but to re-establish contact with an interesting young female student of the college he had met earlier in New York. A pretty, blonde-haired girl just turned twenty-one, her name was Janina Martha Lepska, and she was from a family of Polish immigrants. He was always attracted to a woman with an unusual voice, and was charmed by the slight accent with which she spoke English. She was a graduate student from Bryn Mawr who had transferred to Yale with the intention of studying the history of philosophy, and while Fowlie was busy teaching she and Miller were able to use his apartment to become better acquainted. The two of them made a trip to Bryn Mawr to visit Paul Weiss, another of Henry's intellectual admirers, and then split up briefly, Lepska to return to New Haven and Henry to visit Richard Osborn at Bridgeport. They were re-united at New Haven, and by mid-October had agreed to conclude their brief courtship in marriage.

Before returning to California, however, Miller had one or two other visits to make. After Yale, he went to see yet another of his academic admirers, Professor Herbert West of Dartmouth College. Here he did agree to give a lecture, to one of West's classes consisting mainly of apprentice seamen and midshipmen who were studying at the college under the Navy V-12 programme. He caused something of a sensation by telling his young audience that 'the Nazis are no different than you are. They're fighting for the same things that you're fighting for.' One youth asked him what he believed a man's aim in life should be, to which Henry replied: 'To satisfy your own impulses and fulfil your own desires.' He pointed out to them that they were 'not in uniform because you want to be but because there's an authority that forces you to be. The only authority I believe in recognizing is the authority of one's own will.'

The taoist subtleties of his argument were lost on the FBI men who visited him and Professor West the day after this lecture, and they opened one of their files on his 'anti-American activities'. The incident was followed a few weeks later by a critical article on Miller in a New York magazine, *New Currents*. The journalist, Albert Kahn, wrote a monthly column exposing writers and cultural heroes whom he deemed fascist and anti-semitic, and on the evidence of the lecture, and a study of Miller's published writings, Kahn unhesitatingly classified him with Gide, Pound and Hamsun as guilty on both counts. It was probably the first time since the days of his battles with Michael Fraenkel that Miller found his provoking ways taken so seriously. Kahn fastened especially on a call in one of Henry's articles for 'real traitors, *traitors to the human race*,' and made the unanswerable point that the German Nazis had been betraying the human race in Europe with great efficiency for several years now. Kahn had wilfully mis-understood him, though Miller's way of speaking and writing always left him open to such misunderstanding, and the experience confirmed him in his horror of public speaking. It exposed him too openly to an uncontrollable world where Miller-friendliness could not be guaranteed. They understood him better in California, and that was where he headed now.

291

Miller and Janina Lepska made their way slowly and circuitously westward, calling in on Emil Schnellock at Fredricksburg, Virginia, and making an attempt to marry there which was thwarted by some missing papers. From Fredricksburg they went on to Washington, where they saw Caresse Crosby and Huntington Cairns, then on to Boulder, Colorado to visit Henry's former landlords at Beverley Glen, the Neimans. By the time they reached Denver the documentation was in order and at the city hall on December 18th 1944 Henry and Lepska were married.

CHAPTER FOURTEEN

1944–1951
Life on the lost horizon

1

Psychological theories are hardly necessary to explain why a man of fifty-three should want to marry an attractive girl of twenty-one: one or two pointers suggest, however, that in marrying someone so young Miller was also making an attempt to start life over again from the beginning. The adolescent experience with Cora Seward, the girl he wanted so badly and never won, had taught him the dangers of putting a woman on a pedestal. From Pauline Chouteau he had learnt the joys of sex, and in Beatrice Wickens he felt he had married a woman who climbed up onto a pedestal of her own accord. June Mansfield had offered him what he thought might be the ideal combination of friend and lover, but his sexual conservatism proved too great in the end, the burden of equality beyond him.

The long relationship with Anaïs Nin had been in many ways an ideal arrangement, offering sexual pleasure and intellectual and spiritual companionship with none of the burdens and banalities of ordinary personal responsibility. Henry, however, almost in spite of himself, remained addicted to the state of marriage, and without the hope of permanence and eventual respectability that relationship, too, was doomed to failure. With this wealth of experience behind him he might have felt that he had a fair chance of finally getting it right at the age of fifty-three, and it is interesting to note that Lepska, uniquely among the women in his adult life, had the blond, Nordic looks that recall his descriptions of Cora. The death of his father and the serious illness of his mother must also have had a sobering effect on him, and made him realize that time was passing.

Superficially the two did not have a great deal in common. Lepska was an educated, even intellectual woman, according to Huntington Cairns 'the only female Hegelian I know'. Miller had enjoyed Nin's intelligence but his aversion to education was getting stronger by the year. What they did share was a lack of spiritual complacency: Henry was still, in his fifties, searching for the unifying theories that would provide a coherent explanation of life, and Lepska, in her adolescence, had passed through a phase of intense religiosity during which her parents had had to restrain her from running away from home to become a nun. From Henry she may have been hoping for guidance, maturity and the essential emotional and intellectual stability which his calm exterior often suggested he possessed, while Henry, famous and thirty years older than his wife, probably hoped that he would be able to control her without too much difficulty, and that this second attempt to settle down and start a family would be a greater success than his earlier one.

In their first year together they lived in the cabin on Partington Ridge, where a daughter, Valentine, was born on November 18th 1945. Early in 1946 the owner of the cabin, Keith Evans, returned from the war and the family had to move to a shack in the old convict settlement at Anderson Creek. The living conditions were primitive, the roof leaked and Lepska had to cook on an old wood-burning stove. However, they invested $100 in necessary repairs, painted the ceilings and walls white and the doors and window sashes blue, and with its bright yellow kitchen the place soon resembled a doll's house. Neighbours provided them with rugs, chairs, a round table and a phonograph with some records. Varda gave Henry two collages to hang on the walls. 'Too bad the convicts couldn't have lived this way!' he wrote to Schnellock.

There was no local medical care for Lepska and the baby, so Henry was often left alone at the house while she travelled to Berkeley for check-ups. He spent the time breaking coal and sawing wood, in preparation for the rain, and doing water-colours, so besotted by the pleasures of fatherhood that he did little writing that year. Sometimes he walked over to Slate's hot springs with the family's laundry. The place functioned as a sort of social club, and he got to know many of the other residents there.

Miller already had numerous friends in Big Sur and the surrounding areas, including an eccentric 'white witch' and Christian Scientist named Jean Wharton for whom he developed a particular fondness. She lived in a house on Partington Ridge which he had always admired, and when she decided to move to a smaller house she put it on the market at $6000. There were no takers but, aware of Henry's liking for the house, she offered it to him and his family. He explained that he could not afford her price, but she let him have it anyway on the understanding that he would pay when he was able to. In February 1947 the family moved in.

The house, a thousand feet or so above the coastal highway that ran along by the Pacific, was one of a dozen or so cottages on the Ridge. It had a small shack at the back which Miller used for a studio, and a run-down garage for the car he still didn't own. Its connection with the highway was a one-lane dirt track with branches off towards the other dwellings. There were no shops in the area, and the local mailman ran a small grocery business for the residents from his van. This house remained Miller's home for the next fifteen years. During their second year there Lepska gave birth to their son, Henry Tony.

2

One reason Henry felt he could now try to settle to a permanent home and a regular way of life was that he had achieved his ambition: he was a famous writer. In the process he had justified to himself in the holy name of Art all those crimes he felt himself guilty of – the disappointment he had caused his family in not taking over the tailor-shop; the desertion of Beatrice and Barbara; the betrayal of June with Anais Nin. The three Paris-written books with which he had achieved this were therapeutic acts of literary violence which had left him free to indulge the milder sides of his character, and his reawakened interest in religious philosophies and the occult increasingly flavours his life and letters throughout the 1940s. Lawrence Durrell, who soon became his only remaining contact in the world of conventional literature, was puzzled and amused by what seemed like an anomalous development in a man who had once seemed so impatient of hypocrisy and humbug, but found an explanation in the belief that it was, after all, a not unnatural reaction to the gross materialism of the American way of life. Certainly there was an element of rejection in Miller's cultivation of the bizarre and the ridiculed, but his interests in the field of eccentric religions and philosophies had a longer pedigree, stemming from the days of Bob Challacombe and Benjamin Fay Mills, and the attempt as a young man to abandon the corrupt city and return to the soil which brought him to the fruit farm at Chula Vista.

Though he was to revise *Sexus* in the late 1940s, the original manuscript was written in 1942, and with it he came to the end of his attempts to find some kind of meaning in sex by writing about it. In a sense this had only been part of the larger search for a meaning or a pattern to life which had bothered him since his schooldays. Much of his petty lying, his editing of reality and his enthusiasm for the pretensions of astrology was directed to proving that such order existed, and that the details of his own life demonstrated its existence. In his letter of April 1939 to Huntington Cairns, he claimed: 'the circle of my philosophical wandering is completed. I am liberated from all metaphysical speculation. The half-way station, so to speak, was

295

Sinnett's "Esoteric Buddhism", which I left off reading in the Brooklyn Public Library at the age of twenty-two or three, I imagine – perhaps earlier – and resumed just a year ago here in the Villa Seurat, at the page where I had left off.'[1]

He received an assignment from *Town and Country* to review French and English war literature for them in the autumn of 1945 which gave him the chance to read Gertrude Stein, Rex Warner's *The Aerodrome*, Vercors, Sartre and Camus's *L'Étranger*, among other books. He was glad of the $500 and wrote amusingly of Stein that 'the woman who has spent forty years of her life in Europe today sounds more than ever like a Midwesterner,'[2] but responded most enthusiastically to Claude Houghton's edifying *'All Change, Humanity!'* Paradoxically, for someone who always spoke of idealists with contempt, he detested the Warner novel because in it mankind's 'new leaders are . . . represented as men of power instead of men of truth, or peace, or good will'. Though he did continue to read literature, and could see the greatness in Carson McCullers, for example, his taste in reading from this time onwards tends to be for occult or edifying books well outside the mainstream of literature. *The Flying Saucers Are Real* by Donal Kehoe; *Choose Life: the Biblical Call To Revolt* by Eric Gutkind; *Crisis and Resurrection: A Prognostic of Destiny* by Samuel Greiner; *A Treatise on White Magic* by Alice Bailey and *Interlinear to Cabeza de Vaca: The Power Within Us* by Haniel Long are typical titles he would enthuse over in letters to friends. Such books appealed to the prophetic strain in his character that was first stirred by Walt Whitman's shamanistic poetry, the philosophical works of Grant Allen and Edward Bellamy's hugely successful and influential utopian novel of the 1880s, *Looking Backward*.

Miller's religious enthusiasms did not sap his business sense, however. When George Leite began experiencing some difficulties in his dealing with the Gotham Book Mart, Miller gave him this advice: 'Steloff – yes, I know this line of hers! When you want anything out of her, play the spiritual flute, she loves it.'[3] In Steloff's case the spiritual flute meant his own old favourites, Madame Blavatsky and Theosophy. A curiosity from this period concerning Blavatsky is the letter Miller wrote to his co-seeker Emil Schnellock about her. Schnellock was now running the Art Department at a college of the University of Virginia and slowly declining into alcoholism. In 1944 Miller wrote him a gentle letter breaking the 'disillusioning news' about the Mahatmas of *The Secret Doctrine*: a book he had recently come across proved beyond doubt that 'Koot Hoomi' and 'Mahatma Morya' were the Madame's own inventions and that she had herself forged the written testaments attributed to them on the subject of the existence of other planes of being. By the time of a similar experience in the 1950s, with T.Lobsang Rampa, author of the best-selling *The Third Eye*, Henry's faith had become stronger. The news that Rampa was not a Tibetan monk at all but an English plumber from Devon named Cyril Henry Hoskins did not seem to him to compromise the essential truth of the book's account of a Tibetan upbringing. 'True or false, it's a wonderful book' was his reaction.[4]

3

By 1946, Schnellock was writing to Miller about 'the little band of your followers who knock on my door to see your books and manuscripts – a growing band'.[5] Some of these people actually left their homes to come and live near Miller on Big Sur. A typical example was a biochemist from Chicago named Robert Fink, one of the thousands of men who came under the sway of the *Tropics* while serving in the army. Fink wrote Miller a fan letter, later visited him in person and began supplying him with used clothes and small sums of money. Eventually, in 1949, he and his wife moved out to California where they could help him more efficiently.

The first and, according to Big Sur residents the MacCollums, the best of all the disciples was Emil White, an Austrian who had been captivated by *The Cosmological Eye* while working at a bookshop in Chicago. One of Miller's begging circular letters had fallen into his hands and he had begun raising money for Miller in Chicago literary circles and forwarding small sums of around $3 a time – not much, but in those days enough to eat for a week if one were prudent. He was not to know, of course, that Miller was not prudent. After meeting his hero in Chicago, White had to disappear to Alaska for a while to avoid being drafted into the army. They corresponded and, sensing the extent of White's devotion, Miller urged him to come and live close by. He told him not to worry about money, he would take care of that. This was in 1944, before Miller met Lepska, and as the farce of the celibate relationship with Sevasty Koutsaftis and the mail-order bride June Lancaster showed, Henry was not much good at picking up women on his own. White was a successful womaniser, and Henry had always needed such men in his life, from William Dewar and Joe O'Reagan in New York to Wambly Bald and Alfred Perlès in Paris. 'I'll use you as a decoy for cunt in Carmel,' he told White. 'You go in and fetch them out to the country.'[6]

White duly came and moved into a three-room cabin down on the coast-road, a thousand feet below the Ridge, where he operated as a watch-dog for Miller, weeding out the fans from those who only wanted to go up and stare at the monster behind what one newspaper reporter referred to as 'the cult of sex and anarchy' which was allegedly taking root in Big Sur. Visitors like D.H.Lawrence's widow Frieda, with whom Miller was now corresponding, and the daughter of his old friend Blaise Cendrars, who turned up one day in the company of one of his Hollywood movie friends, were waved on up. White otherwise made himself useful by chopping wood for Henry, answering fan mail and doing little odd-jobs. Miller developed a passion for the novels of Herman Hesse at this time, particularly *Siddhartha*, and he was in the habit of drifting over to Emil's to be read to from the original German version of the book. As for White, he helped himself royally from the women who turned up looking for the wild man of the *Tropics* and found instead a doting father and would-be sage who was, as a later visitor, Dylan Thomas, put it, 'fond of commonplaces'.

White was only the most dedicated of the stream of men who came and went in Miller's life after he settled on the mountain. Sometimes these were confused souls with personal problems, often connected with alcohol, who enjoyed Henry's tolerance of their wild behaviour and his attempts to save them from themselves. Others were aspiring writers and artists who hoped that being acquainted with such a man would be both lucky and profitable. One such was an Israeli artist named Bezalel Schatz, who later became Miller's brother-in-law, with whom he produced a large coffee-table book consisting of an illustrated chapter from *Black Spring* done by a silk- screen process. Miller rewrote the chapter by hand, trying to reflect the mood of the content by varying his own writing, and the book was sold by subscription at $100 per copy.

There is no sense in supposing that Miller minded being used in this way. A master at self-promotion himself, to him it all seemed quite natural and above board. He was a gifted user of other people and was not above schooling them now and then in the correct way to handle him. 'You seem to regard a friend as one who does something *for you*,' he rebuked Bern Porter once. 'Wouldn't it be better to look upon him first and foremost as one whom *you do something for*.' Bezalel Schatz was by this definition 'a tremendous friend. There is nothing he omits or forgets to do for me.'[7] Then there were other, less formal relationships, such as the one with the art critic of the *New York Evening Sun*, whom Miller described as 'an old man – forget his name – good friend of mine'.[8]

Many of those who were attracted to Big Sur during the 1940s were nakedly proud of knowing 'a famous man'. Fink was inclined to boast that 'Henry Miller is one of my closest friends and a man whom many consider a saint', while to another correspondent he confided that Miller was 'only a saint in the sense that he is as nearly complete a human being as the world has ever seen, since maybe Leonardo da Vinci'.[9] Miller protested to an outside world of journalists and friends like Durrell that he was certainly not a saint, yet he did little to ridicule the pronouncements of such as Fink.

The appearance of Bern Porter's *The Happy Rock* in 1945 only made matters worse. Apparently intended by Porter as something between a *festschrift* and a fanclub magazine, this collection of essays and sentimental tributes to Henry from friends and admirers came down quickly and heavily on the side of the magazine. A terse refusal to contribute from the poet Kenneth Patchen was its only redeeming feature. Patchen denounced the whole thing as a bandwagon, and with a directness worthy of Miller himself urged the author of *Tropic of Cancer* to kick the 'sloppy-eyed nobodies' (ie the rest of the contributors) off it and drive the wagon down the nearest sewer. 'For God's sake, Miller', he concluded, 'the important thing is not to be liked by these people!'[10] Like the coffee-table book with Schatz, it can only have strengthened the suspicion in certain quarters that Henry was a literary charlatan.

To certain correspondents, notably Wallace Fowlie, Miller claimed that he did not approve of *The Happy Rock*, that he had known nothing about it and that when he did find out had not wanted to spoil Bern Porter's fun by forbidding it. However, what he said depended very much on to whom he was writing. Fowlie, a practising Catholic, had became an ikon of purity for Miller, and in writing to him Henry always played 'the spiritual flute'. It was unthinkable, for example, that he would ever have urged Fowlie to leave his job at Yale to come to California and act as his decoy for 'cunt in Carmel'. Durrell heard the same protestations of innocent non-involvement from Henry, whereas Schnellock could be trusted to understand every facet of the Miller personality. Schnellock, with his memoir *Just A Brooklyn Boy*, was the star contributor to *The Happy Rock*, and in May 1944 Miller wrote urging him to report any attempts Bern Porter might make to edit his contribution. Around this time he was also trying to persuade Schnellock to write his biography, and had plans to travel to England where he hoped to find someone willing to commission such a book. 'That I collaborated with you will not be mentioned,' Miller assured him,[11] adding that Schnellock's essay on him was so good that he didn't want to 'tamper much with what you wrote'. Despite his ceaseless attempts to get someone to publish Anais Nin's diaries, the prospect that somebody might actually one day do so was beginning to alarm him, and a biography written by Schnellock, with Henry looking over his shoulder, would be his insurance against the emergence of an unsatisfactory portrait. 'It will be your version versus Anais – if the diary is ever published,' he told his old friend.[12] Even the title of Porter's anthology, underscoring the portrait of the writer as Taoist sage, was chosen by Henry. He also took an active interest in the assembly of a book entitled *Of, By and About Henry Miller* which was published by a bookseller named Oscar Baradinsky from his Alicat Book Shop in Yonkers in 1947. An idea of Miller's own, for a book of photos featuring 'HM and "associates",' never got off the ground, although something very like it eventually appeared in 1972 as *My Life And Times*.

So Henry did not kick anybody off his bandwagon, but just let it roll. As far as he was concerned, he was simply enjoying the fruits of promotion, after years of hard work, from the congregation to the pulpit. Hence his use of the word 'holograph' when referring to his handwritten letters, and hence also his willingness to sign and send out a 'holograph' form letter like the one promoting the 1944 publication of *The Angel Is My Watermark*, a 'book' consisting of an original water colour of his, a photographic copy of 'An Open Letter To All And Sundry', the chapter of *Black Spring* from which the title derived, six black-and-white reproductions of his own paintings and several photographs of himself in the act of painting them. The whole cost $50 and was put out, Henry told potential buyers, 'in a spirit of homage by friends of Henry for his friends'.

Miller could laugh at many aspects of himself and his reputation, but his status as an artist and a sage were taboo. There is never a hint of irony or self-ridicule on the subject; nor on the subject of the many other minor publishing ventures of this and subsequent periods in which old letters, scraps of notepaper and notebooks were packaged like holy relics for sale to the faithful. The need to be surrounded by fans rather than friends, and to see his name and even his handwriting in print in the smallest of small magazines perhaps indicates the true extent of the lack of self-confidence he felt in himself as a 'real' writer and illustrates his psychic need of the whole circus of fame simply in order to go on believing in the reality of what had happened to him. In a letter to Alfred Perlès, written shortly after arriving in Greece in 1939, he described his thoughts as he wandered the streets of Athens: 'I have many reflections during these promenades, not least of which is that it is altogether phenomenal that I, Henry Miller, should be prowling about these precincts.'[13] But why should this be so phenomenal? Such thoughts echo the sense of astonishment with which he found himself at the Gare Saint-Lazare in Paris in 1928, and long before that even, on his disorientated adolescent trek westward to Chula Vista in 1913. It is an odd attitude, suggesting that his life seemed to him at times a kind of scarcely credible hypothesis that required constant authentication from the outside world in order to prevent the whole thing – life, man and name – from simply vanishing into thin air.

4

On the domestic front matters were not going well. It became clear almost immediately that Henry and Lepska were not suited. She found him wilful, irresponsible and unreliable, while he chafed under her attempt to bring order and routine into their lives. His many male friends in the region were always a diversion, but life as a family man was once again proving dull. He was therefore pleased to receive a letter late in 1945 from Conrad Moricand, then living in Switzerland whence he had fled during the war. Moricand was the man largely responsible for convincing Henry that the study of astrology was to be taken seriously, and with his circle of artistic and occult friends he remained in Henry's eyes an impressive and exotic man. Moricand was destitute, and after receiving several more letters Henry offered to help him emigrate to the United States, giving the firm assurance that he would look after him 'for the rest of his life'. Lepska was opposed to the idea, but Henry talked her into it.

The arrangements took several months to complete, during which time Miller supported Moricand to the tune of $1000, which represented his entire royalties from the sale of his books in America during the preceding six months. When Moricand's papers were finally in order, Henry paid for his ticket on the plane from Geneva to London, and on the *Queen Mary* from England to New York. The last leg of the trip, again at Henry's expense, was the flight to join his hosts in California. This was real altruism: Henry had nothing to gain from Moricand, and only hoped that the experience of life on Big Sur might cure him of his misery.

Moricand arrived early in 1947 and was given Henry's old writing-room in which to live. One of his first actions was to tack curtains over the windows to keep out the draught. He complained of the cold and left an oil-stove burning all night in his room. The fact that there was no bath tub in the house bothered him, and he did not seem to like children much.

Within weeks of Moricand's arrival it became obvious that the experiment had failed. Miller was bored and disappointed by a man

301

whom he had never been personally close to, even in Paris. Moreover his nature was such that he disliked talking about personal problems with anyone, and rather than discuss the melancholic disaster that Moricand's life had become he gave him Zen-like proddings to stop complaining, pull his socks up and be happy. Moricand, alas, was no searching youngster, nor even a robust oldster. He was a sixty-one year old man on the slide, and he felt he had been humiliated by fate. Henry's suggestion that he pull his weight by teaching French to his two year old daughter did not got down well, and soon Moricand began to hate his host.

Seeing that his own brand of Zen magic was not having much effect on Moricand, Henry one day sent him up to see the white witch, Jean Wharton. Some hours later Moricand returned in disgust, bearing the copy of Mary Baker Eddy's *Science and Health* which Wharton had pressed on him. Miller, for whom the word 'crank' had no place in his vocabulary, later delved into the book himself and found Mrs Eddy a 'great soul, filled with a great light'.[14]

Moricand's health was poor and deteriorating. From the start of his stay he had been complaining of itches and sores on his legs, and in March Miller agreed to take him to see a specialist at Salinas County Hospital. He booked him into a room at the Serra Hotel in Monterey which cost $4 per day, and continued to support him throughout March and April while he worked to persuade him that it would be in the best interests of all concerned if he returned to France. By the end of May he estimated that the had, since 1945, spent about $3000 on Moricand.

Moricand wanted to go back to Paris as much as Henry wanted him to go, but on certain conditions. One was that Henry would use his influence to get him a job there with the Obelisk Press. Another was that Henry would arrange for him to be paid a lump sum of money from his accumulated French royalties on arrival in Paris. Miller would agree to neither term, and the experiment in philanthropy degenerated into an unpleasant farce which involved both the Swiss and the French consuls in San Francisco before it all fizzled out and Moricand disappeared from his life for good, consumed with hatred for his would-be benefactor and muttering '*Quel farceur*' between gritted teeth as he left. He was finally deported in 1949 and returned to Paris, where he lived out the last five years of his life in loneliness and poverty. He died on a houseboat, moored on the Seine, which his rich parents had endowed for the use of the Parisian *clochards*.

'The whole story deserves a book,' Miller wrote to Monsieur Bertrand, the French consul, and in due course he produced *A Devil In Paradise*, written and published two years after Moricand's death in 1954. Like most of what Miller wrote, the account has its moments of great hilarity and sharp self-insight, but in the end the picture is too one-sided. One begins to suspect character-assassination, and to feel a sneaking desire to hear Moricand's version of events, as one would like to have heard Wambly Bald's, or Beatrice Miller's. In a final thrust at the already dead Moricand, Miller recalls a story he told after supper one day, prefacing the account with a description of how his little daughter snatched a piece of bread from Moricand's plate and of how Moricand, eyes blazing, at once snatched it back from her. Later on, when the child had gone to bed, Moricand began his tale of an adventure he had in Paris once which began as he followed a woman and her young daughter through the streets. As the tale unfolded, Miller became aware that Moricand was describing the development of his erotic fascination not for the mother but for the daughter. 'The thought of what was passing through his mind made me shudder,' he wrote. Mother and daughter booked into a hotel, closely followed by Moricand. Signals pass between the two adults, the mother discreetly leaves the room, Moricand enters and . . . Miller listens in horror, unable to dismiss from his mind an image, which he has conjured himself, of the child sitting on the bed in a state of innocent disarray and 'nibbling at a piece of pastry' as Moricand triumphantly reaches the climax of his story: '*Je l'ai eue.*'[15] At this Miller feels his hair stand on end and realizes that he is in the presence of Satan himself. Not even his inspection of Moricand's collection of pornographic drawings, with its scenes of child rape, nuns masturbating with religious artefacts, tortures, coprophagic orgies and so on apparently prepared him for this. His outrage at Moricand's story is a unique expression in his writing of disgust at an aspect of human sexual behaviour and, coming at the end of his description of Moricand, the incident creates an atmosphere of complete aversion towards the man which rules out any sense of pity the reader might feel for him. For Miller, all was fair in love, war and literature. Accused later by an admiring critic of moralizing at Moricand's expense, Miller admitted the charge, and in doing so revealed again the surprisingly deep influence of *Lost Horizon* on his attempt to become a sage. His gesture in trying to save Moricand, he wrote to Thomas Parkinson, had been 'perhaps all unintentionally inspired by that film which I saw at least a half-dozen times – 'The Lost Horizon'. That part particularly where the hero leaves his Paradise in order to save his brother.'[16] One might almost hazard a guess that Moricand's major failing in Miller's eyes was not his paedophilia, but his resistance to Henry's charisma.

303

The major publications of the immediate post-war period were the collection of essays *Sunday After The War* in 1944, which contained 'Reunion in Brooklyn', *The Air-Conditioned Nightmare* in 1945, and its companion piece *Remember to Remember* two years later. *Remember to Remember* bears the subtitle *The Air-Conditioned Nightmare Volume Two*, though the title piece mostly harks back to happy days in Paris. The pen-portraits of Varda, Beauford Delaney, Jasper Deeter and Abe Rattner are bland, but some of the other pieces are excellent, notably the satirical 'Astrological Fricasse' and the fanatically pacifist 'Murder the Murderer'. Particularly fine is 'The Staff of Life', an essay ridiculing the American mania for refined bread and the whole fear of life which underlies it. The ending is a splendid example of the kind of inspired surrealist rant at which Miller excelled.

He also wrote in 1946 the first part of a long essay on Rimbaud for New Directions Year Book number 9. A second part was published in the 1949 Year Book, both under the title 'When Do Angels Cease to Resemble Themselves?', though the complete book, as *The Time of the Assassins*, was not published in English until 1956. Rimbaud became a great favourite of Miller's once he had managed to overcome the association of the name with Mara Andrews' enthusiasm and the Henry Street basement. As was frequently the case with Miller's literary heroes, it was the life as much as the work that inspired him. Rimbaud died in November 1891, the month before Henry was born, and a near-coincidence of this sort hinted at a possible transmigration of souls. He also identified with Rimbaud in his hatred of his mother. What inspired him most of all was the way Rimbaud had apparently succeeded in making a journey all the way through the world of literature and emerged on the other side of it. This was by now his own great dream.

With the assistance of Lepska, he struggled for some time to produce his own translation of *Une Saison en Enfer*. Typically his ideal for the project would have been a translation done without reference to the original, simply relying on his recall of the mood of the work. Eventually this was abandoned in favour of the study, for which he prepared himself thoroughly by reading most of the extant works on Rimbaud and having three separate horoscopes for his birth drawn up. He also benefited from a conversation with Stephen Spender, whom one of his society admirers, Mrs Ruth DeWitt-Diamant, brought up to see him one day. Spender brought news of a recently-published study of Rimbaud. Miller also corresponded with Wallace

Fowlie on the subject. For all this background labour the result was not a factual work, nor yet a critical study, but a spiritual biography, reminiscent in some ways of a book Henry greatly admired, J.W. Sullivan's *Beethoven: His Spiritual Development*. What emerges is a description of Rimbaud as a proto-Henry Miller, someone who, in writing his greatest work, 'stood so clearly revealed to himself that he no longer had need for expression on the level of art'.[17] Though a very different piece of work, the Rimbaud essay looks forward to the novella *The Smile At The Foot Of The Ladder*, published in 1948. Both mark a further move in the direction first indicated by *The Colossus of Maroussi*, away from the violence of the *Tropics* and *The Air-Conditioned Nightmare* and towards a world in which wisdom rather than literary mastery was the preferred goal.

The Smile At The Foot Of The Ladder was written in response to a request for a text to accompany some drawings from circus life by Fernand Léger. One of Miller's childhood ambitions had been to be a clown, and among his friends he had always had a reputation for being exactly that, in the circus rather than the Shakespearian sense. Further, two books written by his friend Wallace Fowlie, *Clowns and Angels* and *The Clown's Grail*, had made a considerable impression on him at this time. Miller agreed to the commission.

The clown story is unusual on two counts in Miller's writing, being a third person narration and being an account of events which are manifestly fictional. Paradoxically the novella seems to offer more insights into Henry Miller than much of his overtly biographical writing. There is a revealing and touching description of the accidental way in which the hero, Auguste, stumbles on the trick which brings him world fame. At a certain point in his act he forgets what he is supposed to be doing next, and while trying to remember the next trick he sits down in the ring at the foot of the ladder and feigns ecstasy. The public roar with laughter, and his name is made. Auguste's astonishment at the spread of his fame for this stunt, which thereafter becomes the highlight of his act, might well reflect Miller's own astonishment at the rapid spread of his fame after *Tropic of Cancer*. The book was, after all, written almost by accident, while he was trying to work out how to turn *Crazy Cock* into a commercial success. And if *Tropic of Cancer* is a burlesque novel, it is also a circus novel, childlike in the way Chagall's paintings of circuses are childlike, but done by a more cynical child. Auguste's description of the circus and the clown's rôle in the ring would serve equally well as a description of the world of *Tropic of Cancer* and its inhabitants:

The life in the arena was a dumb show consisting of falls, slaps, kicks – an

305

endless shuffling and booting about. And it was by means of this disgraceful rigolade that one found favour with the public. The beloved clown! It was his special privilege to reenact the errors, the follies, the stupidities, all the misunderstandings which plague human kind. To be ineptitude itself, that was something even the dullest oaf could grasp. Not to understand,when all is clear as daylight; not to catch on, though the trick be repeated a thousand times for you; to grope about like a blind man, when all signs point to the right direction; to insist on opening the wrong door, though it is marked *Danger*! to walk head on into the mirror, instead of going around it; to look through the wrong end of a rifle, a *loaded* rifle![18]

Presently Auguste tires of his fame and runs away to live a life of anonymity as a circus hand in a small travelling circus. He puts up the tent and mucks out the animals while the averagely-talented Antoine gets an averagely enthusiastic ovation for his clowning each evening. One night he falls ill and Auguste is persuaded to deputize for him. He has what seems to him the happy idea of creating a wonderful new reputation for Antoine by wearing Antoine's costume and make-up in the ring, but performing with all the talent of the great Auguste. The act is a sensational success, but the plan ends in tragedy: Antoine hears what has happened and dies of a broken heart.

Miller's enthusiasm was legendary among his friends, but this tale illustrates some of the pitfalls of enthusiasm, and of indulging the desire to change certain things, such as another man's reputation, which are better left alone. In his own life Miller made this mistake many times, and in portrait essays like 'The Amazing and Invariable Beauford Delaney', 'Varda: The Master Builder' and 'A Bodhisattva Artist' (about the painter Abe Rattner), portraits intended as promotional tributes to little-known artists who also happened to be personal friends, he consistently performed the curious trick of making them all, in the end, essays about Henry Miller. He requisitioned reputations and spoiled them by a generosity of spirit which came close to being patronizing, and a prodigality in the use of superlatives which could only create suspicion in the big world beyond the confines of Miller-friendliness.

Sexus, written early in the 1940s but not published until 1949, was on more familiar ground. The numerous sex scenes in the book made publication in the United States out of the question and it appeared in two volumes in Paris, again published by the Obelisk Press. Two French translations were put out simultaneously by *Editions de la Terre de Feu*, one expurgated, the other complete. The latter edition was seized by the police almost immediately on publication.

306

Censorship thus denied the book a public critical reception, and the personal responses he did get were negative. Lawrence Durrell was particularly disappointed. Somewhat to Miller's annoyance, Durrell insisted on regarding the Greek, American and Rimbaud books as marginalia, and had been keenly looking forward to a book along what he considered Miller's main, autobiographical line of development. The excerpts from *Sexus* that appeared in the 1944 collection *Sunday After The War* augured well, but when he read the full-length work he put their friendship at risk by telling Miller that his book was 'disgracefully bad' and that it was liable to ruin his reputation unless he withdrew it immediately and revised it.[19] Durrell was in a difficult position, having agreed to three or four invitations to review the book in literary magazines and being unwilling either to slaughter it or to put on the old pal's act and lie about it.

Miller's response to Durrell's letter was remarkably calm. He assured him that his professional criticism had no bearing on their friendship, and even encouraged him to go public with it if he so wished. The disturbance rumbled on for a few letters but presently subsided, with Durrell quickly grabbing at Miller's suggestion that the root of the problem was that he had perhaps succeeded *too well* in his attempts to convey the poverty and sterility of his life with June in the 1920s in Brooklyn and Greenwich Village.

Few writers, known or unknown, would have forgiven such an attack on their professional competence from a friend, and in all honesty one has to suspect that this might have been a special dispensation for Durrell and that a similar attack from another quarter would not have been met with such equanimity. No matter: even one such gesture is admirable, and illustrates the unusual pliancy of Miller's personality, and his unorthodox courage. Another demonstration of this was his consistent and vociferous support for a campaign to secure Céline's release from prison in Copenhagen, where he was being held on charges of collaborating with the Germans during the Nazi occupation of France. He signed a petition drawn up by an American journalist named Milton Hindus and urged others to do so, and even agitated for a time for the publication in the United States of Céline's banned *Bagatelles pour un massacre*, which he persistently referred to as *Massacres pour une bagatelle*, until he discovered that it was actually an anti-semitic tract.

Miller felt a fierce, protective admiration for Céline. Along with Knut Hamsun, his other great hero among the European moderns, Céline had lived out the consequences of his anti-democratic beliefs in a way that turned his life into a genuine tragedy. Miller's temperamental – if not artistic – similarity to both writers was great; yet he knew that both of them, in cutting themselves off completely from the despised 'mob' and paying the price of its hatred, had displayed a courage which he perhaps wished he possessed himself but knew he did not. 'The world is full of people who are right,' Céline wrote to him once. 'That's why it's so NAUSEATING.' Hamsun had the same horror and suspicion of the righteous, and so did Miller. What prevented him joining them was the quality Anais Nin had noted in him early in their relationship – his desire to be liked by people. What he *could* do was to remind anyone who might be trying to forget it of the most important fact of all about Céline – that he was 'terrific – and I don't care whether he's a Fascist or a Democrat or a shit-house cleaner. *He can write.*'[20] Two other favourites, Blaise Cendrars and Jean Giono, were also accused of being fascists and generally worthless human beings and dead men as writers after the war, and Miller defended both with a similar intransigence.

6

Even by his own surreal standards, Miller's personal economy during the period of his marriage to Lepska was chaotic. In 1948 he was timidly participating in a $5 chain-letter scheme under a false name, wearing cast-off shirts and trousers given to him by a Hollywood tycoon and complaining to the Swiss consul of how he had to buy shirts for Moricand while being unable to afford to treat his wife to the new shoes she so badly needed. Yet at the same time he talks of having spent $3000 on Moricand within the last two years. The explanation for the paradox is that he had discovered, to his considerable astonishment, that he had become a rich man, thanks to the European sales of his Paris trilogy.

Jack Kahane had assured him he would have an income for life from *Tropic of Cancer* as early as 1937, but the outbreak of war altered the situation dramatically. While Henry was in Greece he received word from Maurice Girodias, Kahane's eighteen year old son and heir who had taken over the firm after his father's death in 1939, that he would be sending him the sum of one thousand francs a month for the foreseeable future. With the fall of Paris, that future turned out to be a very short one. Henry never received even a first instalment of these royalties.

Yet Obelisk had continued to trade during the war. Miller's books turned out to be popular with the German soldiers, and even more popular with the Americans who replaced them when liberation came in 1944. Sales of the books exploded, and French translations of the

Tropics and *Black Spring* in 1945 and 1946 were critical and commercial successes. By December 1945, Miller could write to Durrell that £3000 was waiting for him in Paris, although he was unable to touch it because of restrictions on the export and import of currency.

Throughout 1946, Miller's main official source of income at Anderson Creek was a $50 monthly allowance that he received from James Laughlin of New Directions, publishers of all his full-length works in America since *The Cosmological Eye* in 1939. In addition to this he made over $2000 that year from sales of his water-colours. A frugal man might have lived comfortably on such an income, but Henry was not a frugal man. Though the rent at the shack was only $7 a month, he had a family and a Moricand to support, tobacco, wine, food and a million postage stamps to buy. He even owed money to the Big Sur mailman for groceries.

To the surprise of his associates and writers, Maurice Girodias turned out to be an able businessman, and late in 1946 he sent off the 300,000 francs (about $2000) which enabled Henry to buy the house from Jean Wharton and the following year return to Partington Ridge. Even with this money gone he was still worth 4,470,000 francs by the middle of the year, and was desperately trying to think up ways of getting hold of it. Durrell and Perlès sent him a telegram from Scotland urging him to invest in some old chateau before an impending succession of devaluations of the franc wiped his money out, and Anais Nin's banker husband Hugh Guiler offered him the benefit of his advice. The devaluations duly came, cutting the value of the royalties owing by about a third. Severe currency restrictions continued. Early in 1948 Girodias wrote offering to let him have between $500 and $700 per month if Miller could persuade enough friends visiting France to buy francs for dollars.

Miller wanted his earnings all right – 'Now struggling with might and main to get my money out of France'[21] he told Schnellock – but not enough to make sure he got it. With a little professional help it would have been relatively easy to sort this problem out, but possibly the prospect of having too much money worried him. One of his sustaining articles of faith was that artists should not only be poor but be seen to be poor. They should live in hovels, wear second-hand clothes and write on a battered old typewriter, this being the modern equivalent of a worn-down stub of a pencil. A form of financial *anorexia nervosa* was the mark of Miller's authority as rebel, repudiator and sage, and any drastic change in his personal economic position would have presented him with a major identity problem. He had grown fond of himself just as he was. Sudden wealth could only

309

complicate matters. It all left him only nominally a professional writer, with earnings from his six New Directions publications for 1948 and 1949 at $650 per year.

7

A further drain on his resources was caused by June's re-entry into his orbit. In the middle of 1947, after a silence of almost fifteen years, Miller received the first of a number of distressing letters from her. In the interim she had married Stratford Corbett, that man 'considerably your junior' whom Osborn had reported seeing her with before the Millers' divorce. Anais's astrologer had been gravely mistaken in his predictions of a happy life for her. She was separated again, living alone in squalor and poverty in a Clinton Avenue apartment which she called 'Excrement Hall'. She weighed less than 75 lbs. First news of her plight came in a letter from his old friend Emil Conason in which he described the former taxi-dancer and bohemian queen as a 'perambulating skeleton' with 'gaunt eyes sunk deep into bottomless sockets'. From Esther Elkus, Conason had heard that June was trying to live on $60 a month in an apartment where the rent was $42.50, and had reverted to a state of complete withdrawal from the world. 'I don't hope to find you anxious to give of your precious self,' Conason concluded bitterly, but nevertheless hoped that Henry might send a thousand dollars in trust for her to Esther Elkus. He doubted that he would, however, presuming that Henry would 'rationalize in your inimitable fashion' and consign June to the care of his 'beloved providence'.[22]

Conason's letter shows the ambivalence that those closest to Henry were capable of feeling towards him, the way in which they operated with a double image of him as saint and devil. It also shows how little anyone really knew how much June had meant to him. Written seven years after their relationship was over, and after the heat had gone from the affair with Anais Nin, the notebooks Miller kept on his *The Air-Conditioned Nightmare* journey across America contain a handful of stray references to his second wife which are persuasively personal in their tone. One such reads: 'Sit here dreaming of June. Where now, little June? Are you happy?' Another describes his meeting in Mobile, Alabama, with a waitress whose voice was so beautiful that he could only compare it to June's. Later, in Hollywood, he imagined sending her a telegram telling her he loved her, signed 'Valentine Valentino'. Miller's agitated sexual romanticism would continue to try to disprove it for the rest of his life, but such sentiments

310

suggest that his love for June was a real, personal, individual love, and that other and subsequent women never managed to affect him in a comparable way.

He responded quickly to Conason's letter, began corresponding with June again, sent her small sums of money when he could, diverted debts to her and got a Brooklyn friend, William Allen, to deliver her a winter coat and food parcels. Conason gave her medical assistance, pleased and relieved to find that his old friend was not the super-humanly heartless monster he sometimes appeared to be in his fiction.

8

Henry and Lepska's marriage, which seems never to have been happy, came to an end soon enough. Perhaps it never had any chance. One of the great paradoxes about Miller is the way he ceaselessly sang the praises of living in the present yet in his most important writing obsessively revisited the far past – and not, apparently, to lay ghosts there, but to relive the happiness and intensity of former years. Obsessively re-enacting his love for the fictional June in *Sexus* and then *Plexus* – which was well under way by 1948 – and with the added complication of the reappearance of the real June in his real life, he did not give the present and its inhabitants, including his own wife, much of a chance.

Another disruptive ghost appeared one day in the summer of 1947 when Anais Nin drove out to see the Millers. The reunion was not a success. She was embarrassed by Henry's searching for an ease and a warmth which she felt was no longer possible between them, and she noted the tension between him and Lepska, and the way in which he criticized Lepska for her silence. He assumed that Anais was running away from her life in New York and she had to make it clear to him that this was not the case. She cut the visit short, later recording that it marked the end of the intimacy that had once existed between them.

Later Miller described the marriage as seven years during which he was permanently grouchy, irritated, depressed or in a temper.[23] Even when he was not working he preferred the company of his children, especially his daughter, whom he doted on, or of his friends, to that of his wife, for a wife could never be a friend. In 1947, over a year before the birth of their son, the couple had considered separating, and a final parting was only a matter of time.

Some of their most frequent arguments concerned discipline. Henry had a work hut away from the house and in *A Devil in Paradise*, a book which is laced with references to the wretchedness of the

311

marriage, he wrote that Lepska would rebuke him if she found him out strolling when he was supposed to be writing. One of the few positive facts about poor Moricand's presence in the middle of the cross-fire was that they could use him as a medium through which to address each other in civilized fashion. Lepska must also have been puzzled by the way in which Moricand's desire for a shirt of his own took precedence over her need for a new pair of shoes. The pathological horror of discipline bred in Miller by his childhood struggles with his mother had never left him, and he refused to discipline the children. He would prefer to have given them the kind of upbringing and education he once outlined to a horrified Beatrice for Barbara, which was in substance an education that consisted entirely in following one's nose through life. His journey towards anti-intellectualism was well-nigh complete by this time. As a politician his world-view had never been simpler: what he longed for was 'a world-wide revolution. . .but against all the damn governments that exist.'[24] It was his ability to externalize his problems, or perhaps simply to forget about them, in such passionate and satisfying flights of violent verbal fancy that stood him in good stead when Lepska eventually did leave him, in June 1951, for a Romanian biophysicist with a PhD who had been staying as a guest of their neighbours. With her departure, the experiment of trying to live a normal family life came to an end for good.

CHAPTER FIFTEEN

1951–1959
The Rosy Crucifixion: in search of lost youth

1

After Lepska left, Miller tried briefly to cope with the children on his own. Valentine was now aged six and Tony four, and he found the task exhausting. He made an attempt to enlist the aid of two of his men, Emil White and Walker Winslow, but here discipleship recognized its limits and both at once left Big Sur, White on an extended holiday, Winslow for good. The children had a reputation for being undisciplined and a young nanny whom Miller tried to persuade to look after them walked off the job within twenty-four hours. Finally he gave up and sent both children to live with their mother until he was in a better position to look after them. Lepska took them East with her to stay with her parents in New York. Later she and her new man, together with Valentine and Tony, moved into a house on Kennebec Avenue in Long Beach, California.

Henry did not wait long to replace Lepska. For some time he had been corresponding with the sister-in-law of his friend Bezalel Schatz, a young woman named Eve McClure who lived in Beverley Hills. Like so many of his readers, men and women, Eve had fallen in love with the Henry Miller of the books. She sent him her photograph, from which he could see that she was attractive, dark-haired, and facially not unlike another of his Hollywood fans, Ava Gardner. In the spring of 1952, after a visit to the children in Long Beach, he called in to say hello to his penpal. The meeting was a great success, and on April 1st Eve moved in with him at Partington Ridge.

Eve McClure was born in 1924, the year in which Henry and June married. At the age of seventeen she had been married to a former film-star nearing sixty, so she had some experience of life as the young lover of an elderly man. Her father, five years Henry's junior, disapproved of her new liaison. She was accounted a good woman by all who knew her – warm-hearted, loving, hardworking, skilled in the domestic arts, a good cook and hostess, an unpretentious woman proud to be the helpmate of a man whom she considered a genius. Miller was delighted with her and despatched almost suspiciously ecstatic letters to his friends with the news that a new life had begun. He was supremely happy, he wrote, every day was like a gift, the new wife was a glutton for work, a wonderful companion and the first real mate he'd ever had. Perhaps most important of all from his point of view, the arrival of a new woman meant that he was able to have the children for most of that summer at Partington Ridge.

His books continued to sell well in Europe, where the Germans, Danes and Swedes joined the French in buying native language translations of his works. Braving his anglophobia, the English had also taken Henry Miller to their bosom, and in 1950 Penguin sold 50,000 copies of a paperback edition of *The Colossus of Maroussi*. The Japanese market, which later became a major source of income for him, opened up in 1953 with an English edition of *Tropic of Cancer* and a Japanese translation shortly afterwards. He still played at being poor, however. He kept a card index with the names and addresses of friends and other useful people, and would write to a selection of them now and then with a request for used gloves, preferably kid or pigskin, size 8½, warm underwear ('but not *itchy wool*') and thick winter trousers. As Eve had fallen in love with the man in the books, it was the least he could do.

2

The advent of a new lover after seven years of irritability and depression with a woman he had been unable to control required a celebration. Since parting from Lepska, Henry had been looking forward to returning to France. Most of his real friends were still in Europe – Brassai and Reichel in Paris, Durrell working as press officer at the British Embassy in Belgrade, Fred Perlès married to a Scotswoman and living in Somerset, England – and all of them exerting discreet pressure on him by letter to return and rejoin them. The divorce from Lepska came through in November, confirming the provisional arrangement they had made to have joint custody of the children, with Henry taking care of them during the summer months. Lepska, Henry and the children had Christmas together at Long Beach, and on December 29th, Henry and Eve set off for a seven-month holiday in Europe which was part-honeymoon and part triumphal parade.

They went first to Paris, where many of Miller's pre-war friendships were renewed. He quickly became tired of the nostalgia, complained frequently of being homesick and was distressed by the dramatic change that had taken place in the cost of living in France. Eve, however, making her first trip to Paris, loved it, and was thrilled to meet people like Léger, Man Ray, Brassai, the actor Michel Simon and the jazz musician Mezz Mezzrow. Presently they travelled south and had a few days on the Riviera before moving on to La Ciotat in the Bouches-du-Rhône at the end of the month to stay with Michel Simon, then on again to Die, where they were Albert Maillet's guests.

After a while they were joined by Eve's sister and her husband, Bezalel Schatz, and the party of four went on from Paris to Brussells to see one of Henry's innumerable pen-friends, Pierre Lesdain. Lesdain's brother put a chauffeur-driven car at their disposal, and they spent an enjoyable few days driving round the country and drinking 'the best beer in the world'. Travelling as always stimulated Henry's imagination, and after observing the Belgians for a while he came to the conclusion that they were 'neither fish nor fowl – more like potato balls'.[1]

In May they motored into Spain, picking up the French writer Joseph Delteil and his wife along the way at Montpellier. For Henry the high point of their Spanish visit was meeting Alfred Perlès again in Barcelona – the first time the two had seen each other since 1938. From here the party motored on to Toledo, where Henry was struck by the bellhops at the hotel, beautiful little boys about twelve years old – 'if I were a pederast I could fall in love with them'[2] – and to Cordoba, Granada and Segovia, where he saw and of course conversed with an apprentice matador practising bullfighting on a bicycle. They passed through Andorra on their way out of Spain and returned to Paris via Montpellier.

In Paris, Henry and Eve called on Maurice Vlaminck, a painter whom Miller held in especial awe because he had been a professional bike racer in his youth. Vlaminck did most of the talking during the visit, and Miller listened in silence, trying to imagine how Vlaminck, now a huge man weighing sixteen stone, had ever managed to fit his bottom on to a slim Brooks saddle. He became quite obsessed by the image. Many years later, he concluded his own account of the meeting with the observation that his great regret was that he had never seen Vlaminck mounted on a bicycle. Not even during the Six Day races at Madison Square Gardens in the 1920s had he seen a rider remotely approaching Vlaminck's size.

Before returning to Big Sur, Henry and Eve made a quick trip to England to see Alfred Perlès at his home in Wells. Miller's anglophobia was in retreat by now, mellowed by the success of his books, by Perlès's equally strong anglomania and by his fondness for English pubs. The party drank a great deal of wine during the reunion, a factor which greatly raised Perlès's standing among the corporation dustmen who afterwards collected the empty bottles outside his back door.

315

The Millers also went to Stratford-on-Avon, but the outstanding literary pilgrimage of the trip was to the home of John Cowper Powys at Cae Coed, Corwen, in Wales. Miller and Powys had been corresponding for some three years, ever since Miller had decided to write about Powys in *The Books in My Life*, Henry's autobiographical account of his life as a reader. Powys was deeply flattered to hear how much he had influenced Henry in his youth, and amused to hear Henry's account of how he and Emil Schnellock had argued with him at such length after one of his Labour Temple lectures that in the end his brother Llewelyn had been obliged to intervene. Miller was equally moved by the meeting, and similarly flattered to discover that his old idol was now his fan. Indeed, the visit looks in some ways to have been another example of Miller's ceaseless attempts to give his life at least the appearance of meaningful pattern by establishing as many connections as possible between the far past and the present. It was also an opportunity for him to confirm his loyalty to the past, for he was proud of the fact that he had never become disillusioned with the heroes of his boyhood and adolescence.

Miller's days as a terrorist and sex-fiend were behind him now, and though Powys apologised to him for his 'old-maidishness' Henry was, at a guess, more interested in hearing Powys's theory on the lost continent of Atlantis than in discussing sexual mores. Together Miller and Powys were two of the most significant connecting links between the upsurge of millenial mysticism of the decades round 1900 and similar tendencies observable as the year 2000 approaches, and yet apart from a narrow but intense coincidence of interests in the occult they were light years apart in their literary tastes: at one point Miller looked over Powys's bookshelves at the Homer, Virgil, Dante, Villon, Rabelais, Shakespeare, Marlowe, Greek dramatists, Ovid, Longinus and Lucretius and surprised his old hero by asking him, did he ever look at them now and then? 'Why Henry, I read them all once a year,' Powys replied, the answer astonishing as much as the question had. Later Powys sent him, through the post, one of his stout blackthorn walking sticks which became a treasured souvenir of the occasion.

Thus the trip, which had begun in complaints of homesickness for Henry, ended on a successful note. Eve had greatly enjoyed the holiday too; but her letters home to Bob and Edie Fink present a disturbingly mixed picture of her attitude towards her companion. On the one hand she still idolized Henry as a genius and spoke of her obsessive love for him. 'He is like the Holy Grail for me,' she wrote, and described in similarly religious terms how his touch on her head or a pat on her arm were like benedictions. The future seemed to her 'a path of pure golden light'.[3] Yet a deep unease is present too in her references to his 'silent love, where woman is concerned. I don't think he would choose it to be so, for him or for the woman he loves, but that's the way it is.' She recalls a letter Lepska wrote to him in which he was 'reviled and castrated coming and going for his selfishness, ineptness, and lack of this and that'. Lepska's chief concern and frustration had been 'the books' and the difference between the two Henry Millers, a difference which was a major psychological factor in dictating the quality of his personal relationships.

In her letter Lepska accused Henry of hypocrisy in depicting himself in fiction as someone able to give of himself verbally to his woman, whereas in life her experience had been that he was neither able nor willing to discuss anything with her. Her criticism recalls Anais Nin's observation that Henry would never admit that a problem needed to be discussed. If she seemed troubled he would go no further than to ask, uneasily: 'Is everything alright?' 'I'm a monomaniac. Me no argue,'[4] he wrote once to Durrell, an attitude that is bound to create difficulties in a marriage. Eve was trying to come to terms with the idea of union with a man who apparently had no intention of establishing an intimate bond with her, a Strindbergian male supremacist who wanted not love but adoration. 'My own belief,' she wrote to the Finks, 'is that he has never been able to give of himself verbally.' Yet she fought her misgivings, and praised him as a man 'so tender, so gentle and so damned masculine. What a combination!'[5] At the end of the year she married him, in a civil ceremony, at Ephraim Doner's house in Carmel Highlands.

In August, about six weeks after their return to Big Sur, Eve's father died of a heart-attack. Fortunately she had seen him just two weeks before his death, and he had given his blessing to her relationship with Henry.

Miller had enjoyed the year enormously by the time it ended. It was his turn for the children that summer. Eve had already made him a leather jacket, and now she made moccasins for the children from foot patterns which Lepska had sent her.

3

Now that Miller had a permanent home it was easier for his past to catch up with him. Apart from corresponding with June he was now also writing regularly to Barbara, his daughter by his first marriage, whom he had not seen for some thirty years. Beatrice had married again and taken the name Sandford, and in 1954 the family was living

317

in Hollywood with no idea that Henry had also made his home in the area. In a magazine put out by Safeways supermarkets, ironically called *Family Circle*, Barbara had read an article about Big Sur which mentioned her father, and had written the letter which restored contact between them.

Friends like Richard Osborn, Joe O'Reagan and Ostergren had been providing Henry with occasional scraps of information about his first family over the years. He knew that, in the late 1930s, Barbara had won a prize 'for writing', and had had one or two pieces published in a magazine. Later information indicated that Beatrice was struggling financially, and that Barbara, who had inherited both her parents' musical talent, was helping her mother out by giving piano lessons herself. On Miller's return to New York from Greece in 1940, one of his reasons for keeping a low profile among former acquaintances had been a tip from Ostergren that Beatrice was using a private detective to try to track him down for payment of back alimony. In November 1941 he received news that Barbara was ill which briefly panicked him – according to Anais Nin, he took his daughter's illness as the visitation of divine punishment on him. Still he could not bring himself to see Barbara personally, but tried to reach her through inter-mediaries. A journalist on *Colliers* magazine who interviewed him turned out to be an acquaintance of hers, and could tell him that his daughter did not hate him, as he had assumed, and that she was in fact proud of possessing a copy of his first American publication, *The Cosmological Eye*. He toyed briefly with the idea of getting Wallace Fowlie to set up a meeting in New York but in the end preferred to leave it up to fate. Had Barbara not taken the initiative in 1954, father and daughter might never have met again.

After the initial correspondence, Henry invited Barbara to visit Partington Ridge. She arrived in June and stayed with the Millers for a few weeks. The re-establishment of a personal relationship with his first child after a lapse of almost thirty years was a source of great pleasure to Miller, and after her departure father and daughter remained in regular contact.

With Beatrice, however, there was no possibility of a reconciliation. She was holding on to his love-letters to her until he became famous, at which time, Henry presumed, she would sell them. 'Hates my guts,' he wrote to one of the many collectors with whom he corresponded. 'A real monster.'[6] Lepska also remained resistent to Henry's charm; his tentative efforts in 1954 to buy out her half-share of the house on Partington Ridge were rebuffed.

June was the only ex-wife who remained under Henry's spell. He stayed in sporadic touch with her throughout the 1950s through two of his readers in New York, Annette and Jim Baxter, who took a personal interest in her welfare. Through the Baxters he learned that in the early 1950s she had again spent a brief period in a mental hospital after a period of irrational behaviour and hallucinations. By the time she left she was slightly crippled by a fall sustained while receiving ECT treatment. The Baxters were both keen readers of Miller's work, and enjoyed being shown around some of the old Village haunts by June, though at Henry's request they were careful not to mention *The Rosy Crucifixion* to her. She had not, apparently, read any of his books after *Tropic of Cancer*. Their response to meeting June in person says something about the depressing fate which real-life models of fictional characters have to endure once the author is finished with them: so struck were they by June's candour and her becoming poise, they told Henry, that 'had we not been well acquainted with Mona, we might even have failed to credit June with Mona's capacity for guile'.[7]

The Baxters did what they could for her. Jim Baxter was a doctor and got her occasional work as night attendant for some of his patients, and they and the Conasons made sure she ate properly, helped her to move from 'Excrement Hall', arranged for her to have false teeth fitted on Welfare. ('Received my teeth,' she wrote to Henry, 'and feel as if I'm eating around someone's glass skull. Well here goes another of my senses, no sense of taste.'[8]) They invited her to spend Thanksgiving and Christmas with them, and also rescued from her chaotic safe-keeping several versions of Miller's 'Tony Bring' manuscript *Moloch* which they might have done better to let her lose. June's life since parting with Henry had not been easy, yet her spirit remained good, and she harboured no ill-feelings towards him: 'I envy Eve,' she wrote, 'and all those who have the privilege of living around you.'[9]

June's fate was to be studied: after Miller and Nin it was Annette Baxter's turn. A psychologist by profession, she began making notes for a book on June, but these were lost, along with all the Baxter's other papers, in the fire which killed her husband and herself on Fire Island.

4

The only woman who exerted a comparable influence to June's on Miller's life was his mother Louise. She was dying of cancer and in January 1956 Henry and Eve flew to Brooklyn to nurse her through her last days. Nothing illustrates better the unresolved hopelessness of the relationship between mother and son than the fact that the relationship with Eve was kept secret from Louise because Henry was afraid she would disapprove. Back in 1951, after Lepska had left Henry and taken the children to stay with her parents in New York, Louise met her two grandchildren for the first time and wrote enthusiastically to Henry of their visits, and of how much she loved her grandchildren and her daughter-in-law, and how she hoped that he would always have a happy home. Neither Henry nor Lepska had apparently told her that the marriage was over. Before leaving Big Sur, Henry gave instructions to his friends to address their letters to Eve McClure, not Eve Miller, and when they were together at the house Eve was to pretend to be the girlfriend of Henry's New York friend, Vincent Birge.

Eve was horrified by conditions at Decatur Street and at the filth and poverty in which Louise and Lauretta, now aged sixty-one, were living. Against his mother's will, Henry employed a night-nurse to look after her, precipitating a full-scale row in which he was torn between admiration for her spirit – scarcely able to talk, paralyzed on one side and with her kidneys giving out – and outraged anger over the incredible stubbornness with which she still battled him. 'What a scene!' he wrote. 'Almost had to club her down in bed.'[10] The main problem was to ensure that she had nourishment regularly every hour. Without it she became weak, listless and, in Miller's frustrated summary of other effects, 'abysmally stupid, stubborn and narrow-minded. Worse than Lauretta.'

In the end she held out until March 21st before dying. Miller was called to the hospital early in the morning, spoke with a charming Italian intern, and returned jubilant to his hotel. The funeral took place four days later in a snowstorm in Evergreen Cemetery, and Henry told Emil White that it was one of the two best days he had known since arriving in New York. The first was the day on which she died.

Thus the most influential relationship in Miller's life came to an end. In part the difference between them was temperamental. Miller found his mother conventional, dull, unimaginative and unforgivably stupid. He remembered with particular disgust the preposterous injunction she would use to try to get mad Tante Melia to behave herself: 'Remember that you are an American.' Beyond this there was also a strong streak of sexual unease and even disgust in their relationship. In the mid-1930s, during which he carried out his first extensive scrutiny his own early life in connection with the writing of *Black Spring*, he believed that he had come to understand, for the first time, just how decisive and destructive a rôle Louise had played in his sexual life. He blamed her for the timidity that had prevented him from approaching

320

Cora Seward like a human being and from taking her 'like a man'; and saw both a revenge and an incestuous consummation in his subsequent affair with Pauline Chouteau.

'Never,' he wrote, 'in the case of any woman I loved, did I have the slightest realization of the role my mother played.'[11] He blamed her in retrospect for alienating him from his father, for trying to involve him in their quarrels on her side, for waking him up the middle of the night to go out and look for his father – in other words, for her attempt to get him to usurp his father's position in the house. He blamed her too for the emotional pressure she had exerted on him to force him to join the family business as his father's minder when she knew that this was not what he wanted. When, later, Henry rebelled, rejected these rôles and set off on his impractical and eccentric journey through life as a writer, Louise reacted by treating him as a small boy. We easily become what we are told we are, and in many respects Miller duly remained a small boy for the rest of his life.

The legacy of the failure of their relationship was a fear and a hatred of his mother which he extended to include all mothers. For a while he looked for solutions to the problem in Freud, but abandoned that avenue of exploration soon after realizing that the Freudian synthesis was too simple and unsatisfying to hold him. The more fluid world of literature offered the hope of making his own discoveries, and the extensive study of D.H. Lawrence and the protracted attempt to write a book about him in the 1930s was another attempt to get to the heart of the oedipal problem intellectually. In the end, however, he discovered that the way to deal successfully with all problems was simply to starve them to death by neglect.

Such a discovery was bound to create difficulties once other people became involved. For the women he married, it meant that he was unable to open himself to them as an equal and a friend. A close relationship with a woman meant always, in the end, a struggle to establish and maintain dominance over her. This attitude, so at variance with the literary self-portrait of himself as the adorer of Woman and the prophet of complete submission to Her, misled both Lepska and Eve into thinking that Henry was the right man for them. Only Anais Nin, with the bolt-hole of her marriage to retreat to, was able to tolerate it in order to harvest the sides of Miller's personality that she could use. The overall result was that a man who was on first-name terms with half the reading public of the world continued to have great difficult in achieving intimacy with those closest to him.

Lauretta remained a problem after Louise's death. Hers was a peculiarly cruel fate – not mad, yet incapable of looking after herself. 'Better insane than feeble-minded,' was how Henry viewed the situation. He struggled with the unfamiliar burdens of responsibility, made enquiries about the possibility of hiring a companion to share the house on Decatur Street with Lauretta, but eventually decided to sell it and take his sister back to California with him. They found a place for her in a residential home in Pacific Grove which, with its several televisions, its chapel and its complement of ladies of her own age, provided for all Lauretta's needs. The fees were $200 a month, but these were comfortably covered by the $7500 Miller received from the sale of the house.

5

Miller knew well enough that the great majority of the hundreds of people he knew and corresponded with were not friends so much as fans; he retained a clear sense of the distinction in his own mind, and had no more real friends than the average person. The continued respect of friends from his earliest days was especially important, and the knowledge that he had retained Conason's admiration by his spontaneous show of concern for June meant much to him. The durability of his friendships with Conason and Schnellock was important to him on another score, for it appeared to demonstrate that neither the considerable fame he had achieved by now nor his lengthy sojourn in Europe had changed him. He was still 'just a Brooklyn boy', and everything was just as before between Conason and himself, 'except that I wrote a few books between times'.[12]

He enjoyed the same equality with Alfred Perlès, who visited Big Sur in late 1954 to write the final chapters of his biography *My Friend Henry Miller*. Perlès was 'the friend I love best', Miller wrote once, 'a cure for anyone. I miss him as I never missed a soul.'[13] The subject of the biography took his usual proprietorial interest in how he was to be presented to the world, and the manuscript copy of the book in the UCLA archives shows some amusing editorial changes. Perhaps the best is the alteration, in Miller's hand, of Perlès's unequivocal statement: 'He hasn't read a pornographic book in his life' to read: 'I don't think he has read a pornographic book in his life.' Another interesting feature of *My Friend Henry Miller* is the way in which Perlès disguised the relationship between Anais Nin and Miller by introducing her into the story under her real name, as a close friend, and inventing a character named 'Liane de Champsaur', said to be a choreographer, as Henry's great love and benefactress in the 1930s in Paris. Yet Nin, still determined to keep all record of her long-time infidelity with Henry a secret from her husband, broke with Perlès over what she considered to be an inadequate disguising of herself.

Cheerfully inaccurate in matters of biographical fact, the book turned out to be a good 'instinctivist' portrait of its subject. For all his fondness for Miller and his high praise for his writing abilities, Perlès was never sycophantic, and always severe on his friend's pretensions to sagehood. Writing to him once in praise of their mutual friend David Edgar, Perlès commented: 'The finest thing I can say about Edgar is that he is not a trickster like everybody else, including you and me.' He had just read through a nineteen-page letter Edgar was writing to Miller and noticed that there wasn't a single word about himself in the letter: 'even his misspellings are not personal'.

Perlès was not much impressed by Henry's Big Sur gang, describing them later as 'genial morons'. What did please him was to see his old friend as sheepish as ever in money matters. By this time Miller had an account with the Bank of America, and so his own cheque-book, yet he still managed to look like a guilty embezzler whenever he tried to cash his cheques, blushing and diving into his pockets in search of identification long before being asked to do so by the cashier. Perlès thought Miller happy enough in his mountain hideaway, but felt that what he was lacking was stimulation. He was among those old friends who most consistently urged Henry to return to Europe to settle, and privately felt, as Michael Fraenkel did, that he was selling-out by opting for the easy satisfactions of guruship in California.

With another old friend, Emil Schnellock, Henry continued to correspond until Schnellock's death in 1959. Schnellock remained loyal to the last and was pathetically grateful to his old friend for the way 'you generously bestow upon me the guardian of posterity by publishing your letters to me',[14] a reference to the appearance of *Semblance of a Devoted Past* in 1944. Joe O'Reagan also retained fond memories of Miller, and when he died in 1961 left him $1500 in his will. Emil Conason, who died in 1966, was the only one of Henry's Brooklyn friends, apart from Harold Hickerson, to break into print. His *Salt-Free Diet Cookbook*, published in 1949, was in its own special way a piece of avant-garde literature.

Meanwhile the fan-club side of Henry's life was growing larger every day. There were two aspects to this. On the one hand, there were official undertakings, like the collection of Milleriana started by Lawrence Clark Powell at UCLA in the early 1950s, and the formation of a Henry Miller Literary Society in Minneapolis in 1954 at the instigation of a former journalist named Eddie Schwartz. Though both were primarily fan institutions (the Society newsletter referred to Miller 'affectionately' as 'the Master') they were also intended to mobilize opinion in the struggle against literary censorship by establishing the fundamental seriousness of Miller as a writer.

The other kind of fan expressed him or herself personally in the form of a letter which duly became part of the UCLA collection. Many of these supporters were people who turned Miller into their agony uncle, and wrote to thank him for the way in which his books had enriched their lives; some were cranks who solicited his backing for ideas intended to save the world, such as killing everybody over twelve years of age and allowing the children to make a fresh start; many were women who accompanied their letters with photographs of themselves nude, and quite a few were struggling or already-failed writers who liked to apply Miller's stories of his struggle to become a writer to their own lives. Some of these no doubt did go on to become writers, but many were only people passing through a phase. A typical letter came from a woman who wrote that until reading *The Colossus of Maroussi* she had felt guilty in considering herself a writer; after reading the book, however, she realized 'that it is Love and not Words which make a Writer'. Many admirers proposed a visit, like the man who threatened to arrive bringing with him a large collection of records ranging from Bach to Prokofiev, 'with some Robeson and Burl Ives in case conversation lags'. Many were young, and refreshingly honest: one youth wrote to tell Henry that he too was 'beset by the same passion that lifted some to a greatness they often resent. But never mind that. I don't have your stamina and your capacity to experience earth's sordid cities. They revolt me.' Others sounded a note of touching defiance, like the man who wrote of his many novels and plays about life at sea and in the logging camps which remained unpublished because they 'do not lie down and roll over thereby hoping to please'.

Henry, with his persistent portrayal of himself as a failure, was an ikon for such men and women. It was readers such as these who responded to yet another of his absurd begging letters that was sent out in February 1955, claiming that he would be 'sunk' unless each of the fifty recipients of the letter sent him a dollar a week until the 'crisis' was over. The famous let him down, Valerie Fletcher answering on behalf of T.S. Eliot and declining to help with a pointed remark about how Eliot himself was obliged to give lectures and readings when in the States in order to defray expenses. A Bill Fountaine, however, photostated Miller's letter and circulated copies of it among his own friends. This was at a time when Miller frequently received lump sums of money – $530 from France, $950 from Japan – from the sales of his books abroad.

Perhaps those who benefited most from Miller's willingness to correspond with his readers were two long-term prisoners, Edwin Becker and Roger Bloom, with whom he exchanged letters regularly for many years. These were warm, friendly, newsy letters about his family life, his past, his travels, his writing, containing good advice about what to read, bad advice about how to write and counselling always endurance, optimism and hope when requests for parole were turned down. These letters show Miller in the most characteristic of all his rôles, as the Great Encourager. Friends like Emil White, Anais Nin and Alfred Perlès also wrote to Bloom and Becher, and even Miller's children joined in: 'I'm going to the skin doctors and get my eight warts off,' Valentine told Roger Bloom. 'Do you have any warts?' Miller even put on a suit one day and travelled to see the Governor of Ohio State Penitentiary to try to persuade him that Bloom, who was serving life sentence for bank robbery, was now fully rehabilitated. His efforts finally succeeded and in 1966 Bloom was released after a correspondence that had lasted ten years.

6

The mid-1950s were happy years for Miller. He enjoyed having his children to stay during the summer, wrote his books, corresponded with his readers, visited Lauretta and took her out riding in his old Cadillac, went to the cinema as often as possible and believed the Wild West really was like that. Eve removed the burdens of the practical side of his life, aided by Robert Fink, Emil White, and Vincent Birge, who had moved to the coast from New York to be closer to him. Between them they acted as his secretaries, chauffeurs, handy-men and minders. He took his brisk morning, noon and evening walks, carrying the shillelagh Powys had sent him, got out the hoe to battle with the rattle-snakes when they came too close to the house and struggled to keep the poison ivy at bay. Eve grew their vegetables and there was good wine with the evening meal each day. They lived very much as the idealist hippies of the 1960s would try to live, although Henry had long-since capitulated on the question of schooling, and even took a responsible interest in conditions at the school Valentine and Tony attended during their stays with him: on his own initiative he wrote a letter to the local governor complaining that the driver of the school bus had not been paid for two months and that the lighting and the toilets in the school were wholly inadequate.

When in oriental mood he often wore a mandarin's skull cap presented to him by one of his admirers, and when he felt Grecian he donned a set of Greek robes he had acquired. A Hebraic talisman given

325

to him by Bezalel Schatz, now living in Jerusalem, hung always around his neck, though for a long time he had no idea what the inscription on it meant. Such details hardly concerned him: one of the many carefully chosen letter-headings and mottos he used on his stationery consisted of eight beautifully exotic Chinese characters which, when translated, turned out to be a formal request to honoured customers kindly to pay their bill before the end of the year. Even when he wasn't aware of it, his every communication contained a request for money.

Fink, who knew an accountant fan of Henry's, relieved him of the burden of doing his own income tax, and between them they made the happy discovery that Miller's total expenditure for 1953 at $6881 almost exactly matched his gross income $6872.75. An original Miller water-colour was all the payment the accountant required. In 1954 the arrival of electricity to replace candle power on Big Sur was a major event, and Fink, a gifted electrician, made a superb hi-fi set for Miller to replace his old hand-cranked Victoria. In spite of having once written an enthusiastic 'boost' for his old friend Edgard Varès in *The Air-Conditioned Nightmare*, Miller's tastes in music were conventional and romantic, and he was especially fond of Ravel and Scriabin. Fink also treated him to a green mountain jeep.

Miller had by this time become a hero to a whole generation of young American writers. Some, like Norman Mailer, Saul Bellow, John Updike and James Baldwin valued and admired him for personal qualities such as the courage and honesty of his sexual writing, without being influenced by his style or his religious preoccupations. Others, like Jack Kerouac, Allen Ginsberg, John Clellon Holmes, Lawrence Lipton, Kenneth Rexroth, Lawrence Ferlinghetti and the rest of the Beat poets, rejoiced especially in his anti-Americanism and anti-materialism, and Miller was largely responsible for the upsurge of interest in Zen buddhism and oriental religions and philosophies which was a characteristic of the Beat movement. Michael McClure was among those who visited him at Partington Ridge, and Kerouac and Ferlinghetti made arrangements to dine with him one day at Ephraim Doner's house in Carmel Highlands. Kerouac began drinking, however, and they never made it. Henry was a great fan of Kerouac's writing, and even contributed a diffident preface to *The Dharma Bums* in which he confessed: 'when I read of "spontaneous Bop prosody" I raise an eyebrow. These lads can tell me things.'[15] Perhaps he didn't realize that it was he, with what Ginsberg called his 'great natural wordslinging,' who was largely responsible for the emergence of "spontaneous Bop prosody". Curious and sad that, in the end, few of his most ardent admirers among the young writers were able to follow the Henry Miller course the whole way: Kerouac,

326

who died young of cirrhosis of the liver, once wrote to him that 'you wont and I wont die of "fatty tissues around the heart" like H.G. Wells'.[16]

Politically speaking, Miller's attitude remained essentially what it had been in the 1930s. Passionately distrusting the efforts and motives of professional politicians, he held firmly to the correctness of a position expressed in one of the final chapters of the *Tao Te Ching*, a vision of a world of small and peaceful countries whose inhabitants shun the use of all time- and labour-saving inventions, eat well, dress comfortably and travel as little as possible:

Though adjoining states are within sight of one another, and the sound of dogs barking and cocks crowing in one state can be heard in another, yet the people of one state will grow old and die without having had any dealings with those of another.

When he did express an opinion on some current topic his instincts were usually sound – the Russian invasion of Hungary seemed to him 'a new low for civilisation',[17] and he sent a parcel of clothes to the Hungarians as he had sent similar parcels to the Poles and the Germans in the immediate post-war years. Though he recognised the theoretical appeal of communism to the poor, he was firmly convinced that it was impossible to put into practice owing to the limitations of human nature. Nevertheless, as a good anti-American, he applauded in due course the triumph of Fidel Castro in Cuba.

The overall effect of his refusal to make a hobby of current affairs was that it made him to an unusual degree master of his own happiness. He saw how easy it was for an ordinary person to get anxious and worked up about the horrors of life, and his practical advice to anyone who had allowed themselves to become distressed to the point of neurosis was always to stop reading the newspapers for a while, turn off the radio and prepare themselves a large meal, with all the trimmings.

It was perhaps easier, in those mostly pre-television days, to successfully live out a philosophy of detachment like this. Even so there were times when, like most Americans, he became convinced that the war in Korea would escalate into a universal confrontation between capitalism and communism, and then he would indulge in frantic prophesies of an imminent Third World War and the bizarre realignments of power that would follow.

Astrology retained its interest for him, and as his popularity grew his endorsement of the study made him a target for proselytes. Sidney Omarr, a well-known writer of syndicated astrological columns for newspapers, even wrote an astrological study of him, entitled *Henry*

Miller: His World of Urania, and there have been other such studies. 'Astrological Fricasse', the amusing essay Miller had written ridiculing astrology during his Hollywood days, presented Omarr with an obvious problem, but he was able to get round it by explaining to his readers that the story was actually Miller's way of attacking *abuses* of astrology. In any case, Miller himself contributed a preface to Omarr's book – unwillingly but at great length – in which he maintained that similar studies of other famous men, such as Dostoevsky, Rimbaud, Da Vinci and Gilles de Rais, would greatly add to our understanding of them.

Another vivid and eccentric interest at this time was in the subject of flying saucers. He read books on the subject, and wrote a fan-letter to the author of one in which he requested permission to visit him: 'I will not deny that your testimony struck me as well-nigh incredible,' he wrote, 'but as I have been witness to many incredible events and happenings in my lifetime I have no desire to be critical.'[18] He even hesitantly claimed a near-sighting of his own, recalling that he had seen 'what purported to be a saucer phenomenon, but far out on the horizon, at dawn, and without the aid of glasses'. Other stops along the way in what the journalist Jonathan Cott once called Miller's 'cosmic tourism' were the Scientology of L. Ron Hubbard, the apocalyptic studies of the Essenes, Christian Science, Kahlil Gibran, White Witchcraft and the modern hinduism of Sri Ramakrishna. Perhaps in consistently cultivating a world of multiple and constant revelation he was hoping to ward off both any possibility of existential boredom, and the fear that the last revelation might simply be emptiness. A melancholy but oddly-attractive statement in the essay *My Life As An Echo*, in suggesting that the search for synthesis had become an end in itself, seems to hint at such a solution: 'Any theory, any idea, any speculation can augment the zest for life so long as one does not make the mistake of thinking that he is getting somewhere.'[19]

7

In among all the letter-writing and the spiritual exploring, Miller was still finding time to write books. After publishing *Sexus* he worked quickly to produce *Plexus*, but laid it aside early in 1950 for *The Books In My Life*, which was published by New Directions in 1952. *Plexus* appeared in 1953 in Paris in a two-volume limited edition of 2000. The year 1956 was a good one: an English edition of his Rimbaud book was published as *The Time of the Assassins*; a rewritten version of *Quiet Days in Clichy* was published by Girodias's

Olympia Press; and *A Devil in Paradise*, the account of Moricand's visit to Big Sur in 1948, appeared in English and French editions. It appeared again the following year as a coda to *Big Sur and the Oranges of Hieronymous Bosch*, a series of meditations, essays and portraits on the subject of life at Big Sur.

Of the works peripheral to the main task – the writing of *The Rosy Crucifixion* – *The Books in My Life* represents a particularly happy discovery of an autobiographical form in which Miller's dreamy, folksy memories of vanished burlesque halls, dead entertainers and forgotten film-stars mingle charmingly with meditations on the pleasures of reading on the toilet, sexual polarity, passionate appreciations of personal favourites like Rider Haggard, Blaise Cendrars, Jean Giono and Cowper Powys, and fragmentary auto-biographical glimpses into his early life as a worker and as the unhappy, duty-bound lover of Pauline Chouteau. His love of books and reading is infectious, and in its highly subjective way more likely to promote a healthy and independent interest in literature than the clinical dissections of professional critics for whom the adolescent love of literature degenerates with the passage of time into routine contempt for 'the job'.

Big Sur and the Oranges of Hieronymous Bosch aimed to present Big Sur as a paradise on earth, and had the predictable effect of attracting yet more beats, beatniks, would-be artists and other 'fools, idiots, bores, pedants and readers whom you blush to think have read you' to his door. This is much the most 'cultist' of Miller's works, larded with references to white witches, flying saucers, Mary Baker Eddy and so on, and unless one is personally sympathetic to these enthusiasms it makes for dull reading. The neighbours he describes and the life he leads do not appear to be particularly interesting, and the attempt to cast Moricand as a devil who has 'forsaken Paradise' fails, principally because one can never believe Big Sur really is the Paradise Miller claims it to be.

The most enjoyable section of the book is the 'Chama Serial', a story he makes up for his children about a little girl who lives on her own in a posh hotel in New York. This incorporates the children's own responses to Charma's adventures, and comic accounts of the narrative tight-spots into which Miller's improvising fantasies lead him, and of how he frees himself from these, usually by means of one mighty bound. It probably gives us quite a good picture of the casualness of his actual writing processes. Had he wished, he might have been a fine writer of children's books.

Early in 1959, Miller finished *Nexus*, the third volume of *The Rosy Crucifixion*. Like its predecessors, it was published by Girodias's company in Paris which, after a period as the Olympia Press, had reverted to the name under which it had been founded by Jack Kahane, the Obelisk Press. After *Sexus*'s account of the break-up of his marriage to Beatrice and the beginnings of his subsequent marriage to June, *Plexus* continues with the story of the first two years of this marriage and Miller's earliest attempts to become a writer after leaving the job at Western Union. Mara Andrews enters the scene towards the end of the book and *Nexus* details the effect she has on Miller's wife and on their marriage. After Mara and June's trip to Paris in 1927, and June's return on her own, the marriage appears to be recovering. *Nexus* ends with the couple embarking for Paris in 1928 on money obtained from the writing of *Moloch*.

Miller's aim was to complete the Proustian circle and write a fourth volume which would deal with this first French trip, the return to New York for one year and then his departure for France on his own. This would presumably have ended with a description of him sitting at Michael Fraenkel's desk at 18 Villa Seurat and writing: 'I am living at the Villa Borghese,' the opening line of *Tropic of Cancer*. Miller made several attempts to write this fourth book but finally abandoned the task.

The Rosy Crucifixion is certainly a unique human document. Among other things it is a fine folk history of Brooklyn and New York in the 1920s, containing all that was left out of newspapers of the time and practically nothing that was in them. While its form and its range of contents, from sex to religion, might recall other memoirs like Frank Harris's *My Life and Loves*, its style is unique. Miller was an early enthusiast for Japanese films like *The Seven Samurai*, and the style of the trilogy explains this affinity; in both, the axe rather than the knife is the favoured weapon, and events and emotions are described with childlike explicitness and exaggeration. The characters grunt and grimace and scowl, slap their thighs when laughing, posture and strut when proud or angry and when sad bury their heads in their hands.

Miller's long years of practise as a letter-writer and as a first-person narrator had made him a master at creating a feeling of intimacy between himself and his reader, and a master, too, at dealing with his own limitations as a novelist. Like a comic juggler he was able to win the sympathy of his audience by his very ineptness, bungling trick after trick while retaining the ability to astound between times with passages of astonishing and haunting power. With sound tactical sense he usually placed these at the end of his chapters. Chapter nineteen of *Sexus* concludes with one such flight, a vision of life in a Jewish ghetto:

In another cellar an old man sits in his overcoat on a pile of wood, counting his beard. His life is all coal and wood, little voyages from darkness to daylight. In his ears is still the ring of hoofs on cobbled streets, the sounds of shrieks and screams, the clatter of sabres, the splash of bullets against a blank wall. In the cinema, in the synagogue, in the coffee-house, wherever one sits, two kinds of music are playing – one bitter, one sweet. One sits in the middle of a river called Nostalgia. A river filled with little souvenirs gathered from the wreckage of the world. Souvenirs of the homeless, of birds of refuge building again and again with sticks and twigs. Everywhere broken nests, eggshells, fledglings with twisted necks and dead eyes staring into space. Nostalgic river dreams under tin copings, under rusty sheds, under capsized boats. A world of mutilated hopes, of strangled aspirations, of bullet-proof starvation. A world where even the warm breath of life has to be smuggled in, where gems as big as pigeon's hearts are traded for a yard of space, an ounce of freedom. All is compounded into a familiar liver paste which is swallowed on a tasteless wafer. In one gulp there is swallowed down five thousand years of bitterness, five thousand years of ashes, five thousand years of broken twigs, smashed eggshells, strangled fledglings . . .

The effect of a passage like this, suddenly surging out of a prose that is often lax and pedestrian, can be both exhilarating and disorientating. It is like waking suddenly to find oneself high on a mountain with no path in sight, nothing to indicate the means of ascent. A look back through the preceding pages to find the point of take-off will rarely succeed, and in the end one simply has to shrug and forge on, leaving behind all dull expectations of knowing exactly what is supposed to be happening. Plot-like themes or story-lines emerge now and then in the books; there is one involving the dance-hall owner Harcourt, and Henry whistles and curses and shakes his head in astonishment at each fresh revelation of this man's cunning; yet it is hard to fathom what this Harcourt is supposed to be up to, or what any of it has to do with Henry.

The characters can be similarly disorientating: without even the excuse of unfamiliar names, it can be as hard for a reader to keep track of who is who in *The Rosy Crucifixion* as in any Russian novel. Ulrics and Stanleys and Curleys and O'Maras and O'Rourkes appear and as suddenly disappear, indistinguishable from one another and all talking like Henry Miller. Emil Schnellock, the model for Ulric in *Sexus*, once commented cautiously on this phenomenon: 'I will not say

331

that I am glad that you are working on my portrait,' he wrote 'I remember of course, how more than once you told me you would write of me as Olivier to your Christophe, and in a thousand ways you have done so. . . . I am not forgetting to thank you for making Ulric in his talk of the artist (to Dewar) speak with the tongues of angels, and in the inspired voice of Henry Miller.'[20]

Disingenuously, Miller claimed to Lawrence Durrell that in writing *Sexus* he had been trying to recapture 'a poverty and sterility . . . which few men have known', and that had he been 'a braggart and an egotist I might have written more gloriously'.[21] Yet readers of the book cannot help but notice that Miller invariably promotes himself as right, healthy, and always correct in his exchanges with the other characters. The Kronskis and O'Maras and Ulrics are men of straw, and their primary rôle in life is to be wrong so that Henry can correct them. The technique is similar to that employed in the *Chuang Tzu*, a series of parables loosely strung together with the aim of demonstrating the sage's sagacity. The narrator of *The Rosy Crucifixion* is Pinnocchio in reverse, the only real person in a world of ventriloquist's dummies. Henry had other aims in writing *Sexus* too; he recommended it to one of his female readers once with the assurance that the book 'will give you a thrill all over'.[22]

There are many fine eccentricities in *The Rosy Crucifixion*. *Nexus* is prefaced, without identification, by the closing lines of Gogol's *Dead Souls* in the original Russian, a language which Miller himself could not read and which, at a guess, few of his readers could. Here and there the text has footnotes to explain a point of Brooklyn geography, or an unusual use of the word 'moon', and on several occasions he reminisces fondly but in obvious confusion about some of his favourite characters and incidents from Knut Hamsun's novels. June Miller, who at the beginning of *Sexus* is known as Mara, later changes her name to Mona without explanation. One might toy with the resonances of these names – the rôle of 'Mara' in Buddhist mythology, the associations of enigma with the name 'Mona' – but without much self-confidence. Miller did not have this kind of artistic self-consciousness, and while we are just possibly meant to hear the fiction at the end of the 'crucifixion', the fact that another character in the trilogy is called O'Mara is surely not intended to suggest any kind of association with the narrator's Mara. These oddities are all part of the books' charm, and bring to mind a comment by the ever-astute Perlès, that his friend Henry Miller was essentially an amateur writer, a Sunday writer, a man writing – astonishing thought – for the fun of it.

The difficulty with such autobiographical fictions is that they do not profit from repeated reading. They are not like symphonies or great novels that offer more with each successive experience of them. Rather they offer less, until at a certain point as readers our only means of enlivening the experience is to cease looking *with* the story-teller and instead look *at* him. Miller knew the feeling well himself, and disliked it. A passage in *The Colossus of Maroussi* describes how he sat one day listening to one of Katsimbalis's (the 'Colossus's') monologues when, suddenly and inexplicably, he found that he had detached himself from the story and was coolly observing the story-teller. The experience left him feeling 'foolish and impotent, as one does when one succeeds in destroying the power of illusion'.[23] Yet a knowledge of the writer's biography makes such detachment unavoidable in the end, and one begins to look outside the book for answers to some of the riddles within it.

The intrusively intense pro-semitism of the trilogy, for example, notably the ten-page section in *Sexus* sparked off by the death of 'Mona's' father, really only makes sense in the light of the knowledge that Miller felt guilty about certain passages he had written about Jews earlier in his career in the unpublished *Moloch*. He remained deeply disturbed by the accusations of anti-semitism periodically levelled at him on the basis of his published writings, and in a specially-written preface for a French translation of his 1935 letter *Aller Retour New York* he wrote that in this new edition he had toned down the 'harsh, seemingly unjustified references to the Jews' from the original version, explaining that he had 'caricatured, fulminated, abominated and blasphemed to my heart's content throughout the great body of my writings. I was more extravagant and reckless with my language in those early months of 1935 when this was being written, because I was younger, and more thoughtless of others.' The trilogy contains no such explanation. Rather than express regret about his previous attitudes, rather than admit his instincts had led him astray in this matter and simply admit that Jews are just like everyone else, some good and some bad, he chose to fill it with pro-semitism, like some ptolemaic astronomer preferring to build his equations ever higher rather than simply scrap them and start anew.

Biographical information is interesting, but too much of it can spoil the tale and turn a first-person novel into a case-study. As a folk-history of immigrant Brooklyn during the years of Miller's youth and early manhood, *The Rosy Crucifixion* is a treasure-trove of memories, pastimes and social attitudes. As a novel the trilogy lacks the narrative detachment and self-conscious artisty that might have turned it into a working-class version of Proust's *A la recherche du temps perdu*. Better, in fact, simply to concede that the work is closer to therapy than art, and accept that all Miller was trying to do was capture the intensity of his past happiness and communicate it to others. Among its most enjoyable qualities are the absurd informality of the sex scenes which exult in the fact that 'Celia shits', and which assuredly rescued many a young man from the paralysing effects of over-sensitivity in his first encounters with women; the hilarious surrealism of the language, and the strong sense the story conveys of what it is like to be another person; the consistent promotion of the idea that life is enjoyable, and that happiness has little to do with money; above all, perhaps, a curious, elegiac quality, which has something to do with the way the trilogy insists on the importance of the triviality and the banality of everyday life in the face of the often quite spurious claims made on our conscience and our attention by the television, radio, film, newspaper and pop music industries, and its affirmation of our right to indulge now and then in shameless sentimentality, vulgarity, and entirely private memories and fantasies without feeling that in doing so we are letting the rest of the world down.

As to the truth of it all, who can say? Perhaps not even the author knew by the time he had finished reinventing his life. William Dewar and Emil Conason did not recognize themselves as portrayed by their old friend. Neither did Schnellock, but then he realised that Henry was playing all the parts himself. As for Miller, he was haunted for a long time by the fear that Beatrice might sue him for what he had written about her in his books if they ever became available in America.

CHAPTER SIXTEEN

1959–1970
Everybody's hero, everybody's villain

1

Nexus turned out to be end of *The Rosy Crucifixion* and the end of Miller's literary involvement with June Mansfield. Considering that the work was projected in 1927 and finished in 1959, he had paced himself nicely, and the great story had kept him going for most of his adult life. Other old men approaching seventy might have taken up gardening, or drinking. Always an unpredictable man, Miller embarked instead on a particularly eventful, disruptive and interesting decade. The climax was the final acceptance in his home country of the *Tropics* and his other sexual writing. The recurrent motives were women and travel.

In April 1959 he took the first of several trips to Europe in company with Eve and the children. It looked like a good way of spending the 540,000 francs that his European agents Hoffmann were holding for him in France. They rented a flat on rue Campagne-Première, close to the Montparnasse cemetery, within fifteen minutes walk of Miller's old home at the Villa Seurat. Here they stayed for a few weeks, sightseeing and visiting old friends, before going on to see Henry's Danish publisher Hans Reitzel in Farum, on the outskirts of Copenhagen. Back in France again they went to see Albert Maillet, a writer friend, at Die, where they bought an old Fiat in which they motored south, in the company of Alfred Perlès, for a prolonged stay with Lawrence Durrell. Durrell had rented a flat in Sommières for them overlooking the market-place, and on moonlit nights Miller would roller-skate in the square. With the publication of Durrell's *Justine* in 1957, and *Balthazar* and *Mountolive* the following year, Durrell had finally achieved critical and financial success after some twenty years of relative obscurity. Miller, who had done everything he could to further his friend's career during its earliest days, was personally delighted for him, and the reunion was also a celebration. Professionally speaking, however, Durrell's novels after *The Black Book* were too crafted and complex for Henry's tastes, which were by now almost directly anti-literary.

They went sightseeing to Saint-Rémy to visit the house where Nostradamus was born, to the Gorges du Tarn, and to Les Baux, which had inspired Dante in writing the *Inferno*, and visited Joseph Delteil, another of Henry's many French literary friends, at his home near Montpellier before returning to Paris for a few last days and then home to California.

Miller did not enjoy the trip at all. In July he had written to Emil White that he had 'wonderful moments every time I see Durrell. Apart from that it is a nightmare.'[1] A letter to Durrell shortly after his return conveyed a similar sense of unease and a rare self-doubt:

I'm going through some sort of crisis. Never felt more desolate. Yet underneath very hopeful. Two nights ago I got up in the middle of the night with the firm intent of destroying everything – but it was too big a job. So I'll hang on and finish *Nexus* (Vol.2)* then see. Writing seems so foolish, so unnecessary now. (Not yours, of course, but mine.) As for you, I feel such a glorious future for you. You've just opened the vein. And with what a salvo! Go on, you bring joy everywhere. As for me, I seem to feel that all I have done is to create a booby-hatch.[2]

There was more talk of a 'crisis of some sort', and in the autumn of 1959 Miller was indulging in a favourite daydream of travelling to the East to visit Japan, Siam and Burma. He even made arrangements to fly to Japan in April 1960 but was distracted by the arrival of an invitation to be one of the judges at the Cannes Film Festival. He had been indiscriminately fond of films all his life, and accepted with alacrity the chance to get away from the scene of his depression, see a few films and be fêted by the French. He travelled to Europe alone this time – or so he wished Eve to believe.

In fact, with the assistance of Vincent Birge, he was joined in France by a woman named Caryl Hill Thomas, a divorced mother of two with whom he had been having an affair for some months. Hill was a waitress at Nepenthe, a restaurant built on the site of the Log House, Miller's first Big Sur home where he had lived briefly in 1944 with Lynda Sargent. Birge recalls Hill as pretty but shallow, and believes she was primarily attracted to Miller's fame.

They met twice at the bar and on the third occasion Miller took his old love along to meet his new one, subjecting Eve to the same humiliations as Pauline Chouteau, Beatrice Miller and June Miller had been obliged to endure. Eve, who had been having problems with alcohol for some time, got drunk and Miller went outside to wait for her in the car. Hill, presumably at a prearranged signal, joined him there.

*This refers to the projected conclusion of *The Rosy Crucifixion*

In December and January, Eve was frequently away from home, tending to her dying mother at Berkeley and the subsequent funeral arrangements. This gave Hill and Miller ample time to consolidate their affair. Miller believed that he was conducting himself discreetly, but the Big Sur community was a small one, and Eve knew as well as everyone else what was going on. Yet she also knew that her husband was not a promiscuous man. He was not even a conqueror of women, but simply a man who had never outgrown his addiction to the excitements of 'falling in love'. Seven years of close attachment to one woman had been his upper limit ever since his marriage to Beatrice. Eve hoped that the affair with Hill was just the return of this periodic wave, and that if she allowed him to have his fling it might prove satisfaction enough and ensure the survival of the marriage in the long run. The joint trip to France, however, was a heavy humiliation to bear.

Miller provided reports of his European trips for the newsletter of the Henry Miller Literary Society, and his description of the 1960 tour contained a complaint that the thirty-two films he had to sit through at Cannes were 'poor, and all of them too long'. His personal favourite among them was the Japanese entrant *Kagi (Odd Obsession)*. Unsurprisingly, he made no mention of the fact that he was accompanied by his mistress on the trip, nor that on the day of his arrival in Cannes he received a letter from Eve requesting a divorce.

Hill and Miller spent an uncomfortable week with the Durrells at Sommières, went on to Milan and Pisa, where Henry lavished empathic affection on the leaning tower; to Florence to visit the house in which Dostoevsky had written *The Idiot*; and then to Paris, where Miller cut short the trip and flew home alone to deal with the divorce. Within a month of his return he heard that Hill had arranged to marry the man she had been seeing before the jaunt to Cannes. Eve left him and moved in with a neighbour pending the divorce hearing. Henry was left on his own.

2

Women like Frieda Lawrence and Frank Harris's Nellie knew only too well the hazards of being married to a writer of sexy books, and perhaps the problem did cross Eve's mind as she sat in the summer of 1952 reading *Sexus* and feeling the size of Henry's myth. Even so, few women of thirty-six with a husband nearing seventy would have given serious thought to the prospect of losing him to still younger woman; but Miller was a unique seventy year old, still with a slender, athletic build and with a personal vanity that expressed itself increasingly in the classically well-cut suits and jackets he now wore instead of the second-hand cords, check shirts and boots that had been his uniform throughout the 1940s and 1950s. Their sex-life had not been satisfactory for some time, for which Eve bravely took the blame. 'I never heard her say a word against Henry,' Vincent Birge recalls.

Like most people who knew the couple, he regarded the end of the marriage as a tragedy for her. She was young enough and innocent enough to have fallen for an image, the open, honest, warm, even paternal 'Henry Miller' of the books, only to discover, as Lepska had done, that being a Happy Rock was a full-time business. There was no way into him, not even for a wife – perhaps especially not for a wife. Throughout their marriage her husband had remained a disturbing enigma: 'You mustn't take Henry amiss,' she wrote to one acquaintance. 'He is one of the most thoughtless, tactless men in the world . . . at the same time the most sensitive, giving, understanding. He's a prism. But he never *intends* to hurt another.' Returning an unread manuscript to a friend on Henry's behalf she offered her personal apologies: 'He can't always live his own truths, high visions . . . believe me, do I know! . . . I am his wife (I could raise the hair on your head, m'dears).'[3] Miller's philosophical ideal of steadiness, 'rockness' and personal inviolability, whether it was the result of his taoist convictions or just plain egoism (and it could easily have been a coincidence of the two), was incompatible with the successful conduct of a normal marriage. In the face of such an ideal Eve could not help but feel emotionally superfluous to her husband's needs, and it may have been this sense of exclusion which slowly turned her from a social drinker into an alcoholic.

She struggled to keep up a good front in the community, however, and to hide the extend of her hurt and disappointment, enabling Henry to adopt a familiar posture of sheepish, guiltless fatalism: 'No matter what one expects,' he lamented, 'it's always a blow. Maybe we will be better friends now – certainly I have no bad feelings – how could I?'[4] As grounds for her divorce Eve opted for 'desertion', which she found 'less messy than "mental cruelty" and what not'.[5] He had always dominated her so completely, even when she was drunk, that he was mildly surprised to discover that she intended to apply to the court for alimony.

3

By this time Miller's emotional life had degenerated almost wholly to the level of pure play, and his first thought on regaining his personal freedom was to realize in physical form his lifelong spiritual fascination with the East. 'Next amourette must be Oriental,' he wrote to a young friend.[6]

Before organizing this, however, he made what turned out to be a last serious attempt to fall in love again. He travelled to Europe for a third time for the specific purpose of seeing Renate Gerhardt, a young German woman whom he had met at the offices of his German publisher, Rowohlt, while touring Europe in the spring with Caryl Hill.

Accompanying him on the trip this time as his companion, secretary, translator, interpreter, chauffeur, ping-pong opponent and minder was Vincent Birge, an admirer who had written to him early in the 1950s after reading *Tropic of Cancer*. Birge was a radio operator on TWA intercontinental routes, and as such he knew where to get the best rates of exchange for Henry's accumulating French royalties in Paris, and had often helped him to get access to these. He had also done some book-smuggling for him. A loyal, honest, modest and practical man whose own marriage was faltering, he had reasons of his own for wanting to get away from America and made an ideal companion for Miller. 'I wonder what we're going to do for women,' Henry wrote before they set out. 'If we were a pair of homos the situation would be perfect, what!'[7] They were not a pair of homos, of course, but Eve was certainly onto something when she remarked that she was glad he had Vincent along to look after him and keep him content, 'instead of some ill-chosen woman'.

They left Big Sur on September 24th and flew from Los Angeles to Paris, where they stayed for a fortnight and socialized with old friends Georges Belmont, Man Ray, Brassai, Maurice Nadau and Maurice Girodias, who was enjoying a great success with Nabokov's *Lolita*. Henry read the book, but found it hard going. There was too much art in it for him.

From Paris the two men went to Die to pick up the Fiat which had been in storage there since Miller's trip with Eve in 1959. Albert Maillet had arranged for the car to be serviced before they arrived, and passed on to them an ominous warning from the mechanic who did the job that it was a wreck and that the motor was 'about to collapse'. Nonetheless, they set off for Germany, departing in a snowstorm on a route that took them through Grenoble, Besançon, Colmer and Strasbourg, into Germany and on to Darmstadt and Minden. He found Minden especially lovely and wondered how his grandfather Heinrich Müller could have left such a place for New York. Armed with a letter from the Miller family historian, his Aunt Mary Smith of

Brooklyn, he searched the archives at the Rathaus for dates of family significance and to his chagrin found none. (On his return from the trip Emil Conason teased him that this was because he came from a family of renegade Jews.) The following day, on October 19th, they reached Reinbek-bei-Hamburg where Renate lived and where Rowohlt Verlag had their offices. While the car went into the garage for running repairs, Miller courted Renate.

She was a widow with two young sons, Titus and Ezra, an attractive woman of thirty-six with the dark, sensual looks that Miller had favoured ever since the days of Pauline and Beatrice. Her job as the purchaser of foreign rights at Rowholt Verlag had brought her into contact with Henry's books, and she admired them greatly. Their reunion in the autumn confirmed his impressions of their first encounter in the spring. Henry was in love again, and everyone had to know. The urgent announcements of delirious happiness he dashed off to his friends had a familiar ring: a new life had begun, he had at last found the right woman, he had not been so profoundly happy in years. Eve used inverted commas herself when she wrote to the Finks to tell them that Henry was 'in love' again. . . .

Renate's German nationality was certainly a factor in Henry's interest in her. For the first time since leaving France in 1939, he was seriously thinking about returning to settle in Europe. Perhaps life with a German wife would provide him with what must have seemed to him the greatest synthesis of all – the return to the pre-Brooklyn roots of the Müller family which would wipe out that sense of almost shameful rootlessness which he felt as an American. The attempt to trace his genealogy in Minden was one expression of this hope. Another was the effort he made to revive his knowledge of the German that he had heard spoken so much in his early childhood. Before leaving Big Sur he had taken a Living Language course, and for a time tried to speak in German with Renate. He soon gave up, complaining that it was a language more suitable for elephants and rhinoceroses than human beings. For a joke, he wrote a short article in nonsense German and sent it to his friend Gilbert Neiman for inclusion in *Between Worlds*, a review Neiman edited in Puerto Rico. 'Neiman thinks it means something,' he wrote to his daughter Val, 'and is trying to get it translated. He has a Viennese philologist working on it. Ssh! Mum's the word!'[8]

After about a fortnight at Reinbek, during which Henry visited Mölln, the birthplace of Til Eulenspiegel and played frequent ping-pong with the employees at Rowohlt, he and Birge set off for three weeks' sightseeing together with Emil White, who was in Europe making his leisurely way to Israel. They visited the house where

Goethe was born in Frankfurt and spent an enjoyable week in Vienna. The highlight of the month, however, was undoubtedly Miller's brief stay at the home of Georges Simenon, near Lausanne, where he had the pleasure of meeting and dining with Charlie Chaplin. White and Birge rented a room at a nearby hotel, where Henry rang them to apologize for Simenon's refusal to include them in the invitation to meet Chaplin. White in particular was heart-broken, and consoled himself by seducing Simenon's maid the next time he visited the house. Miller also met Erskine Caldwell and the Icelandic writer Halldor Laxness on this trip, but did not like them particularly.

At the end of November the three men split up. White continued on his way to Israel, Birge drove to Paris in the Fiat and Miller flew back to Hamburg to be with Renate. Over the Christmas period the two decided that they wanted to live together, and in March Birge was summoned to Reinbek to pick up Henry and begin the search for the ideal spot where he and Renate and the four children could settle. The basic requirements were a mild climate, in a place where the cost of living was moderate, with English-language and German-language schools in the vicinity and with adequate medical facilities at hand. At seventy, Henry's health was beginning to show small signs of breaking down, and he was concerned that he might have a murmuring heart.

In search of such a place the two men set out on a trip that lasted three months, navigating back and forth across France, Germany, Switzerland, Austria, Spain, Portugal, Italy, Lichtenstein and San Marino with the aid of an inscribed atlas given to them by Renate. At a conservative estimate, the car broke down seventeen times, in spite of the fact that at Miller's insistence Birge checked the level of the electrolyte in the battery daily, a task that involved unloading a complete set of spare tyres and tubes, snow chains, shovel and tow-rope which Miller had also insisted they take along with them. It was useless for Birge, a fairly competent mechanic, to protest that such daily checks were unnecessary. He was more inclined to worry about the loud screeching noise the car made in third gear, and was not convinced by Miller's explanation that the noise was a regular feature, intended by the Fiat designers to let the driver *know* that he was in third gear.

The trip had its memorable moments, including a visit to Mont-pellier museum where Miller was allowed to try on Rabelais's gown; dinner with Joseph Delteil and his American wife, Caroline, just two days after Delteil had seen an apparition of St Francis in his garden; a performance of Ionesco's *Rhinocéros*; and a visit to Cervantes's house at Valladolid. However, although the search did turn up two areas that seemed to meet the modest requirements, in the Ticino and in Gibraltar, Miller rejected both in the end as being too perfect – the same criticism as he levelled at Mozart's music.

He had never really been enthusiastic about the search anyway. Almost from the start he had been afflicted by a curious and profound depression which caused him to spend much of his time in bed. There were many possible causes of this: suppressed guilt over the casual way in which he had jettisoned Eve; signs of impending old age, including the possible heart murmur, failing sight in one eye and a bad fall while out walking in Biarritz that damaged his leg and was the beginning of a recurring problem with his thigh; fear that the onset of sexual impotence was nigh; and the old, paralysing horror that always overtook him when he had to take a decision. Once again his reference point in describing his condition was the film he and Durrell had seen together six times in Paris in 1937: 'It's almost as if, in quitting Big Sur, I walked out of my true paradise – and now, like the hero of *Lost Horizon*, I am fucked!' He confided to Birge that he hoped Durrell might solve his problems for him by simply telling him where to live, and for that reason hung around Sommières for two weeks in April waiting for his friend to return from a trip to London. Durrell could not help him, however, and Renate would not. 'What can we do?' she wrote in answer to one of his pathetic letters. '*I* cannot choose a place for you! *You* must find it.'[9]

Worst of all, at the end of May, Miller had to put aside his long-standing plans for the children to join him for the summer. He explained his decision to Emil White:

Had to cancel the children's trip – was near a breakdown – and am still rocking – full of anguish, guilt, doubt, indecision, frustration – a real neurosis. I feel desolate. I have become in very essence the Wandering Jew. I don't know where to turn, what to do. Some days I think I ought to just go and put myself in the bughouse. I can't stop thinking – and no matter what I think – no solution. But don't tell people, *please*, about my condition.

ps. I'm waiting to hear what Eve and Lepska will do for the children. I feel so guilty, so heartbroken over it, I could kill myself. But that wouldn't do anybody any good.[10]

When they first met, Renate had noticed that Henry behaved in a hesitant, almost shy way with her. This caused her to act passively towards him, and give him what turned out to be a false impression of her as basically submissive. With that disarming honesty of which he was capable he told her early on in their relationship that what he needed above all was to be worshipped from afar by a woman,[11] but as the weeks of the pointless odyssey dragged by and the letters passed back and forth between them, it became obvious that Renate was not interested in any relationship that did not assume complete equality between them. 'I love to listen to you,' she had written to him once, 'and shall probably never know what I love more: to read you or listen to you'. By June 1961 she seems to have made up her mind that it was perhaps better just to read him. When he returned she made it clear to him that she no longer thought marriage between them a good idea. like Henry, she was a firm believer in astrology, and both of them afterwards used the predictions of their respective astrologers as a way of shifting the blame for the failure of the relationship from themselves on to the malignant operations of the stars and planets. Henry had apparently been particularly unlucky with a bad passage of Saturn over his Radix, and one has to suspect that he was secretly not too disappointed to hear it. To emigrate and make yet another fresh start in life in his seventy-first year was a daunting prospect.

The two continued to correspond for some years, and on Miller's subsequent trips to Europe in the 1960s they met occasionally. In 1962 they even spent a few days together on Mallorca when Henry served as one of the judges for the literary *Prix de Formentor*. The aura of emotional game-playing that surrounded Miller gradually began to affect Renate too. She became fascinated by the mythologized version of June that Henry had created in his books, and questioned him frequently about her. At one point in their correspondence she even began to play a June-like rôle in his life. Rowohlt had declined to publish *Just Wild About Harry*, an extremely bad play Henry had written over the Christmas period at Reinbeck in 1960, and suggested to him that he tear it up and forget about it if he wished to avoid ruining his reputation. Under the circumstances Renate allowed herself to be tempted to set up a small company to publish it herself. Later the company ran into financial difficulties, and she sent a succession of wild letters to Henry describing her impending in-carceration in a dank debtor's prison unless he sent her a large cheque at once. Henry obliged, finally putting the affair on the kind of footing he understood best when dealing with women.

Henry's confessional and exponential urges dominated his person-ality so completely that, in the end, Renate proved no more successful than any other wife or lover had been in persuading him that a private life of secrets and intimacies shared by just two also has its pleasures. His suggestion in 1965 that she lend the water-colours he had given her for an exhibition of his paintings surprised and hurt her; and she was even more dismayed when he later suggested that she could raise money by selling his love-letters to her to some institution or college library. Her own intimate letters to him duly found their way into the

343

archives at UCLA, with an accompanying note in Henry's hand decreeing that these were not to be read until after his death. His death, not her's.

4

A hidden element in the depression that struck Miller in 1961 was that in the spring of that year he had become, overnight, a rich man. In May, almost thirty years after it was written, *Tropic of Cancer* was legally published in the United States. After a preliminary discussion over lunch in Paris in June 1960, involving Miller, Rosset and Girodias – at which Miller was shocked at the extravagance of the two young tycoons in ordering pigeon paté at 1000 francs for starters – he signed a contract with Barney Rosset of Grove Press. This took place on February 18th 1961 at the Atlantic Hotel in Hamburg, and gave Rosset the rights to publish both *Tropics* in the United States. In return Miller received an advance against royalties of $50,000. He and Birge had been correcting proofs of both books during April and May of their trip, and as publication date loomed he worried increasingly that he might be arrested, tried, fined or even imprisoned on his return to the States. Possible repercussions arising from the invented episode about killing a boy with a rock in *Tropic of Capricorn* bothered him too, and he was plagued by a return of his fears that a former wife – in this case June – might sue him for what he had written about her in the book.

From its modern beginnings in 1956, the movement to abolish the censorship of literature in the United States had proceeded with great rapidity. In essence, the lawyers responsible for the defence of the two books central to the issue – D.H. Lawrence's *Lady Chatterley's Lover* and Miller's *Tropic of Cancer* – concentrated their arguments on attempts to overthrow the traditional legal definition of what constituted obscene literature. This had nothing to do with the literary value of the work in question; for most practical purposes it simply involved the application of the Hicklin rule, with its definition of obscenity as matter liable to deprave and corrupt 'those whose minds are open to such immoral influences, and into whose hands a publication of this sort may fall'. There had been liberal modifications of the rule and, by the end of the 1940s, the practice of proceeding against a book on the basis of isolated passages within it rather than on the tendency of the whole to 'deprave and corrupt' had lost ground, at the same time as the realization spread that the phrase 'into whose hands [the book] may fall' effectively set the mark of ethical maturity in a society at the level of its children. Neverthless, the Hicklin rule remained the guiding principle in deciding whether a book was liable to arouse lustful thoughts in its readers or not. The Roth decision of the Supreme Court in 1957* appeared to confirm the view that obscene literature was not protected under the First Amendment's guarantees of 'freedom of speech or of the press'. In a written opinion, however, a gratuitous observation by one of the judges that obscenity was 'utterly without redeeming social importance' provided the loophole that lawyers for liberal publishers like Rosset were able to exploit to discredit traditional definitions of the term and provide new ones.

Grove had published an unexpurgated *Lady Chatterley's Lover* in America in 1959 which had been seized and ruled 'obscene and nonmailable' by the Postmaster General. On appeal, counsel for the publishers argued that the implication of the Roth opinion was that only those things which were 'utterly without social importance' could be called obscene, and so deprived of the protection of the First Amendment. The further implication – that anything *with* social importance *was* guaranteed constitutional protection – was an important factor in the decision of federal district court judge Bryan to allow the appeal and to permit *Lady Chatterley's Lover* to pass through the US Mails. The government appealed against his decision, but on March 25th 1960 the Court of Appeals affirmed Bryan's finding.

In the wake of his victory, Rosset felt that the time was right to proceed with his plans to launch Henry Miller's most notorious book. He held back briefly, awaiting the verdict in a case involving a painter named Dorothy Upham who had notified Customs that she would attempt to enter the United States carrying a copy of *Tropic of Cancer*, and was now trying to recover it through the courts after it had been duly confiscated. The prospect of pirate editions forced his hand, however, and in June 1961, Grove published the book, shortly before the Judge in the Upham case ruled that *Tropic of Cancer* was 'not obscene' and freed it for importation into America. Independently of this the federal agencies had concluded that the decision to lift the ban on *Lady Chatterley's Lover* also implied constitutional protection for Miller's book and on advice from the Department of Justice, Customs raised its import ban and the Post Office permitted *Tropic of Cancer* to pass through the mails. In June, Val Miller wrote to tell her father that she had bought a copy of his book at the bookshop at Reed College, Oregon, and Miller wrote to Roger Bloom in jail in Ohio that it was 'another great victory – and an easy one. Something is happening to

*Samuel Roth was a publisher of cheap, straight pornography who was prosecuted in New York under the Comstock Act.

America – all of a sudden the barriers are down. I never thought they would be so indulgent towards me.'[12]

He was mistaken, for the book's extraordinary adventures were not quite over yet. Its resilience over the preceding thirty years, however, had provided it with almost mystical powers of survival. Following the failure of the tentative attempts to get Harcourt Brace and Simon and Schuster interested in publishing *Tropic of Cancer* during 1934 and 1935, and of Miller's attempts to arrange a pirated edition that would allow him to collect royalties on it, the novel appeared in pirated editions in Shanghai and in Vienna. These versions were of indeterminable size and he earned nothing from them. The only translation before the Second World War was into Czechoslovakian, in an edition with a specially drawn cover by Matisse. Denoel had a French translation ready by 1938, and made so many promises to publish the book without actually doing so that Miller finally lost his patience with him and the two almost came to blows: '*Je vous emmerde!*' cried Denoel, to which Henry replied, in English: 'Go fuck yourself!'[13] Denoel liked the book well enough, but in the end had no desire to repeat the difficulties he had encountered as the publisher of Céline's novels.

Tropic of Cancer went through five legitimate editions in Paris before the first pirated version of the book appeared in America. This was the so-called Medusa edition of 1940, published by Jacob R. Brussells and was printed on Lexington Avenue. The ruse of writing 'Imprenta de Mexico' on it failed to mislead the authorities, and Brussells served a two-year sentence in jail for his involvement in the project. Miller knew about this edition. The bulk of the two thousand copies were sold through Francis Steloff at the Gotham Book Mart and through Ben Abrahamson in his bookshop in Chicago at $10 per copy. It has been suggested that Miller received a lump sum of $1000 from each of the booksellers instead of a ten per cent royalty on sales, but he makes no reference to any such windfall in his letters, and the story is probably apocryphal.

Miller's attitude throughout was one of straight intransigence: he preferred to see the book pirated rather than bowdlerized. He made his position very clear to Frank Dobo back in 1938. Dobo, who by that time had returned from Paris to New York, had suggested publishing a book consisting of printable excerpts from *Tropic of Cancer* and *Black Spring*, but Miller would have none of it:

To make the public wait all these years and then give them a diluted, modified version of my works is hardly very strategic – it might prove to be a boomerang. A lot depends on the publisher, which publisher, and what his attitude is towards me and towards the public he caters to. I don't want to deal with any shrewd opportunist devils, such as there are aplenty in New York. You see, I have waited a long time to be accepted *in toto*, not in part. And the longer I hold out the better my hand is, vis-a-vis America. . . . Strategically, the longer I withold the books from the American public the more prestige I acquire, willy-nilly. My tactics all along have been just the reverse of the usual American tactics. I have played my hand like a Chinaman. . . . If America never capitulates I can get along without her. I am not trying to become a millionaire. I am trying to preserve my integrity, to write as I please, and to take orders from no one – except God, who is my boss.[14]

In 1945 Denoel finally published Henri Fluchère's translation of *Tropic of Cancer*, and the French authorities made an immediate attempt to suppress the book. French writers, many of them personal friends of Miller, mounted a successful campaign in his defence, and depositions from some of these same defenders were assembled by the American Civil Liberties Union for a campaign in 1950 to free *Tropic of Cancer* for import into America. This had to be abandoned in October when the judge refused to admit the depositions. Three years later, the United States Court of Appeals, sitting in San Francisco, upheld a ban on both *Tropics*. *Sexus*, in the meantime, had been banned in France, and in 1956 was banned in Norway.

In 1955, Frank Dobo put forward another plan. He suggested that Henry sign a contract with a legitimate American publisher for publication of both *Tropics* which would then appear in expurgated versions. After these had been on the market long enough to earn some money, Henry could then 'discover' the ruse and salve his conscience by complaining that he had been tricked by an unscrupulous publisher. Though Dobo guaranteed strict secrecy in the matter he doubted whether Miller would agree to the plan, and he was right.

While it would be unnecessarily cynical to suppose that Miller had no idealistic motives in taking this all-or-nothing attitude, it would be naive to suppose that he had not been aware from the start that, if he succeeded in writing a book good enough to be appreciated and rude enough to be banned, it would achieve far more for him in terms of prestige than merely writing yet another good book. *Tropic of Cancer* had become a legend during its years in the wilderness, and by 1949 combined sales of the *Tropics* in English were well over one hundred thousand in Europe alone. There was no reason why it should not go on selling forever – as long as it remained on the forbidden list. Thus Miller, in a letter to Durrell in 1958, urged him not to compromise in order to get *The Black Book* published: 'It will *stay in print*, if banned. Whereas with the others, it will get raves and then die a quick death.'[15]

347

With courageous honesty he wrote to Emil White that he feared the consequences of publication: 'Rosset is killing the goose that laid the golden egg. I mean, unwittingly. He'll make a killing and then my name'll be forgotten.'[16]

If ever a man lived by the maxim that it is better to travel hopefully than to arrive, it was Henry Miller. His whole literary persona was based on the perception. He had become addicted to travelling, and suddenly and unexpectedly to arrive after so many years posed special difficulties for him. The $50,000 from Grove Press, with the prospect of much more to come, removed his financial worries, real and imagined, once and for all, but left him with a whole set of new problems. One was this fear that his reputation would disappear. Another was the realization that his identity as the suffering artist dissolved completely in the money. The problem had surfaced once before, when Maurice Girodias wrote to him in 1946 with the news that he was holding a fortune in French francs for him. The fact that the money was 'over there' enabled Miller to deal with the problem on that occasion largely by ignoring it. No such option was open to him this time, however. He realized that he could no longer play with any conviction the rôle of starving artist that had sustained and delighted him for so many years. This caused his anxieties to mount: would the public still be prepared to take him seriously as a critic of American mores and materialism, now that the ultimate authority of poverty and rejection had been taken from him? Did the dramatic changes in his circumstances mean he would have to reinvent himself all over again? If so, could he still do it?

Poverty may have been swept aside for ever, but the rejection lingered awhile. In spite of Henry's confident reference to an 'easy' victory, within six months of publication the forces for dullness and repression had gathered. Grove followed up the hardback edition of the book with a paperback in October 1961. Paperback books were then regarded as *in essence* subversive literature, since they retailed to the masses at a price which they could afford. Police officials in Chicago and surrounding areas began a systematic intimidation of booksellers who stocked the new edition. Arrests were made. A storm of litigation was hurled at the novel, and suddenly *Tropic of Cancer* was on trial in fifty-three separate court-rooms across the United States. To some it looked as though the censorship lobby had discovered a new tactic: to take the offending publisher and his book to court so many times that in the end the cost of defending it simply bankrupted him.

The showcase trial was at Cook County Court in Chicago, where Elmer Gertz defended it before Judge Samuel B. Epstein. Gertz, who had written a book on Frank Harris in his youth, worked hard to present Miller as someone whose writings revealed him to be fundamentally a religious man. Among his witnesses he had managed to get hold of a young Lutheran preacher who was a particular admirer of Henry's books. On February 21st 1962, Judge Epstein reached his verdict: *Tropic of Cancer* was not obscene 'under the law'. His reasoning seems quaint today, with its description of a society in which the 'coverall bathing-suit is being replaced by the bikini, and the ballroom dance of old has been replaced by the Twist', and his assertion that *Tropic of Cancer* would not cause an increase in juvenile delinquency because sexual offenders 'have such a low educational background they don't read books of this literary calibre'. Neither did the prosecution read books of this literary calibre either: during the course of the trial Gertz discovered that all except one police chief had read a total of one paragraph of *Tropic of Cancer* – the famous 'prose ode to Tania at the top of page 5'.[17]

Chicago was only a battle, not the war. The Superintendent of Police lodged an appeal against Epstein's verdict, and a 'Statement in Support of Freedom to Read' signed by two hundred authors and publishers was issued in July. Later in the month the Supreme Judicial Court of Massachusetts cleared the book. Minor aggravations, convictions, appeals, acquittals, continued for the next two years. In the midst of it all, in September 1962, Grove Press slipped *Tropic of Capricorn* on to the market, complete with the section entitled 'The Land of Fuck'. All the attention of the puritans was focussed on *Tropic of Cancer*, and its twin never became the subject of prosecution in the United States.

As it had in the United States, *Lady Chatterley's Lover* paved the way for Miller's books in England. Emboldened by Rosset's success, Penguin Books published an unexpurgated edition of Lawrence's novel in 1960 which was challenged by the Director of Public Prosecutions under the Obscene Publications Act of the previous year. As England has no written constitution, the lawyers acting for the publishers found it necessary to use other tactics than their American colleagues to support their contention that the book was 'not obscene'. Among other things they assembled a collection of thirty-five witnesses for the defence, including university professors, priests, head teachers, journalists, writers and even two of the Members of the Parliament responsible for passing the Act. Penguin won their case. The grounds for acquittal, however, were subjective rather than legal, and heavily biased towards the experts' endorsement of the alleged literary and moral qualities of Lawrence's novel. The absence of the simple emphasis on freedom of expression which had formed the basis of the decision in the American courts thus left the British government with considerable discretionary powers to proceed against other novels, powers which it made use of later in the decade – against Hubert Selby junior's *Last Exit to Brooklyn*, for example – as the sexual revolution gained pace. John Calder's first English edition of *Tropic of Cancer*, however, published in March 1963, was left in peace, as were subsequent editions of Miller's novels.

The numerous American cases against *Tropic of Cancer* proceeded. In July 1963 the California Supreme Court ruled that the book was not obscene, the New York Court of Appeals that it was. In June 1964 the Illinois Supreme Court reversed Judge Epstein's finding, the US Supreme Court reversed a Florida court's conviction of the book, and on July 7th the Illinois Supreme Court withdrew its June ruling and reinstated Judge Epstein's original decision. The book was free.

To his great relief, Miller was never required to participate personally in any of these trials. He had a life-long horror of public speaking and, in 1934 when the book was first published, he suffered for some time from nightmares in which he found himself standing in the dock, hopelessly trying to defend it before a sea of unsympathetic faces.

The closest he came to experiencing the nightmare in real life was in the summer of 1962, when conspiracy charges were filed in Brooklyn against himself, Grove Press and three booksellers. The somewhat bizarre aim of the case was to show that Miller, in 1934, had conspired with Rosset, then twelve years old, and the three Brooklyn retailers to 'prepare and author' a book which was to 'depict and represent acts and scenes wherein the sexual organs of both male persons and female persons were to be portrayed and described in manners connoting sex degeneracy and sex perversion and were to be of such a pornographic character as would tend to incite lecherous thoughts and desires'. The retailers and Rosset both appeared in person before Judge Manuel Gomez, who dismissed the retailers and released Rosset on bail of $500. Gomez, however, was especially keen to see the Brooklyn boy himself in his courtroom. When Henry showed no signs of wanting to make the trip from California – not even when the district attorney offered to pay his travelling expenses – a bench warrant was issued for his arrest. Brooklyn threatened to start extradition proceedings against him if he refused to come voluntarily, but with the Supreme Court decision of June 1964 that *Tropic of Cancer* was not obscene the conspiracy charges were finally dropped.

It was the end of an era for the United States, and coincidentally the end of an era for Henry Miller personally. Having given away the address of Paradise back in 1957 in *Big Sur and the Oranges of Hieronymous Bosch*, he found the place overrun with proto-hippies, homosexuals and other would-be tenants anxious to find their real selves. His revived notoriety made him once again something of a tourist attraction, and he was pestered by disturbed people whose company he did not enjoy. With no woman to help him look after the children now that he and Eve had parted, and with the collapse of the projected return to Europe and marriage with Renate, there was nothing to keep him in Big Sur anymore. In September 1962, after seventeen mainly good years, he came down from the mountain and moved into a furnished room at 661 Las Lomas in Pacific Palisades.

5

Six months later, in February 1963, Miller, with Valentine and Tony, now aged eighteen and fifteen respectively – and for a while their mother and her third husband – moved into the two-storey Georgian house at 444 Ocampo Drive, Pacific Palisades, which was to remain Henry's home for the last eighteen years of his life. He paid $77,000 for it.

More than anything else he ever did, the move from the rustic simplicity of life on Big Sur to this wealthy, upper-class suburb of Los Angeles, with its swimming pools and its clipped hedges, palm trees and oleander bushes surprised those who thought they knew Henry Miller well. His sudden interest in the problem of income tax also seemed at odds with the contemptuous indifference with which he had formerly regarded money. He quickly discovered a tax dodge that enabled him to combine business with pleasure, and soon after moving into Ocampo Drive began producing huge quantities of water-colours for donation to non-profit-making organizations. He wrote to Elmer Gertz asking him to suggest any institutions which might be persuaded to accept such 'gifts' from him and Gertz replied promising to see what he could do, though 'that is the sort of letter I never expected Henry Miller to write'.[18] Henry boasted that between March and July 1963 he had churned out 115 such paintings, and was hoping for an appraisal of between $200 and $250 apiece from the tax authorities. Emil White, whose love for Miller was not blind (he sometimes referred to his friend in letters to third parties as 'the Mahatma') wrote that it was 'unbelievable what this tax business has done to him (and to many others, I suppose). But who would have ever dreamed that HM would show so much concern over such matters. Hasn't written a

351

thing, and I wouldn't be surprised if he doesn't even finish *The Rosy Crucifixion*.'[19]

Despite this, Miller remained essentially inept and amateurish in his financial dealings. 'Everybody has been bleeding me since I came into money,' he wrote to Hans Reitzel in 1963, and three years later he claimed to have made loans totalling $75,000 which had not been paid back. Yet as fast as he spent or gave money away it rolled in. *Black Spring* and *Tropic of Capricorn* sold in huge quantities in the wake of *Tropic of Cancer's* notoriety, and in 1965 Grove Press published paperback editions of *The Rosy Crucifixion* which went straight to the top of the US best-seller lists. Miller could boast of one hundred separate translations of his books, including seventeen of *Tropic of Cancer* alone.

Such massive popular acclaim inevitably led to a noticeable backlash against Miller among intellectual critics. Back in 1957 he had been elected a member of the National Institute of Arts and Letters. The citation read by Louise Bogan stated: 'His boldness of approach and intense curiosity concerning man and nature are unequalled in the prose literature of our time.' Now that Henry was rich and famous, however, and the battle for freedom of expression temporarily won, it was no longer necessary for the literary Establishment to present a united front.

Though nothing could take away from him the loyal statement made by Lawrence Durrell that *Tropic of Cancer* was the equal of *Moby Dick* and that 'American literature today begins and ends with the meaning of what Miller has done', nor Karl Shapiro's description of Henry as America's greatest living author, nevertheless a firm and unofficial campaign was soon under way to point out that neither of these claims were accurate. Cyril Connolly had been one of *Tropic of Cancer's* most enthusiastic supporters in its early days, and his own book *The Unquiet Grave*, published in 1945, owes a clear debt to Miller's. Reconsidering Miller's work in 1963, however, Connolly found *Tropic of Cancer*: 'an interminable rhapsody deriving from Lautréamont, Whitman, Joyce, Lawrence and Céline . . . which now leaves me cold. It is not profound, it is adolescent egomania, and much of it could be cut.'[20] Connolly was honest enough to admit that when a critic revalues downwards a book he admired in his youth, it is often simply because he is an older rather than a better critic, but unfairly revalued the book downwards anyway. Miller never made this mistake, which is what makes *The Books In My Life* so enjoyable, even if he does overestimate the importance of his loyalty to the favourite reading of his boyhood and adolescence.

James Gould Cozzens also criticized *Tropic of Cancer* as adolescent, as though this were a fault in itself. He wrote that it 'really addresses itself to the young – or better, the non-adult who can still be shocked and still find being shocked an exciting literary experience'.[21] Horace Gregory showed a better understanding of the true nature of the book by calling it 'Huck Finn in Paris', and Gael Green, who was among the first to suggest, on the strength of the books alone, that Henry might be a misogynist and a puritan, also emphasized the adolescent quality of the Miller character in *Tropic of Cancer* by describing him as a post-graduate Holden Caulfield.

None of this criticism bothered Miller, if he were even aware of it. He was a big star by now and greatly enjoyed the fuss that was made of him at the Writers Conference in Edinburgh to which he was invited in August 1962. Colin MacInnes made a speech in fulsome praise of him to which he responded with the uncharacteristically arty statement that he didn't see why they were discussing the novel at all, the novel had been dead for a hundred years anyway, why didn't they talk about water-colours instead? Among the many other writers present at the conference were Stephen Spender, Mary McArthy, Lawrence Durrell, Norman Mailer, Angus Wilson, Malcolm Muggeridge and Rebecca West. At Edinburgh, Henry had hoped to shake hands with yet another of the heroes of his youth, Bertrand Russell, but Russell failed to turn up, so the meeting between the intellectual and the visceral fathers of the permissive society never did take place. Henry did meet William Burroughs twice, however, and Burroughs has left an amusing account of the occasion:

I met him at the Edinburgh Literary Conference in 1962 at a large party full of literary people all drinking sherry in the middle of the floor and he said 'So you're Burroughs'. I didn't quite feel up to 'Yes, Maître' and to say 'So you're Miller' didn't seem quite right, so I said 'A long-time admirer' and we smiled. The next time I met him he did not remember who I was but finally said 'So you're Burroughs'.[22]

Miller's success at Edinburgh was recorded by Anthony Blond, who wrote in *Books and Bookmen* that 'if Henry Miller was the hero of the week, William Burroughs was the heroin'.[23] His association with Edinburgh continued into 1963, when the Lord Chamberlain closed down a production of *Just Wild About Harry* during the Edinburgh Festival on the grounds that it was obscene, nicely illustrating the ultimate futility of the practice of censorship by providing this poor play with a spurious notoriety and immediate demands for the rights to perform it elsewhere in Britain and Europe.

Miller was certainly the most well-known writer in America at this time, and the 1960s produced a rash of books on him. The most widely read of these was probably William Gordon's *The Mind and Art of Henry Miller*, which Gordon published in 1967 after a nerve-wracking correspondence with his subject. 'I only wish you had got in touch with me before you started the work,' Miller complained to him. 'A few days with you, talking things out, would have made a tremendous difference.'[24] Gordon's objective approach alarmed Miller, especially his insistence on making a distinction between 'hero-Miller' and the actual, real-life author. Miller stonewalled every attempt to find a presiding artistic self-consciousness in his books with his old cry that he was just a man trying to tell the story of his life, which prompted Gordon to reply: 'if the quartet (ie *The Rosy Crucifixion*) is no more than the story of your tragic love-life it is far less a work than I think it is. Some critics, including a few who have given me a hard time, feel that you are in fact writing only a record of events, and that it is not worthwhile writing about you at all.'[25] A later book by Jane Nelson took a similarly serious line on Miller, and calls to mind the gentle advice Miller once offered to his French biographer F-J. Temple: 'I think, Jacques, that you attribute too much purpose and direction to my actions sometimes. I was never very single-minded.'[26]

Ihab Hassan's *The Literature of Silence: Henry Miller and Samuel Beckett*, published in 1967, was an interesting and bold study. Hassan did not believe Miller to be an artist like Beckett, but he recognised that what the two writers had in common was the struggle against the tyranny of silence. Beckett once said that his aim in writing was to make a scratch on the silence, which is close to something Miller told Anais Nin in 1931, that his ambition was to 'leave a scar on the world'.[27] Other books included Annette Kar Baxter's *Henry Miller, Expatriate* which appeared in 1961; Walter Schmiele's biography in German; and the biography in French by Miller's friend F-J. Temple, which was published in 1965. Richard Ellmann, already well-known for his biography of James Joyce, tried for some time to persuade Miller to allow him to write his life-story, and even made a start on his research, but met with such resistance to the project from its subject that he gave up in the end.

6

Henry's fears that June and Beatrice might sue him over their literary portraits in his works proved unfounded, but he still worried that one of his four ex-wives might decide to publish an unflattering account of life with him. In sending a copy of Françoise Gilot's memoir of her life with Picasso to Eve with the comment that he liked all the personal stuff – 'so revealing and so humorous. His weaknesses make him more human, what!'[28] – it seems as though he might have been trying to pass on the hint to Eve: here is how to write about life with a genius.

June also received her copy of Gilot's book, probably for similar reasons. Again his luck held: June, like all the women in his life so far – wives, daughters, and mistresses – showed a sense of pride and privacy which, at a purely personal level, formed an impressive contrast to Henry's relentless exposure of intimacies. She remained in love with him, and forgave him everything. Anaïs Nin was another matter, however. June became very angry over her appearance in Nin's famous diaries, the first of which was published in 1966. This volume began in 1931, with Nin's meeting Henry and June, and becoming briefly infatuated with June. Some New York admirers of Miller had approached June unofficially, prior to publication, on behalf of the publishers, Harcourt Brace, to find out how she would react to being publicly exposed in this way, and found her unexpectedly obstinate. Eventually they talked her round, although they advised Miller not to mention any of this when he wrote to her, in case she felt that she was 'being pressured, or that there's some conspiracy etc',[29] which of course is exactly what there was. No wonder she suffered paranoid breakdowns.

What bothered June most was the way in which Nin, with breathtaking dishonesty, had expurgated her published diary to remove all evidence of the part she had played in the break-up of the Miller's marriage. With the major motivation for her distressed and confused behaviour during the final break-up of her marriage in Paris omitted, June inevitably cut a ridiculous figure. She called Nin a 'distorted, sad woman', and ridiculed her for writing so much about trivialities, saying that 'the world needs more intelligent, intellectual literature'. It was probably the appearance of the Nin diary in 1966 rather than *The Rosy Crucifixion* which prompted her to agree to be interviewed by a journalist named Kenneth Dick for a book he was writing on Miller. In this she tried to give her account of their life together in New York in the 1920s and Paris in the early 1930s. The result was discreet and factually similar to his, though by no means identical. Her chief concern was to make it clear that she had only ever been a skilled flirt and never the promiscuous mythomaniac of Miller's imagination. Miller nevertheless made a point of describing the interview as 'purported' and denounced the book as 'treacherous'.

June made no mention to Dick of the reunion dinner she and Henry had eaten together at her New York apartment in September 1961 while Henry was on his way back from the nightmare European trip and the fiasco with Renate. It was not a success. He cut short the evening, appalled by the physical deterioration in June and depressed by her anxiety to please him. Yet he had been impressed by her courage and told Emil Conason afterwards that he would have put a bullet through his head long ago had he been in her situation. June found him 'young, rakish, dapper', and in his presence felt 'old and insignificant'.[30] 'He seems so removed from everything,' she told Conason.

Changes were taking place in his family life. Lauretta died in the summer of 1963, and early in 1964 his daughter Valentine married and left home. Later in the year his son Tony went off to study at a military academy in Carlsbad, California. Lepska and her husband moved out of the house, taking most of the furniture with them, and went to live in Pasadena. In August 1966 Miller learnt that his third wife Eve had died. After drifting through a period of promiscuity that made her the butt of some unpleasant jokes in the Big Sur community, she married a local widower. Perhaps unwisely, she did not make the clean break with Henry that Lepska had done but continued in the vaguely humiliating rôle of friend, even answering some of his fan mail for him now and then. Her drinking grew worse, and it was this which killed her in the end.

In his own account of his reaction to the news Miller described how he sobbed all morning before going off to play ping-pong at a friend's house – 'and then began an afternoon and evening during which I was as gay as I have ever been. I ended up in a restaurant with four Canadian girls at my table and one on my lap. Still merry, more alive than ever.'[31] However, a friend who was in the house with him when he received the news recalls that Miller collapsed on the floor sobbing and had to be helped to bed, where he remained for some days. Miller wanted to see himself, and wanted others to see him, too, as Chuang Tzu, who beat a drum and sang on the day of his wife's death, and explained to his shocked visitors that she had gone to lie down peacefully in a vast room – 'if I were to follow after her bawling and sobbing, it would show that I don't understand anything about fate. So I stopped.'[32] But as Eve herself ruefully observed, Miller couldn't always live up to his own truths and high visions.

7

With the move from Big Sur to Pacific Palisades Miller replaced an old set of friends with a new one, though the friendships remained largely morganatic. Bob Fink and his wife were unhappy reminders of life

356

with Eve, and Fink was not a welcome visitor to the house on Ocampo Drive. Vincent Birge, who, after returning from Europe, had moved into the old house on Partington Ridge, began to feel that Miller was taking him for granted and presently left the circle to go back to France. Bern Porter, Miller's earliest bibliographer and one of the keenest exponents of the cult of the off-print, the special edition and the holograph reproduction that played such an important part in establishing the Miller legend, was now 'pest number one', while Eddie Schwartz, President of the Henry Miller Literary Society, had defected when the astrology and the flying saucers became too much for the newspaperman in him to swallow. Emil White remained where he was when Miller moved, and the successor to Dewar, O'Reagan, Wambly Bald and White in the rôle of 'decoy for cunt' in the Hollywood phase of Miller's life fell to a stunt man and stand-in for the actor Dean Martin named Joe Gray. Gray was a former boxer from Brooklyn whom Miller described admiringly as 'absolutely natural, and he doesn't give a shit about anybody'.[33] He used to take Miller out driving sometimes just to demonstrate the ludicrous ease with which he could pick up a woman, any woman at all, and the ease with which he could get rid of her too.

Their friendship was the kind of relationship that could baffle Miller's more serious supporters. In *Collector's Quest*, a correspondence between J. Rives Childs and Henry Miller, the scholarly and pooterish Childs recalled an occasion in 1963 when Gray visited him in Nice on Miller's recommendation. Gray told Childs he was making a study of Rimbaud and was especially anxious to meet the renowned Rimbaud expert, Henri Matarasso. Childs duly made an appointment, and accompanied Gray to Matarasso's villa where they looked over Matarasso's collection of Rimbaud treasures, with Childs acting as Gray's interpreter. 'It struck me as curious,' he wrote later, 'that Gray should be making a study of a French poet when he was unable to speak or read French with any ease. Gray left either that day or the day following and I never heard what became of his project.'[34] If it had been anyone else but Miller involved, one would almost suspect that Childs was being sent up.

It was Gray who was instrumental in introducing Miller to the Hollywood parties-and-starlets circle which Henry frequented for a time after the move. Miller found it thrilling to meet film stars, and flattering to be met by them. He wrote enthusiastically to his friends of his latest coups, though his enthusiasm puzzled June. She wondered if his boasting about his actress friends was an attempt to taunt her. In one letter he even wrote a numbered list of the actresses he had dined with in the recent past. These included Elke Sommer, Jennifer Jones,

Kim Novak, Ava Gardner, Carrol Baker, Gia Scala and Diane Baker. All of them impressed him as 'fascinating, genuine, sensitive souls. Not just "stars".'[35]

He appreciated the bizarre, unreal side of Hollywood life, as when a model arrived in his garden one day to pose as a living Venus de Milo for a few hours; but after a while he grew tired of hearing recitations from *The Nazz*, Lord Buckley's 'beat' version of the gospels, and of the maunderings of people high on marijuana. He began spending more time alone at home, and he told Fred Perlès that his life now reminded him of the Villa Seurat days, only without the laughs.

He rode his bike slowly along the flat roads around his home and watched television. He was particularly fond of professional wrestling and ball games, and surprised to see how many of the players were black. He also acquired a better grasp of world affairs than at any time previously in his life. He had retained his status as a hero to the young, and received a steady trickle of pilgrims at the house on Ocampo Drive. One day in October 1963, Joan Baez brought Bob Dylan to meet him after playing a concert at the Hollywood Bowl. The two men played some ping-pong together, but Dylan was in taciturn mood and for most of the evening kept his back turned to his host. Afterwards Dylan wrote a poem about the meeting in which he recalled the way Miller continually referred to him as 'the poet fellow', and commented that even his worst enemies never put him down in such a mysterious way.[36] Miller was fascinated by Dylan's personality, but on the whole he preferred people like Betty Ford, the female bullfighter, killer of over 400 bulls; or Christine Jørgensen, the first person in Denmark to have a sex-change operation whom he met in a Hollywood bar one day.

Miller was still more than capable of making his own fun. To Alfred Perlès he wrote:

Every once in a while the spell comes over me and I hypnotise people with my talk. Happened recently to me at a dinner for some politician. After the talk I was cornered by senators and other legislators, drank eight whiskies in a row, then it came over me. I grabbed one of them by the lapels – he was a cripple – and I prophesied what his life would be – it was so touching that the tears ran down his face and he kissed my hand. Then I kissed him on the brow. Everyone astounded, naturally. Myself above all.[37]

But what he really needed to fill his days was the oriental 'amourette' he had been tracking before he was diverted by the pseudo-serious affair with Renate Gerhardt. Early in 1966 he found her.

Over the years, Miller's fondness for ping-pong had developed to the stage where it had become a life-art. Playing a 'steady, defensive, zen-like game', he used it as a means of keeping fit, of locking horns with newcomers, and – finally – as a courting technique. Fittingly, his passion for the game was the cause of his meeting the woman who eventually became his fifth and final wife.

In February 1966, at the house of Dr Lee Siegel, a friend and regular opponent, he met Hiroko Tokuda. A pretty Japanese girl of twenty-seven, she had only recently arrived in California from Japan, where she had taken singing rôles in a number of films. She made her living playing the piano in a Hollywood bar called the Imperial Gardens.

Hoki, as she was universally known, had the same professionally flirtatious ways June Mansfield had once cultivated in her days at Wilson's Dance Hall, and Miller again became infatuated with an image of the *femme fatale*. He began frequenting the Imperial Gardens to listen to her as she played her way through a repertoire of sentimental love-songs, and one night, when Joe Gray drove them home in his car, Hoki sat on Miller's knee and allowed him to rest his hand between her legs. Henry took the gesture seriously. Well aware of the superficial impossibility of a relationship between himself, now seventy-five years old, and a woman young enough to be his granddaughter, he nevertheless threw himself into a courtship of her that was both pathetic and cold-blooded, inundating her with love-letters to which she hardly responded at all. These became longer and more intense as the months went by, and more and more baffled and frustrated as it remained clear that Hoki was neither seriously interested in his 'love' nor even charmed by him. She would not indulge him in his boasting, and when he tried to make her jealous once by telling her that he had recently received three separate proposals of marriage in the post she only smiled ironically and offered him a congratulatory handshake. Her response hurt and even shocked him. His hope was that she would turn out to be like the Japanese women of Western fancy, who treat old men with exaggerated respect and do exactly as they are told. Alas, she was no more this than James Hilton's Shangri La was really Tibet.

Yet he forged on, hurling his protestations of love into the same vacuum. His persistence paid off after a year, when the girl found herself in need of a pro-forma marriage partner in order to secure a permanent work-permit for herself. Henry gallantly stepped in with an offer of marriage which was accepted. Edie Fink made Hoki an engagement ring which broke the first time she wore it. Henry mended it with tape. He had great faith in graphology at this particular time, and sent off samples of his fiancée's handwriting to various experts for analysis. The wedding took place on September 10th 1967, and the following week the couple travelled to Paris for a honeymoon.

Hoki had stayed out late drinking with her friends on her wedding night, a gesture that set the pattern for the almost three years in which this marriage lasted. Miller, whose bad hip made it difficult for him to negotiate staircases, now slept in the small maid's bedroom on the ground floor, while Hoki occupied the upper floor. At his insistence she had given up her job at the Imperial Gardens, but she spent most of her evenings and nights away from home anyway, playing Mah Jong and drinking with her friends. She also took a series of extended holidays in Japan, at Henry's expense, during which she tried to establish a career as a pop singer on Japanese television.

Miller showed great patience with her in his attempts to persuade her to consummate the marriage. He bought her a white Jaguar sports car, used his influence to get her interviewed in European newspapers and paid for holidays in Europe and Hawaii. But it was no use, Hoki refused absolutely to have sex with him. They had a huge and decisive row on the subject one night which ended with her pleading with him not to force her to it. To complete his humiliation, during one of her trips to Japan she made the conditions of her marriage clear in a magazine interview she gave to a local journalist.

The highlight of 1968 was a visit from Lawrence Durrell in the spring. Hoki took Durrell along to Disneyland, and all three watched the race riots on television together. After Durrell left, Miller tried his hand at writing pop-lyrics for Hoki's songs and watched more television, drumming his way through the commercial breaks on his son Tony's drum. A bout of food poisoning laid him low for a few days in April, and he wrote to Durrell that it made him 'feel like that old 'un in *Lost Horizon* – remember, the Belgian with one leg off, who was supposed to be 140 years old?'[38]

The following year, in July, he and Durrell met up again when he travelled to Paris with Hoki and Puko, one of two young girlfriends of Hoki's who were now sharing the house in Ocampo Drive with them. The purpose of the trip was to follow progress on the shooting of Joseph's Strick's film version of *Tropic of Cancer*. Here Miller had a reunion with one of the original characters from the book.

Eugene Pachoutinsky was an emigré Russian writer who was playing the piano in a cinema when Miller met him in 1930. Miller was homeless at the time, and for several nights Pachoutinsky allowed him to spend the night in the cinema manager's office after the place had closed for the day. The pair made a point of sharing a drink in the same little café near the *Cinéma Vanves* where they had often sat forty years earlier.

By this time Miller had given up his attempts to persuade Hoki into his bed, and in the many letters written to her on her travels he sometimes even referred to himself stoically as her 'old goat'. She finally left him in May 1970, when she moved to Marina del Rey and opened a boutique in Beverley Hills. In return for the white Jaguar and his help in financing her brief showbiz career, she had fed his desire to relive the masochistic ecstasies he had known during his life with June. These were duly converted into literature in the form of *Insomnia*, a 'holograph' account of the adventure which was published, with original water-colours by Miller himself, in 1970, and received their monument with the publication after his death of a collection of the letters Miller wrote to Hoki. The experience of such complete sexual failure, even if it were of his own devising, had led him to read and reread his old favourite Knut Hamsun. *Victoria* and *Mysteries* became again his bibles and his scripts as he revived the rôle of the tragic lover of the enigmatic woman. Hamsun's Nagel, with his tricky diffidence and his driven rôle-playing, remained the character with whom Miller most closely identified in literature, and when *Mysteries* was reissued in 1971, his heartfelt appreciation of the novel appeared on the front page of *The New York Times Book Review*.

Every bit as important to him at this time was *Victoria*. The mood and even the imagery of Victoria's last letter to her lover Johannes, which she writes on her death-bed 'with God reading it over my shoulder', were everywhere apparent in *Insomnia* and in Miller's own letters to Hoki. Hamsun, however, was in his thirties when he wrote *Victoria*, and his characters were still younger. Miller's letters – full of charm, humour, absurdities and Millerisms – were the work of man in his late seventies, and as love-letters they were doomed to parody. The cumulative effect of reading them is like watching a man pedalling furiously on an exercise bicycle and finally tumbling from the saddle, exhausted and bewildered at having got nowhere at all. The sheer impossibility of the affair was its greatest attraction, and Miller would become abusive and angry when friends, thinking to save him from himself, tried to point out to him what he knew perfectly well – that Hoki was simply using him. Henry was 'in love' again, as Eve Miller would have put it, and that was all that mattered. Indeed, he enjoyed writing love-letters so much that sometimes he wrote them and laid them aside without even bothering to post them.

361

The 1960s were Miller's great decade. His faith that *Tropic of Cancer* would force its way into American society on its own terms was vindicated, and he was amply rewarded financially for his patience. White, middle-class society rightly hailed him as one of its greatest rebel-heroes, and with books like *The Air-Conditioned Nightmare* he had proved himself one of the most efficient feeders of the masochistic instinct which helps society to keep itself and its progressive liberalism under constant review. He was a hero to young and old, men and women alike, and his influence was everywhere apparent on the literary scene in Europe and America.

For the first time in two hundred years, *Fanny Hill* became legally available in the bookshops, as did Walter's *My Secret Life*, Frank Harris's *My Life and Loves*, the *Kama Sutra*, *The Perfumed Garden* and a host of similar works. Contemporary writing made possible by the appearance of *Tropic of Cancer* in America included William Burroughs's *The Naked Lunch*, John Rechy's *City of Night*, Hubert Selby junior's *Last Exit to Brooklyn*, Norman Mailer's *An American Dream*, Philip Roth's *Portnoy's Complaint*, John Updike's *Couples* and the novels of Charles Bukowski. In Europe he opened the way for the confessional sexual writing of authors like Agnar Mykle, Jan Cremer, Stephen Vicenzy and Suzanne Brøgger. It became permissible to show pubic hair, breasts and buttocks on the screen. Besides *Tropic of Cancer*, *Quiet Days in Clichy* was filmed in a version by the Danish director Jens Jørgen Thorsen, with music by Country Joe and the Fish. Miller was amused to discover that the actor who portrayed him in the Danish film was homosexual. The hippie culture of the early and mid-1960s was permeated by his own interests and enthusiasms and attitudes, most obviously in the slogan 'Make Love, Not War', the contempt for politics and politicians and the reverence for the gurus and artefacts of Indian spiritual life. In the realms of so-called 'straight' society many a middle-aged man left his wife and family in search of an imagined real self after reading the *Tropics*. Once the floodgates were opened, however, the shock effect of the *Tropics* and *Sexus* paled surprisingly quickly beside the sadistic outpourings of a book like Hubert Selby's *The Room* or the excesses of John Rechy's novels about homosexual life and drug-taking.

At eighty years of age, Miller was an avuncular and much-loved figure throughout the world. He corresponded with Thomas Merton in his retreat ('Dear Father Louis – or can I just call you Tom?)[39] and took instructions in the art of silk-screen printing from the nuns at the Immaculate Heart College, Hollywood. The Italians gave his collection of essays *Stand Like The Hummingbird* an award as the Best Book of 1970. His reputation as a great liberator and prophet of sexual good health seemed assured until the advent of an unforeseen revival of the feminist movement. In *Sexual Politics*, Kate Millett's analysis of the history of sexual mores published in 1970, she devoted a section to the ideological criticism of recent and not so recent novels, limiting her selection to the work of male writers. Several examples of Miller's sexual writing were reproduced in the book and, along with D.H. Lawrence and Norman Mailer, he stood accused of being a modern apologist for an attitude of enduring male hostility towards women.

In her book, Millett showed a generous appreciation of other aspects of Miller's writing besides the sexual. She even referred to the literary establishment's 'scandalous and systematic neglect of his work'. For the purposes of her argument, however, she confined her analysis to those descriptions of sexual encounters from *Black Spring*, *The World of Sex* and *Sexus* which had once seemed, to men and women alike, the 'good bits'. Her conclusion was a judgment: that Henry Miller was 'a compendium of American sexual neuroses'.

Whether the analysis was correct or not must remain a matter of opinion and temperament rather than demonstrable fact. Certainly her description of Miller's sexual personality would have been more convincing had she been able to describe for her readers the better way and better times that were providing her with her yardstick of sexual normality. Moreover, many were taken aback by the sinister interpretation she put on Miller's use of words like 'muff' to describe the female genitals, and felt that her objection to his use of sexual slang, on the grounds that it was a secret language of oppression, was hardly to be distinguished from the puritanical objections raised against his use of taboo words since the 1930s. Another weakness of her analysis was a failure to appreciate the extent to which the 'Henry Miller' whom she was considering was not a typical man, but rather a fantasy figure whose anarchic clowning and preposterous sexual boasting provided valuable light relief from the strains of responsible living for the Prufrocks which so many men are at heart. There was also a monstrous paradox to consider: that Miller, in his writing as in his life, had rejected every aspect of the rôle developed by society for the male – as worker, provider and head of the family – and with an almost frantic consistency urged his readers likewise to reject their socio-sexual destinies. Millett ignored this; yet, for his part in destroying the rôle-model of *paterfamilias* alone, Miller ought logically to have been hailed as a hero to the burgeoning feminist movement.

At one level, *Sexual Politics* was a sympathetic and even idealistic plea for greater tenderness in the world. What attracted public attention, however, and turned the book into a best-seller, was its often abrasive 'sex-war' tones. It changed the rhetoric of liberalism and in doing so set the tone of the intellectual debate for the ensuing decade. With this book as their reference point, female sociologists and critics undertook a mass revaluation of the works and reputations of most well-known male writers, and in the process Miller suffered badly. Soon it became a grave social blunder to admit that one had ever enjoyed *Tropic of Cancer* at all, and before he quite knew what had happened, Henry found himself beneath the wheels of the revolution that he had himself helped to set in train.

CHAPTER SEVENTEEN

1970–1980
'I regard myself as a history of our time'

1

The trip to Paris that Miller took in June 1969 to observe progress on the filming of *Tropic of Cancer* turned out to be the end of his long love-affair with the city, and with Europe. His health had been slowly breaking down since the onset of trouble with his hip joint during the long car tour with Birge in 1960. The pain was at times severe enough to bring on depression, and the onset of arthritis aggravated his discomfort. In addition, his concern about his heart increased considerably, and he was taking digitalis regularly. Even so, he was still robust enough to ride his bike, play ping-pong and swim in his heated swimming pool. In March 1969, he was operated on for a prostate gland condition; what finally slowed him down was a series of operations in 1972 to remove a right-side artery and replace it with an artificial one. His body rejected it and in a third operation he went into shock and lost the use of his right eye. By 1974 he was using a walker, and spending much of each day in bed.

Back in 1963 he had complained to Renate Gerhardt of the onset of impotence, and in his marriage to Hoki she had never given him the chance to find out whether he was right or not. Though he could not rival the sexual longevity of Chaplin, Casals and Picasso, he continued to play at romantic love with unattainable and ambitious young women. He was, as ever, prodigal with his celebrity, and there was no shortage of Hollywood starlets like the Chinese Lisa Lu, or Brenda Venus, who were willing to indulge an old man in return for the chance to play a rôle in a real-life myth. Miller used these relationships to live out a life of vivid sexual imaginings. Brenda Venus, the last in a line of darkly exotic women that extended from Beatrice through June to Anais Nin and Eve McClure, excited his fancy particularly, and in letters charmingly spiced with metaphysical observations and heavy-duty reading lists he would give her detailed descriptions of how she had been conducting herself in his dreams: 'Without the slightest blush you lightly touch your cunt with your right hand. Then . . . with two fingers of each hand you open the crack between your legs and you show me the small lips that tremble like a little bird. The juice flows liberally; your thighs gleam. Without saying a word you put your hand in my trousers and catch my flute (or the bollard if you prefer).' Finally she cries out: 'Fuck me, Henry, fuck me! Shove it in to the hilt. I'm so horny.' To which Henry responds: 'God give me the power, the strength, and I will kiss you endlessly.' Some quaint sense of delicacy decreed that he render such dialogues in French. After his death, and at about the same time as she published *Dear, Dear, Brenda*, a selection of some of the 1500-plus letters that Miller had written to her over the four years of their correspondence, Brenda Venus posed for *Playboy*. 'It had to be in good taste,' she explained to the magazine's caption writer. 'I did it as if I were a Greek goddess, an imaginary creature. I wanted to play it like an actress. I think Henry would be proud.'[1]

Another of his imaginary partners was a woman from Bradford, Pennsylvania, whom he never even met in person.[2] On her own initiative she had been supplying him with photographs of herself ever since the mid-1950s. To begin with these were relatively mild 'cheesecake' studies, but as time passed she became increasingly daring in her posing, and by the 1970s the pictures were directly pornographic. Whilst living with Eve, Henry had gently tried to discourage her approaches. Now, however, he actively urged her to be ever more adventurous in her posing and made specific suggestions about the kind of positions he would like her to assume. He studied the photographs with a magnifying glass, he told her, though he did not add that after he had done so he sent them on up the hill for Emil White to look at. Though his fascination with pornographic photographs was obviously erotic, it seems to have been largely free of that desire to see women humiliate themselves which is often said to be the chief need of the consumer of pornography. In *The World of Sex* Miller wrote: 'Perhaps a cunt, smelly though it may be, is one of the prime symbols for the connection between all things,' and this informal expression of desire for synthesis in the sexual world parallels his obsessive quest for a similar synthesis in the metaphysical worlds of Madame Blavatsky, Oswald Spengler, Freud, astrology *et al*. That the searcher got somewhat bogged down in his search is undeniable; yet the belief that enough concentrated staring at the entrance to the womb might one day produce a transcendent moment of revelation never quite deserted Miller. His immersion in the world of cerebral sex also had its psychologically banal sides: another of his correspondents was a former lover who, at his request, enclosed a lock of perfumed

366

pubic hairs with one of her erotic letters. Miller sent her, in return, a batch of his fan mail to read.

Of the flesh and blood women in his life, his third wife, Lepska, remained one of his few personal enemies. Her sin was to have had the stronger personality, and in his eighty-fifth year he still day-dreamed of pushing her over a cliff if he thought he could get away with it. June finally disappeared from his life in February 1977 with a short note telling him that she was going to live with her brother Herman somewhere in the Arizona desert. She preserved her silence to the end, and in some quarters acquired a mythic status of her own that exceeds Miller's. Miller, Anais Nin and Alfred Perlès all created and published their own portraits of her, and in the literature of recent times perhaps only Neal Cassady, the Dean Moriarty of Kerouac's *On The Road* and the hero of Tom Wolfe's *The Electric Kool-Aid Acid Test*, has been as comprehensively mythologized.

Anais Nin visited Miller in Pacific Palisades in 1962, and again in 1972 and 1973, after Miller's major surgery. Divorced from Hugh Guiler and living in California with her long-time friend Rupert Pole, she had belatedly obtained the recognition she craved as a writer with the publication of successive volumes of her 'Diaries'. She was elected to the National Institute of Arts and Letters in 1974, by which time she was suffering from the cancer which eventually killed her early in 1977.

Of all Miller's serious relationships with women, that with Nin was certainly the most successful. On the evidence of her diaries she was a pompous woman, with none of Miller's deflationary sense of humour. Yet she was clearly the *yin* to his *yang*, and shared with him a willingness to live out sexual desires rather than allow them to be stifled by a morality in which neither of them believed. Under the circumstances, the relationship succeeded precisely because they never attempted to live together as man and wife. In spite of his addiction to marital status, Miller's experience of monogamous marriage had been an unmitigated disaster, and when in 1974 a renegade Mormon with twelve wives fell foul of the law Miller wrote a heartfelt letter in defence of the man's rights to the editor of the *Los Angeles Times*.

He continued to enjoy an affable relationship with the children of his marriage to Lepska Miller. After Valentine's marriage ended in divorce in 1966, she toyed for a while with the idea of being a film actress, and later Miller gave her money to open a ski shop in Aspen, Colorado. She remained in California, however, and after a protracted adolescence that included arrest in 1967 on a charge of possessing marijuana she eventually took up residence in her father's old home in Big Sur.

Tony Miller's decision to attend military college in 1964 baffled Miller, though as a reaction to an upbringing with little paternal discipline it had its own logic. Bafflement turned to pride, however, when Tony honoured the Miller family tradition in pacifism by deserting from the US army rather than risk being drafted to Vietnam. After two years in hiding in Paris and Montreal he returned to California with plans to write a book about his experiences. Later he moved into Ocampo Drive as his father's minder-cum-secretary. Henry enjoyed life with his son: 'If I go outside, I'm nobody again. Here, I'm king and I do what I like. This is my domain, my territory, and we have a sweet, peaceful, contented life here.' Tony Miller introduced his father to some of his own favourites among the newer American writers, and at his recommendation Henry read and enjoyed the novels of Kurt Vonnegut junior. Nothing, however, could match his enthusiasm for Isaac Bashevis Singer, the great literary discovery of Miller's final years.

Tony was among those most fiercely opposed to Miller's marriage to Hoki, which finally ended in divorce in 1977. Indeed, none of Henry's children have inherited their father's enthusiasm for the institution of marriage. Barbara, the eldest, eventually abandoned her adolescent ambitions of becoming a writer, and presently settled for the less risky life of a real-estate agent.

2

Miller continued to write, but the attacks on him and other writers by female sociologists and critics hit his reputation hard. Norman Mailer was the chief target of these attacks, but Miller was number two on the list. Male writers in general ignored their female attackers, but in 1976 Mailer published *Genius and Lust: A journey through the major writing of Henry Miller*, a hastily assembled selection of extracts from Miller's books, with comments by Mailer, which was intended as both a tribute and a defence. Miller liked Mailer personally, but not his writing. 'I never read a thing Norman Mailer ever wrote,' he told a journalist. 'Not even the thing he wrote defending me against the feminists. I started to read it, but I couldn't stand it. . . . You see, I hate the New York type – ultra-sophisticated, analytical, critical of everything.' He was undoubtedly influenced in his dismissal by Mailer's description of *The Rosy Crucifixion* as 'one of the greatest failures in the history of the novel, a literary cake as large as the Himalayas which fails to rise,' and Mailer's irreligious view that *The Colossus of Maroussi* was a deliberate attempt on Miller's part to sweeten his image in the eyes of Americans in order to pave the way for legitimate publication of the *Tropics*.

The rise of the phenomenon of ethnic protection opened up another area in which Miller's books, with their casual use of 'ethnic slurs', became vulnerable to the attacks of orthodoxy-sniffers. Where George Orwell's self-censoring liberal of the 1930s worried that some of his thoughts might accidentally be fascist, his counterpart in the 1970s and 1980s agonized over the fact that he might unconsciously be a racist. Miller, growing up in Brooklyn, was the product of an abrasive linguistic culture in which a boy's sanity and survival depended on his ability to give and take verbal abuse. In a gesture of working-class loyalty he had remained on those streets – linguistically speaking – all his life, practising a life-art the rules and subtleties of which made it morally incomprehensible to the liberalisms of the late twentieth century. In the 1970s, anti-rascists inaugurated a campaign for the censorship 'in a good cause' of the written and spoken word which achieved many disquieting successes in extending the definition of thought-crime. Yet Miller never apologized for himself, preferring to remain true to a statement made in *Black Spring* in 1936, that he regarded himself as 'a history of our time'. This loyalty to the truth of his own upbringing, right or wrong, was an important aspect of the subjective honesty he had always tried to practise. Saul Bellow avowed a similar point of view when he described for a journalist his own upbringing in the Chicago melting-pot at the beginning of the century: 'There were no apologetics back then. Everything was out in the open. The absence of an idea of defamation was liberating. Nobody was immune. We took abuse in return for freedom of opinion. It is a far less open society since ethnic protection came in.'[3]

Under the circumstances, Miller's books sold poorly, and his relationships with his publishers became increasingly acerbic. The rights to *Insomnia* had been taken over by Doubleday and the book reprinted in 1974 with disappointing results. Miller's pride could not accept that he was no longer an author who attracted the public interest, and he blamed the company's marketing strategy for the poor sales. New Directions, owners of the rights to publish his books in paperback, also received letters rebuking them for their failure to promote his books.

His several Japanese publishers over the thirty years of his success there were the target of his particular ire. The experience with Hoki had cured him of his illusions about her countrymen, and he wrote and attempted to insert in a number of European newspapers an abusive and intemperate open letter to his Tokyo publishers, accusing them of cheating him out of thousands of dollars in royalties since the early

1950s. His suspicions may have been well-founded, but by the time he joined the aggressive American literary agency Scott Meredith in 1976, the economic complications that had arisen were too remote in time and space for them to do much about the situation. The $10,000 he received in 1971 from the Tokyo *Weekly Post* for an article on the death of Yukio Mishima was some compensation for his disappointment in the Japanese.

Capra Press, a Santa Barbara publishing house run by an admirer of Miller's named Noel Young, came to his rescue in his last years, publishing a number of short essays and sketches he wrote during the 1970s. Young showed great indulgence to Miller, whose literary judgment was becoming eccentric even by his own liberal standards. *Sextet*, published in 1977, contains the collected shorter works of this last period. Perhaps the most remarkable of these is *Mother, China and the World Beyond*, an indescribable but unforgettable description of a reunion and reconciliation with his mother in 'the Beyond'. As they talk over their relationship together, Louise tells him among other things that she is taking guitar lessons from Segovia, and that she hopes to be reincarnated as a black man. Henry can only smile, and reflect that his mother has come a long way since he knew her on earth. She even apologises for having opposed his wishes so often: 'As I told you, son, I was a very stupid woman.'[4] Yet *Mother, China and the World Beyond* is not a sign of incipient senility, and could as easily have been written between customers at the tailor-shop during the Great War, or while taking a vacation from 'the Land of Fuck' in 1938, as during Miller's eighty-sixth year.

1975 saw the publication of the *Letters of Henry Miller and Wallace Fowlie*, a modest volume spanning the period 1944–1972. This was the fourteenth separate occasion on which Miller's correspondence was made public, and by the late 1980s the figure had risen to eighteen volumes, large and small. The final figure may even be higher. Many commentators have observed that the letter was Miller's natural form, intimate, unstructured and at least apparently spontaneous. Yet of all these collections only those involving Lawrence Durrell, Anais Nin and Emil Schnellock are really worth reading for their own sake. The remainder simply repeat a dull ritual involving a star and his fans.

The main achievement of the last decade was his *Book of Friends*, published in three volumes between 1976 and 1979. The prevailing tone of these reminiscences of old friends and vanished Brooklyn monuments is mellow, although now and then the old terrorist still manages to raise his stick and takes a crack at somebody. The study of Joe O'Reagan, for example, ends with a wonderful and gratuitous swipe at the Catholic priesthood. The chapter on his best friend – his bike – also hits a splendid note in its last lines, quoting Rabelais on the curative power of laughter, and concluding that there is precious little of it today: 'No wonder the drug pushers and the psychoanalysts are in the saddle.'[5]

3

Most of the friends Miller wrote about in these volumes were either dead or obscure. Of the obscure ones many seem to have been friends in the special sense in which Miller used the term to mean loyal and devoted admirers of his person and work. He demanded a recognition of superiority from those around him, and there were few exemptions from the demand. Lawrence Durrell, who visited Miller several times during these last years, was one, and Vincent Birge recalls that the only time he saw Miller take a back seat in a gathering of friends was when Durrell was present. However, friendship with another strong and intellectual personality on a day-to-day basis always proved problematic. Gerald Robitaille, a French-Canadian writer with whom Miller had corresponded since the early 1950s, moved to California in the 1960s to join him as his secretary, and too-quickly found himself undergoing casual humiliations at the Master's hands or, on one occasion, his feet, as Miller ordered Robitaille to cut his toenails for him while he sat by the pool in the sunshine chatting with Lawrence Durrell.

Like so many would-be writers and artists who drifted into Miller's orbit, Robitaille entertained hopes of being able to use the connection to further his own literary ends. Like the rest of them, he soon found that a recommendation from Henry Miller to a publisher was no recommendation at all. As Miller himself ruefully admitted once, not more than three or four of the hundreds of recommendations he made to publishers had ever resulted in a book being printed. Robitaille and his wife returned to Europe in 1969, and in 1970 Robitaille published his 'indiscreet essay' *Le Père Miller*, which is not especially indiscreet, but which nicely captures in its title the monstrous, Ubu-esque side of Miller's personality.

Miller's personal charm remained undiminished to the end, and there was no shortage of admirers ready to ease his last years, helping him to wash and dress, cooking for him and helping him in and out of his swimming pool. Valentine's friend Twinka Thiebaud moved in for a time as his housekeeper and cook, and during her four years with Miller observed at close quarters his enigmatic ideas on socialising.

Governor Jerry Brown of California visited them one day in August 1978 and Miller, apologizing beforehand for his impertinence, welcomed the governor with the announcement that he had 'always held the opinion that politicians are rather at the lowest rung, at the bottom of the barrel of humanity, so to speak,' before offering him a glass of wine. Despite the greeting – or because of it – the governor enjoyed the meeting, and stayed for over two hours. Living without the worry of a wife's aesthetics Miller had been able to turn his suburban home into a boy's dream. The walls of his bathroom and one wall and the ceiling of an upstairs guest room were covered in collages, posters, poems and quotations written in coloured inks. Guests were encouraged to add to the graffiti.

On days when guests were expected for dinner Miller would be woken from his afternoon nap at about seven o'clock. Presently he would make his way to the kitchen to find out what was on the menu and enthuse about the delicious smells of the food. 'Health foods' were taboo in the house. Once, tiring of a friend's repetitious warnings about the dangers of cholesterol, he wrote out a list of his favourite fatty foods and pinned it up on the kitchen cupboard with the message 'NO HEALTH FOODS PLEASE' across the bottom. He rarely dressed for dinner, and after swallowing a handful of vitamins and tuning his hearing aid he made his way to table wearing just pyjamas, dressing gown and orthopaedic shoes.

Miller had inherited his father's love of professional entertainers, and the guests were often film stars, like Jack Nicholson, whose work he had seen and admired. He continued to identify with characters and stories on the screen, and had become particularly fond of Nicholson after seeing his performance in *Five Easy Pieces*. Miller even wrote a brief appreciation of this film which in so many particulars resembled the story of his own life – of the talented man (even a half-talented pianist, as Miller had once been) full of life and charm, and a fascinated self-disgust at the ease with which he can manipulate people's emotions, who walks out on his wife and his old life on a whim, looking for the moment-by-moment excitement of an unknown future to keep him from boredom. Miller even suggested that Nicholson would be ideal in the part of Nagel, if any Hollywood producer ever thought to make a film of *Mysteries*.

Another welcome guest at his dinner table was Erica Jong. After reading her confessional novel *Fear of Flying* in 1973 Miller inundated her with admiring letters and wrote – unsolicited – a preface for the French version of her book. So struck was he by the evident influence of *Tropic of Cancer* on her novel that when they met in Los Angeles in 1974 he even suggested – nicely ignoring the fact that he was still alive

– that she was his reincarnation in female form. In an appreciation written after his death, Jong recalled that she was too 'bookish' for Henry to make a pass at. He did tell her that he now and then 'copped a feel' from some of the many young women who came and went in the house, 'though not of *my* breasts,' she quickly assured her readers.[6]

Henry was still regularly consulting his horoscope and told a Los Angeles *Free Press* journalist who interviewed him in 1976 that he had recently been contacted by his Swiss astrologer with the news that Uranus was in conjunction with Scorpio. The usual great things were to be expected.[7] On the subject of the existence of God and our knowledge of what happens beyond the grave he retained what can only be called an open mind. Like Elvis Presley, he seemed to believe that his fame came from God, not from people; and like Elvis he was known to try out his psychic powers occasionally. During his stay in Denmark in 1961 with his publisher Hans Reitzel, he met the graphic artist Palle Nielsen. Nielsen had a bad stammer which Henry was convinced he could cure for him. He spoke a lot to him and looked into his eyes, but at the end of the day Nielsen was still stammering. The long search for his own version of the order and pattern in creation that Spengler and Blavatsky had found eluded him in the end, and writing to a young English fan in 1974 he declared that he was moving closer to Gnostics, and was inclined to believe, with them, that the planet Earth was merely a cosmic error. His 'air-conditioned night-mare' trip across America, especially what he had seen of the Amish People and the Baha'i, had convinced him that the existence of cults – indeed of any and all minority groups in American society, including blacks and Indians – was the best guarantee that society would not be destroyed by too much rationalism and too much uniformity, a condition that must account in part for the automatic response of support he offered every crackpot religious and philosophical idea he came across in later life. His spontaneous attraction to frauds, from his boyhood hero Schliemann the archeologist through Madame Blavatsky and Frank Harris and on to L. Ron Hubbard, Adamski and Lobsang Rampa, is an odd and even touching index of his credulity. He developed a defensive fondness for exposed charlatans which continued into the 1970s, when he wrote to a young admirer praising Gurdjieff as a 'rogue, but a charming rogue,' and placing him above both Thoreau and Krishnamurti on account of his sense of humour. Figures like Gurdjieff and Rampa/Hoskins were, in the end, merely great entertainers in Miller's world, close relatives of the burlesque artists of his early years like Dr Walford Brodie who, with the assistance of Mystic Marie, could make electricity spark from his fingernails. Colourful and amusing frauds who clambered down from the stage to the streets, they drew a clamorous and excited public behind them whom they perhaps duped, but never harmed.

A list Miller provided in 1960 of the ten books which had most influenced him includes only Balzac (the Balzac of *Seraphita*), Céline and Gide (as Dostoevsky's biographer) from the world of established literary greats. The rest of it reads almost like a study-course for would-be New Agers; nor did the revelation that Madame Blavatsky was a fraud stop him from including her *Voice of Silence*. A second listing in 1977 almost redresses the balance: Lao Tzu is named as the greatest writer of all times, but Rabelais, Nietzsche, Whitman and Proust are all high on the list. Dostoevsky is there too, even if Marie Corelli, Louise Miller's great favourite, just pips him for eighth place.

In 1976 the French awarded Miller the *Légion d'honneur*, a welcome sign of respectability, and in pursuit of further respectability, not to say money, he devoted much effort in 1978 to a campaign to win the Nobel Prize for Literature for himself. All his European publishers were contacted and asked to write to the committee in support of his candidature, and Durrell wrote a long letter urging his old friend's case in Stockholm. It was unseemly behaviour, naturally, but then practically everything Miller ever did was unseemly in one way or another. In the event the prize for 1979 went to Isaac Bashevis Singer. Singer was the tenth name on Miller's 1977 list of all-time-great writers. He had become an object of hero-worship for Miller in his final days, and Miller genuinely rejoiced in the committee's decision.

By 1980 Henry realized that the Armenian soothsayer he met in Greece back in 1939 must have been wrong, and that he was not going to emulate Lao Tzu and live forever after all. On May 8th, aware that he had not long to go, he spent two hours dictating farewell letters to his friends with the assistance of his last minder, William Pickerill. He took especial care with the messages to Lawrence Durrell and Alfred Perlès, his oldest surviving real friends. 'See you in Devachan, Joey,' he told Perlès. Brenda Venus also received a last letter in which Miller, perhaps worried that God might be reading it over his shoulder, took a firmly chaste leave of her: 'Tonight I will hold you in my arms,' he told her, 'and I will leave you *intact*.'

Capra were planning to publish an edited version of his massive, unfinished book on D.H. Lawrence that summer. Miller had not looked at the fifty year old manuscript for decades, but on glancing at the first page he indicated that he was deeply impressed and gave the editors involved permission to proceed. Not long before the book was ready Miller died, snoozing off at 4.35 on the afternoon of Saturday June 7th. By a will dated October 11th 1978 the bulk of his estate,

374

including books and manuscripts valued at over $500,000, went to his three children, while Lepska inherited his half-share of the house in Big Sur. His clothes and his hundred neckties went to Pickerill. He had enjoyed his thirty-two thousand, three hundred and four days on earth, and no doubt he continues to enjoy himself in whatever version of the Beyond he has gone to. Perhaps he is slowly reading his way through the Akashic Record, the history of Everything That Has Ever Happened which, according to Madam Blavatsky, is written on the ether. Perhaps he is helping his mother with her guitar lessons from Segovia, or standing in line for the next flying saucer, listening in pleased wonder as those waiting with him – Whitman, Hamsun, Rabelais and Dostoevsky – pass the time in conversation about everything under the sun except politics.

*

Two years ago, in conversation with Alfred Perlès, I asked him how he would sum up his friend's character. He refused to be drawn, saying that to psychoanalyse Miller 'would be like sexing him'. Almost at once he added: 'He was not a psychopath – I am more a psychopath than he was.' It was a curious and revealing addition. As a label 'psychopath' is not so much an explanation of character as an admission of moral bewilderment, and Miller was nothing if not morally bewildering. The ugly excesses of behaviour associated with the term 'psychopath' make it an unsatisfactory description of Miller's character, and the uncomfortable truth is that he appears to make little sense to any moral system, unless it be the absence of system of taoism and zen buddhism. In *Genius and Lust* Norman Mailer reluctantly attempted the task of psychoanalysing Miller on the basis of his published works. His conclusion was that Miller was 'narcissistic', and in terms of conventional wisdom few would be inclined to dispute this finding.

As a popular American sage Miller has had numerous successors, many them grazing in the lucrative pastures of the New Age philosophies which he and Aldous Huxley sowed during their years in California. Yet most, from the earnest Shirley MacLaine to the informal and folksy Robert Fulghum, remain closer to Dale Carnegie than Henry Miller. Few seem able to reproduce his mixture of honesty and humour, and fewer still are prepared to risk the implication of his best moments: that all the searching for real selves and deep meanings in life is finally just a diverting and enjoyable way of passing the time.

As a writer it is clearer now that Miller was only occasionally an artist. In the 1930s, when he was making his breakthrough, he worked harder at his craft, and the results show to best example in *Tropic of Capricorn*, a book that remains a deeply satisfying amalgam of social criticism, personal confession and pure raving. After his return to America he settled all too often for the easy victories of mere self-expression.

Perhaps Miller's major achievement was that, with *Tropic of Cancer*, he began the process of building a bridge across that 'frightful gulf' which Orwell wrote of in 1939, between the Establishment 'intellectual' with his authorised version of culture, and the interested 'man in the street' who simply stumbled his way towards a culture of his own devising. Miller's first mass readership was among GIs and working men, men who might normally have turned away in embarrassment at the mere mention of words like 'art', 'culture', and 'spirit'. In the easy, colloquial writing style he mastered, using the vocabulary of the street corner and the workplace, he nevertheless performed the surprising feat of getting such men to listen to him and consider for themselves the importance of such abstractions. The growing democratisation of the arts in this century, the gradual disappearance of notions of 'high art' and *avant-garde* art, and the acceptance as art of new, previously-overlooked or despised forms of expression on the basis of a subjective appreciation that these simply *work* are all phenomena prefigured by Miller's career. His successor in this respect has been Bob Dylan, whose cultural frame of reference stretching from Robert Johnson to Smokey Robinson via T.S.Eliot – a modern parallel to Miller's own easy mingling of influences, from Marie Corelli to Frank Fay and Arthur Rimbaud – is regarded as enriched rather than eccentric.

Miller no longer shocks. Not even the appearance of the hard-core pornographic *Opus Pistorum* in 1983 attracted much attention in America, although in 1988 a British evangelical charity calling itself 'Christian Action Research and Education' tried to persuade the Director of Public Prosecutions to proceed against the book. Had he done so it would have been the first case of its kind in Britain since the trial of *Last Exit to Brooklyn* in 1968. That he did not is hardly surprising. In a world of filmed pornography featuring real men and women performing real acts, the pornography of the written word is nowadays of almost exclusively antiquarian interest.

In sum, Miller was an original man, neither good nor bad, but hugely himself. His helpless explorations in the realms of human weakness brought therapeutic relief to a million strangers and considerable distress to those most closely associated with him. This almost palpable humanity resides in the vigorous abandon with which he enacted the rôles of both Don Quixote and Sancho Panza in the course of a single lifetime, mingling the Don's desire for sainthood with what Orwell called Pancho's love of 'safety, soft beds, no work, pots of beer and women with "voluptuous figures"'. Miller was the reader's 'unofficial self, one spirit that rejects all prevailing orthodoxies, and cries out against the tyranny of the Correct Opinion'. Perhaps he should have won the Nobel Prize for Literature. His name among the list of Nobel laureates might have functioned as a permanent reminder not to take the business of literary prizes too seriously, and it would also have rounded off nicely the career he had outlined for himself, back in 1928, of a 'purposeful literary buffoonery'. Generally speaking, there is not enough of this. Certainly we need our great writers to have serious faces, to be righteous, and to save us from ourselves. What we don't need is for them to be too serious-faced and righteous. When this happens our need is for someone to sneak up behind them and finish off their sable gowns with a dog's tail, just to keep the world in perspective. Since his death, Miller's matchless talent for this kind of refreshing irreverence has been sorely missed.

Notes

Chapter One

1 'I did not belong to any environment', letter to William Gordon, August 27th.

2 'a little boy', *My Life and Times*, p202.

3 'talking without continuity or point', *Crazy Cock*.

4 'whether good or bad', *Book of Friends*, p56.

5 'heroism and puke, disease and medals,' *Saga of the Streets*, p26.

6 'integrated picture of the whole subject,' *The Books In My Life*, p180.

7 'your loving son, Henry,' letter of March 28th 1899.

8 'why did they have beards?' *Hamlet Letters*.

9) 'every other Jewish boy in the area,' *Brooklyn is America* by R.F. Weld, p105.

10 'cause it to fade away,' *Stand Still Like the Hummingbird*, p46.

11 'what a calamity!' *The Book of Friends*, p91.

12 'Chemistry.' Letter to the author from senior registrar Thomas F. Jennings at City College, June 20th 1989.

Chapter Two

1 'a thing that had been used too roughly,' *Black Spring* notebook.

2 'told himself that it wouldn't recur,' *Henry and June* by Anais Nin, p263.

3 'my Bright Green Wind,' *The Books In My Life*, p127.

4 'maybe a good corporation lawyer,' preface to Sidney Omarr's *Henry Miller's World of Urania* and *My Life and Times*, p188.

5 'than anyone in this wide world,' letter to Charles Keeler, December 9th 1916.

6 'the only thing of its nature obtainable in my American environment,' *Saga of the Streets*, section on B.F. Mills.

7 'mystic side of my nature,' *Ibid*.

8 'And they supply it,' *Ibid*.

9 'unnecessary to make the trip,' *Tropic of Capricorn*, p138.

10 'hands were torn and cut by the branches,' *Reflections*, editor Twinka Thiebaud, p23.

11 'they took a liking to me,' *Reflections*, p23.

12 'on their way to a Mexican whorehouse,' *My Life and Times*, p190.

13 '*hot* welcome,' *June* notebook, section entitled 'Pauline Fiasco'.

14 'hopeless to evade my destiny,' *Saga of the Streets*.

15 'I turn my strength into spiritual conquests.' *Ibid*.

16 'This is where we sleep,' *Stand Still Like the Hummingbird*, p49.

17 'am tongue-tied. I can't do it . . .' *Tropic of Capricorn*, p308.

18 'He regularly came home drunk,' *My Life and Times*, p193.

19 'violation and must pay the penalty,' *Saga of the Streets*.

20 'his little boss tailor way,' *Black Spring* notebook.

21 'his father a drunken bum, *Reflections*, p21.

22 'my father whose life is destroying her,' *Saga of the Streets*.

23 'Caruso,' *My Life and Times*, p195.

24 'reading Lao Tzu in the middle of that crazy family!' *Face to Face with Henry Miller*, Conversations with Georges Belmont, p41.

25 'wistful regret expressed in *Sexus*,' *Sexus*, p61.

26 '19th century dramatists of most European countries,' Letter to William Gordon, August 17th 1966.

27 'Miller's own heart,' *Frank Harris* by Philippa Pullar, p347.

28 'first contact with a great writer,' *My Life and Times*, biographical appendix.

29 'see his greatness. Am I near-sighted?' Letter to Charles Keeler, December 9th 1916.

30 'a grim reality about their writing that appeases me,' *Ibid.*
31 'He was like an oracle to me,' *The Books In My Life*, p135.
32 'He pierced the veil time and time again.' *Ibid*, p137.
33 'worse than having an artistic temperament, it is thinking you have one,' letter to Charles Keeler, December 9th 1916.
34 'usually on an empty stomach,' *The Book of Friends*, p134.
35 'his failure to make an early start as a writer,' *My Life and Times*, p187.

Chapter Three
1   to 'bring her out into any clear, open sexual relationship,' *Sexus*, p202.
2   'the dark acts masturbating each other,' *Black Spring* notebook.
3   'the better the fuck,' *The World of Sex*, p85.
4   'on the sex note,' letter to William Gordon, September 1966.
5   'our sex life more exciting,' *Ibid.*
6   'coarse language during the act of love-making,' *Henry and June* by Anais Nin, p246.
7   'saboteurs of progress,' *Nexus*, p314.
8   'during his ten years in London,' *My Life and Times*, p188.
9   'perhaps have a home of my own, after a fashion,' letter to Charles Keeler, December 9th 1916.
10 'but we feel we can't trust you,' *Book of Friends*, p68.
11 '*converted* to it, otherwise it makes no appeal,' *Semblance of a Devoted Past*, p29.
12 'one hand tied behind the back,' *Remember to Remember*, p340.
13 'Get married, you silly bastard,' *This is Henry, Henry Miller from Brooklyn*, editor Robert Snyder, p50.
14 'a dying calf,' letter from Agnes Snyder to Henry Miller, January 1960.
15 'never the hero,' Dewar interview, *Henry Miller: Colossus of One* by Kenneth Dick.
16 'a feeling almost of nausea,' *The Books In My Life*, p278.
17 'didn't give a fuck,' *Tropic of Capricorn*, p284.
18 'ritual shave and haircut,' *Ibid.*
19 'Rochester for honeymoon. Bitterness, sorrow etc.' *June* notebook.
20 'its startling conclusion,' *Sexus*, p23.
21 'so they told me,' *Tropic of Capricorn*, p285.

22 'Bennie Epstein, and Beatrice had other plans,' *June* notebook.
23 'she had TB as well as her son,' *Tropic of Capricorn*, p307.
24 '"Make it a honeymoon trip," she says laughingly,' *The World of Sex*, p86.
25 'the old-fashioned trunk,' *Sexus*, p211.
26 'a bit of Leiderkranz,' *Ibid*, p213.
27 'wistful smile of the hypochondriac,' *Ibid*, p211.
28 'committed suicide long ago,' *The Books In My Life*, p290.
29 'toy theatre built for him by an uncle,' *Plexus*, p127.
30 'a spotlight,' *The Books In My Life*, p289.
31 'unfettered expression,' *Autobiography* by John Cowper Powys, p474.
32 'the perverse and the forbidden,' *The Books In My Life*, p303.
33 'just diluted crap,' *Black Spring*, p107.
34 'poison of Pauline,' *Saga of the Streets.*
35 'abortive, thoroughly incomprehensible,' *Remember to Remember*, p338.
36 'like receiving a thousand dollars,' letter to Val Miller, June 1953.

Chapter Four
1   'undelivered telegrams in his pocket,' *Inside Western Union* by Mike Rivise, p133.
2   'putting them back on salary,' *Tropic of Capricorn*, p41.
3   'pocketed the difference in the cost,' *Inside Western Union*, p217.
4   'Abandon Hope All Ye Who Enter Here,' *Tropic of Capricorn*, p293.
5   'exactly the same – or worse,' *Ibid*, p20.
6   'hold a telegram in his hand,' *Ibid*, p27.
7   'no sense of decency, no respect for me,' *Moloch.*
8   'it's the Jew in him that's talking now,' *Crazy Cock.*
9   'a dentist's office,' *Tropic of Capricorn*, p257.
10 'puzzled me all my life,' *Black Spring* notebook.
11 'wisdom, intuition and experience,' *The Books In My Life*, p86.
12 'in many respects to *Hunger*,' Hamsun article, Sommières, July 2nd 1959.

379

13 'what it was to fail,' *Tropic of Capricorn*, p32.

14 'more than three people around,' letter to Geroge Leite, February 14th 1944.

15 '*That's totem and taboo!' The Happy Rock*, edited by Bern Porter, p11.

16 'waited for me an hour, I understand,' letter to Huntington Cairns, April 30th 1939.

17 'without wasting a deal of valuable time,' *Moloch*.

18 'before he leapt to the sidewalk,' *The Happy Rock*, p10.

19 'themselves as his friends,' *Ibid* p22.

20 'been worth a pretty sum!' *Ibid* p21.

21 'I'd stand her up against a fence and do what I could,' *The World of Sex*,' p90.

22 'Henry's conquests were exaggerations.' Interview with Dewar in *Henry Miller: Colossus of One* by Kenneth Dick.

23 'and on revolving chair,' *June* notebook.

24 'the short skirts she wore,' *June* notebook.

25 'American white woman,' *Book of Friends*, p278.

26 'didn't know she was a negress?' *The Happy Rock*, p13.

27 'of the lost and of the damned,' *Tropic of Capricorn*, p310.

Chapter Five

1 'brass and hollow gut,' *Tropic of Capricorn*, p311.

2 'devour them at one gulp,' *Sexus*, p10.

3 'waiting to meet me again,' interview with June in *Henry Miller: Colossus of One*.

4 'for the sake of writing a story,' *June* notebook.

5 'with a god,' *Sexus*, p15.

6 'Do they have souls of their own?' *Henry and June* by Anais Nin, p212.

7 'to discuss "the case" with me,' *The Happy Rock*, p13.

8 'any mishap, any tragic happening,' *Ibid*, p13.

9 'having her meet June,' *June* notebook.

10 'might struggle for hours,' *Sexus*, p17.

11 'still water "running deep",' letter from Henry Miller to Emil Schnellock, August 26th 1923.

12 'whenever I had acquired what I needed,' *Black Spring* notebook.

13 'of learning as Wellesley,' *Sexus*, p315.

14 'of master and slave,' *The Books In My Life*, p245.

15 'they were shiftless and worthless,' *Inside Western Union* by Mike Rivise, p160.

16 'take them off and dry them,' *Ibid*, p216.

17 'to make myself heard,' *Sexus* p248.

18 'bother to answer the telephone,' *Ibid* p335.

19 'my head in the noose again,' *Ibid* p371.

20 'rôles with the Theatre Guild group,' *Just Wild About Harry*, p8.

21 'her name in bold clear letters,' *Sexus*, p375.

22 'short, powerful, disruptive,' *Ibid*, p314.

23 'the marriage state,' *June* notebook.

24 'broken up into apartments,' *Plexus*, p9.

25 'invited the first kiss,' *Henry and June* by Anais Nin,' p220.

26 'wonderful not to be jealous anymore,' *Sexus*, p349.

Chapter Six

1 'NY *Journal* and Hearst Papers,' *Henry Miller: Letters to Emil*, p10.

2 'writing is not your forte,' *Semblance of a Devoted Past*, p22.

3 'book about Jesus-the-carpenter,' *Sexus*, p25.

4 'Hotel Bossert for a 48 hour rest,' interview with June in *Henry Miller: Colossus of One*.

5 'unpleasant situation arising,' *Letters to Anais Nin*, p39.

6 'I sell myself – my work,' letters from Henry Miller to Emil Schnellock, February 2nd 1925.

7 'the world for posterity,' interview with June in *Henry Miller: Colossus of One*.

8 'sympathetic conversationalist or listener,' *Ibid*.

9 'daughter of Lesbos,' *The Improper Bohemians* by Allen Churchill, p217.

10 'purposeful, literary buffoonery,' *Henry Miller: Letters to Emil*, p11.

11 'some guy who knows a little less than I do,' *Ibid*, p14.

12 'We bathed in turn at the kitchen sink,' *Plexus*, p217.

13 'the subject to one another,' *Ibid*, p217.

14 'Gertrude Stein,' *Ibid*, p234.

15 'as useful as possible,' *Ibid*, p282.

16 'that sort of thing,' *Ibid*, p290.
17 'smelly feet,' *Ibid*, p285.
18 'wolves and my good friends,' *June* notebook.
19 'in the corner of my mouth,' *Gliding Through the Everglades*, p44.
20 '100,000 easily,' *Black Spring* notebook.
21 'the editor of a dictionary,' *Ibid*, p367.
22 'old-fashioned sink,' *Plexus*, p369.
23 'hostess and mistress of ceremonies,' *International Herald Tribune*, November 5th 1982.
24 'the door behind us,' *Ibid*, p379.
25 'even loan her money,' interview with June in *Henry Miller: Colossus of One*.
26 'it's Bodenheim, stupid,' *Crazy Cock*.

Chapter Seven
1 'fighting in the same cause,' *Exiles Return* by Malcolm Cowley, p66.
2 'passionless women to be the norm,' *Freud and the Americans: The Beginnings of Psychoanalysis in the United States, 1876–1917* by Nathan G. Hale, Junior, p40.
3 'for the sake of truth,' *Ibid*, p44.
4 'safeguard to virtue and truth,' *Ibid*, p24.
5 'caused 15 suicides,' *The Erotic in Literature* by David Loth, p145.
6 'sex before marriage as those born before 1900,' *Freud and the Americans: The Beginnings of Psychoanalysis in the United States, 1876–1917* by Nathan G. Hale Junior, p476.
7 'addicted to the marriage state,' *June* notebook.
8 'Lesbians present were especially called for,' *Greenwich Village – 1920–1930* by Caroline Ware, p253.
9 'strangers to find their way,' *Ibid*, p237.
10 '. . . . think it indifference,' *June* notebook.
11 'She outweighed and outreached me,' *International Herald Tribune*, November 5th 1982.
12 'like a bullfrog,' *Cyril Connolly* by David Pryce-Jones, p118.
13 'rather talented unhappiness,' *Ibid*, p211.
14 'to seek someone else,' *June* notebook.
15 'pages cut or torn,' *My Life and Times*, p143.
16 'not only defiant but insulting,' *Crazy Cock*.

17 'achieve the insuperable,' *Crazy Cock*.
18 'place was permanently cold,' *Henry and June* by Anais Nin, p46.
19 'What are bad thoughts?' *Crazy Cock*.
20 'the subject of Paris,' *Plexus*, p79-100.
21 'lurked in their grasps,' *Crazy Cock*.
22 'something rare and beautiful,' *Ibid*.
23 'lowest had recourse to,' *Ibid*.
24 'I thought I was a man,' *Ibid*.
25 'bathtub and urinated on Mara,' interview in *Playboy* magazine.
26 'a mother's for a child, that's all,' *June* notebook.
27 'they were invincible,' *Crazy Cock*.
28 'than the epileptic or the neurotic?' *Ibid*.
29 'with which to combat nature,' *Ibid*.
30 'strangle them under brassieres,' *Ibid*.
31 'the ladies to conduct themselves like whores,' *Ibid*.
32 'how he would dominate a bull,' *Exiles Return* by Malcolm Cowley, p223.
33 'it has bereft me of emotion,' *Henry Miller: Letters to Emil*, p13.
34 'Paris. Eternally Paris.' *June*, notebook.

Chapter Eight
1 'kissing Roland seemed preposterous to me always,' *A Literate Passion* by Anais Nin and Henry Miller, p49.
2 'alien to me, something I did not know,' *Henry Miller: Letters to Emil*, p123.
3 'the proper limits are,' *Sexus*, p362.
4 'Miller claimed to be exploring,' February 2nd 1928, Celia Conason's archive.
5 'a jackass for punishment,' Celia Conason's archive, undated.
6 'in Spain or France,' May 4th 1928, Celia Conason's archive.
7 'beauty, like Garbo's,' *Anais: An International Journal*, Volume 8, 1990.
8 'Night after night,' *A Literate Passion* by Anais Nin and Henry Miller, p41.
9 'some thirty years later,' *Who Am I? Where Am I? What Am I Doing Here?* for *Holiday* magazine.
10 'small boy in his presence,' *Ibid*.
11 'three-horse carriage to Cernauti,' letter to Frank Dobo, October 22nd 1958.

12 'poverty, of misery, around us,' *A Literate Passion* by Anais Nin and Henry Miller, p39.

13 'taking its subject matter for granted,' *Exiles Return* by Malcolm Cowley, p304.

Chapter Nine

1 'you could cut it with an axe,' *Letters to Emil*, p17.

2 'with two wops,' letter to Schnellock, April 14th 1930.

3 'who we are! (*Whom am I?*)' Letter to Emil Conason, Celia Conason's archive.

4 'an awfully good time,' *Letters to Emil*, p51.

5 'of remaining here longer,' *Ibid*, p57.

6 'something wrong with him,' letter to Schnellock, December 4th.

7 'more bohemian than this,' *Letters to Emil*, p61.

8 'forms which invariably bring results,' *On the Left Bank*, p88.

9 'sufficient to last a year or so,' letter to Elkus, October 20th 1930, Celia Conason's archive.

10 'confessions in plain Millersque language,' *Letters to Emil*, p65.

11 '*tout-à-fait Parisien maintenant*,' *Ibid*, p64.

12 'as any of them,' *Ibid*, p68.

13 'chronic state of intoxication,' *The Happy Rock*, p28.

14 'my heedlessness,' *Ibid*, p28.

15 'hope of selling them,' letter of January 1st 1932, reproduced in *My Life and Times*, p151.

16 'one of my WU "nuts",' letter to Schnellock, April 11th 1933.

17 'Henry wept,' *The Happy Rock*, p36.

18 'deafening noise, and the blinding lights,' *Letters to Emil*, p81.

19 'one of his own invention,' *Ibid*, p114.

20 'edifying pastime, as you can see,' *Ibid*, p82.

21 'Four and a half minutes,' *Ibid*, p85.

22 'the mainspring of *Tropic of Cancer*,' *Hamlet Letters*, p98.

23 'love me for myself,' *Crazy Cock*.

24 'an old spell,' *Ibid*.

25 'purple writing, trash, pulpy,' *Diary of Anais Nin*, Volume 1, p108.

26 'fuck everything!' *Letters to Emil*, p80.

27 'a lousy newspaperman,' Frantz to Richard Ellman, November 6th 1968.

28 'snappy kid appearance,' *Lost Generation Journal*, 1974; Bald interview.

29 'critical etc etc,' undated letters to Emil Conason, Celia Conason's archive.

30 'art of living by his wits,' *My Friend Henry Miller*, p13.

Chapter Ten

1 'I feel I am not living,' *Diary of Anais Nin*, Volume 1, p5.

2 'June was in ecstasy,' *Henry and June*, p37.

3 'bored with her life, so she took us up,' *Ibid*, p27.

4 'only ugly thing I have heard her say,' *Ibid* p27.

5 'cruel, cold ideas of using you,' *Ibid*, p203.

6 'I would not promise unless I were to give,' *Ibid*, p30.

7 'debts which she never intended to pay,' *Ibid*, p30.

8 'What a spectacle!' *Letters to Anais Nin*, p19.

9 'the creature who provokes it,' *Ibid*, p31.

10 'never then be the least jealous,' *A Literate Passion*, p29.

11 'actual excursions are fairly limited,' *Letters to Anais Nin*, p31.

12 'Only whores can appreciate me,' *Henry and June*, p56.

13 'he's not for *you*, Joey,' *Henry Miller's Complete Book of Friends*, p251.

14 'hundred-percent-man,' *Henry and June*, p268.

15 'latent homosexual,' *Ibid*, p161.

16 'go after him with a whip,' *Anais: An International Journal*, Volume 8, p8.

17 'infinitely more valuable to the world,' letter to George Leite, February 14th 1944.

18 'I love June and I love you,' *A Literate Passion*, p46.

19 'I would lose faith in you,' *Ibid*, p50.

20 'nor do I want to see her back,' *Ibid*, p69.

21 'wasn't anguish that prompted it,' *Ibid*, p100.

22 'honey on his mouth,' *Henry and June*, p156.

23 'almost more sensual than June,' *Ibid*, p219.

24 'always a great evaluator,' *A Literate Passion*, p103.

25 'any drama, nor any compromise,' *Ibid*, p110.

26 'false, false, false'. *Diary of Anais Nin*, Volume 1, p134.

27 'both of them,' *Ibid*, p135.

28 'She had none,' *Anais: An International Journal*, Volume 2, p4.

29 'I want rest – won't you give me peace,' *Ibid*, p6.

30 'that's my gift to you,' *A Literate Passion*, p121.

31 'awed by it,' *Ibid*, p130.

32 'creative lying', *Letters to Emil*, p106.

33 'your last chapter for your book!' *Diary of Anais Nin*, Volume 1, p157.

34 'strong, undefeated, imperishable,' *A Literate Passion*, p213.

Chapter Eleven

1 'wished to use in his writing,' *Henry and June*, p169.

2 'just a *character*,' *Letters to Emil*, p108.

3 'one man he trusted implicitly,' letter to Schnellock.

4 'you can fuck,' *Henry and June*, p109.

5 'equal in every way,' *Letters to Emil*, p107.

6 'Chinese in housekeeping matters,' *My Friend Henry Miller*, p81.

7 'bourgeois who holds a purse carefully,' *Henry and June*, p101.

8 'subsequent polishing,' *My Friend Henry Miller*, p60.

9 'poor, wrong words etc,' undated letter to Walter Lowenfels.

10 'who's going to know the difference?' *Lost Generation Journal*, Fall 1974, p41.

11 ' "I Sing the Equator." ' *A Literate Passion*, p80.

12 'he entered the room and began to talk,' *The Happy Rock*, p41.

13 'is hostile to,' undated letter to Lowenfels.

14 'saying for the moment,' letter to Schnellock, October 14th 1932.

15 'on the contrary to *remain* himself,' *The Happy Rock*, p44.

16 'Means everything.' Undated letter to Walter Lowenfels.

17 'to see if they are inked enough,' *Letters to Emil*, p120.

18 'mysterious, *big*, and I'm in heaven,' *Ibid*, p132.

19 'very "Albertine". *Very*.' *Letters to Emil*, p133.

20 'I realize it now only too well,' *A Literate Passion*, p177.

21 'Please *date* your letters!' *A Literate Passion*, p202.

22 '*Lady Chatterley* and *Ulysses* were "lemonade" ', *Letters to Anais Nin*, p65.

23 'who will never be born,' letter to Schnellock, April 11th 1933.

24 'a study of him,' letter 'to Emil and Joe', June 6th 1933, Celia Conason's archive.

25 ' "Influence" of Lawrence on Miller,' *Letters to Donald Windham 1940– 65*, editor Windham, 1977.

26 'great poetry . . .' *Saga of the Streets*, Celia Conason's archive.

27 'probably have disgusted Lawrence,' *My Life and Times*, p156.

28 'considerations of form,' letter of May 26–30th 1933 to Bradley, quoted in *D.H.Lawrence*, editors Hinz and Teunissen, Santa Barbara, 1980.

29 'Lawrence book is finished,' *Letters to Anais Nin*, p253.

30 'five times greater in England,' letter from Rebecca West to George Orwell, February 22nd 1946.

31 'saint, creamy voiced,' *Henry and June*, p243.

32 'Excellent neighbours,' letter to Schnellock, August 27th 1934.

33 'separate us in December,' *A Literate Passion*, p107.

34 'have my fling,' *Letters to Anais Nin*, p77.

35 'the American hospital just the same,' *Ibid*, p78.

36 'premonition of imminent death,' *A Literate Passion*, p228.

37 'philologists and etymologists,' *Hamlet Letters*.

38 'tampering with me. No sir!' *A Literate Passion*, p268.

39 'a German spy,' *Henry and June*, p268.

40 'a deadly aim.' *Letters to Anais Nin*, p81.

41 'just by wanting,' undated letter to Hilaire Hiler.

42 'serious work,' *Letters to Anais Nin*, p80.

43 'a sort of reinforced hedgehog position,' *My Friend Henry Miller*, p107.

44 'Is that clear?' *Letters to Anais Nin*, p64.

45 'It is in the piss and dung,' Chuang Tzu, *Basic Writings*, translator and editor Burton Watson, p16.

46 'the thing broke loose,' *Letters to Emil*, p145.

47 ' "democracy" and "freedom" – illusions', *Ibid*, p145.

48 'longing and envy,' letter to Hilaire Hiler, November 29th 1934.

49 'birth to in August was his,' the Diary of Anais Nin, Volume 1, p346, and letter to the author from Rupert Pole:

'Anais knew the child was Henry's and should not be brought into the world.'

Chapter Twelve

1   'You are weak, Henry,' *A Literate Passion*, p270.
2   'you had spilled the beans,' *Ibid*, p243.
3   'nothing between you and Henry,' *Ibid*, p266.
4   'by quite a wide margin,' *Ibid*, p282.
5   'no one on board had heard of', letter to Hiler, January 5th 1935.
6   'stop "exhibiting",' *Ibid*.
7   'reception from the little prick,' letter to Dobo, November 8th 1935.
8   'changing for the worse,' letter to Dobo, September 15th 1936.
9   'So fuck them!' letter to Dobo, April 14th 1939.
10 'Spengler's predictions' undated letter to Hiler, 1935.
11 'weeping about,' undated letter to Emil Conason, late 1934.
12 'keep a fancy terrier,' letter to Dobo, March 16th 1939.
13 'complimentary copies,' letter to Dobo, October 21st 1935.
14 'alone if needs be,' letter to Schnellock, October 1935.
15 'sane and without kinks,' letter to Olga Rudge, December 1st 1934.
16 'good son of a bitch,' letter to Hiler, September 1935.
17 'intelligent and just,' letter to Hiler, October 21st 1935.
18 'prejudice on my part – dunno,' *Ibid*.
19 'a lot of sad ruminants, eh wot?' letter to Hiler, October 12th 1935.
20 'shorn of future menace,' letter to Hiler, November 20th 1935.
21 'fuck these guys,' letter to Hiler, November 20th 1935.
22 'always the attack,' letter to Hiler, November 29th 1934.
23 'my Jewish acquaintances,' *Hamlet Letters*, p121.
24 'a real racist can never afford,' undated letter to Dobo.
25 'unpleasant to the policeman,' Rebecca West, in a letter to George Orwell, February 22nd 1946.
26 'solely to retrieve some dough,' *The Durrell–Miller Letters 1935–1980*, edited by Ian S. MacNiven, p14.
27 'frighten and depress,' Michael Fraenkel, in a letter to George Orwell, February 14th 1936.
28 'source and mainspring of my vitality,' *Hamlet Letters*, p133.
29 'lost in the rush – like father!' Letter to Schnellock, July 6th 1936.
30 'on a greater scale,' Walter Lowenfels, epitaph for Michael Fraenkel, in UCLA.
31 'party labels,' Orwell, April 17th 1940 for *20th Century Authors*, NY 1942.
32 'copy-book for my generation,' *The Durrell–Miller Letters 1935–1980*, p2.
33 'practically nothing, I should say,' *Ibid*, p41.
34 'more suitable for my "admirers",' *Ibid*, p40.
35 'when they get drunk,' letter to Schnellock, November 4th 1938.
36 'derelicts, vagabonds, psychopaths,' *The Happy Rock*, p58.
37 'typing with the other,' *Ends of the World* by Cecily Mackworth, Manchester 1987.
38 'I ram my prick down her throat,' letter to Schnellock, October 1935.
39 'the sea you make,' *A Literate Passion*, p307.
40 'feel their life empty,' *Ibid*, p308.
41 'I don't know,' letter to Schnellock, January 8th 1938.
42 'repay or help,' *Ibid*.
43 'in ten minutes. A fact!' letter to Dobo, April 14th 1939.
44 'above the messenger boys,' undated letter to Conason, 1934. Celia Conason's archive.
45 'with these pigs,' letter to Conason, November 23rd 1934, Celia Conason's archive.
46 'and in my sleep,' *Hamlet Letters*, p163.
47 'temperamental – and terribly earnest,' *The Durrell – Miller Letters 1935–1980* p101.
48 'to become the monster I am,' letter to Hiler, April 1936.
49 'ecstatically about it and probably will,' *Letters to Anais Nin*, p161.

Chapter Thirteen

1   'nothing unusual about it,' *Colossus of Maroussi*, p195.
2   'in the presence of a holy man,' letter from Huntington Cairns to Miller, July 9th 1941.
3   'metaphoric barn-dancing with him,' *The Durrell–Miller Letters 1935–1980*, p133.

4   'to sexual intercourse very truthfully and clearly,' letter to Morton Czabel, December 17th 1939.
5   'he is prolix,' letter from Wallace Stevens to Henry Church, April 27th 1939.
6   'whose address wasn't stated,' *Letters to Anais Nin*, p139.
7   'loaded gun at the head of America,' letter to Hiler from Barbizon Plaza Hotel, 1935.
8   'white people too,' *Letters to Anais Nin*, p205.
9   'the religious groups will recreate America,' *The Air-Conditioned Nightmare* notebook.
10 'collectors was of the grossest sort,' George Barker in a letter to the author, March 5th 1990.
11 'but I doubt it strongly,' *Collector's Quest*, p33.
12 'three such fine restaurants,' *Conversations with Eudora Welty*, editor Prenshaw, 1984.
13 'feel sorry you're involved,' *A Literate Passion*, p325.
14 'People say they stink,' *Letters to Anais Nin*, p251.
15 'treason to say anything against America,' *Ibid*, p279.
16 'stand in the way of returning to me,' *A Literate Passion*, p336.
17 'excuse for doing whatever pleases you,' *Ibid*, p329.
18 'put money in my pocket,' *Letters to Anais Nin*, p325.
19 'Her name meant, in Greek, "revered one",' letter to Schnellock, June 12th 1943,' See *Henry Miller's Complete Book of Friends*, p285.
20 'not *in* love with you,' *My Life with Sevasty*, unpublished manuscript.
21 'unreserved love and admiration,' *Sexus*, p28.
22 'I would become a hermit,' *Letters to Anais Nin*, p297.
23 'A trembling rock,' letter to Schnellock, March 29th 1944.

5   'a growing band,' Emil Schnellock to Henry Miller, 1946.
6   'and fetch them out to the country,' undated letter to Emil White.
7   'omits or forgets to do for me,' letter to Walker Winslow, marked 'Sunday morning'.
8   'good friend of mine,' letter to Oscar Baradinsky, January 1946.
9   'maybe Leonardo da Vinci,' Robert Fink, in a letter of August 3rd 1963.
10 'not to be liked by these people,' *The Happy Rock*, p124.
11 'will not be mentioned,' letter to Schnellock, 1943.
12 'your version versus Anais,' letter to Schnellock, May 10th 1944.
13 'prowling about these precincts,' letter to Alfred Perlés, October 30th 1939.
14 'a "great soul, filled with a great light",' *Big Sur and the Oranges of Heironymous Bosch*, p360.
15 'the climax of his story, "Je l'ai eue".' *Ibid* p363.
16 'in order to save his brother,' letter to Thomas Parkinson, July 30th 1958.
17 'expression on the level of art,' *The Time of the Assassins*, p43.
18 'the wrong end of a rifle, a *loaded* rifle!' *The Smile at the Foot of the Ladder*, p29.
19 'withdrew it immediately and revised it,' *The Durrell–Miller Letters 1935–1980*, p233.
20 '*He can write*,' letter to Emil White, Hollywood, Saturday 1942.
21 'my money out of France,' letter to Schnellock, July 4th 1947.
22 'beloved providence,' undated letter from Emil Conason to Henry Miller.
23 'irritated, depressed or in a temper,' *The Durrell–Miller Letters 1935–1980*, p261.
24 'the damn governments that exist,' letter to Frank Dobo, April 14th 1948.

Chapter Fourteen
1   'the page where I had left off,' letter to Huntington Cairns, April 30th 1939.
2   'like a Midwesterner,' *Town and Country* magazine, August 1945, p68.
3   'the spiritual flute, she loves it,' letter to George Leite, June 14th 1945.
4   'True or false, it's a wonderful book,' letter to Roger Bloom, March 17th 1958.

Chapter Fifteen
1   'more like potato balls,' letter to Emil White, April 20th 1953.
2   'pederast I could fall in love with them,' letter to Emil White, May 5th 1953.
3   'path of pure golden light,' letters from Eve Miller to Bob and Edie Finks, February 8th and 13th 1953.
4   'I'm a monomaniac. Me no argue.' *The Durrell–Miller Letters 1935–1980*, p116.

5   'What a combination!' Eve Miller to the Finks, February 13th 1953.

6   'a real monster,' letter to Tullah Hanley, August 20th 1956.

7   'capacity for guile,' letter from Annette Baxter to Miller, November 3rd 1956.

8   'no sense of taste,' letter from June Corbett to Miller, November 18th 1957.

9   'of living around you,' June Corbett to Miller, June 24th 1957.

10 'Almost had to club her down in bed,' letter to Emil White, February 14th 1956.

11 'the rôle my mother played,' *Saga of the Streets*, Celia Conason's archive.

12 'wrote a few books between times,' letter to Emil White, February 25th 1956.

13 'I miss him as I never missed a soul,' letter to Gerald Robitaille, April 1st 1954.

14 'your letters to me,' letter from Schnellock to Miller, 1949.

15 'these lads can tell me things,' Preface to *The Dharma Bums* by Jack Kerouac.

16 'like H.G.Wells,' Jack Kerouac to Henry Miller, undated.

17 'a new low for civilisation,' letter to Dobo, November 30th 1956.

18 'I have no desire to be critical,' letter of September 12th 1954.

19 'getting somewhere,' *Stand Still Like The Hummingbird*, p82.

20 'inspired voice of Henry Miller,' letter from Emil Schnellock, 1946.

21 'I might have written more gloriously,' *The Durrell–Miller Letters 1935–1980*, p233.

22 'the book "will give you a thrill all over".' Undated letter to Tullah Hanley.

23 'destroying the power of illusion,' *The Colossus of Maroussi*, p34.

Chapter Sixteen

1   'it is a nightmare,' letter to Emil White, July 30th 1959.

2   'create a booby-hatch,' *The Durrell–Miller Letters 1935–1980*, p348.

3   'raise the hair on your head, m'dears,' Eve Miller to Gerald Robitaille, February 26th 1959 and March 18th 1959.

4   'I have no bad feelings – how could I?' Henry Miller to Eve Miller, May 22nd 1960.

5   'messy than "mental cruelty" and what not,' Eve Miller to Henry Miller, May 27th 1960.

6   'next amourette must be Oriental,' letter to Gerald Robitaille, July 27th 1960.

7   'a pair of homos,' letter to Gerald Robitaille, September 12th 1960.

8   'Ssh! Mum's the word!' Letter to Valentine Miller, February 14th 1961.

9   '*You* must find it,' Renate Gerhardt to Miller, Easter Monday, 1961.

10 'that wouldn't do anybody any good,' letter to Emil White, June 7th 1961.

11 'worshipped from afar by a woman,' Renate Gerhardt to Henry Miller, November 7th 1960.

12 'so indulgent towards me,' letter to Roger Bloom, June 30th 1961.

13 'Go fuck yourself!' letter to Frank Dobo, April 14th 1939.

14 'except God, who is my boss,' letter to Frank Dobo, April 6th 1938.

15 'get raves and then die a quick death,' *The Durrell–Miller Letters 1935–1980*, p317.

16 'my name'll be forgotten,' letter to Emil White, June 27th 1961.

17 'prose ode to Tania at the top of page 5,' *Lost Generation Journal*, Winter 1974, p22.

18 'letter I never expected Henry Miller to write,' Elmer Gertz to Henry Miller, November 30th 1962.

19 'if he doesn't even finish "The Rosy Crucifixion",' letter from Emil White to Vincent Birge, February 4th 1966.

20 'adolescent egomania, and much of it could be cut,' in *The Evening Colonnade*, London 1973, article written in 1963.

21 'still find being shocked an exciting literary experience,' *Notebook*, August 30th 1961.

22 'so you're Burroughs,' *Conversations with William Burroughs*, editor Bockris.

23 'William Burroughs was the heroin,' *Books and Bookmen*, October 1962, pp26–27.

24 'would have made a tremendous difference,' letter of William Gordon, August 26th 1966.

25 'worthwhile writing about you at all,' *Writer and Critic, A Correspondence with Henry Miller*, editor William Gordon, Louisiana State UP, 1968.

26 'I was never very single-minded,' Miller to Frédéric-Jacques Temple, June 27th 1965.

27 'leave a scar on the world,' *Henry and June*, p224.

28 'His weaknesses make him more human, what!' Letter to Eve Miller, August 22nd 1965.

29 'that there's some conspiracy etc,' letter from James A. Baxter to Henry Miller, October 3rd 1965.

30 'felt "old and insignificant",' June Corbett to Emil Conason, October 26th 1961, Celia Conason's archive.

31 'Still merry, more alive than ever,' *Letters by Henry Miller to Hoki Tokuda Miller*, editor Joyce Howard, p23.

32 'I don't understand anything about fate. So I stopped.' *Chuang Tzu*, translated and edited by Burton Watson, p113.

33 'he doesn't give a shit about anybody,' *Henry Miller's Complete Book of Friends*.

34 'never heard what became of his project,' *Collector's Quest*, p168.

35 'Not just "stars".' letter to Roger Bloom, August 7th 1965.

36 'in such a mysterious way,' *Another Side of Bob Dylan*, cover.

37 'astounded, naturally. Myself above all,' letter to Alfred Perlès, September 30th 1964.

38 'the Belgian with one leg off, who was supposed to be 140 years old?' *The Durrell–Miller Letters 1935–1980*, p426.

39 'can I just call you Tom?' Letter to Thomas Merton, July 31st 1964.

Chapter Seventeen

1 Feature in *Playboy* magazine, July 1986.

2 'never even met in person,' see *Henry Miller's Complete Book of Friends*, p303; 'Louella'.

3 'ethnic protection came in,' *The Independent*, Saturday, February 10th 1990, p29.

4 'a very stupid woman,' *Mother, China and the World Beyond*, p176.

5 'the psychoanalysts are in the saddle,' *Henry Miller's Complete Book of Friends*, p214.

6 'though not of *my* breasts,' *Black Messiah*, 1981, editor John Bennett, p35.

7 Los Angeles *Free Press* July 30th – August 5th 1976, interviewed by Jonathan Kirsch.

Bibliography

Aldington, Richard and Durrell, Lawrence, *Literary Lifelines*, ed MacNiven and Moore, NY 1981.

Anderson, Sherwood, *Winesburg, Ohio*, London 1947.

Bald, Wambly, *On the Left Bank, 1929–1933*, ed Benjamin V. Franklin, Ohio 1987.

Barrow, Robin, *Happiness*, Oxford 1980.

Benavides Rodolfo, *Dramatic Prophecies of the Great Pyramid*, Mexico 1970.

Bodenheim, Maxwell, attributed, *My Life and Loves in Greenwich Village*, NY 1961.

Brown, J.D., *Henry Miller*, Ungar, NY 1986.

Buche, Maurice Richard, *Medical Mystic, Letters of Doctor Buche to Walt Whitman and His Friends*, selected and edited by Lozynsky, Detroit 1977.

Carroll, Peter N. & Noble, David W., *The Restless Centuries: A History of the American People*, Minneapolis 1979.

Céline, Louis-Ferdinand, *Death on the Instalment Plan*, London 1966.

Charney, Maurice, *Sexual Fiction*, London 1981.

Childs J. Rives, *Collector's Quest: The correspondence of Henry Miller and J. Rives Childs, 1947–1965*, ed R.C. Wood, Charlottesville 1968.

Chuang Tzu, *Basic Writings*, translator and editor Burton Watson, NY 1964.

Churchill, Allen, *The Improper Bohemians. Greenwich Village in its Heyday*, NY 1959.

Cowley, Malcolm, *A Second Flowering. Works and Days of the Lost Generation*, London 1973; *I Worked at the Writer's Trade, 1918–1978*, NY 1978, *Exiles Return. A literary saga of the 1920s*, NY 1951.

Crick, Bernard, *George Orwell: A Life*, London 1980.

De Camp, L. Sprague, *Lost Continents: The Atlantis Theme in History, Science and Literature*, NY 1970.

Dostoevsky, Fyodor, *The Idiot* NY 1969.

Durrell, Lawrence, *The Big Supposer. An Interview with Marc Alyn*, NY 1974.

Eaton, Walter Prichard,*Theatre Guild: The First Ten Years*, Brentano 1929.

Edmiston, Susan and Cirino, Linda D., *Literary New York: A History and Guide*, Boston 1976.

Ford, Hugh, *Published in Paris: A Literary Chronicle of Paris in the 1920s and 1930s*, NY 1988.

Fowlie, Wallace, *Letters of Henry Miller and Wallace Fowlie 1943–1972*, NY 1975.

Goldman, Emma, *Living My Life*, Volume 1, NY 1931.

Gordon, Wm.A., *The Mind and Art of Henry Miller*, London 1968.

Haight, Anne Lyon; updated and edited by Chandler B. Grannis, *Banned Books, 387 BC to 1978 AD*, 4th edition, NY 1978.

Hale, Nathan G. junior, *Freud and the Americans: The Beginnings of Psychoanalysis in the United States 1876–1917*, Volume 1, NY 1971.

Hamsun, Knut, *Hunger*, London 1967; *Mysteries*, London 1973.

Harris, Frank, *My Life and Loves*, Paris, undated.

Hassan, Ihab, *The Literature of Silence – Henry Miller and Samuel Beckett*, NY 1967.

Haynes, Jim, *Thanks for Coming: An Autobiography*, London 1983.

Knapp, Bettina, *Anais Nin*, NY 1978.

Langridge, Derek, *John Cowper Powys: A record of achievement*, London 1966.

Lao Tzu, *Tao Te Ching*, translated by D.C. Lau, 1963.

Lawrence, D.H., *Lady Chatterley's Lover*.

Loth, David, *The Erotic in Literature*, NY 1962.

Mailer, Norman, *Advertisements for Myself*, NY 1960; *Henry Miller: Genius and Lust, Narcissism*, American Review number 24, 1976.

Martin, Jay, *Always Merry and Bright: The Life of Henry Miller*, Santa Barbara 1978.

McAlmon, Robert & Boyle, Kay, *Being Geniuses Together 1920–1930*, London 1984.
McCullough, David W., *Brooklyn – and how it got that way*, NY 1983.
McGilchrist, Ian, *Against Criticism*, London 1982.
Millett, Kate, *Sexual Politics*, NY 1970.
Mitchell, Edward, *Henry Miller: three decades of criticism*, NY 1971.
Mitgang, Herbert, *Dangerous Dossiers. Exposing the secret war against America's greatest authors*, NY 1989.
Morehouse, Ward, *Matinée Tomorrow: Fifty Years of Our Theatre*.
Morton, Brian N., *Americans in Paris*, Ann Arbor 1984.
Nelson, Jane, *Form and Image in the Fiction of Henry Miller*, Detroit 1970.
Nin, Anais, *Henry and June: From the unexpurgated diary of Anais Nin*, edited by Rupert Pole, London 1987; *Journals*, edited by Stuhlmann, London 1967.
Orwell, George, *Inside the Whale: Selected Essays*, London 1957; *The Collected Essays, Journalism and Letters of George Orwell*, Volumes 1,2,3,4, London 1968.
Perlès, Alfred, *The Renegade*, London 1943; *My Friend Henry Miller*, London 1955; *My Friend Alfred Perlès*, Coda to an unfinished biography, London 1973; *Scenes From A Floating Life*, London 1970.
Powys, John Cowper, *Autobiography*, London 1949.
Pullar, Philippa, *Frank Harris*, London 1975.
Rabelais, *Gargantua* and *Pantagruel*, 1955.
Read, Herbert, *The Tenth Muse*, London 1957.
Rembar, Charles, *The End of Obscenity*, London 1969.
Rodgers, Cleveland & Rankin, Rebecca B., *New York: The World's Capital City*, NY 1948.
Root, Waverley, *The Paris Edition 1927–34*, 1989.

Rosenstone, Robert A., *Romantic Revolutionary: A biography of John Reed*, NY 1975.
Rushdie, Salman, *Outside the Whale*, Granta number 11, Cambridge 1984.
Saint Augustine, *The Confessions of St Augustine*, NY 1969.
Scenes Along the Road, edited by Ann Charters, *Photographs of the Desolation Angels 1944–1960*, NY 1971.
Shifreen, Lawrence J., *Henry Miller: A bibliography of secondary sources*, Scarecrow author bibliographies, Metuchen NJ 1979.
Shinkman, Elizabeth Benn (ed), *So Little Disillusion. An American correspondent in Paris and London 1924–1931*, McLean 1983.
Snyder, Robert, *This is Henry, Henry Miller from Brooklyn*, Los Angeles 1974.
Sobel, Bernard, *A Pictorial History of Vaudeville*, NY 1961.
Temple, F-J., *Henry Miller: Qui suis-je?*, Lyon 1986.
Waley, A., *The Way and Its Power: the Tao Te Ching and its place in Chinese thought*, London 1977.
Ware, Caroline Ferar, *Greenwich Village 1920–1930*, Boston 1935.
Weigel, John A., *Lawrence Durrell*, NY 1966.
Weld, Ralph Foster, *Brooklyn is America*, NY 1950.
Wexler, Alice, *Emma Goldman: An Intimate Life*, NY 1984.
Whitman, Walt, *Leaves of Grass*, NY 1954.
Wickes, George, *Americans in Paris 1903–1939*, NY 1969.
Wickes, George, *Henry Miller*, University of Minnesota Pamphlets on American Writers number 56, Minnesota 1966.
Widmer, Kingsley, The Literary Rebel, Carbondale, Illinois 1965.
Wilson, Edmund, *The Shores of Light*, London 1952.
Winslow, Kathryn, *Henry Miller: Full of Life. A memoir*, Los Angeles 1986.

Index

392

393